Stepping over the Color Line

Stepping over the Color Line

African-American Students in White Suburban Schools

Amy Stuart Wells and Robert L. Crain

Yale University Press

New Haven and London

Printed in the United States of America.

Library of Congress Cataloging-in-Publication Data

Wells, Amy Stuart, 1961–
    Stepping over the color line :
    African-American students in white
    suburban schools / Amy Stuart Wells and
    Robert L. Crain.
      p.   cm.
    Includes bibliographical references and index.
    ISBN 0-300-06760-7 (cloth : alk. paper)
    1. School integration—Missouri—Saint Louis Metropolitan Area—Case studies.
2. Afro-American students—Education—Missouri—Saint Louis Metropolitan Area—Case studies.   3. Suburban schools—Missouri—Saint Louis Metropolitan Area—Case studies.
    I. Crain, Robert L.   II. Title.
    LC214.23.S22W45   1997
    379.2′63′0977865—dc21   96-43906
                                             CIP

A catalogue record for this book is available from the British Library.

The paper in this book meets the guidelines for permanence and durability of the Committee on Production Guidelines for Book Longevity of the Council on Library Resources.

10 9 8 7 6 5 4 3 2 1

To Todd, Nan, and all the children of St. Louis City and County, for the love and encouragement we require today and the hope we have for tomorrow.

The Negro needs neither segregated schools nor mixed schools. What he needs is education. What he must remember is that there is no magic, either in mixed schools or in segregated schools. A mixed school with poor and unsympathetic teachers, with hostile opinion, and no teaching concerning black folk, is bad. A segregated school with ignorant placeholders, inadequate equipment, poor salaries, and wretched housing, is equally bad. Other things being equal, the mixed school is the broader, more natural basis for the education of all youth. It gives wider contacts; it inspires greater self-confidence; and it suppresses the inferiority complex. But other things are seldom equal.
—W. E. B. Du Bois

Contents

Acknowledgments

This book was a true labor of love, a total of seven years—five years of research and two years of writing—in the making. So many individuals and organizations helped us along the way, giving time, energy, and resources to this project, that we never will be able to convey all of our gratitude. And while we have endeavored to be true to the complex and often contradictory ways that people we interviewed understood school desegregation in St. Louis, the conclusions drawn in this book are our own, and we take full responsibility for them.

First, we would like to thank the Spencer Foundation for its support of this study, and we remain forever grateful to the late Lawrence Cremin, the former president of Spencer who believed, until his untimely death in 1990, that research on school desegregation could still contribute to the public debate on racial inequality. The Spencer Foundation also awarded the first author a Dissertation Year Fellowship, which was instrumental to the research and writing of this book. With so little funding available for school desegregation research in the past fifteen years, the Spencer Foundation has helped to fill a significant void by funding studies such as this one, and we are greatly indebted to the organization.

We would also like to thank the entire staff of the Voluntary Interdistrict Coordinating Council (VICC) in St. Louis for providing us with critical data and information. Funded by the state of Missouri under the court order, VICC is a consortium of school districts in metropolitan St. Louis. The VICC staff is responsible for recruiting African-American students from the city to transfer to suburban schools, and white students from the suburbs to attend magnet schools in the city. VICC also assists suburban schol districts in their efforts to work with the transfer students. Thus, the staff is placed in the unenviable position of trying to make the St. Louis desegregation program work in spite of the racial politics and tension that often envelops them.

Susan Uchitelle, the executive director of VICC, is a remarkable woman who is extremely committed to the children of St. Louis, particularly the African-American children in the city. Without her assistance, this book would not have been possible. She provided us access to files in the VICC office and to data from the student achievement and attitudinal studies commissioned by her office. Because of her precarious position as both an appointee of the court and an advocate for a politically contentious program, she is not quoted directly in this book. Despite her absence in the text, she is the strongest and most important visionary of this story, and someone who, we believe, will go down in history as a central character in the fight for racial equality in this country.

We would also like to give special thanks to Ron Franklin, director of data at VICC, for assisting us with logistics and analysis. Other VICC staff members who provided moral and technical support at various points along our journey include Sharon Heisel, Carol LaDriere, Laverne Michom, Rosemary Smith, Tracy Snow, Dan Watson, and Vicki Williams. And in memory of Judy Katz, former executive secretary of VICC, we would like to honor the courage and conviction of all the VICC employees, without whom there would not be a story of inter-district school desegregation to tell.

Thank you also to Evelyn Busby, Mary Baily, and especially Tamala Turner, three graduate students from Washington University in St. Louis who accompanied the first author on her interviews with the African-American students and parents. We could not have found more dedicated or caring interviewers. Thank you also to the students and staff at Columbia University who helped with the transcription of hundreds of interview tapes.

Encouragement and advice for this project came from countless generous colleagues and associates across the country, especially Jomills Braddock, Peter W. Cookson, Jr., Herbert J. Gans, Robert McClintock, Lamar P. Miller, Gary Natriello, Jeannie Oakes, James Rosenbaum, and Harrison White. Many of these colleagues read and commented on various sections of the book; others provided guidance at perilous moments in the writing process.

We owe a special thanks to Gary Orfield, who read and commented on several sections of the book and who, along with William Taylor, provided us with a great deal of important background material.

We cannot adequately express our gratitude to the more than three hundred people of the state of Missouri and of St. Louis city and county who allowed us to interview them. They gave us not only their time but also their valuable insights into the desegregation program. In particular, we would like to thank the students we interviewed for their openness and honesty, and for their willingness to teach us about the world through their eyes.

In addition, many people, including those at the Missouri State Department of Education, the St. Louis public schools, and the law firm Lashly & Baer, shared valuable documents and data with us. We also offer a special thanks to E. Terrence ("Terry") Jones, dean of arts and sciences at the University of Missouri–St. Louis, for providing us with a copy of his results from a 1998 survey he conducted for the *St. Louis Post-Dispatch*. We also thank Dean Jones and UMSL's Public Policy Research Centers for their helpful 1993 focus group studies of students involved in the desegregation plan. In addition, we thank Robert W. Lissitz of the University of Maryland for his evaluation of student achievement in St. Louis, as well as the helpful work of James Dixon's Education Monitoring and Advisory Committee.

We would like to acknowledge Gladys Topkis at Yale University Press for her patience, perseverance, and belief in our project. Also, Heidi Downey at Yale has been wonderful to work with on the production end of the this long process, and we thank her for her encouragement. And thank you to the anonymous reviewer of our manuscript for helpful and constructive feedback.

Most hearty and heartfelt thanks go to Stuart P. Wells and Ann B. Wells, the parents of the first author, who, as longtime residents of the St. Louis metropolitan area, provided critical support for this project, including lodging, inspiration, and literally hundreds of local newspaper clippings that helped to fill in gaps in our research and provide the much needed background and color for this book. In many ways and on many levels, this book would not have been possible without their support. To them the first author owes her drive, determination, interest in politics, and love of the English language.

And last, we thank our spouses and partners in life, Todd W. Serman and Nan Guptill Crain. Todd, who painstakingly read two drafts of this manuscript and caught many early flaws, has always been a supportive and understanding husband and has given so much of himself to his wife's various causes. Nan has also been a source of comfort and encouragement at critical points along the way. We cannot thank them enough for their undying love and their belief in our work toward social justice.

Introduction

There is no doubt, in the writer's opinion, that a great majority of white people in America would be prepared to give the Negro a substantially better deal if they knew the facts. But to understand the difficulty the Negroes have to overcome in order to get publicity, we must never forget the opportunistic desire of the whites for ignorance. It is so much more comfortable to know as little as possible about Negroes, except that there are a lot of them in Harlem, the Black Belt, or whatever name is given to the segregated slum quarters where they live.
—Gunnar Myrdal, *An American Dilemma*

School desegregation policy should never have been expected to overcome the obstacles confronting it in American society. In saying this, we do not mean to imply that desegregation has been a failure. In fact, there is mounting evidence that African Americans who attend desegregated schools are more likely to achieve at higher rates and have higher aspirations than those in segregated schools and are more likely to go on to college and secure high-status jobs (see Grissmer, 1996; Schofield, 1989 and 1991; Wells and Crain, 1994).

Nor do we intend to insult people committed to the ideals of integration. Indeed, this book is written for and about them.

What we do mean is that school desegregation is a radical strategy that conflicts with virtually every cultural and structural element of our society. As one of a handful of civil rights policies aimed at stripping away years of racial inequality, school desegregation is an irregularity, a form of particularism in which one group is specially treated because of its race in a society dedicated to universality, or the idea that all people, regardless of race or class, will be treated the same (Lipset, 1963).

School desegregation is an affirmative action policy assuring African-American and Latino students access to schools that their ancestors could not attend. In an era increasingly referred to as "post-desegregation," such policies are seen as incredibly out of sync with core American values (see Kunen, 1996). And perhaps they are. But rather than accept the prevalent beliefs and deny the benefits of a policy that challenges them, we have chosen to reexamine these core values in a critical and historical light to better understand the purpose of school desegregation.

Most civil rights legislation and court cases focused on giving African Americans the same opportunities as whites to achieve in a white-dominated society. Under such policies, blacks were suddenly unshackled and then expected to compete in a contest in which whites had a 200-year head start—a contest for which whites had written the rules and constructed the meaning of "merit" on their own terms.

In 1965, President Johnson put forth a similar argument when he commented about blacks and racial equality, "You do not take a person who for years has been hobbled by chains and liberate him, bring him up to the starting line of a race and then say you are free to compete with all the others, and justly believe you have been completely fair" (cited in Berman, 1996). School desegregation policies, on the other hand, are intended to work retroactively, dismantling a separate and unequal educational system created when segregation was legally sanctioned in the South and ignored in the North—a system so entrenched that without government intervention it would continue long after Jim Crow. Thus, school desegregation has been but one policy designed to chip away at an embedded structure of two racially separate and highly unequal societies—separate in housing, employment, and social interaction.

In describing the accomplishments and shortcomings of one school desegregation plan we provide insight into a much broader dialogue on the role of race in America. St. Louis, Missouri, and its suburbs demographically resemble many midsized, late-twentieth-century metropolitan areas in the United

States. What makes St. Louis unique is an urban-suburban school desegregation plan that has blurred but not erased the color line between white and black communities. The story of school desegregation across city-county borders illustrates how truly separate and unequal our society has become and how difficult it is for the educational system alone to change that. The story of St. Louis and its struggle to undo years of segregation and discrimination through one vulnerable school desegregation plan also highlights why this is a struggle worth fighting and why St. Louis may now be, as a result, better poised to face the twenty-first century than are most other metropolitan areas.

In 1968, President Johnson's commission on civil disorders, the Kerner Commission, investigated the causes of urban riots. The commission's report emphasized that the legacy of discrimination had created two separate societies: a black ghetto condemned by whites but largely maintained by white institutions, and the more familiar white society. More than two decades later the National Research Council's Committee on the Status of Black Americans reported that "there are striking resemblances between the descriptions of 1968 and the position of black Americans reflected in our findings" (Jaynes and Williams, 1989, p. x).

It would be foolish to assume that desegregation of public schools could solve all the racial problems of a society that has for so long accommodated racial inequality in the way that many families accommodate alcoholism: periodically worrying about the problem while regularly contributing to the cause. In the past three decades, despite African Americans' hard-earned progress in education and the growth of the black middle class, the two separate societies continue to coexist. Even in instances where black ghettos become increasingly Latino in many cities, they remain separated from white neighborhoods. These separate societies minimize the effects of such policies as school desegregation by providing racially isolated suburbs to which whites can flee. Suburbs are, in turn, justified as the accumulative result of private choices that people make about where to live and who their neighbors are—choices that the government has no right to regulate. "Thus, at the core of black-white relations is a dynamic tension between many whites' expectations of American institutions and their expectations of themselves" (Jaynes and Williams, 1989, p. 5).

Public schools are uniquely situated at the confluence of government policy and private lives. Despite their public funding and democratic governance, schools play an important role in the private decisions we make about how we prepare our children for adulthood. Thus, school desegregation has forced many whites to retreat from their commitment to equality in order to rationalize their behavior. In doing so, they turn to some of the basic principles of our nation: the American Creed.

Whites' reliance on the Creed to explain their resistance to race-specific policies is paradoxical given that the Swedish economist Gunnar Myrdal predicted fifty years ago that the Creed would lead the United States toward a solution to the "Negro problem." Myrdal described the Creed as belief in the essential dignity of individual human beings, the fundamental equality of all, and certain inalienable rights to freedom, justice, and fair opportunity. To understand how this Creed, once a mantra for the civil rights movement, became a rationale for opposition to such policies as school desegregation is to understand why racial segregation and inequality have become as much a part of our culture as the Fourth of July.

RACE AND THE AMERICAN CREED

Myrdal (1962) described the "American dilemma" as the ever-raging conflict between the American Creed and the subordinate position of blacks in society. "For practical purposes," he wrote, "the main norms of the American Creed as usually pronounced are centered in the belief in equality and in the rights to liberty"—ideals that represent the nation's early struggle for independence (pp. 8–9). The reality that Myrdal encountered in his travels was, however, vastly inconsistent with these norms. He wrote that racial inequality was perhaps the most glaring conflict in American society and the greatest unsolved task for its democracy (p. 21). "The very presence of the Negro in America; his fate in this country through slavery, Civil War and Reconstruction; his recent career and his present status; his accommodation; his protest and his aspiration; in fact his entire biological, historical, and social existence as a participant American represent to the ordinary white man in the North as well as in the South an anomaly in the very structure of American society" (p. lxix).

Myrdal believed, however, that the United States was on the verge of a major political effort to grant equal rights to blacks and bring the realities of day-to-day life in line with the general precepts of the Creed. The end of World War II and the return of African-American soldiers who had risked their lives to fight racism overseas brought the American dilemma into sharper focus. The civil rights movement of the 1950s and '60s exposed the hypocrisy of a country that professed to stand for liberty and justice for all while systematically denying a large segment of its population the choice of where to sit on a public bus.

The Supreme Court ruling in *Brown v. Board of Education,* the Montgomery, Alabama, bus boycott, the marches in Selma and Birmingham, and the March on Washington were symbols of the struggle of African Americans and the growing acceptance among whites of equal opportunities for all Americans. The civil rights movement peaked with the passage of the Civil Rights Act of 1964 and the Voting Rights Act of 1965 (Orfield, 1988). The Civil Rights Act restricted discrimination in employment and in all institutions receiving federal aid, including schools, and authorized the Justice Department to sue on behalf of minorities if discrimination occurred. The Voting Rights Act promised the broad expansion of the black electorate in the South by nullifying unfair restrictions on voter registration.

Orfield contends that these advances in the mid-1960s were attributable to a "liberal" political consensus of blacks and whites who supported the same universal standard for blacks in terms of access to voting, jobs, education, employment, and public facilities. This political consensus and the move toward equal opportunity validated Myrdal's prediction that Americans would address the dilemma and attempt to live up to the Creed's ideals of equality and liberty. But there were limits. Policies aimed at bringing African Americans up to the same universal standards did little to remove vestiges of *prior* discrimination. The voting rights legislation, for instance, gave African Americans the same right to vote as other Americans, but it did not reverse the prior actions of white politicians elected when blacks were denied access to the polls.

Mounting opposition to Jim Crow laws symbolized movement toward a "color-blind" society. By 1965 only 25 percent of white adults surveyed said they favored "strict racial segregation," and the percentage who said blacks "should have as good a chance as white people to get any kind of job" rose rapidly, from 42 in 1942 to 95 in 1972 (Pettigrew, 1994, p. 54). Color blindness slowly became a societal goal, one that most whites value because it fits their conception of the Creed. What the color-blind perspective does not do, however, is acknowledge the vestiges of hundreds of years of racial inequality.

As growing numbers of whites tried to make good on the Creed by supporting the abolition of explicitly racial statutes, it became increasingly clear that stronger government intervention would be needed to solve the problem of the color line—the impenetrable boundary between black ghettos and the rest of the world. Orfield (1988) argues that by the mid-1960s, racial segregation in urban America was so entrenched, so encompassing that it could not be overcome by simple "equal access" laws but would yield only to bold race-specific policies in housing and education.

In education, for example, when the Civil Rights Act of 1964 instructed the federal government to cut off funding from racially discriminatory schools, many districts reassigned students—black or white—to the school closest to their home. This universal or color-blind approach to student assignment integrated parts of the rural South, where black students had been bused past all-white schools to more distant all-black ones. But it left segregation virtually untouched in the cities, where housing remained highly segregated because black migrants from the farms were given access to housing only in isolated ghettos (Orfield, 1988, p. 317). Thus, efforts to desegregate schools in these urban districts would have to rely on a legal or political rationale that went beyond universality—it would require a more race-specific agenda.

The vast majority of Americans were not then and are not now ready to move beyond a universal or equal opportunity agenda to a more proactive particularistic or race-specific one designed to produce equal results. Whites who had been convinced of the need for the original, equal access demands of the civil rights leaders simply did not understand or accept the need for the shift in focus of the civil rights movement: "a shift, that is, *from struggles over acquiring basic civil rights to struggles over actually redistributing educational, economic, political and social resources*" (Bobo, 1988, p. 85, emphasis in original). Most whites supported the objectives of the first struggle; few supported the objectives of the second.

Liberal whites did support some community-based "social welfare" policies, such as preschool, compensatory education, and job training. But the basic assumption was that "no fundamental economic or racial change was essential. Opportunities existed; the need was simply to prepare blacks for jobs and forbid discrimination" (Orfield, 1988, p. 328). Bolder policies, such as housing integration, school desegregation, and affirmative action in employment—policies aimed at dismantling segregated systems to assure more equal *results*—faced strong resistance from whites who felt that enough had been done.

These bolder efforts were politically less feasible, partly because they targeted both northern and southern cities and thus would affect northern whites who had supported solving the "Negro problem" when it was a southern issue but not when whites too were implicated in creating racial inequality. They were unfeasible also because of the sudden increase in ghetto violence beginning in the summer of 1965 with the Watts riots, which erupted a mere five days after President Johnson signed the Voting Rights Act. Anger over the broken promises of the civil rights movement and, from blacks' standpoint, the futility of "equality" amid systematic housing segregation and lack of employment opportunitites exploded onto the streets of urban America for all the world to see but for few to understand. This was, according to Orfield (1988), the turning point in the civil rights movement and the beginning of the end of the integrationists' dream. In the years following, as race riots broke out in other cities and as such policies as school desegregation moved north, whites convinced themselves that racial inequality was simply the product of blacks' lack of motivation or their immoral culture, not anything white society had created. Soon many whites would turn their backs on the issue of racial inequality, and they have not faced the issue since.

The abandonment of the race issue is in part a result of whites' inability to distinguish between a society structured in a way that promotes racial inequality, regardless of the level of individual prejudice, and a society composed of racist individuals. Most whites do not see the need for bold, proactive policies because they do not see that our society continues systematically to deny blacks a fair chance at housing, education, and employment. Yet if whites could not understand this thirty years ago, they have even more difficulty understanding it today. As a result, the current separate and unequal societies continue to reproduce themselves, and the greatest of all American dilemmas lives on.

THE COLOR LINE: AN INVISIBLE STRUCTURE

Forty years after Myrdal defined the American dilemma, Jennifer Hochschild (1984) revisited the Creed and racial inequality in her study of political resistance to school desegregation. She offered a more critical analysis than Myrdal's and suggests that racism is not simply an anomaly within an otherwise healthy liberal democratic body but a part of what shapes and energizes that body. "American society as we know it exists only because of its foundation in racially based slavery, and it thrives only because racial discrimination continues. The apparent anomaly is an actual symbiosis" (p. 5).

By racism Hochschild does not mean personal dislike or denigration of another race. "Individual prejudice is neither necessary nor sufficient for racism to exist," she explained, because people and institutional requirements may systematically discriminate without anyone so intending. "Thus to assert that American history and contemporary politics are deeply racist is not to accuse individuals of harboring evil thoughts; it is to say that our society is shaped by actions in consequence of racial differences—actions that usually elevate whites and subordinate blacks" (p. 2).

In distinguishing between racist individuals and a system of racism, Hochschild demonstrates how U.S. institutions, economic patterns, governmental agencies, and geographic arrangements predetermine personal choices and interactions. We have inherited this racial structure from earlier generations, from those who created the urban ghettos and those who were forced to live in them. We no longer see or question this color line, and thus we perpetuate it, often unknowingly.

The color line envelops us all, limiting the housing we rent or purchase, the schools our children attend, the transportation we have access to, and the network of friends and associates with whom we share information. It explains why whites who move to Los Angeles do not look for housing in Watts and why the New York City public school system, which serves mostly black and brown children, has less than half the per-pupil funding of schools in many of its mostly white suburbs. It explains why whites can obtain million-dollar mortgages to buy suburban estates and why African Americans and Latinos are denied far smaller loans to purchase inexpensive bungalows. The color line perpetuates a political system in which blacks lack access to better-paying jobs, and in which toxic chemicals are most likely dumped in predominantly African-American or Latino neighborhoods. It explains why urban communities have few grocery stores that sell fresh vegetables at reasonable prices while suburbs host mega-supermarkets with bushels of fresh produce and "smart buys."

Although the color line was established at a time when blatant discrimination was ignored if not condoned, the structure has remained. Its stability does not imply that all individuals who live and work within it are bigots or that we do not sometimes regret that it exists. But our actions are influenced by the presence of race despite the best intentions of individuals, many of whom are not prejudiced and do not subscribe to negative stereotypes (Blauner, 1994).

Thus, when whites buy homes in all-white neighborhoods they contribute to a structure of racial segregation that isolates African Americans and Latinos in poverty-stricken neighborhoods. They reinforce the color line even if they do not harbor hostile feelings, beliefs, or stereotypes about African-Americans or Latinos. They could be kind, decent, and hard working, going about their business of realizing the American Dream: a home in the suburbs, personal equity, and a good return on their investment. Still, they perpetuate a societal structure that is inherently unequal, a structure that greatly benefits whites economically and socially.

Thus, racism has been interwoven into the fabric of society so that prejudicial attitudes are no longer required to maintain racial oppression (Blauner, 1994). In the 1960s the term "institutional racism" was coined to describe a form of racism in which assumptions of white superiority unconsciously shape the functioning of social institutions (see Blauner, 1994; Carmichael and Hamilton, 1967; Finkenstaedt, 1994; Jankowski, 1995). A clear example of this is seen in the housing market, where the unstated assumption that all-white neighborhoods are superior to mixed-race or all-black ones drives property values and institutional lending practices.

Discrimination occurs when privilege becomes institutionalized—embedded in the norms and informal rules of corporations, unions, schools, and professions. Thus the labor market remains segregated through many seemingly benign practices, such as word-of-mouth recruitment networks. The subtle ways that institutions exclude, admit, evaluate, and promote individuals are often driven by narrow and not necessarily pertinent criteria (Feagin, 1989). Yet as racism becomes institutionalized, whites are less aware of it and more likely to assume that racial issues are a thing of the past (Blauner, 1994).

THE VIEW FROM THE SUBURBS

Because most whites do not see insidious racism or its effect on the structure of society, they resist policies that give disadvantaged racial groups preferential treatment and deny the need for government intervention. This resistance is based not merely on the benefits whites derive from the status quo; it also reflects the cultural framework through which they view the world, allowing them to rationalize lingering racial inequality by blaming blacks for not trying to succeed.

Whites support the general principles of equality and integration, as long as the government does not play a major role in assuring that they are achieved. Thus "specific policies aimed at improving the social and economic position of blacks" are generally not acceptable because whites believe that blacks should pull themselves up by their own bootstraps (Bobo, 1988, p. 88). Similarly, a national survey found that support for "integrated schools" rose from 42 percent in 1942 to 95 percent in 1983, while an overwhelming majority of whites continued to oppose government efforts to desegregate schools (Bobo and Kluegel, 1993, p. 444). Gary Orfield's (1996) review of the literature on public opinion toward school desegregation also shows a large majority of parents in favor of racial mixed schools to help prepare their children for a diverse society but a small minority in favor of student assignments to schools outside of their neighborhoods.

Differences in whites' reactions to policies banning flagrant discrimination and those sanctioning government enforcement of civil rights laws relate to the degree of government intervention into whites' private lives necessary to achieve each goal. Sniderman and Piazza (1993) found, for instance, that while virtually no whites disagree that blacks should have the right to vote or use public accommodations, they are highly resistant to fair housing legislation, which makes it illegal for a homeowner or landlord to refuse to sell or rent housing to a person based on race or religion. "What distinguishes fair housing on the equal treatment agenda is the call to use the force of law to back the principle of equal treatment in a private context—to intervene in decisions white people would ordinarily take to be their own business" (p. 123). Fair housing legislation then is an "un-American" government curtailment of property owners' freedom to choose to whom they will sell their homes. It violates the principle of universality by assuring access to the housing market for one particular group and crosses the boundary between the role of government and the rights of private people. In his campaign to become governor of California three decades ago, Ronald Reagan told the California Real Estate Association that fair housing was wrong because the "right of an individual to ownership and disposition of property is inseparable from the right of freedom itself" (Orfield, 1988, p. 327).

Reagan drew on a cultural theme that is fundamental to the Creed and the American concept of equality. The founding fathers, for instance, believed strongly in the rights of property owners. "The man who owned property was inherently an individual of merit" (Finkenstaedt, 1994, p. 10). Of course "property" then included African-American slaves. Today it includes valuable real estate in the suburbs that descendants of slaves were until recently legally barred from purchasing and are continually denied access to by property owners and lending institutions.

Armed with the Creed, whites resist preferential treatment for blacks to compensate for past discrimination, including such policies as affirmative action and school desegregation. Four out of five whites oppose affirmative action in employment or education (Sniderman and Piazza, 1993). These data concur with other studies that found whites' opposition to race-conscious policies does not vary much with education, age, or region of the country— factors that usually influence political views—leaving little reason to anticipate increased support in the future (Bobo and Kluegel, 1993).

School desegregation policy, as part of a race-conscious agenda, has never been color-blind or universal. Early desegregation court orders reassigned students—mostly black but some white and Latino students as well—to more distant schools in order to dismantle a system of segregation and assure black students' access to the higher-status schools. More recently developed desegregation plans allow parents and students to choose among racially mixed schools, but districts under court-ordered desegregation must manipulate these choices to assure racial balance (Wells, 1993).

As a more aggressive policy, school desegregation represents exactly what whites dislike about particularism and affirmative action: the infringement on their long-held freedoms and liberties to control their personal lives. In particular, they cherish the right to send their children to any school they choose, even when such action perpetuates a segregated and unequal educational system. Judges' orders for white parents to send their children to desegregated schools are perceived as unjust, though few if any white parents complained during prior decades when they were told that their children must attend racially segregated schools.

Historian John Hope Franklin (1993) illustrates the paradox of whites' resistance to government intervention on behalf of blacks after centuries of race-specific policies and intervention that assisted powerful whites. "Until 50 years ago, however, the intervention was on behalf of a small segment of society that was using government to facilitate its programs to concentrate the major part of the nation's wealth in a relatively few hands" (p. 18).

Most whites do not see it this way. They voice opposition to school desegregation and similar particularistic policies in terms of "reverse discrimination." They claim that government is denying them the same basic freedoms that the civil rights movement assured for blacks, and thus such policies are antithetical to the Creed. Thus, whites' perceptions of fairness and equality, while not monolithic across social classes, ethnic groups, political ideologies, or regions of the country, tend to be similar in terms of the meaning and implications of the American Creed, which allows for the elimination of de jure segregation but not the vestiges of that segregation. Most whites believe that the race-conscious agenda is distinctive in its moral challenge to fundamental American values. Because "the principle of preferential treatment runs *against* the Creed" (Sniderman and Piazza, 1993, p. 177).

Much of the political impasse in the past two decades regarding government efforts to improve the life chances of African Americans is due to a belief on the part of most whites that what began in the 1950s as a civil rights movement in sync with core national values is now in direct conflict with them. In a liberal democracy, policies considered to be in conflict with core values are likely to be short-lived and to be undermined along the way so that the intended beneficiaries of such acts no longer want them. Thus, we hear of many African Americans who, in reaction to whites' resistance to school desegregation or affirmative action, no longer support such policies (Bell, 1987; Carter, 1991). After years of whites' resistance and efforts to resegregate students in desegregated schools into separate and unequal classes (Oakes, 1985), it is no wonder that some blacks have lost hope in the goal of integration.

Some social scientists contend that whites use the Creed as a tool to warrant whatever fits their self-interest (Wellman, 1993). But we argue that whites' attitudes are not simply the outgrowth of narrow self-interest but rather the ideological heart and soul of the nation, supported by such broad cultural themes as individual responsibility, materialism, unfettered competition, and undying belief in the economic system as fair and meritocratic despite evidence to the contrary. These prevalent themes legitimize racial inequality by blaming the victims of racism for not succeeding in a society that depends on their failure. Victim blaming is perpetuated by a normative belief that economic success is the measure of one's worth, a belief that makes many whites fearful of falling from their working- or middle-class status and concerned that government intervention on the part of African Americans will be at their expense, economically and socially (Newman, 1993; Edsall, 1991). This consumerism and materialism is what Cornel West (1993a) refers to as "market morality," in which "the market begins to hold sway in every sphere of a person's life, lead[ing] to meaninglessness and hopelessness in poor communities. Among working-class people, it leads to self-paralyzing pessimism as they feel their standard of living and quality of life is declining" (p. 18).

Finkenstaedt (1994) traces this American tendency to use economic criteria to measure individual worth to the Protestant beliefs of our founders— that is, the "materialistic ethic," or the association of worldly success with divine election (p. 10). Through this lens, the African-American poor are not the product of discriminatory practices: "They are simply men, women and children who are unable to meet the demands of materialistic society and who do not enjoy its benefits because of their innate disabilities. . . . They deserve their lot" (p. 11).

Tied to this materialistic ethic is strong belief in "human agency," or the ability of individuals to overcome obstacles, and in "individual responsibility," or the commitment of each person to take care of his or her "own." These beliefs prevent many whites from seeing how they themselves benefit from "group" interests. For instance, they do not generally see the role that big business plays in national policy, nor do they recognize the existence of a congressional block representing the suburbs. This inability to see anything above the level of the individual or the family prevents whites from acknowledging that their privilege comes from the power of their group. Instead, they credit their own hard work and ingenuity for their success, and the laziness of others as the primary cause of their failure. These cultural themes explain intense political resistance to race-conscious policies. Whenever an effort is made to redress a wrong done to a certain group, some members of the group that has never experienced a wrong tend to feel aggrieved. "They are displeased simply because justice has at long last been done to the group whose disadvantaged position provided new opportunities for those who now protest what they call reverse discrimination" (Franklin, 1993, p. 71).

Thus, while few whites still subscribe to beliefs that racial inequality results from inborn inferiority, the prevalent ideologies of our society allow whites to see racial inequality as the result of whites' work ethic and blacks' lack of such ethic, of whites' commitment to individual responsibility and blacks' refusal to accept it (Kluegel, 1990). Once the legal barriers to equality were lifted and blacks were guaranteed the right to vote, to use public facilities, and so on, it was then up to blacks to achieve the kind of success that whites had achieved with the same rights, albeit 200 years earlier.

By the early 1980s, the Reagan Revolution had legitimized a new political majority comprising strange bedfellows—corporate elites, working-class Catholics, white southerners, suburbanites in the Sunbelt, and middle-class Americans who were united in their opposition to government efforts to provide access for all to the nation's resources and opportunities. President Reagan and his political descendants have blamed poor African Americans and, more recently, Central American immigrants, for the declining fortunes of working- and middle-class whites. They have focused the attention of white voters on the federal government's role in their loss of control over school selection, university admissions programs, hiring, promotion, and so on, leading to a strong antigovernment sentiment manifested in everything from Proposition 209 in California to the bombing of the Oklahoma City federal building.

The natural outgrowth of this antigovernment political movement was the New Right, with its emphasis on moral issues—such as the decline of traditional family values—as the primary cause of social decay and poverty in the ghettos (Franklin, 1993; Edsall, 1991; Klatch, 1990). The government was seen as condoning and even promoting this "immorality" through a welfare system that "rewards" single mothers (Murray, 1984; Bennett, 1992). Sniderman and Piazza (1993) found that "merely asking whites to respond to the issue of affirmative action increases significantly the likelihood that they will perceive blacks as irresponsible and lazy" (p. 103).

Less socially conservative whites believe that the erosion of liberty, not of morals, should be of utmost concern. From their perspective, each individual is endowed with free will, initiative, and self-reliance; thus the solution to the nation's economic and social problems is greater economic and political liberty through less government involvement in individuals' daily lives (Klatch, 1991). Responding to both of these antigovernment strands, more policy makers at the state and national level stress getting government out of Americans' lives—a euphemism for cutting government programs designed to help the poor and people of color.

We found plenty of whites in St. Louis who agree with these tenets—for either moral or economic reasons or both—and thus resist government involvement in their lives, especially when it comes to where or with whom their children attend school. We refer to these whites as "resistors"—some of of whom are narrow-minded, others of whom simply choose to understand racial inequality as blacks' unwillingness to help themselves.

In St. Louis, as in most cities, there are also liberal whites who realize that past discrimination probably has something to do with current despair in the black ghettos. They tend to have sympathy for the 50 percent of all African-American children who are growing up in poverty, but they do not recognize the structural and cultural elements of society that perpetuate this situation. Many live in the suburbs and do not see the link between the suffering of the poor and the structure of the society in which it takes place. These whites, whom we call the "sympathizers," frequently favor such social policies as Head Start preschool centers and special job training programs in inner-city neighborhoods, as long as these policies do not affect their own personal freedoms or choices.

The final group of whites we refer to are the "visionaries"—a small minority of white people who see the bigger historical and structural picture of society. These whites recognize the depth of racial problems and inequality; they acknowledge the existence of the color line and understand that whites helped create it and continue to perpetuate it. They also see that much of the ideology around the Creed reflects efforts to explain away racial inequality. These whites support more radical racial policies, such as school desegregation.

On the white side of the color line, people generally fit into one of these three perspectives—resistors, sympathizers, or visionaries—which signals their understanding of the role of the government in dealing with racial inequality. Some whites fluctuate in their stance, depending on the issues, but only visionary whites see the symbiotic relation between the structure and culture of society and the problem of the color line.

THE VIEW FROM THE INNER CITY

In this book we also present other, more discerning lenses through which to examine lingering inequality between whites and African Americans. As Blauner (1994) notes, there are at least two languages of race in America—black and white—which signify separate systems of understandings about social reality and which incorporate different views of the centrality of race and racism to America's very existence, past and present. "Blacks believe in this centrality, while most whites, except for the more race-conscious extremists, see race as a peripheral reality. . . . The intellectual power of the African-American understanding of race lies in its more critical and encompassing perspective" (p. 24).

This more contextual perspective of blacks generally allows for greater discernment in explaining the mixed results of the civil rights movement in the United States, results that include impressive gains in the educational achievement and attainment of African-American students and substantial growth in the number of blacks—currently about 40 percent—who are considered middle class (Grissmer, 1996b; Jaynes and Williams, 1989; Sigelman and Welch, 1994; Wellman, 1993). On the other hand, signs of the unfulfilled promises of the movement abound. Income gaps, for instance, between whites and nonwhites remain even as differences in educational attainment decrease. In California, the gap between Anglo and African-American or Latino earnings is wider among the most educated in each racial group than it is among members of these racial groups with little education (Hubler and Silverstein, 1993). Half of all African Americans under age eighteen live in poverty (Terkel, 1992), and 25 percent live in "severely distressed" neighborhoods, defined by high levels of poverty, unemployment, and high school dropout rates (Annie E. Casey Foundation, 1994). Segregation and isolation of African Americans in housing, and therefore in education and employment, remain more pronounced than they do for any other group (Orfield, 1993; Massey and Denton, 1993).

The signs of unfulfilled promises are vivid in statistics on African-American males, who have the lowest life expectancy of any group in the United States and whose unemployment rate is more than twice that of white males. Among men with college degrees, blacks are three times more likely to be unemployed than are whites. Nearly 25 percent of black men between the ages of twenty and twenty-nine are in jail and are likely to remain there longer than whites who have committed the same crimes (Terkel, 1992).

From the perspective of the segregated and isolated inner city, where schools lack even basic college preparatory courses, the Creed and the American Dream it supports seem a cruel hoax. From this vantage point, middle-class subdivisions are distant and somewhat surreal. Many African Americans lack transportation to the jobs that have disappeared from the cities and reappeared in suburbs, as well as knowledge about those jobs to begin with. A growing number of African Americans respond to whites' dismissal of racial inequality and emphasis on blacks' immoral behavior with hostility and violence, which only reconfirm whites' negative views (Wilson, 1996). Many reject the dominant bootstrap culture and abandon the goal of integration, calling for separate institutions and adopting an "oppositional identity" defined as antiwhite (Fordham and Ogbu, 1986; Blauner, 1990; Bell, 1987). From this standpoint the dominant view of an accessible American Dream represents an ahistorical perspective and ignores the powerful role that the intergenerational transmission of advantage plays in our society. It denies that so much of what hardworking whites, particularly baby boomers, have accomplished is due in part to what many of their parents were able to provide for them—for example, years of formal education and personal wealth and property.

Of the different perspectives presented by the African Americans we interviewed, we call those with this more oppositional view the "separatists." Beginning with the black power movement of the 1960s, vocal and highly visible African Americans have developed a resistance-based cultural identity that incorporates a sophisticated critique of the American Dream. These separatists believe that the answer to the economic and political plight of African Americans is segregated solidarity—blacks supporting black-owned businesses and sending their children to all-black schools run by black educators (Bell, 1987; Adair, 1984). These separatists shun integration as a goal, partly because it comes with real political costs to African-American politicians and professionals who depend on a segregated power base.

Efforts to integrate housing and education are seen by separatists as divesting African Americans of their leadership roles in education and politics. This has been an argument against racial integration for many years. Myrdal (1962), for instance, noted that black professionals—preachers, teachers, doctors, lawyers, and businessmen—had built their economic and social existence on the segregation of their people, in response to the dictates of white society. "To state the situation bluntly: these upper class Negroes are left free to earn their living and their reputation in the backwater of discrimination, but they are not free to go into the main current of the river itself. On the one hand, they are kept fully aware of the wider range of opportunities from which they are excluded by segregation and discrimination. On the other hand, they know equally well how they are sheltered by the monopoly left to them in their little world apart" (p. 29).

In addition to these real political and professional issues, African Americans have also been faced with hostile responses to their entry into white schools and neighborhoods. Thus, we find that many blacks resist such policies as school desegregation, fed up with efforts to integrate into white institutions where they are frequently unwanted and accepted under unfavorable terms.

Yet while this separatist ideology has supported the careers of some black professionals and fostered a greater sense of community, as Wilson (1987; 1996) explains, this sense of community has been fractured over the past several decades by the exodus of the black middle class from the inner city, leaving low-income blacks more isolated from jobs and opportunities than ever. Furthermore, in a society in which most resources are controlled by whites, the separatist ideology can take African Americans only so far. As we demonstrate in this book, separate can never be equal in a society divided along racial lines, especially when people on one side of the line hold the vast majority of wealth.

We encountered, in addition to the separatists, other groups of African Americans, including a large number who were "beat down," resigned to their fate on the bottom of a very stratified society. These blacks exhibited what West (1993b) calls the "nihilistic threat born of both economic deprivation and political powerlessness and the related psychological depression, personal worthlessness and social despair so widespread in black America" (pp. 12–13). West writes of this nihilism, resulting from years of degradation, as a plague within an otherwise culturally rich community. We encountered several blacks who appeared caught in this beat-down syndrome. They tended to be those who quietly ignored social policies, such as school desegregation, designed to help them cross the color line. They spoke of a fear of interacting with whites, a fear born of their sense of powerlessness and alienation from the larger society. Some had experienced negative encounters with whites and had given up hope that they might be treated as equals.

The third group of African Americans we encountered harbored a "white is right" attitude. West (1993a, p. 27) calls this the "narrow assimilationist position" of blacks who define whiteness as good. "The closer I get [to whites] the better I feel. There is a tradition in black America like that." Some of the African Americans we interviewed are assimilationists. They tried hard to cross the color line and act as model white students and parents, only to be treated as less than equal by whites and accused of selling out by blacks. Many of the black assimilationists we interviewed had only negative things to say about members of their own race; they had developed a kind of "raceless persona" to help them achieve in a white world (Fordham, 1988).

But we found that the number of true assimilationists is quite small and that many of the African Americans we interviewed struggle endlessly to maintain their self-esteem in a society that rarely values their cultural heritage or contributions. Caught between black separatists and white racists, these African American "visionaries" struggle to be understood without selling out. They, like white visionaries on the other side of the color line, are the heroes and heroines of this book.

WHAT THIS BOOK IS ABOUT

The issues we raise here are complicated and insidious. The freedom of whites to segregate themselves in the suburbs creates a separation that has been legitimized by our culture and thus seems so innocent, so American.

This is a highly segregated society against which such policies as school desegregation and the individuals who believe in them must continually struggle. This means that the mechanisms of social change are individual agents—federal judges, educators, parents, and students. Given the persistence of the color line, these individuals and the policies they support are not supposed to win very often. They are swimming against a tide so unrelenting that even minor progress must be applauded.

We applaud the efforts of individuals who struggle against a racist system. Thus, this book is not filled with national statistics documenting the disparity in average incomes or rates of out-of-wedlock births for white versus nonwhite Americans. This is a case study of the creation, implementation, and impact of a 1983 federal court order that imposed a unique inter-district school desegregation program on a highly segregated metropolitan area, linking the mostly poor and black St. Louis City to its whiter and wealthier suburbs by allowing city students to transfer to suburban schools. The 1996–97 school year is the thirteenth year of this program, and all but two of the sixteen suburban school districts receiving city students now have enrollments that are at least 15 percent black. Eleven of these districts were virtually all-white when the program started.

In our five-year process of studying the St. Louis urban-suburban desegregation program and interviewing more than 300 educators, policy makers, parents, students, lawyers, and judges, we learned through their eyes just how entrenched the color line is and why people on both sides of that line lack the will to erase it. This book is their story.

The first of three parts, "The Politics of Race and Education," presents a broad historical overview. In Chapter 1 we revisit the creation of the color line. Using St. Louis as a case study, we depict the exodus of the white middle class from the cities and urban public schools of the nation. St. Louis resembles other metropolitan areas in terms of racial segregation, but it has many distinct features that exacerbated the separate and unequal experiences of blacks and whites. In Chapter 2 we provide a history of the St. Louis school desegregation case that resulted in an inter-district program bridging what had been very separate city and suburbs.

Part II, "The City," looks at the desegregation plan from the black side of the color line. In Chapter 3 we describe the decline of the St. Louis public school system, once nationally acclaimed, with 110,000 mostly white students, and now one of the nation's most disparaged districts, serving 42,000 mostly poor and black students. Linking the fiscal and social problems in the city schools to white flight, lack of political will, and decline of St. Louis in general, we argue that race was the most significant factor in the demise of this school district. We also consider the costs and benefits of the metropolitan-wide desegregation plan for the St. Louis schools.

In Chapter 4 we glimpse into the world of the students who remain in their all-black city school instead of transferring to a suburban school. Ironically, most of these "consumers of urban education" and their parents consider suburban schools "better" than city schools but say that they have made their school choices based on factors other than quality of education. These students and parents generally appear beat down, although some of them subscribe to a separatist ideology.

In Chapter 5 we focus on the African-American students who transfer from the city to suburban schools and succeed academically and sometimes socially. Our interviews with these students reveal that their success in suburbia is often related to either sustained parental support and encouragement or to a special talent—academic, athletic, or artistic—that is recognized and valued by whites. While some of the students and parents described in this chapter fit the description of assimilationists, many are visionary. These are generally the more savvy students and parents—those with a clear idea of how the suburban schools, much more than segregated city schools, will help them achieve their long-term goals.

In Chapter 6 we portray black students who transferred to suburban schools but ended up back in a city school or out of school altogether. Some of these "return" students found the social and academic demands of suburban schools too great, and some rebelled against what they considered unfair treatment by white educators. Compared with the African-American students who thrive in the suburban schools, these students tend to receive less parental support and direction. Their parents often appeared beat down as hopes of their children's success in a white-dominated world recede.

Part III, "The Suburbs," presents the story of the desegregation plan from the perspective of the mostly white educators, parents, and students who live in the county. In Chapter 7 we examine the political resistance of educators and parents in the suburbs to the desegregation plan. The whites described in this chapter are, for the most part, resistors.

In Chapter 8 we focus on suburban educators who see black students in their otherwise white schools as an asset rather than a liability. Within their stories lie some of the best-kept secrets of the St. Louis desegregation plan. Often isolated and unknown to one another, these visionary educators are striving to change the status quo in their classrooms, schools, and districts. They credit the transfer program with prompting them to reexamine their assumptions about teaching and learning and to thus improve their schools in ways that benefit all students.

In Chapter 9 we look more closely at how the white parents and students in the suburbs view the desegregation plan. Because there is no strong pro-integration stance on the part of state and local leaders, most of the white taxpayers in suburban St. Louis do not realize that their local school districts derive financial and educational benefits from the desegregation program. We did find that the white suburban students who live with the desegregation plan tend to become, with every school day, more accepting of the program than do their parents. The whites portrayed in this chapter represent a mixture of resistors and sympathizers, yet there is hope that some of the white students will be the next generation of visionaries.

In Chapter 10 we offer our conclusions and recommendations for policy makers, educators, civil rights advocates, parents, and voters. Without trying to second-guess the lawyers and judges who designed this program, we recommend some changes in the St. Louis plan based on knowledge gleaned from our research. We hope these suggestions will be helpful as society reconsiders school desegregation and school choice policies.

The story of the struggle in St. Louis over race and school desegregation forces whites, African Americans, Latinos, Asians, and Native Americans all over the United States to question their separate and unequal lives. Through the men, women, and children of St. Louis who, because of a federal court order, now associate with people they would have never known, we tell of fear, alienation, and misunderstanding. We also tell of blacks and whites who strive to find a middle ground where race does not splinter them into antagonistic groups but where differences are appreciated and understood as historical social constructs.

This is a story of hope and possibility, of lessons learned and mistakes best not repeated. We commend the people of St. Louis, who, for better or worse, have wrestled with racial issues that people in other metropolitan areas have been unwilling to touch. Most important, this is a story that depicts how far we as a nation still have to go, how encompassing our solutions must be, and how quickly we need to act. We emerged from this study not with all the answers but with a clearer understanding of the problems as far more intricate and embedded than most people in our "meritocratic" and "color-blind" society are willing to admit.

PART I

The Politics of Race

I

Creating the Color Line:
White Flight and Urban Ghettos

Housing is an outward expression of the inner human nature, no society can be fully
understood apart from the residences of its members.
—Kenneth Jackson, *Crabgrass Frontier*

If ever a place symbolized the past and present problems of urban America,
it is St. Louis, a once-grand city encircled by affluent suburbs. Known as the
Gateway to the West, St. Louis stands at the crossroads of the nation, where
southern politeness meets northern refinement, where East Coast tradition
encounters West Coast individualism, and where the muddy Missouri River
converges with the mighty Mississippi. The city fans out from the Mississippi
River on the eastern edge of Missouri, a state that defies categorization and
borders eight diverse states, including Nebraska and Tennessee. Most north-
erners consider Missouri a part of the South, and southerners think of it as belonging to the Midwest. In fact, Missouri has several distinct regions and has
been called a microcosm of the complexity that characterizes U.S. history
(Christensen, 1988). St. Louis, Missouri's oldest city, embodies this confluence
of cultural themes that represent American society.

The metaphor of St. Louis as a reflection of the nation is especially poignant in relation to racial issues and the history of African Americans. Missouri in general and St. Louis specifically have been at the center of several events shaping the country's racial landscape over the past 175 years. From the Missouri Compromise of 1820, which dictated the future of slavery, to St. Louis' Pruitt-Igoe housing project, an emblem of failed urban policies, this centralized state and its quintessential city have repeatedly reminded Americans of inherent contradictions in our nation's efforts to eliminate racial inequality. St. Louis, where a bold statue of Ulysses S. Grant stands less than a mile from the Robert E. Lee Riverboat, is referred to in African-American folklore as a southern city with a northern exposure. This mixture of north-south identity has produced an odd form of racial politics in St. Louis that often appears progressive while maintaining the status quo.

W. E. B. Du Bois (1969) predicted in the early 1900s that the problem of the American twentieth century would be the problem of the color line, and the demographics of St. Louis today are testimony to his wisdom. According to the 1990 Census, of the 232 largest U.S. metropolitan areas, St. Louis is the eleventh most racially segregated (Farley and Frey, 1994), the result of nearly two centuries of denial on the part of most St. Louisans that the color line not only exists but remains a formidable barrier. The end of twentieth century finds St. Louis City a shadow of its former self, deserted by whites who sought the American Dream in suburban townships with their own school systems, governments, and zoning ordinances.

This is the setting for the city-suburban school desegregation plan that we describe and analyze in this book; this is the color line over which African-American students who participate in the desegregation plan must step every school day. Some of these students step lightly so no one in the suburbs will hear them or learn of their journey; others roll like thunder onto the fairly tranquil suburban campuses, carrying with them anger and frustration borne of the history of their people. Many suburban whites look at these often loud and disruptive students with disgust, as if black youths had written their own history and created their own sense of frustration and hopelessness while whites stood by innocently. This is the misunderstanding that comes from living on opposite sides of the color line for far too long.

IN THE BEGINNING, THERE WAS RACE

In 1764, French fur trappers from New Orleans founded St. Louis as a trading post eighteen miles south of the confluence of the Mississippi and Missouri Rivers. With them came African slaves. Later, Spaniards brought slaves to work in the nearby lead mines. When the United States purchased the Louisiana Territory from France in 1803, there were 10,340 people residing in what is now Missouri, including 1,320 blacks (Kirschten, 1960).

With slavery legally sanctioned in the new territory, whites from southern states, especially Kentucky, Tennessee, and Virginia, migrated there, bringing slaves and pro-slavery politics with them. They settled in the central farming region of Missouri, known as Boonslick, along the shores of the Missouri River. Farmers in Boonslick, nicknamed "little Dixie," used slave labor for the production of tobacco, hemp, corn, and livestock. By 1820, Missouri was the only midwestern territory with significant numbers of slaves, who accounted for about 15 percent of its population (Confluence, 1989).

While slave-owning whites were migrating to rural areas of Missouri, settlers from the northeast were flocking to St. Louis, where only a few wealthy whites from the South owned slaves. The concentration of anti-slavery Yankees in St. Louis juxtaposed with southern slave owners in the rural areas helped shape an urban-versus-rural political antagonism that continues to this day. Attitudes toward slavery across Missouri in the early 1800s were said to mirror those in the nation at large: mixed and heated (Christensen, 1988, p. 95). It is only fitting that, as the northernmost territory allowing slavery—an institution on which most of its urban citizens were not dependent—Missouri and its struggle for statehood would intensify the national debate over race and liberty.

This debate over slavery escalated each time a new state was admitted to the union, especially with states such as Missouri, which were not clearly northern or southern. The Missouri Compromise of 1820 admitted Missouri as a slave state but stipulated that every future state north of Missouri's southern border was to be free. Some historians believe that this famous compromise postponed the Civil War for a generation (Christensen, 1988, p. 95), but it also left Missouri surrounded, except along its southern border, by free states. This position would assure that Missouri and its largest city would remain at the center of the nation's racial tensions.

The Missouri Compromise directed the legislature to keep freed slaves out of the state, and in the 1830s those freed slaves who did reside in Missouri were frequently hired out by authorities (Orfield, 1985).

Between 1840 and 1860, St. Louis experienced an influx of anti-slavery German immigrants as the city's population increased from about 6,000 to nearly 160,700. By 1860, nearly a third of St. Louisians had been born in Germany (Christensen, 1988; Primm, 1990). With the German influx, the abolitionist movement in St. Louis expanded, and the conflict between pro- and anti-slavery forces grew fierce, gaining national attention.

In 1836, one of the first martyrs of the abolitionist cause, newspaper editor Elijah P. Lovejoy, was attacked by a pro-slavery mob in St. Louis after publishing articles condemning the lynching of a mulatto steamboat steward. The pro-slavery vigilantes followed Lovejoy to Illinois and eventually killed him, throwing his printing press into the Mississippi River (Christensen, 1988; Primm, 1990). A few years later, St. Louis slave Dred Scott traveled with his master to Illinois. On returning to St. Louis, Scott sued for his freedom, arguing that because he had been in a free state he was therefore free. While the lower court agreed with Scott, the Missouri Supreme Court overturned not only the lower court's decision but several of its own prior decisions when it ruled that the "voluntary removal of a slave by his master to a state that prohibits slavery does not entitle the slave to sue for his freedom in the courts of this state." The case was appealed to the U.S. Supreme Court, which held on March 7, 1857, that "a Negro, by Missouri law, a slave, could not bring suit for his freedom in a federal court," thereby denying Scott the right to sue in federal court because Negroes, enslaved or free, were not citizens (Joiner, 1971; Primm, 1990, pp. 241–243).

These events inflamed the debate over slavery, and Missouri, sharply divided between pro- and anti-slavery forces, was a microcosm of the national turmoil. Throughout the 1850s, many St. Louisians, including Ulysses S. Grant, freed their slaves. The number of slaves in the city declined dramatically from 20 percent of the population in 1840 to less than 1 percent in 1860 (Kirschten, 1960; Primm, 1990). By the outbreak of the Civil War, less than one-fourth of white Missourians owned slaves, and two-thirds of the state's 114,931 slaves were owned by planters in little Dixie. Free blacks outnumbered slaves in St. Louis, and a small black aristocracy had integrated into the city's high society.

The true tragedy of the Civil War—brother fighting brother and neighbor against neighbor—was perhaps no place more vivid than in Missouri. During the war, the pro-slavery governor, Claiborn Fox Jackson, and several legislators fled to Arkansas and established a government in exile to represent Missouri in the Confederacy. Meanwhile, the Union army declared martial law on Missouri and established a provisional state government. Families and communities were split, with 40,000 Missourians fighting for the Confederacy and 110,000 for the Union. As a state divided over slavery and one of the southernmost states controlled by the Union, Missouri was third, behind Virginia and Tennessee, in the number of Civil War battles or skirmishes (Christensen, 1988; Primm, 1990).

On January 11, 1865, the Missouri legislature freed the last 45,000 slaves in the state, most of whom lived in little Dixie, where postwar survival was

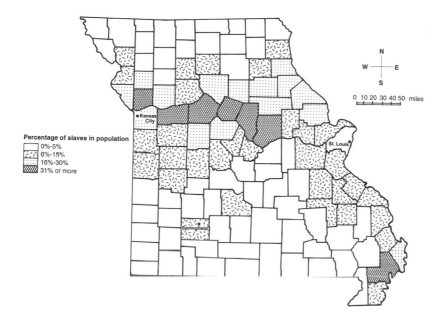

Figure 1.1 Slavery in Missouri, by County, 1860
Source: State Maps on File: Midwest. © Facts on File 1984. Reprinted with permission by Facts on File, Inc., New York.

difficult. Soon many of these former slaves would migrate to the promised land—St. Louis.

THE BIRTH OF THE URBAN GHETTO

One of the greatest demographic shifts in U.S. history—the migration of African Americans from the farms to the cities and from the South to the North during the century following the Civil War—occurred so gradually that its impact is almost incomprehensible. While historians disagree over which years constitute *the* "great migration" of blacks out of the rural South, demographic data show large waves between 1915 and 1930 and again from 1940 well into the 1960s. According to Grossman (1989), about half a million blacks left the South between 1916 and 1919 to start anew in northern cities; nearly 1 million more followed during the 1920s. Between the early 1940s and the late 1960s, more than 5 million blacks left the South for the cities (Lemann, 1991). Within the broader background of these peak migration periods was a constant 100-year flow of blacks into urban areas—in the North and South—that was greeted by an increasingly sophisticated system of housing segregation. According to Massey and Denton (1993), no racial group in the history of the United States has experienced the sustained level of residential segregation that has been imposed on blacks.

Residential segregation, once condoned by law and still upheld by custom, remains at the heart of racial inequality in the United States. This intense separation of living spaces produces more than feelings of rejection and degradation among African Americans; it has major consequences for their life chances by denying them access to employment, personal financing, home equity, a better educational system, and the social networks that make upward mobility possible. According to Massey and Denton, "Residential segregation is the institutional apparatus that supports other racially discriminatory processes and binds them together into a coherent and uniquely effective system of racial subordination" (p. 8).

For whites in the 1990s to understand how housing segregation and thus an entire structure of racial subordination became so entrenched during the past 150 years—at a time when whites were supposedly becoming more open-minded about race—requires a broad historical perspective. It requires the realization that most of the houses built in the days of legal segregation are still standing, which means that the unwritten rules of the housing market created during that era (concerning the value of property in a given neighborhood, and so on) continue to shape peoples' most important economic decision: where to purchase a home.

But examining current conditions from a historical perspective and conceptualizing privilege as something passed down from generation to generation runs counter to most white Americans' perceptions of the world. For instance, a 1969 report from a conference of St. Louis–area leaders noted, "There is a determined mood in the white community to use the safeguarding of middle-class values which may be otherwise worthwhile as a means of blocking pressure for social change" (Human Development Corporation, 1970, p. 14). Whites must reexamine the urban ghettos they constantly critique and recognize that their ancestors helped to create the inner cities of today.

According to Hirsch (1993), the present-day black ghetto was created in three stages: between emancipation and the New Deal in 1933; between 1933 and 1968, a time of growing federal presence in urban affairs; and in the current post–civil rights era. In each of these eras St. Louis was at the center of the racial divide.

The Great Migration and the Meek Metropolis

In 1860, about 90 percent of the 4.5 million blacks living in the United States were slaves living in the South, heavily concentrated in the "black belt" (the cotton-growing states, from Mississippi to Georgia) and the "tobacco belt" (Kentucky and Virginia). By 1940, the percentage of blacks living in the South had declined to 77, and by 1970, only 53 percent of blacks called the South home. Yet the "urbanization" of blacks was even more dramatic than their movement north. In 1880, more than 87 percent of blacks were farmworkers, usually sharecroppers; by 1981, only 1 percent of the nation's 26.5 million blacks were working in farming (Hirsch, 1993, pp. 66–67). This migration of African Americans out of the rural South—the only home most had known on this continent—had major cultural, social, and political impacts on the nation (Grossman, 1989).

Being both northern and southern, Missouri was a place to migrate from *and* to. The first wave of black migration occurred within state borders as former slaves moved eastward from little Dixie to St. Louis shortly after the Civil War. In fact, historians note that the national migration of blacks from the farms to the cities began with this early transition within Missouri (Ahmad-Taylor, 1994). Some blacks tried to migrate to St. Louis from other, more southern states at the time, but city officials were openly hostile. In fact, in 1879, Mayor Henry Overstolz tried to prevent steamboats carrying blacks from the South from landing in St. Louis. He threatened to fine the steamboat companies, and he wired southern authorities warning of the dismal prospects facing black newcomers (Orfield, 1981). Still, the African-American population in St. Louis grew from less than 4,000 in 1860 to more than 22,000 in 1880, well before the larger, cross-country migration of blacks began. By 1900, the black population of St. Louis was surpassed only by that of Baltimore, Philadelphia, and New York (Confluence, 1989; Troen, 1975). Later, with the national migration of blacks, another influx of African Americans from farther south came to call St. Louis home.

The early urbanization of Missouri blacks was accompanied by the premature development of a system of racial segregation in St. Louis. National data show that most African Americans who lived in northern cities before 1900 were not significantly more segregated than members of other ethnic groups (Massey and Denton, 1993, p. 19). Yet in St. Louis, housing segregation rose more quickly after 1860 than in any of the nineteen cities Massey and Denton (1993) examined. For instance, St. Louis' "index of dissimilarity," or the percentage of blacks who must move to create even racial composition across all neighborhoods, was a moderate 39 in 1860. By 1910 it had jumped to 54, and by 1940 it was 93, meaning that in order to create a racially balanced city, 93 percent of all blacks would have to move into white neighborhoods (p. 21). From 1890 to 1930 the percentage of blacks who lived in predominantly black neighborhoods increased from 11 to 47 (p. 24).

In 1870 three of the twelve wards in St. Louis housed 55 percent of the city's African Americans but only 30 percent of the whites. By 1900 the city contained more than thirty wards, and 49 percent of all blacks lived in six of these, next to only 14 percent of all whites. Two of these wards were the most densely populated in the city, with living quarters wedged behind factories and warehouses. Four of the wards were overcrowded and contained crumbling and poorly constructed boardinghouses, tenements, and shanties. "Landlord discrimination, high rents and white persecution were obstacles to blacks moving to better neighborhoods" (Confluence, 1989, p. 13).

The patterns of racial segregation that emerged in St. Louis were not simply products of Southern racial politics. Although Southern Democrats controlled the state government, race relations throughout Missouri and in St. Louis reflected both northern and southern norms (Christensen, 1988, p. 99). During the era of state-enforced, or de jure, segregation across the South, the Jim Crow laws in Missouri were perhaps least extreme. For instance, while blacks attended separate schools and while many restrooms and restaurants were for whites only, Missouri blacks were rarely denied the right to vote, and public transportation was not segregated. This relative freedom is reflected in a well-known expression of blacks who migrated from Mississippi to St. Louis: "I'd rather be a lamppost on Targee Street [in St. Louis] than be mayor of Dixie" (Troen, 1975, p. 81).

James Buford, president of the St. Louis Urban League, recalled that in the 1950s, when he was a young boy, his mother would remind him to use the bathroom before they went downtown, where there were no public restrooms for blacks. Yet Buford and his mother did not have to sit in the back of the public bus, and they could eat in most restaurants but only at certain counters. Not until 1965, under threat of federal intervention, did the Missouri legislature pass the Public Accommodations Act, prohibiting discrimination in restaurants, theaters, and all public places (Confluence, 1989).

Buford said that the Jim Crow laws in St. Louis were nothing compared to what he saw in his travels to Mississippi and Louisiana. He said that southern blacks who migrated to St. Louis were usually on their way to Chicago or Detroit but stopped in the Gateway City because it was so much better than where they had been—"always just enough good jobs, always just enough of everything" to keep them from traveling on. But as the migration of blacks from the South continued, St. Louis and other northern cities developed sophisticated patterns of segregation that would prove more enduring than the Jim Crow laws. St. Louis maintained aspects of a southern-style de jure segregation system, particularly "separate but equal" schools, even as it developed a more insidious northern-style de facto system of segregation that was not legally sanctioned but strongly supported by customs and actions. Terry Jones, dean of arts and sciences at the University of Missouri–St. Louis and a historian of the city, explained the mix of northern and southern racial policies: "You could argue that we have the worst of both worlds racially—that we have the southern tradition as incorporated in our laws being a former slave state and of being a state that had a constitutional mandate for educational segregation and which used the state court system to enforce restrictive covenants—all southern attributes. And yet we have the kind of northern indifference to race. . . . So we have this lack of social interaction of any kind really, which is a northern attribute, and then you have the southern laws."

In their study of housing segregation, Farley and Frey (1994) note that one of three major factors affecting present-day segregation in cities is the region of the country in which they are located. Region matters, because in the nineteenth century, states in the Northeast and Midwest granted city officials substantial authority to expand city boundaries by annexing outlying areas. In fact, the adjustment of local boundaries through annexation became the "dominant method of population growth" for large northern cities (Jackson, 1985, pp. 140–141). Greater New York City, for instance, was created in 1898 when Manhattan annexed Brooklyn—once the fourth largest city in the United States—Queens, Staten Island, and the Bronx. Other cities, including Minneapolis, Cleveland, and Pittsburgh, expanded through a series of small additions. St. Louis increased its area from 4.5 to 14 square miles in 1856, to 17 square miles in 1870, and eventually to 61 square miles in 1876 (Jackson, 1985, p. 143). During the nineteenth century most residents in outlying areas welcomed this annexation because they identified with their neighboring cities and because the merger brought sewers, schools, water, and police services, which poor rural communities could not finance on their own. This strategy of northern city growth worked for many decades, until the surrounding communities decided they were better off as separate political entities.

In the South, however, cities rarely had the authority to annex surrounding communities, in part because of racial politics. In the late nineteenth century, southern legislatures feared that black voters would join poor whites in a populist movement, so the legislatures vested authority in countywide governments, which were subject to state control, and transferred power from cities to counties, diluting urban votes. Paradoxically, this metropolitan form of government inhibited racial segregation by precluding the formation of autonomous suburbs (Jackson, 1985).

By the early 1900s, in the absence of metropolitan governments in the North and Midwest, opposition to urban annexations mounted, and residents in outlying areas formed independent suburban communities. They developed their own land-use regulations, zoning, ordinances, police forces, and public schools. With no state-sanctioned segregation to dictate who lived where, suburbanites built an elaborate de facto system of segregation through an animosity toward blacks that indicated neighborhoods, parks, and schools were for whites only. After World War II, blacks continued to flow from farms to cities, more suburbs were incorporated, and the "centrifugal movement" of the white middle-class to suburbia began (Jackson 1985, p. 147).

In spite of Missouri's southern history of slavery and Jim Crow, the pattern of urban annexation and the eventual city-suburban divide was characteristically northern—but ahead of the northern trend. The urban-suburban dividing line was drawn in 1876 with the city's final annexation of land and vote to separate from the county, making it one of the first independent U.S. cities (Jackson, 1985, p. 143). In seceding from the then-rural county, city residents unknowingly locked their beloved St. Louis into a pattern of urban decline well before such decline became the national norm. Paradoxically, the 1876 vote was in part driven by city residents' fear that the end of Reconstruction would return political control of the state to the strongly Confederate little Dixie region. Thus, city voters wanted to assure independence and less state interference in local matters; the Unionist majority in St. Louis was willing to let the Confederates run the state if they could run their city (Faherty, 1976). A new state Constitution was adopted the same year, making St. Louis the first city ever granted constitutionally guaranteed home-rule status (Primm, 1990). Under this new charter, St. Louis County was granted 506 square miles, compared to the city's 61, which St. Louisians believed was more than enough to accommodate the city's growth (Faherty, 1976).

Today, the shape and size of St. Louis City are the same as those specified in the 1876 Constitution. The entire city, except a narrow strip to the north, may be circumscribed by an eight-mile semicircle spread eastward from the Mississippi River. Surrounding the city is St. Louis County, with its distinct suburban communities and conglomeration of towns and governments.

While the city leaders were obviously wrong in their prediction that 61 square miles would leave enough room to expand, in the short run the city was one of the largest and fastest growing in the country. In 1870 it was the fourth largest city in the nation behind New York, Philadelphia, and Brooklyn, a ranking it would maintain until 1920, when it dropped to sixth behind Cleveland and Detroit. Despite the city's increase in population throughout the 1920s, the rate of that growth began to slow.

Meanwhile, between 1910 and 1920 the population of St. Louis County grew quickly—26 percent growth in the county compared with 12 percent in the city (Tobin, 1976, p. 100). The 1920 Census also revealed that, for the first time since 1870, the black population in St. Louis had accelerated more rapidly than the population as a whole; it grew from 6 percent of the city's 730,000 population in 1910 to 9 percent of the 780,000 population in 1920 (Primm, 1990, p. 441). The great migration of blacks from South to North and from farms to cities had begun, bringing a second wave of black migrants to St. Louis, this time from further south, particularly the Mississippi Delta.

From 1910 to 1930, the black migration into Missouri peaked, as more than 90,000 blacks poured in from other states, settling mostly in the cities. Meanwhile, in-state migration continued, as 102 of the state's 114 counties lost African Americans to St. Louis and Kansas City. At the outbreak of the Depression, these two cities contained about 60 percent of the state's 223,830 blacks, with 90,000 in St. Louis, more than twice the number in Kansas City ("Kansas City," 1971). The increasingly segregated black neighborhoods in St. Louis were overcrowded, and the housing was frequently run down. By the end of World War II, St. Louis led the nation in substandard housing (Confluence, 1989, p. 13).

As more whites moved to the suburbs, St. Louis, like other older cities, sought unsuccessfully to grow. In the 1920s, the business elite—a group known as the Greater St. Louis Conference—led a well-publicized campaign to consolidate the city and the county. If such action was not taken, members of the conference prophesized, the city would shrink in comparison to other

Figure 1.2 Missouri Counties in St. Louis Region
Source: *State Maps on File: Midwest.* © *Facts on File, 1984. Reprinted with permission by Facts on File, Inc., New York.*

great cities. In 1924 residents voted on a city-county consolidation proposal that would have made St. Louis the world's largest city. The plan won a majority in the city, but it was resoundingly rejected by county voters (Jackson, 1985, p. 150). By this time, the city already had a sizable and quickly growing black population, leading some historians to speculate that race was a factor in the county voters' resistance to the merger. A series of efforts to reverse the city-county divide continued into the 1960s, but to no avail (Orfield, 1980a).

The conference's prediction became reality in 1940, when Census data showed that the city's population had declined for the first time in 120 years. Though the decrease was small—less than 1 percent, to 816,048—the rush of city dwellers to the green suburbs had more than doubled the county population during the 1930–40 decade, to 274,230. Eighty percent of new construction in the metropolitan area between 1935 and 1940 occurred outside the city (Primm, 1990, p. 472).

As an extreme example of a national trend, whites in St. Louis were moving toward the outermost boundaries of the city and eventually beyond while more blacks made their way into the city. Blacks in St. Louis and elsewhere continued to be much more segregated than were other ethnic groups, whose ghettos were often "temporary way stations that oversaw the ultimate dispersal—not the increasing concentration—of their residents" (Hirsch, 1993, p. 71). Most cities provided separate settlement houses for white immigrants and black migrants, and blacks had far fewer housing choices than did other newcomers. According to Hirsch, nonracial forces could not have produced the extreme levels of black-white segregation that were in place by the 1930s (p. 70).

By the early 1940s the final and most significant wave of black migration had begun, with the largest decennial black migration from the South occurring between 1940 and 1950 (Hirsch, 1993). Sparked by World War II mobilization, this wave intensified with the mechanization of southern agriculture and New Deal policies forcing farmers to pay minimum wage. Once-essential black farmhands and sharecroppers were no longer needed or wanted in the South. From the Mississippi Delta, where mechanical cotton pickers made sharecropping obsolete, blacks flowed by the trainload into the cites (Lemann, 1991). The massive displacement of blacks in agriculture led to urbanization of blacks in all regions of the country. In 1940, almost two-thirds of African Americans resided in rural areas; in 1950, more than half lived in cities. By 1960, blacks were more urbanized than were whites, and in 1970, only 19 percent of blacks lived in rural areas. Meanwhile, the number of whites in the largest cities peaked in 1960, after which flight to the suburbs became the norm (Farley, 1975). Thus, in a perfectly parallel manner whites suburbanized as blacks urbanized (Hirsch, 1993). The causal relation in this parallel is obvious in histories of cities such as St. Louis.

The black migrants who flooded into St. Louis from 1940 to the 1960s—the third large wave of mostly poor and poorly educated blacks into the city in less than 100 years—arrived in a city trapped between the Mississippi River and a suburban county of small, autonomous, rapidly growing, and fairly homogeneous communities that wanted nothing to do with the increasingly poor and overcrowded city. In 1945, blacks constituted 13 percent of the city's population. By 1957, after an influx of 95,000 blacks, they constituted 30 percent of the population. Although the third wave of black migrants had subsided somewhat by the late 1960s, St. Louis continued to lure blacks. In the early 1980s, the largest single group of migrants to the city was blacks from outside the region (Community Advisory Committee, 1985).

Private Actions with Public Consequences

Although most St. Louis blacks were forced to live in one of four wards during the 1880s, there were a few neighborhoods, recently abandoned by whites, in which the housing stock was decent. One such neighborhood was a tight-knit community northwest of the downtown business district. Originally called Elleardsville after Charles Elleards, a horticulturist who owned the land, the neighborhood attracted German, Irish, and a small number of African-American residents in the mid-1800s. Yet because Elleardsville, eventually called the "Ville," was one of the only established neighborhoods open to blacks, it became a magnet for African-American migrants, especially those with the means to purchase homes. In 1920, 8 percent of Ville residents were African American; by 1950, it was 95 percent black. The Ville became the center of the black community and thus the "cradle of black culture" in St. Louis (Wright, 1994).

The Ville was home to many of the social institutions—churches, schools, a hospital, and small businesses—serving the African-American community in St. Louis. Of these institutions, the public schools were perhaps the greatest symbol of the opportunity that St. Louis offered black migrants. Although Missouri maintained "separate but equal" schools for white and black students, St. Louis provided a free public education to black children that was rich in comparison to that in the rural South. In the Ville, Simmons Elementary School (originally called Elleardsville Colored School No. 8) opened in 1873; Sumner High School, the first black high school west of the Mississippi River, opened in 1874. Yet as more blacks moved in and more schools for black children only were established in the Ville and surrounding areas, more whites began to leave. The John Marshall Elementary School, for instance, was built in 1900 in the Ville for white students. By 1918 it had been converted into a black intermediate school. In this way the segregated housing and educational systems fed off of each other, drawing a color line that would remain long after Jim Crow was gone (Orfield, 1980b).

As blacks continued to pour into St. Louis and concentrate in the few neighborhoods where they had access to housing, the Ville became isolated from the rest of the city, surrounded by neighborhoods of poor blacks and substandard housing. While the Ville remained for many years a vibrant neighborhood at the center of the black community, by 1970 racial isolation and the resulting poverty and lack of employment had taken their toll. Since then, many of its institutions, including the only hospital located in the North St. Louis area and the main employer of black doctors and nurses, have closed down.

While many older black St. Louisians have fond memories of the segregated Ville in its heyday, there is another side to the story of how the entire north side of St. Louis became black and poor. This less appealing side to racial segregation is reflected in the flight of whites, and the jobs and tax dollars they took with them. While segregation may seem tolerable from within caring communities like the Ville, segregation is usually built on discrimination and too often nurtures the concentration of poverty and isolation from opportunity that destroys even the strongest black neighborhoods (Wilson, 1996).

In St. Louis, as in other cities experiencing large influxes of African-American migrants, whites worked to systematically restrict blacks' access to housing. Thus, despite blacks' efforts to move out of the ghettos, they were continually rebuffed, "not by invisible, impersonal or anonymous forces" (Hirsch, 1993) but by explicitly racial restrictions, including racial zoning laws, restrictive covenants, racial steering, redlining and exclusionary zones. "No other group had to face such an onslaught; it was the distinguishing characteristic that separated the black ghetto from the ethnic slum" (p. 73). These restrictions have constructed a color line so deeply etched into our cities that it remains years after the laws were revoked and the private practices forbidden. Again, St. Louis presents one of the worst-case scenarios.

Racial zoning laws were perhaps the most blatant form of racial restriction. These statutes, associated with older Jim Crow laws, legalized residential segregation by forbidding blacks from renting or buying in certain neighborhoods or on certain streets. By the beginning of the twentieth century, these laws were prevalent in cities in Virginia, North Carolina, and South Carolina. By 1916 cities in border states—including St. Louis, Baltimore, and Louisville—had adopted similar zoning laws. In fact, in February 1916, St. Louis became the first city in the United States to enact mandatory residential segregation, via a 3-to-1 vote in a popular referendum. An advocate of the law pointed out in a preelection debate that if the schools and hotels were segregated by law it only made sense to extend the same principle to housing (cited in Orfield, 1981).

In 1917 the U.S. Supreme Court, in *Buchanan v. Warley,* a case from Louisville, invalidated racial zoning laws, though several southern cities attempted to resurrect them in the 1920s (Hirsch, 1993, p. 73).

With racial zoning laws nullified, border cities turned to other strategies of racial segregation. In St. Louis, the City Plan Commission manipulated zoning boundaries in such a way as to keep blacks out of white residential areas and to control the movement of blacks by erecting small residential zones for blacks in the midst of industrial and commercial areas. In 1927 the commission suspended the requirement that parks be built in residential areas so that a playground for black children could be built near their homes in an industrialized area (Orfield, 1981).

Furthermore, in many northern neighborhoods, white property owners had established a set of private agreements, known as racially restrictive covenants, which stated that the residents would not sell or lease their property to blacks or any other racial, ethnic, or religious group deemed undesirable. These pacts were established through the careful orchestration of neighborhood "improvement associations," whose ostensible purpose was to promote neighborhood "security and property values." These organizations attempted to achieve these goals by keeping blacks out through a variety of tactics, including lobbying city councils to close rooming houses that attracted blacks, withdrawing patronage from white businesses that catered to blacks, and collecting funds to buy property from blacks or purchase homes that stood vacant for too long (Massey and Denton, 1993). Yet the most effective tactic of neighborhood improvement associations was to implement restrictive covenants, barring sales or leasing to members of many ethnic groups, usually blacks. In St. Louis there were 316 restrictive covenants by 1930, and 99 percent of these covenants specified blacks alone as the group to be excluded. During years of heavy black migration to urban areas, entire subdivisions were placed under such covenants (Hirsch, 1993; Orfield, 19981).

Property owners who signed restrictive covenants bound themselves and their heirs to the agreements for a specified time. Local improvement associations conducted covenant-writing campaigns, which became vehicles for rallies against black "invasions" of their neighborhoods. It was not unusual for these organizations to exert pressure on potential white sellers and black buyers, as well as on black homeowners residing on the fringes of white neighborhoods. The pressure placed on blacks was often violent, including house bombings, which deterred other blacks from moving into a neighborhood (Hirsch, 1993). Whites who violated the convenants and tried to sell to blacks could be sued for damages by any party to the agreement (Massey and Denton, 1993, p. 36). Furthermore, judges frequently enforced restrictive covenants—that is, until a 1948 U.S. Supreme Court ruling in a St. Louis case, *Shelley v. Kraemer.*

In 1945, a black family named Shelley attempted to purchase a house in a white neighborhood just west of the Ville. The owner, a white man named Bishop, entered into an agreement with the Shelley family despite a 1911 neighborhood covenant that included the Bishop house. The covenant stated, "No part of said property or any portion thereof shall be, for said term of Fifty-years, occupied by any person not of the Caucasian race, it being intended hereby to restrict the use of said property for said period of time against the occupancy as owners or tenants of any portion of said property for resident or other purpose by people of the Negro or Mongolian Race" (*Shelley v. Kraemer,* 1948, p. 4).

Ironically, at the time the covenant was signed by white property owners, five of the forty-seven parcels covered under this agreement were owned by blacks (four of the five had been owned by blacks for more than thirty-four years). Still, the white property owners brought suit against the Shelleys and the Bishops in the Circuit Court of St. Louis City, asking that the Shelley family be restrained from taking possession of the property. The court denied the request on the grounds that the restrictive covenant had not been signed by all of the property owners in the area covered by the agreement. The case was appealed to the Missouri Supreme Court, which reversed the decision, holding that the agreement was effective and that its enforcement did not violate the rights of the Shelley family (*Shelley v. Kraemer,* 1948, p. 6).

On May 3, 1948, the U.S. Supreme Court overturned the Missouri Supreme Court ruling along with a similar decision from the Michigan Supreme Court regarding a restrictive covenant in Detroit. The Supreme Court held that while the private actions of individuals to create such restrictive covenants do not violate the Constitution, the actions of state courts and officials in enforcing such private agreements do indeed infringe on the rights of those barred from purchasing private property. The equal protection clause of the Fourteenth Amendment, the Supreme Court noted, "erects no shield against merely private conduct, however discriminatory or wrongful" (p. 12). But in both the Missouri and Michigan cases, the court ruled, the purposes of the private agreements were secured by the state courts. "The undisputed facts disclose that petitioners were willing purchasers of properties upon which they desired to establish homes. The owners of the properties were willing sellers, and contracts of sale were accordingly consummated. It is clear that but for the active intervention of the state courts, supported by the full panoply of state power, petitioners would have been free to occupy the properties in question without restraint" (*Shelley v. Kraemer*, 1948, p. 19).

The Supreme Court ruling in *Shelley v. Kraemer* left whites and their neighborhood improvement associations free to write restrictive covenants, but it prohibited the state from enforcing such agreements. Twenty years later the Supreme Court, in a case from suburban St. Louis, extended the ban on racial discrimination in the sale or rental of property to *all* actions—private and public (*Jones v. Mayer Co.*, 1968). Still, the *Shelley v. Kraemer* ruling curtailed the use of restrictive covenants because the power of such agreements was vested in the ability of the neighborhood associations to call on the courts to enforce their agreements and punish those who violated them (Massey and Denton, 1993, p. 36). However, white neighborhood associations used other means, including violence and intimidation, to keep African Americans out of their communities. (Franklin, 1993, p. 64).

In fact, during World War II a rash of antiblack violence erupted in cities around the country as defense industry jobs drew white workers off the farms, creating a shortage of housing and severe overcrowding in the cities for blacks and whites alike. White homeowners and tenants increasingly resorted to violence as blacks encroached into their neighborhoods. In Chicago, for instance, whites assaulted forty-six black homeowners between May 1944 and July 1946. And from 1945 throughout the 1950s, large-scale riots over the black occupation of previously all-white neighborhoods erupted in Chicago and Detroit, with lesser disturbances in St. Louis, New York, and Philadelphia (Hirsch, 1993, p. 84). The violence subsided as segregated suburbia blossomed, allowing many whites to flee the cities rather than stay and fight for their urban neighborhoods.

Beyond the violence, racial zoning, and restrictive covenants, local real estate boards and companies acted as gatekeepers, steering blacks into all-black neighborhoods. In 1924 the National Association of Real Estate Boards (NAREB) adopted an article in its code of ethics stating that a real estate agent should never introduce into a neighborhood "members of any race or nationality . . . whose presence will clearly be detrimental to property values in that neighborhood." The president of NAREB drafted model real estate agent licensing guidelines, adopted by thirty-two states, that permitted state commissions to revoke the license of any agent who violated the code (Hirsch, 1993, p. 75).

But the St. Louis Real Estate Exchange went even further than the NAREB code by establishing "unrestricted colored districts" where property could be sold to blacks and declaring the rest of the city off limits to black buyers. These led to a huge demand for housing in black neighborhoods and worsened over-crowding. In 1945, for instance, blacks comprised 13 percent of the population in the City of St. Louis, but they had access to only 7 percent of the housing stock. By 1950, St. Louis had the highest "index of racial dissimilarity," or segregation, of the fourteen largest cities in the country. Ninety-three percent of black families would have had to move to achieve a nonsegregated residential pattern (Orfield, 1981). Eight years later, when blacks comprised 30 percent of the city's population, they had access to only 16 to 20 percent of the housing (Confluence, 1989, p. 13).

To make more money, landlords often divided large housing units in black neighborhoods into small apartments, another practice that exacerbated overcrowding. Rents and home prices in black neighborhood far exceeded those in white neighborhoods. In the North, many cities had dual housing markets—one for whites and one for blacks (Hirsch, 1993, p. 77). These dual markets, coupled with the distinct color line, created great potential for profits along the borders of the ghettos, "guaranteeing that some real estate agents would specialize in opening up new areas to black settlement" (Massey and Denton, 1993, p. 37). This process, which came to be known as racial blockbusting, was skillfully choreographed by real estate agents who made their money by advancing the color line in a systematic fashion. Blockbusting agents would select a neighborhood that looked promising for racial turnover, usually an area adjacent to a black ghetto with older housing and some apartment buildings. The agents would quietly buy a few homes or apartment buildings in the area and rent or sell them to black families. Next they would deliberately increase white fear of a black "invasion" and then offer to purchase or rent the homes at bargain prices (Massey and Denton, 1993). In the meantime, the agents would increase demand for housing by advertising in the overcrowded black neighborhoods and then exploit that demand with inflated prices. In this way, "ghetto building proved profitable" (Hirsch, 1993, p. 77).

Once the racial transition was well under way, property values would fall rapidly, so that whites who were slow to sell and blacks quick to buy ended up losing the most money; the only people who actually gained from blockbusting were the real estate agents. Of course blockbusting would not have proved nearly as profitable had whites not been so resistant to having black neighbors. "Given the intensity of black demand and the depths of white prejudice, the entry of a relatively small number of black settlers would quickly surpass the threshold of white tolerance and set off a round of racial turnover" (Massey and Denton, 1993, p. 38). The heyday of blockbusting and ghetto building ended after World War II, when suburbs began calling whites away from the cities to their own promised land of half-acre lots and white neighbors. But blockbusting continued well into the 1970s in some cities, including St. Louis.

Post–World War II homeowners in the United States can be divided, with few exceptions, into three categories: whites who moved to the suburbs in the early years of suburbanization and made large profits as their homes increased in value; whites who remained in the cities until the black ghettos were knocking on their doors and who then sold their houses at low prices but partially regained their losses in profits on their suburban houses; and blacks and other people of color who were shut out of suburban neighborhoods where property values skyrocketed during the inflation of 1960s and 1970s and who lost money by living in devalued ghetto housing during the same years. In Baltimore—a border city similar in many ways to St. Louis—a brick row house in the ghetto had a market value of only $1,000 to $2,500 in 1970 (Grigsby et. al., 1970).

THE SUBURBAN FRONTIER

The mass migration of blacks northward and into cities was second only to the suburbanization of the white middle class as the most profound social phenomena of twentieth-century America. Jackson (1985) calls suburbia the "quintessential physical achievement of the United States," noting that it is perhaps more representative of American culture than are big cars or professional football: "Suburbia symbolizes the fullest, most unadulterated embodiment of contemporary culture" (p. 4).

While several economic and political factors, including home equity and federal policies, contributed to white suburbanization, we argue that cultural factors, including beliefs about African Americans, perceptions of communities, and interpretations of the Creed, helped shape the economic and political realities that created the urban-suburban color line. Whites' search for local control and personal freedom explain why the majority of voters now live in suburbs, far from the problems of the inner cities that they hear about on the nightly news.

Schneider (1992) writes that suburbanization embodies the preference for the private over the public in all aspects of life—environment, entertainment, and, most significantly, government. Suburban voters, Schneider argues, buy their "private" government so that they can control taxes, spending, schools, and police. "These people resent it when politicians take their money and use it to solve other people's problems" (p. 37). In this way, Schneider notes, sub-urbanites have lost a sense of connection to the larger common good. In fact, a growing number of Americans are now moving into "private" suburban com-munities, which take the concept of suburban life one step further. In these so-called private suburbs, the streets are private and the community is gated. They are governed by a private community association, which may ban every-thing from guns to certain colors of house paint. An estimated 4 million Americans now live in such communities, and the nunmber is quickly growing (Egan, 1995).

The disconnection—physical and mental—allows suburbanites to justify their lack of concern with the problems of the central cities they fled many decades ago. Lewis Mumford wrote that "in the suburbs one might live and die without marring the image of an innocent world, except when some shadow of its evil fell over a column in the newspaper. Thus the suburb served as an asylum for the preservation of illusion" (cited in Jackson, 1985, pp. 155–156).

Racial segregation via suburbanization of whites is consistent with the Creed's commitment to rugged individualism, which justifies the desire for private space. Societal stress placed on material gain means that owning a home is a key element of the American Dream. In the past forty-five years, purchasing suburban housing with federal financing has provided an equity-building opportunity for those veterans and young families with access to neighborhoods and federal funds. Furthermore, home ownership has be-come the way in which people advertise their personal success, which is why they invest their life savings in the housing market. Jackson (1985) notes that historically in the United States "ownership of land has been not just the main but often the only sure basis of power," and the sublime insurance against ill fortune (p. 52).

This penchant for home ownership is not found in other industrialized so-cieties. By the 1980s, about two-thirds of Americans owned their own dwell-ings—double the percentage of homeowners in western Europe. The percentage jumps to 95 percent for two-parent white families living in small cities (Jackson, 1985, p. 7). The single-family dwelling has become the "para-gon of middle-class housing, the most visible symbol of having arrived at a fixed place in society, the goal to which every decent family aspired" (p. 50). Yet simply owning a home is not enough; where that home is located is also an important indicator of wealth. The severe racial segregation of the housing market is an essential element of a society in which social status is partially defined by address and perpetuated by the interaction of property values and public opinion.

These attitudes toward neighborhoods, which in turn drive property values, appear to be more strongly related to the race of the people who live in these neighborhoods than to more practical considerations. Several researchers have found that the racial composition of a neighborhood has a stronger effect on whites' desire to live there than do such factors as location, housing quality, and crime rates (St. John and Bates, 1990. For instance, Taub, Taylor, and Dunham (1984, p. 56) found that even though location, environmental cleanliness, crime, housing quality, and social environment all have statistically significant effects on neighborhood desirability for whites, racial composition is of greater importance. Thus, the presence of black neighbors diminishes desirability even when other factors are held constant. As a neighborhood's black population increases proportionately, whites' desire to live in the neighborhood decreases significantly, implying that "even if neighborhood crime and deterioration were controlled, racial composition would remain an important determinant of neighborhood evaluation" (p. 58). These findings have been replicated, leading some researchers to conclude that "for the bulk of white American society, race continues to play an important role in ascribing group as well as neighborhood status, even after education, income and occupational levels are considered" (Berry and Kasarda, 1977, p. 23).

This relation between whites' views of neighborhood desirability and race raises questions about the demand for local control as a driving force behind suburbanization. If middle-class whites with the resources to move to the suburbs have been, for the past fifty years, seeking local control *and* white neighbors, then why would they not use one to assure the other? While the desire for local control and small government can sound so pure and so American, it can also represent a less favorable view of U.S. culture as circumscribed by race and racial segregation. Strong local control, as history has taught us, is used in discreet and indiscreet ways to maintain the color line.

The consequences of a color line drawn between locally controlled suburbs and poor ghettos is that even well-intentioned whites who would otherwise choose to live in a racially mixed neighborhood are as much at the mercy of this larger social structure as are nonwhites. Real estate agents steer them toward whiter, higher-priced neighborhoods, and they incur real economic costs if they remain in a neighborhood that is changing from white to black or Latino. But even well-intentioned whites are not "victims" of this segregated system in the way that African Americans and Latinos are, because whites usually benefit economically from a segregated housing market as their property, on the white side of the color line, increases in value. Thus they build equity that they will pass on to their children—equity that most African

Americans never have the opportunity to build. Because whites want to purchase homes that will appreciate in value (or at least not depreciate), they must conform to the real estate mantra "location, location, location."

White buyers' demand for white neighborhoods further depresses property values in integrated neighborhoods, increasing the likelihood that future buyers will choose segregation as well. If their neighborhoods show signs of racial tipping, whites are caught in a situation in which their life savings and their social status are threatened. This explains white suburbanites' desire for local control and thus the power to create "exclusionary zones," which ban the construction of low- and moderate-income housing by requiring all single-family units to contain a specified number of square feet of living space (Stahura, 1983, p. 422). Exclusionary zones also include density controls—such as limits on the number of dwelling units per unit of land—designed to guarantee that the neighborhood remain "desirable" (Babcock and Bosselman, 1973; Jackson, 1985, p. 59).

These exclusionary practices, while more subtle than racial zoning or restrictive covenants, date back to the 1880s, when legal agreements written into property deeds required that houses in a neighborhood cost no less than a given amount and be set back from the street a minimum number of feet. These zoning laws ensure that a home in the affected neighborhood would remain too expensive for poor families. Exclusionary zoning can also be used by local governments to force blacks from a suburb by rezoning their neighborhoods as commercial zones or by surrounding them with nonresidential "no-man zones." Exclusionary zoning was not seriously challenged in the courts until the 1970s, but little change results even when plaintiffs win these cases, because the rulings apply only to towns and neighborhoods built after the suit (Stahura, 1986).

In St. Louis, where the legacy of southern segregation meets a northern political geography of separate city and county, the pull of the locally controlled suburbs was particularly strong. By the early 1980s, St. Louis County was divided into more than ninety self-governing municipalities and twenty-three autonomous school districts with carefully drawn boundaries minimizing housing integration and black enrollment in predominantly white schools.

During a 1970 U.S. Commission on Civil Rights hearing on segregation in St. Louis, the chair, the Reverend Theodore M. Hesburgh, noted, "The suburbs are almost all white, while the city is [almost] 50 percent black. Within the city, two separate cities exist, one white and one black. The county contains 100 government units. Nearly all, by separate policies in zoning, subdivision regulation and more subtle private action, maintain the white noose around the city."

White flight and the resulting urban decline was greatly accelerated in St. Louis because of the geographic constraints of the city, the exodus of industry to the suburbs, and the city's predominantly brick housing stock, which is too expensive to repair and too solid to raze. And as whites moved to the suburbs in droves, discriminatory housing practices restricted the ability of black families to follow them. Between 1950 and 1980, St. Louis City lost nearly half its population—from a peak of 856,000 people in 1950 to 453,000 in 1980, and most of these migrants were whites (table 1.1).

The desertion of the city was so rapid that a 1973 Rand Corporation report on economic and social conditions in St. Louis noted, "St. Louis is a city undergoing rapid demographic change. During the 1960s, some areas of the city registered a gradual increase in population, others a precipitous decline; still others underwent an almost total transition from white to black. . . . Each has occurred in a tempo to be measured in years rather than decades" (Morrison, 1973, p. 1). And in the catch-22 of urban decline, the eroding tax base of the city meant that planners could not attract the new industry and jobs needed to revitalize the economy (Community Advisory Committee, 1985).

In addition to rapid population shifts, St. Louis City experienced a net decrease of 62,000 housing units from the early '60s to the mid-'80s. While the southern third of the city remained relatively stable, on the north side and central corridor, where most blacks lived, the city government, with federal support, began a project to remove deteriorated housing. On the land where the housing had stood, a highway was built to provide those who lived in the white and wealthy suburbs but who worked downtown to reach their offices and homes without driving through poor neighborhoods.

Table 1.1. Changing Racial Demographics of St. Louis City and County, 1920–1990

	City Population	Percentage Black	County Population	Percentage Black
1920	772,897	9	100,737	4.7
1930	821,960	11.4	211,593	4.6
1940	816,048	13	274,230	4.5
1950	856,796	18	406,349	4.1
1960	750,026	29	703,532	2.7
1970	622,236	41	951,671	4.8
1980	453,085	46	973,896	11.3
1990	396,685	47	993,529	14

Source: U.S. Census

By building superhighways, the federal government accommodated the cultural forces that enhanced the color line. The Federal Highway Act of 1916 and Interstate Highway Act of 1956 benefited the road, the truck, the private motorcar, and thus suburban commuters. Some argue that construction of the suburbs themselves would have been unthinkable without the rapid postwar construction of the interstate highway system (Hirsch, 1993; Jackson, 1985). By 1960, highway funds represented nearly half of all federal grants to state and local governments. According to Orfield (1981), urban neighborhoods were leveled in the rush to build highways and speed whites' access to the suburbs (p. 47). In the St. Louis area, five major freeways involved a public investment of more than $250 million during the 1960s, with the federal government paying nine-tenths (Orfield, 1981). But the federal government role's in creating the color line was much more strongly felt in the housing market, where billions of federal dollars secured home mortgages for whites in the suburbs and constructed high-rise ghettos for blacks in the cities.

ROLE OF THE FEDERAL GOVERNMENT

Home ownership is the most important source of wealth for most families, and it is this wealth that is generally passed on to the next generation. It is, therefore, important to locate the foundation of today's white middle class in the post–World War II housing boom—a boom from which blacks were systematically excluded. Jackson argues that suburbanization was an ideal government policy because it met the needs of citizens and business interests and it earned politicians votes. "It is a simple fact that home ownership introduced equity into the estates of over 35 million families between 1933 and 1978" (Jackson, 1985, p. 216). The federal policies that fostered home ownership were race-specific, designed almost exclusively to benefit white families and exclude blacks.

HOLC and FHA: Government-Made Suburbs

The federal government began building suburbs during the Great Depression. In 1933, President Roosevelt signed legislation to create the Home Owners Loan Corporation (HOLC), which helped refinance thousands of mortgages that were in danger of defaulting and granted low-interest loans that allowed owners to recover homes lost through foreclosure. HOLC profoundly affected the ability of most Americans to purchase homes by introducing a system of self-amortizing mortgages with uniform payments spread over twenty years or more. Under this system people with moderate incomes could afford homes with incremental mortgages (Jackson, 1985; Massey and Denton, 1993).

The systematized appraisal methods of HOLC, which were adopted by the private housing industry, further transformed the American housing market and contributed significantly to racial segregation. To predict the useful life of the housing it financed and thus the risk associated with loans, HOLC gathered information regarding the occupation, income, and ethnicity of inhabitants, and the age, type of construction, price range, and so forth of the housing stock in a particular neighborhood (Jackson, 1985).

The practice of "redlining" derived from HOLC's four-category coding system. Neighborhoods coded red were considered the highest risk, and prospective buyers in these neighborhoods virtually never received HOLC loans. Areas with large numbers of blacks were "invariably rated as fourth grade and 'redlined'" (Massey and Denton, 1993, p. 52). Private lending agencies still employ similar evaluations, and black neighborhoods—low-income or not—consistently receive the lowest ratings. Thus, blacks still have difficulty securing mortgages or home improvement loans (Stahura, 1983), and the cumulative effects of HOLC's policies can be seen in the many abandoned buildings in inner-city neighborhoods.

In St. Louis, beginning in the 1930s, the rating system strongly favored county over city neighborhoods, despite similarities in the quality of housing stock (Jackson, 1985). Describing one area of St. Louis County, "HOLC appraisers noted approvingly that the area's 4,535 acres, criss-crossed by streams, were 'highly restricted' and occupied by 'capitalists and other wealthy families.' Reportedly not the home of a 'single foreigner or negro.'" This community received a first-grade rating, as did other affluent and mostly white suburbs. The only neighborhoods in St. Louis County receiving the lowest grade were those with African-American residents (see fig. 1.3). One mostly black neighborhood, where homes were small but relatively new and of good quality, was redlined. The HOLC appraisers wrote that the houses were of "little or no value," having suffered a tremendous decline due to the "colored element" now controlling the district (p. 200).

The city fared even worse at the hands of the HOLC appraisers, with black and some working-class white neighborhoods consistently receiving the lowest rating, regardless of the condition of the housing. According to Jackson (1985), in St. Louis, as in every city, "any Afro-American presence was a source of substantial concern to HOLC. . . . Not surprisingly, even those neighborhoods with small proportions of black inhabitants were usually rated Fourth grade or 'hazardous'" (p. 201).

Two federal loan programs—administered by the Federal Housing Authority (FHA) and the Veterans Administration (VA)—worked in conjunction with HOLC to drastically alter the housing market by guaranteeing millions

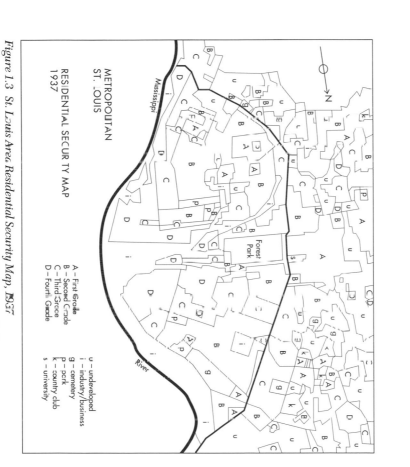

METROPOLITAN
ST. LOUIS

RESIDENTIAL SECURITY MAP
1937

A – First Grade
B – Second Grade
C – Third Grade
D – Fourth Grade

u – undeveloped
i – industry/business
g – cemetery
p – park
k – country club
s – university

Figure 1.3 St. Louis Area Residential Security Map, 1937
Source: Record Group 31, National Archives, Washington, D.C.

of loans by private banks to would-be suburbanites. The FHA was established under the National Housing Act of 1934 as part of the federal government's effort to jump start the construction industry during the Depression. The Serviceman's Readjustment Act of 1944 (known as the GI Bill), created the VA program, which assisted 16 million World War II veterans in purchasing homes. While the FHA and VA did not lend money themselves, they insured long-term mortgage loans, enabling more lenders to make home loans.

Through a number of practices, blacks were excluded from these programs. The FHA regulations forbade insuring loans that would encourage racial housing integration; even after these formal regulations were changed in the early 1960s, the FHA practices aimed at keeping blacks out of white neighborhoods continued (Stahura, 1986, p. 133). Meanwhile, these federal programs were building the backbone of white middle-class America.

Before the advent of the FHA program, prospective home buyers were able to borrow only one-half or two-thirds of the appraised value of the property, paying for at least 30 percent of the home up front. But with FHA-secured long-term loans, lenders were willing to finance mortgages with down payments of only 10 percent. In addition, tax laws allow homeowners to deduct the interest on their mortgage payments from their tax bills. Over the years, these policies have substantially increased the number of middle- and lower-middle-class families who could purchase homes. In some parts of the country, during the postwar housing heyday, it was cheaper to buy than rent because of low-interest loans and federal income tax deductions (Bartelt, 1993).

Between the end of the war and 1972, the FHA helped nearly 11 million families purchase homes and another 22 million improve their properties by pumping nearly $120 billion in mortgage insurance into banks lending to mostly white suburbanites. The percentage of families living in homes that they owned swelled from 44 to 63 percent between 1934 and 1972. By the 1960s almost half of all housing was FHA- or VA-financed. "The middle-class suburban family with the new house and the long-term, fixed-rate, FHA-insured mortgage became a symbol, and perhaps a stereotype, of the American way of life" (Jackson, 1985, p. 206). But the FHA also contributed greatly to current patterns of housing segregation.

At least four FHA policies spurred builders, lenders, and buyers to favor suburban over urban development, which in turn hastened the decay of inner-city neighborhoods: First, the legislation favored the construction of single-family homes over multifamily units, such as apartment or condominium buildings. Second, FHA-insured loans for repair of existing structures were small and of short duration, which meant it was often easier to buy a new home than to refurbish an older one. Third, the FHA relied on the "unbiased professional estimate" of a lending agent regarding the value of the property, the quality of the neighborhood, and the character of the borrower as a prerequisite to any loan guarantee. Through this practice, the FHA allowed lenders' biases toward all-white suburban neighborhoods to strongly affect which loans it guaranteed (Jackson, 1985).

Finally, the FHA set minimum requirements for "ideal homes" by specifying lot size and how far from the street and adjacent structures each unit should be. These minimum requirements for home construction became almost standard in the industry, and private contractors consistently built houses to meet FHA criteria (Jackson 1985, p. 204). In cities where space was scarce, there were few opportunities to build single-family homes meeting these standards. Between 1934 and 1960, homeowners in St. Louis County received more than five times the federal mortgage insurance as city residents.

As it was aiding and abetting white flight from the cities, the FHA was assuring that blacks had a far more difficult time moving out of the urban ghettos. As part of the official policy, FHA agents were concerned about "inharmonious racial or nationality groups" residing in one area, for fear that an entire neighborhood could lose its investment value. To avoid such financial catastrophes, the FHA compiled detailed reports and maps charting the present and most likely future residential locations of blacks and openly recommended the use of restrictive covenants to prevent these relocations. Even after the Supreme Court's 1948 ruling in *Shelley v. Kraemer,* which made restrictive covenants unenforceable, the FHA waited two years before announcing that it would not insure mortgages for homes in neighborhoods with restrictive covenants. Still, the FHA did not prohibit federal assistance to segregated developments

The FHA and VA profoundly affected current housing patterns for two reasons: First, through these loan guarantee programs, the federal government supported the racially biased practices of the real estate industry rather than tried to prevent them. As late as the 1960s, banks and savings and loans benefiting from FHA guarantees institutionalized the practice of denying mortgages "solely because of the geographic location of the property," which discriminated against those who could not buy in white and wealthy areas (Jackson, 1985, p. 217). In following "sound business principles" the FHA delivered itself into the hands of the real estate industry, and the NAREB "ethics" soon found their way into FHA manuals. For many years these manuals demanded restrictive covenants as a precondition for loan guarantees (Hirsch, 1993). Second, not until the 1950s did the FHA begin reversing its segregationist policies and its reluctant twenty-year march toward a more color-blind stance, when it offered too little, too late: "In the 1930s and 1940s, the federal government mandated racial discrimination; through the 1950s and much of the '60s it permitted bias in both the private and public spheres; in the 1970s and 1980s it outlawed most forms of such discrimination, but only after a sustained postwar building boom served as a federally supported centrifuge that separated an outer layer of whites from a dense black core. Attempting to end discriminatory practices in housing in the post–civil rights era is not simply a matter of closing the barn door a little too slowly—the horse had not only escaped, but it had gotten into the trailer, moved down the interstate, and been put out to stud in rural pastures" (Hirsch, 1993, p. 92).

In spite of intense lobbying efforts by civil rights groups during the 1950s, the federal government failed to adopt regulations or pass legislation that would eliminate discriminatory practices in the housing industry until 1966, when the FHA relaxed credit standards for black applicants and encouraged the renovation of older buildings in the cities (Massey and Denton, 1993). But these new policies allowed for fraud as home improvement companies bought properties at low cost, made cosmetic improvements, and then sold them to African Americans at inflated prices approved by the FHA. This pattern led to thousands of FHA repossessions of urban homes from blacks (Jackson, 1985).

The Fair Housing Act of 1968 provided some hope that the federal government was committed to equal access for African Americans by prohibiting several forms of housing discrimination, including refusing to rent or sell property on the basis of race, discriminating in real estate advertising, "blockbusting" through scare tactics, and lying about the availability of units. Two months after the passage of the Fair Housing Act, the Supreme Court ruled in favor of a black plaintiff in *Jones v. Mayer* (1968), the landmark case from a St. Louis suburb. The plaintiff, Joseph Lee Jones, was denied the right to purchase a home built by the Alfred H. Mayer Company because of his race. The Supreme Court ruling in this case went well beyond its *Shelley v. Kraemer* decision by declaring that purely private discrimination, unaided by any action of the government, is unconstitutional according to the 1866 Civil Rights Act and the Thirteenth Amendment, which grants Congress the power to eliminate all racial barriers to the acquisition of property.

Together, the Fair Housing Act and *Jones v. Mayer* promised to restrict discriminatory real estate practices, although neither delivered on that promise. The Fair Housing Act proved to be particularly difficult to implement because of constraints placed on the Department of Housing and Urban Development (HUD). Former HUD secretary Patricia R. Harris noted that under the Act, the department's role was not proactive but reactive, reduced to "asking the discovered lawbreaker whether he wants to discuss the matter" (Massey and Denton, 1993, p. 196). By the 1970s, only a small percentage of complaints filed with HUD or local housing authorities reached formal mediation, and in nearly half of these cases the violators were later accused of continued racial discrimination. "During the 1970s and 1980s, therefore, discriminators had little to fear from HUD or the Justice Department," and victims of racial discrimination were forced to obtain a great deal of evidence and initiate legal proceedings on their own (Massey and Denton, 1993, p. 197).

Meanwhile, housing discrimination had become far more subtle. Instead of racial zoning or restrictive covenants, by the 1970s white developers and real estate agents were steering blacks away from white neighborhoods, and local governments were pricing them out of markets through zoning ordinances. But the exact form of discrimination was less important than the missed opportunities: with the suburbanization of the white middle class almost complete and inflation rising rapidly, first-time home buying became increasingly difficult. Those shut out of the postwar housing boom would have a far more difficult time realizing the American Dream, as white suburbanites sat tight on their half-acre lots with their tax-deductible mortgage payments, watching housing prices skyrocket. In some suburbs, homes that sold for less than $20,000 in the 1950s were, by the 1980s, worth more than five times that amount. The generation of white and black Americans growing up separate and unequal in suburbia and the inner city during the post–World War II housing boom would inherit vastly different amounts of wealth and property from their parents. They would come to understand the world and their positions in it from vastly different viewpoints. White baby boomers do not understand the privileges passed down from their parents and the government's housing policies. In fact, many of them have come to resent their parents' good fortune, regretting that they will not see their own property values increase to the same extent (Newman, 1993). Young African Americans, on the other hand, increasingly resent whites in the suburbs who really believe they got there through hard work alone, without any government handouts.

Public Housing: Government-Made Ghettos

Another major federal contribution to the color line was public housing. The Housing Act of 1937 empowered the U.S. Housing Authority (USHA) to finance and subsidize the construction of public housing units for people who could not afford to rent or purchase homes in the free market. Although USHA did not build the units, it lent municipalities up to 90 percent of the capital cost of a project and subsidized construction and maintenance costs. By 1941, USHA had sponsored 130,000 new units in 300 housing projects across the nation; by 1962, more than 2 million people lived in nearly 500,000 publicly funded housing units (Jackson, 1985, pp. 224–225).

Public housing has historically contributed to racial segregation because of two critical factors: First, publicly subsidized housing is generally perceived to be un-American, a government handout in a nation that emphasizes self-sufficiency. Thus, people who live in public housing are considered undesirable neighbors, the antithesis of our bootstrap culture. Mohl (1993) writes that public housing has been attacked by real estate agents and others as socialistic. The stigma attached to living in public housing leads those with other options to stay away, leaving only the most destitute in the projects. Second, because federal funding for public housing has always been channeled through municipalities, local governments have had discretion over where and when to build projects. Suburban residents could ban public housing from their precincts by simply refusing to create a housing agency or requiring a two-thirds vote on a referendum to build subsidized housing. Under this local initiative model, suburbs simply did not apply for federal funding for public housing construction. Consequently, low-income housing projects were built not on inexpensive land in the suburbs but rather in cities where larger percentages of the poor were residing and where local governments were hungry for federal funds and "slum clearance," and where local officials dared to construct public housing only in segregated areas (Jackson, 1985, p. 225). The unpopularity of public housing and the degree of local control over its development resulted in far fewer units being built than were originally planned. In 1949, urban redevelopment legislation authorized construction of 810,000 public housing units over the next six years, but by 1960 fewer than half of these had been built.

Furthermore, local housing authorities are typically prominent citizens and business leaders who are often more focused on clearing slums and protecting real estate values than on assuring that poor people are properly housed. According to Thomas Jackson (1993), federal urban-renewal and public-housing legislation has benefited private developers and bondholders more than the poor, who were often displaced by slum clearances and relocated in crowded, poorly constructed, and racially segregated projects. And because public housing units were often designed to take up little space and make room for urban-renewal projects, they were frequently the ubiquitous "vertical ghettos," high-rise buildings with few windows and no open space where children could play (Mohl, 1993).

From the beginning, the federal government's involvement in public, low-income housing projects has reinforced racial segregation. Local housing authorities, mired in local racial politics, generally give priority for public housing to residents of the segregated neighborhoods surrounding the new projects (Hirsch, 1993). Despite the 1968 Fair Housing Act, housing authorities are notorious for refusing to place blacks in housing projects in white neighborhoods. This is what happened to Dorothy Gautreaux and three other blacks in Chicago, who in 1966 filed a class action suit in federal court against the Chicago Housing Authority (CHA) and the U.S. Department of Housing and Urban Development, arguing that they had discriminated against black tenants by confining them to second-rate projects in black neighborhoods.

In the case of *Hills v. Gautreaux*, the plaintiffs won the first round of litigation in district court, but when the judge ordered the CHA to build the next 700 units in white areas of the city, the authority responded by halting construction. The case was appealed to the U.S. Supreme Court, which ruled unanimously in 1976 against CHA and HUD, declaring that the entire Chicago metropolitan area, not just the city, was the relevant housing market for the remedy. In June 1981 the district court judge approved an agreement between the plaintiffs and the CHA and HUD, which would allow 7,100 black families to move from the crime-ridden inner city to the suburbs, using federally subsidized housing vouchers (Massey and Denton, 1993, p. 191). In Yonkers, New York, a federal judge ordered the local housing authority to build 200 units of public housing in townhouses in white neighborhoods and to desegregate them with black tenants. This order, in the case of *NAACP v. Yonkers,* was met with some of the most extreme resistance ever shown by a local government to a federal judge.

According to Gary Orfield's 1981 report on housing segregation in St. Louis, the county and outlying suburban areas "have been striking for their rejection of subsidized family housing, location of the small number of units provided for black families in segregated suburban areas, and very active resistance to federal attempts to require production of scattered site public housing as a precondition for receipt of federal community development block grand money" (p. 34). *Park View Heights Corporation v. the City of Black Jack* involved a nonprofit developer who attempted to build a public housing project in an unincorporated area of St. Louis County in the late 1960s. White residents attended public meetings about the pending housing project and spoke openly about keeping blacks out of their neighborhood and schools. They then launched a successful campaign to incorporate their all-white community into a city called Black Jack, and immediately following incorporation the zoning commission of the new town approved an ordinance preventing the construction of such multiple-family dwellings. The developer sued the city, claiming racial discrimination. Seven years later the Eighth Circuit Court of Appeals ruled that the zoning ordinance denied "persons housing on the basis of race" and interfered with the right to equal housing opportunity. On June 23, 1975, the U.S. Supreme Court refused to hear the case on appeal from Black Jack. By this time, however, the developer's federal financing for the complex had fallen through, and skyrocketing inflation made the project prohibitively expensive (see Metcalf, 1988; Massey and Denton, 1993, p. 229).

The resistance of the Black Jack community to public housing is not unusual in St. Louis County, which for decades has failed to succumb to federal and state requirements or requests to build more pubic housing units. In fact, county politicians have used this resistance to HUD regulations to win votes, and in the late 1970s St. Louis County almost lost millions of federal dollars as a result of such noncompliance (Orfield, 1981a). Meanwhile, as communities in the county were trying to keep federally subsidized housing out of their neighborhoods, the city of St. Louis was in dire need of federal funds and was more than willing to build more housing projects to get it. As more of the city's tax base migrated to the suburbs, federal urban programs became "absolutely crucial" for the operation of the city of St. Louis. "HUD used this leverage to push the city into a large-scale housing program" (Orfield, 1981, p. 105). St. Louis made its most indelible mark in the history of public housing with a large project named after two locally prominent men—a black named Pruitt and a white named Igoe. The Pruitt-Igoe project was constructed in the early 1950s, just northwest of the central business district and southeast of the Ville. It consisted of thirty-three buildings, eleven stories tall and containing 2,762 apartments; at its peak occupancy it housed 11,500 residents. The project, which cost the federal and Missouri governments $21.7 million, was touted by housing officials as one of the largest and best-designed projects of the postwar era. It won architectural awards and was viewed as a "high-rise icon of architectural modernism" (Mohl, 1993, p. 16).

Although Pruitt-Igoe was originally to be racially mixed, whites and blacks were to live in separate buildings and separate sections—blacks in the twenty-building Pruitt section and whites in the thirteen-building Igoe section. But the 1954 Supreme Court ruling in the *Brown* case brought an end to overt racial classification by the housing authority, and within a few years of completion Pruitt-Igoe was all black and poor. Whites were reluctant to move in, partly because the project was located in a black part of town. Blacks, however, had few housing options, having lost thousands of homes to the slum clearance efforts. In 1954, the same year Pruitt-Igoe was completed, a city-improvement bond issue passed that allowed the demolition of the homes of roughly 20,000 residents of the Mill Creek neighborhood, 95 percent of whom were black (Wright, 1994). From 1960 to 1965 the city demolished another 12,000 housing units for urban renewal and highway construction. And in the late 1960s, 1,500 to 2,000 low-income families in St. Louis were displaced each year (Human Development Corporation, 1970).

Pruitt-Igoe was built on fifty-seven acres of land set off from the rest of the city; there were no social service organizations, grocery stores, or shopping centers nearby. According to a St. Louis University report on Pruitt-Igoe, the area was "isolated from the main business district and major centers of industrial employment and devoid of commercial activities except the marginal corner-store type of operation" (cited in Orfield, 1981, p. 36). With no job opportunities in the vicinity and virtually no public transportation to jobs in other parts of the city, the project became a mecca for organized crime. And despite their architectural awards, the Pruitt-Igoe buildings were poorly designed: the elevators stopped only on the fourth, seventh, and tenth floors; there were no restrooms on the ground floor; and there was little recreational space for the thousands of children who lived there (Rainwater, 1970; Wright, 1994). Pruitt-Igoe was, in fact, not a modern architectural achievement but the epitome of the government's efforts to house the poor in vertical ghettos (Mohl, 1993; Confluence, 1989).

When Rainwater conducted an extensive ethnography in Pruitt-Igoe in the late 1960s, he found that only blacks desperate for housing were willing to live there. He asked tenants what the government was trying to accomplish by building public housing, and one said, "They were trying to better poor people (but) they tore down one slum and built another; put all kinds of people together; made a filthy place" (Rainwater, 1970, p. 11). The problems of unemployment and crime that plague inner cities in general were magnified at Pruitt-Igoe. Tenants complained of broken glass and trash everywhere, problems that led to infestations of mice and cockroaches; there were numerous fights, thefts, and attacks. Eventually Pruitt-Igoe was uninhabitable (Confluence, 1989; Rainwater, 1970). In a 1974 book on St. Louis, the man who was mayor of the city throughout much of the Pruitt-Igoe fiasco, A. J. Cervantes, wrote about the broken windows and stolen plumbing in what was left of the huge project: "The architectural gem had become a ghost town haunted by muggers" (cited in Orfield, 1981, p. 40).

In 1976, with much media coverage and head shaking on the part of taxpayers who knew the project only as a concrete mass they could barely see from the highway, the grand symbol of U.S. urban policy was razed to the ground. To this day, whites in St. Louis see Pruitt-Igoe as a symbol for blacks' laziness, ungratefulness, and unwillingness to make something better of their lives. In fact, these sentiments extend beyond St. Louis: "The plight of the Pruitt-Igoe high-rise development in St. Louis represented to many people a symbol of the failure of public housing" (Gottlieb, 1976, p. 464). According to

Jackson (1985), "In the mind of the average citizen, the failures of public housing were due to cultural characteristics of the poor themselves, who were seen to be resisting improvement" (p. 229).

THE POST–CIVIL RIGHTS ERA

By 1970 there were about 30,000 people living in public housing in St. Louis City, which had one of the largest programs in the country. There were no families living in public housing in St. Louis County (Orfield, 1981). The Fair Housing Act of 1968 spurred public housing construction; between 1970 and 1973, 1.5 million public housing units nationwide were either built or rehabilitated with federal subsidies. While some of these projects created good housing for poor people, there were many serious problems in the vertical ghettos. Residents of these urban public housing projects were often isolated from the rest of society and employment opportunities, and without hope. The crime and vandalism that characterized the final years of Pruitt-Igoe were not unique to that project.

In St. Louis, meanwhile, the city council adopted a 1971 ordinance to prevent future disasters like Pruitt-Igoe by restricting the concentration of low-income housing in any one neighborhood. The ordinance was ignored, however, as the construction of public housing in St. Louis ground to a halt even earlier than in most cities.

The Fair Housing Act of 1968 also created a subsidized low-income home-ownership program called Section 235. By eliminating down payments and offering extremely low interest rates on relatively inexpensive homes, the law made it possible for poor families to purchase homes for the same or less money than they spent on rent. While the program had the potential to move low-income blacks into less poor and more integrated neighborhoods, and to stabilize racially mixed areas by allowing more whites to purchase homes in the city, a study of the Section 235 program's impact on St. Louis showed that it instead contributed to the growth of the inner-city ghetto and helped low-income whites leave the city for the suburbs. It also left many poor black families with low-quality housing that they had purchased at inflated prices. By 1970, 990 families in St. Louis were living in homes under this program; most of those families were black and most were female-headed with several children. More than one-fourth of the buyers came from public housing projects, and more than half were on welfare. Nine-tenths of the homes sold under the program were in black or racially changing areas. Meanwhile, white participants in the program were purchasing homes in scattered white areas. According to Orfield (1981), there was widespread "knowledge and approval among realtors, local welfare officers, and the local office of the Federal Housing Administration of the fact that black families were being steered by realtors into segregated neighborhoods and areas where the ghetto was expanding" (pp. 56–57).

The New Federal Role in Housing

The demolition of Pruitt-Igoe was a metaphor for the rapidly changing political climate. In January 1973, President Nixon imposed an abrupt two-year moratorium on federal housing construction and rehabilitation programs, reflecting the general public's desire to neglect housing as an issue and to end the federal government's construction of housing for the poor (Gottlieb, 1976; Bartelt, 1993). Growing out of this two-year moratorium was the Housing and Community Development Act of 1974—a new approach to housing policy, unique in that it expressed concern for the concentration of low-income people in central cities and focused on the "spatial deconcentration of housing opportunities" for the poor (Gottlieb, 1976, p. 466).

The law's mechanism for deconcentrating the poor was a housing subsidy known as the Section 8 Rental Assistance Program, referred to simply as Section 8. Through this program, tenants pay up to 30 percent of their income for rent, and any balance is paid by the federal government. Those whose income is between 50 and 80 percent or less of the median income for the area in which they reside are eligible. Landlords must cap the rent at about $1,000 for a two-bedroom apartment, depending on the housing market (Berger, 1993).

Section 8 participants receive certificates from the local housing authority—vouchers that they use in the private housing market. Ideally, in keeping with the deconcentration of poverty goal of Section 8, priority is given to those who find housing in buildings where less than 20 percent of the occupants receive subsidies (Gottlieb, 1976). Currently, Section 8 subsidizes housing for about 2.7 million people (Berger, 1993).

In the 1970s the Section 8 policy represented a change in the federal government role in housing the poor: from a funder of housing projects to a subsidizer of tenants (Bartelt, 1993, p. 150; Sussman, 1990). Yet there is little evidence that the Section 8 program, except in a few instances, is helping to desegregated poor African Americans or Latinos into neighborhoods and housing units with more middle-class families. Many of the Section 8 units are in high poverty areas, and not in buildings with many unsubsidized tenants. The inability of Section 8 to deconcentrate the poor is due in part to resistance by landlords and other tenants to allow low-income families, particularly African Americans, to live outside the ghettos. Court cases frequently are brought by black participants who were steered away from predominantly white neighborhoods by housing agents or real estate brokers (see Berger, 1993). In the *NAACP v. Yonkers* case, the judge cited a litany of illegal activities by local officials promoting racial segregation, including refusal to seek all the Section 8 certificates for which they qualified, despite the pressing need for low-income housing (Massey and Denton, 1993, p. 228).

On the other hand, in the court-ordered remedy for Chicago's *Gautreaux* case, Section 8 vouchers subsidize the rent of black families relocated to the suburbs. In fact, the results of this remedy were so successful in desegregating low-income black families into the suburbs that HUD created, in 1994, a five-city, ten-year demonstration experiment modeled after *Gautreaux* (Berger, 1993). The program, Moving to Opportunity, cost $230 million in its first two years, and it helped 6,200 poor families leave impoverished urban areas.

In St. Louis, the recently built and renovated housing for Section 8 participants is not in racially or even socioeconomically mixed neighborhoods. Rather, the neighborhoods with the largest number of Section 8 voucher recipients are in the poorest areas of the city, especially concentrated in the sparse and blighted neighborhood adjacent to the large vacant lot where Pruitt-Igoe once stood. A 1980 HUD report found that approximately 94 percent of the subsidized family units in St. Louis, including Section 8 units, were located in Census tracts that were more than 75 percent black. Furthermore, despite efforts by St. Louis City to work with the county housing authority to administer the Section 8 program across the metro area, few housing unites were available in the county. In fact, the county housing agency even issued bonds to finance the construction of segregated housing in the city (Orfield, 1981, p. 78). "In contrast to some metropolitan areas, such as Denver, Seattle, Minneapolis, and others which built much of their subsidized housing of the seventies outside the central city, St. Louis' record was bleak" (p. 83).

And finally, the Missouri Housing Development Commission has played an important role in keeping Section 8 participants in segregated areas of St. Louis when it became involved in selecting Section 8 housing for HUD. According to one HUD official, members of the Missouri Housing Development Commission feared retaliation from the state legislature if the agency financed subsidized housing in St. Louis suburbs" (Orfield, 1981, p. 116).

Black Suburbanization—Still Separate and Unequal

In spite of persistent racial segregation in U.S. housing and efforts to keep subsidized housing out of the suburbs, it is no longer accurate to depict suburbs as all white. In the 1960s, the number of blacks in the suburbs increased substantially as the growth rate of blacks in central cities began to decline. Still, because whites continued to flee cities at a much faster rate than blacks, the percentage of the total population that is black increased in most cities (Farley, 1975, p. 169).

Between 1970 and 1980, the percentage of blacks living in the suburbs rose from 16 to 21 while the percentage of blacks living in central cities declined from 58.2 to 55.7 (Massey and Denton, 1988; Hirsch, 1993). The trend toward black suburbanization continues, though it has not had a marked impact on black-white racial segregation (Farley and Frey, 1994). By the end of the 1980s, 30 percent of blacks still lived in Census tracts that were 90 to 100 percent black (Sussman, 1990). According to Massey and Denton (1993), "There is little in recent data to suggest that processes of racial segregation have moderated much since 1980, particularly in the north, where segregation remains high and virtually constant" (p. 223). They note that among the thirty metropolitan areas studied, eighteen had segregation indices considered very high in 1990, and seventeen had experienced no significant change over the prior decade. These metropolitan areas are home to 60 percent of all urban blacks.

Meanwhile, the growth of the black middle class—10 percent of all blacks—suggests that the persistent racial segregation in present-day suburbia cannot be attributed to socioeconomic factors alone. Pettigrew found that in Chicago in 1974, only 8 percent of blacks lived in the suburbs although 46 percent of blacks could afford suburban housing (cited in Rist, 1976). More recent research on segregation has found that once a suburb acquires a visible black presence it attracts more blacks than whites, which leads to neighborhood succession and the emergence of a black enclave (Massey and Denton, 1988). In this way the racial housing patterns of the suburbs mirror those of the urban neighborhoods decades ago. Clearly the black suburbanization movement has not led to the "imminent dispersal of densely concentrated inner-city black populations" (Hirsch, 1993, p. 67).

Farley and Frey's (1994) research using 1990 Census data suggests that while there is a "pervasive pattern of modest declines" in housing segregation within metropolitan areas, African Americans remain far more segregated than Asians or Latinos in the cities or the suburbs. They also found that the degree of black-white segregation varies greatly from one metropolitan area to the next and is strongly related to the age of the city, with older cities being more segregated; the type of industry that is dominant, with manufacturing towns more segregated; and, as we mentioned earlier, by the region of the country, with northeastern and midwestern cities more segregated. In older, industrial cities in the Northeast and Midwest, most blacks live in a few highly segregated areas, with only a handful living in suburbs that are not adjacent to the segregated city (Stahura, 1983). By 1980, none of the industrial cities of the Northeast and Midwest with a black population of at least 200,000 had a suburban population that was even 10 percent black, though there was some growth in the percentage of blacks living in the suburbs of Sunbelt cities. These regional differences in housing segregation are no doubt related to politically autonomous suburbs in the North and Midwest and to the power of their local control.

In addition to age, industry, and geography of a metropolitan area, other factors play a role in perpetuating segregation. Banks and other lending institutions, as mentioned earlier, continue to redline and thus remain instrumental in creating and maintaining segregated suburbs. In the 1960s, at the peak of the suburbanization movement, the suburbs of St. Louis with the largest black populations were redlined and thus home buyers in these areas were regularly denied Federal Mortgage Insurance. In 1967, less than 1 percent of the FHA-insured homes in suburban St. Louis were purchased by black families (Orfield, 1981). A 1989 study conducted for the *Atlanta Journal-Constitution* ranked St. Louis the twenty-third worst out of 100 metro areas for blacks to be approved for home loans. The study found that while blacks are rejected twice as often as whites for home loans nationally, in St. Louis this ratio is almost three to one (cited in Confluence, 1989).

Real estate agents continue to steer prospective homebuyers into black or nonblack housing areas, which keeps the cost of houses in predominantly white communities high and maintains the color line in the city *and* the suburbs. One study found that black home shoppers in two large metropolitan areas had a 38 to 59 percent greater chance of receiving unfavorable treatment compared with white shoppers, and blacks were informed of only 65 units for every 100 shown to whites (Massey and Denton, 1993, p. 99). In addition, a 1991 survey by the Urban Institute found that blacks faced discriminatory hurdles 59 percent of the time when purchasing a home; black renters experienced overt discrimination in 56 percent of their tested encounters (Hirsch, 1993, p. 84).

In the 1960s, the Greater St. Louis Committee for Freedom of Residence sent black and white "checkers," or prospective home buyers, to fifteen white real estate companies and found "extensive manipulation" of the local housing market by real estate agents. The committee noted, "Blatant and subtle methods and techniques of manipulation and discrimination" by the white real estate community resulted in the containment of blacks in designated areas (cited in Human Development Corp., 1970, p. 44). In 1992, in north St. Louis County, which had been experiencing an influx of black families from the city and an out-migration of whites to other sections of the county, an activist group of clergy and members of twenty churches accused local real estate brokers of perpetuating racial segregation by steering prospective white buyers away from racially mixed neighborhoods while scaring white residents into selling their homes (Todd, 1992).

The housing patterns of the St. Louis metropolitan area illustrate how the color line is preserved in spite of the flow of blacks to the suburbs. In fact, St. Louis County, which is now 14 percent African American, is one of five metropolitan areas—along with New Orleans, Atlanta, Washington, D.C., and Memphis—with "notable" black suburban populations. Yet because these metropolitan areas are southern, many of the black "suburbs" are actually long-standing black communities in formerly rural areas that were engulfed by white suburbs (Hirsch, 1993). Another pattern of black suburbanization more common in northern cities occurs when ghettos expand beyond city boundaries into rings of older suburbs, and whites quickly flee (Hirsch, 1993).

In St. Louis, both patterns of black suburbanization developed. St. Louis County contains several black communities that are more than 100 years old and are now incorporated into white suburbs. Originally these were farming communities, and the blacks who lived there were either sharecroppers, hired farmhands, or house servants. The number of such long-standing black communities has decreased, however, since the 1950s and 1960s, when many St. Louis suburbs undertook "urban renewal" projects of their own, regularly displacing black families and redirecting them to subsidized housing in the city of St. Louis. Meanwhile, in a more northern demographic shift, several suburbs that ring the north side of St. Louis City have "flipped" from all-white to all-black in the past twenty-five years. The creation of these newer black suburban and highly segregated communities was aided by the St. Louis County housing authority's efforts to keep the Section 8 units available to blacks contained in mostly black areas, including Weltsten and University City. Furthermore, efforts by real estate agents to make money via block-busting did not end at the city boundary. Rather, whole inner-ring suburban communities were transformed into segregated black suburbs through such tactics (Orfield, 1981).

The suburban St. Louis communities in which blacks live—whether they are former rural areas or former white suburbs—are generally isolated and far less wealthy than their white counterparts. In a 1989 national study of American suburbs, deVise named two predominantly white St. Louis suburbs in his list of the fifteen wealthiest suburbs and one predominantly black St. Louis suburb in his list of the fifteen poorest ("Suburbs, Rich and Poor," 1989).

Unemployment and Urban Decline

Segregation in housing generally attracts little public attention (Massey and Denton, 1993). One explanation may be that some blacks and Latinos prefer to live in racially isolated neighborhoods and enjoy the sense of community, the "consciousness of kind" shared by people of a common culture and history (Foster, 1986). It is, therefore, more difficult for people to see segregation in housing as criminal, the way they might see segregation in employment and education. But as Massey and Denton (1993) explain, all forms of discrimination and segregation are interconnected. Many life chances are inextricably tied to where people live—not just to who their neighbors are, but also the price they pay for their property and thus the personal wealth they acquire. Housing profoundly affects employment opportunities, since where people live determines their physical and social access to the labor market, as information about jobs and careers flows through social networks. The lack of employment opportunities for African Americans obviously does not depend entirely on segregated housing; in the South, for instance, where blacks and whites have traditionally lived in closer proximity, African Americans have had limited employment options. Also, racism on the part of employers and labor unions is not entirely related to where people live. In St. Louis, which was, until the 1980s, known as a union town, black laborers could not get jobs on construction projects in their own neighborhoods (Confluence, 1989). But housing segregation and the mass migration of whites out of cities has worsened the employment situation for blacks. For the past fifty years, businesses have followed whites to the suburbs, moving jobs farther from black ghettos and beyond the reach of people without transportation (Wilson, 1996). In the early days of suburbanization, most employment opportunities outside the city were in retailing, but now manufacturing as well as wholesale and administrative organizations have suburbanized in increasing numbers. In many places the suburban fringe is displacing the central city as the economic focus of the metropolis (Sly and Tayman, 1980).

A drive west from the Gateway Arch to the edge of St. Louis County reveals a growing number of corporate headquarters on the suburban side of the city-county divide. In fact, many of the major corporations that call St. Louis their home—including Monsanto, McDonnell Douglas (the state's largest employer), Mallincrodt, and Emerson Electric—are actually outside the city. Meanwhile, many of the industries that were anchored to the city, such as transportation and shoe and auto manufacturing, have all but evaporated. Between 1947 and 1958 the central city of St. Louis lost 21 percent of its manufacturing jobs and the suburbs gained 42 percent. Between 1951 and 1969 the city lost 37,000 payroll jobs and 49,000 manufacturing jobs while the county added 197,000 payroll and 44,000 manufacturing jobs (Metcalf, 1988). In 1970 alone, St. Louis lost forty-three companies to the suburbs. The percentage decrease in retail sales for 1958 to 1967 in the city was 7.6, while the suburbs enjoyed a 76.2 percent increase (Berry and Kasarda 1977, p. 255–257). The only growth in employment in the city has been in low-paying clerical jobs, especially in the fields of finance, insurance, and real estate (Community Advisory Committee, 1985).

According to the Human Development Corporation (1970), in 1967 St. Louis' central city had the highest unemployment rate for blacks of the fourteen largest poverty areas in the United States. And from the late 1970s to the late '80s, the city's unemployment rate remained consistently well above national and regional averages. During this same time period the city undertook a number of urban redevelopment projects, including the renovation of Union Station into a shopping and entertainment center and the construction of the St. Louis Centre, a shopping mall designed to attract downtown workers. New high-rise office buildings were also constructed under federal and local tax abatement programs. While this redevelopment brought a trickle of suburbanites downtown for shopping, entertainment, and work, the long-term benefits for city residents are not clear. Since the mid-1980s the opening of the St. Louis Centre, Union Station, the headquarters for Southwestern Bell and Edison Brothers Stores, the Adam's Mark Hotel, the Kiel Center, and the TWA Dome football stadium, are said to provide more than 130,000 jobs to the downtown area. Still, most of these new jobs are part-time entry-level positions in the service sector; they provide no benefits nor do they offer enough income to support a family (Wilson, 1996; Aronowitz and DiFazio, 1994).

The 1990 Census data show that 36 percent of St. Louis residents are employed in either administrative support positions, including clerical jobs, or in service occupations; 17 percent in the retail trade industry; and only 15 percent in manufacturing. According to Richard Ward, president of Development Strategies, Inc., jobs in St. Louis are currently concentrated in clerical positions in offices and service jobs in hotels, restaurants, and convention centers. Yet even these low-paying service jobs are not always open to African Americans. In 1986, when the Adam's Mark Hotel opened, developers promised it would provide 700 permanent jobs. A ceremony to mark the opening of the hotel was picketed by members of the Association for Community Organization for Reform Now (ACORN), who charged that while the hotel owners and investors had benefited from the city's generous tax abatements, management had failed to hire low-income and unemployed city residents, particularly African Americans. According St. Louis historian James Neal Primm (1990), the ACORN protest symbolized the larger racial and social class issues inherent in urban redevelopment projects: "The question had arisen repeatedly during the past two decades, especially since the city had blighted the whole downtown area, except for existing new buildings, in 1971, making new constructions and renovation eligible for tax abatement. Was it fair to the residents of St. Louis to pick up the tax bill for wealthy developers? This question was raised by ACORN and other groups seeking quid pro quo in jobs for the poor" (p. 563).

While St. Louis is often cited as a model of recent urban redevelopment, it is not clear to the citizens of this, the now twenty-seventh largest U.S. city, what this redevelopment has done to ease poverty and crime rates. During his unsuccessful 1985 mayoral campaign, Alderman Freeman Bosley, Sr., a black politician from the north side of the city, noted that the success of St. Louis' redevelopment was overrated: "What we get out of it is a beautiful skyline, . . . what we need is jobs, a piece of the action" (cited in Primm, 1990, p. 563).

Furthermore, while suburbanites may venture downtown for sporting events, cultural activities, and shopping (although there is plenty of retail shopping in the county), virtually none of them would like to move to the city, which means that large sections of land are destined to remain empty and that many vacant homes and abandoned buildings will stay dormant. A 1986 survey of St. Louisians found that while only 6 percent of those living in the suburbs would prefer to live in the city, 31 percent of those residing in the city said they would like to move to the suburbs (Urban Land Institute, 1987). This data suggests that the urban-suburban migration may not be over and that the suburban-urban migration that was to follow urban renewal will probably never occur.

To make matters worse, St. Louis, like many western U.S. cities, has never had an adequate public transportation system to help move people from poor and highly segregated areas to where there are jobs. In 1994, the Metro-Link elevated rail line opened with one route from East St. Louis, Illinois, to Lambert International Airport in St. Louis County. Additional Metro-Link lines are planned and may help connect low-income blacks with jobs in the suburbs.

The Urban-Suburban Link: The Only Hope for the Future

Behind the fanfare surrounding its redevelopment projects, St. Louis City continues to shrink in population and vitality. The new tax-free downtown office buildings, sports centers, and retail malls used by the affluent before they retreat to suburban enclaves, will not solve the problems of impoverished black ghettos. Spread out to the north and west of the downtown area is the separate and still very unequal world of most African Americans who call St. Louis home. Amid hundreds of acres of vacant lots and burned-out buildings, they live in dilapidated public housing projects or in homes abandoned by whites years ago. They are circumscribed by a society that created their isolation and now tries to ignore them.

On the south side of the city a shrinking population of white working-class homeowners are clustered in ethnic neighborhoods—Irish, Italian and German. To the east is the Mississippi River, and on city's west side, just south of the black ghetto, is a grand old neighborhood of nineteenth-century mansions where a handful of wealthy and prominent whites live behind tall fences and security systems. Further west lies the mostly prosperous St. Louis County, with its autonomous, locally controlled municipalities and their separate fire departments, police departments, and, most important, school systems. A few poor and all-black suburbs are clustered near the city's northern boundaries, but they, like the city they are tied to, offer little promise of an integrated society.

Kenneth Jackson (1985) points to St. Louis as an illustration of the current dilemma of American society: "Partly as a result of federal housing policies enabling white middle-class to leave the city . . . St. Louis had become by 1984 a premier example of urban abandonment. Once the fourth largest city in America, the 'Gateway to the West' is now twenty-seventh, a ghost of its former self. . . . Many of its old neighborhoods have become dispiriting collections of burned-out buildings, eviscerated homes, and vacant lots. . . . After Chicago, St. Louis is the nation's leading exporter of brick. . . . It is the supreme indignity. Having lost more than 300 factories in the 1970s to the Sunbelt, St. Louis itself is now being carted away" (pp. 217–218).

St. Louis' current condition, in light of its history and position at the crossroads of the nation, suggests that the great divide between black and Latino cities and mostly white suburbs could eventually pull both down. Since World War II, leaders in St. Louis and other metropolitan areas have struck a kind of Faustian bargain between the older cities and the residents of the expanding suburbs: "The cities agreed to serve increasingly as the poorhouses of the metro community as long as the suburbanites—with Washington and the state capitals acting as brokers and intermediates—underwrote the extra costs this role imposes" (Hirsh, 1993). Thus, cities agreed to take federal and state funding and tax abatements in exchange for keeping the poor disconnected from their suburban neighbors; the suburbs agreed to forgo federal and state funding in exchange for continued local control and detachment from the problems of poverty.

But as we can see in post-redevelopment St. Louis, this is not a viable long-term solution. A 1995 study of the best and worst cities for children to live in—based on general welfare criteria such as poverty rates, unemployment, crime, education spending, and pollution—rated St. Louis as one of the ten worst cities (Manning, 1995). A growing number of policy analysts and urban scholars argue that national and state "urban" policies must move away from the traditional concern with reimbursing disadvantaged cities for keeping the poor out of sight and out of mind; they must promote healthier metropolitan regions (Salins, 1994; Wilson, in press).

Before policy makers will embrace metropolitan solutions, suburbanites must agree to relinquish some of the local control they have come to cherish, and African Americans who live in mostly black cities must agree give up some of their political power in isolated and impoverished urban areas. Resistance to such solutions is likely to come from both sides of the color line. Suburban whites will guard their government structures and their racially and economically homogeneous enclaves. And urban blacks who are finally benefiting politically, if not economically, from the concentrated black vote in segregated cities may defend their localism and eschew broader metropolitan solutions that entail state or national government intervention into their communities (Smothers, 1993).

Yet a growing number of visionaries understand that the "problem" of the ghetto is not simply an urban problem. Urban poverty taps suburban prosperity; the two are inextricably linked. A former St. Louis school board member noted that the citizens of metropolitan St. Louis must embrace their beleaguered city. For whites, he argued, the "luxury of being so local," entrenched in small suburban communities, has become a detriment not only to those excluded from suburbia but to everyone in the metropolitan area. "It will strangle us; it has strangled us." As more policy makers define the issues in this way, more metropolitan solutions will be proposed. This is why the Clinton administration has fought to expand Chicago's Gautreaux housing desegregation experiment through the Moving to Opportunity program and why regional initiatives designed to "help spread the burden of inner-city problems and create housing integration" have been created in Portland, Seattle, and Minnesota (Rusk, 1993).

In St. Louis, the move toward metropolitanwide solutions is embodied in one politically fragile school desegregation plan, the result of a unique settlement agreement between the city school system and twenty-three suburban school districts. The plan is a political compromise between a judicial mandate to remedy decades of inferior education for blacks, and whites who insist on sending their children to locally controlled suburban schools.

At the break of dawn each day, a parade of yellow school buses canvases the urban ghetto, picking up black children from communities where white faces are typically seen only on television. The buses carry students west and south, against the daily commuter traffic from the suburbs to the city, and deliver them to 122 suburban schools. For these African-American students, stepping over the color line means more than transferring to a predominantly white school. It means staring 175 years of St. Louis history square in the face. For these students, the bus ride is yet another black migration, this time from the city to the suburbs, but as always, to a place where so few people understand the trouble they have seen.

2

The Color Line and the Court Order

We need to appreciate the importance of legislation, judicial decisions, and executive orders in setting the stage for eliminating the color line. Without them it is not possible for individuals or groups of individuals, however dedicated, to make a good-faith and successful effort to eliminate the color line.

—John Hope Franklin, *The Color Line: Legacy for the Twenty-First Century*

The cause-and-effect relation between housing segregation and school segregation is never clear. The two feed off each other until they are so intertwined that they become one. Whites move to white suburbs because of the reputation of the schools, which is strongly related to their racial composition, and because of the local control they have over these suburban schools. Blacks and Latinos are deterred by economic, social, and political forces from purchasing or renting homes in mostly white suburbs, and thus their children do not attend reputable suburban schools (Orfield, 1980b).

Civil rights lawyers have been far less successful in tackling discriminatory housing practices than in suing school districts for similar acts. Thus, in most communities, school desegregation policies are the only corrective action taken after years of unequal racial treatment in all sectors of society. "The issue of white 'suburbs' was of secondary importance" to the civil rights movement because school board practices were always an easier target (Stahura, 1986, p. 133). This emphasis is ironic, Stahura notes, given that the better educational opportunities were moving out of central cities. Thus, school desegregation plans, generally implemented in urban districts, represent the lone remedy for African Americans—a trickle of a solution pushing against a flood of whites to their separate suburbs.

Untouched segregated housing patterns mean that if children are to attend desegregated schools they have to be transported from one neighborhood to another. These transportation policies have provided opponents of desegregation with symbols—neighborhood schools and busing, for example—of their resistance to court orders. These symbols are powerful because our history of segregated housing has led people to believe that separate schools for white and nonwhite children are the "natural" outgrowth of Americans' freedom to live where they like and associate with whom they wish.

White resistance to school desegregation, some researchers argue, accelerates white flight from cities and thereby increases housing segregation (see Armor, 1972; Rossell, 1990). Still others have noted that cities with no desegregation plans, such as Atlanta and Chicago, have also experienced rapid white flight (Orfield, 1978a; Orfield and Ashkinaze, 1991). In fact, some researchers found that within areas affected by school desegregation plans, housing segregation decreases as families seek integrated neighborhoods so that their children can attend integrated *neighborhood* schools instead of being transported elsewhere (Farley and Frey, 1994). This is especially true in the South, with its countywide school districts. But desegregation plans within a single urban district surrounded by separate suburban districts can lead to increased white flight across district boundaries, increasing housing segregation at the metropolitan level (Pearce, Crain, Farley, and Taeuber, 1995).

The obvious implication of this research is that broad-based, inter-district, or metropolitanwide school desegregation plans are most likely to bring about meaningful desegregation in schools and neighborhoods. But legal precedent related to urban-suburban or metropolitanwide desegregation cases does not favor such remedies, which means that school desegregation has always been legally and logistically easier in southern school districts that envelop an entire county, including the city and the suburbs. "School districts in most Southern states coincide with county lines—which encouraged residential integration in those districts under Federal court order to desegregate because there were no white suburbs to flee to" (Farley and Frey, 1994, p. 35). In addition, housing segregation has traditionally been less severe in the South because Jim Crow laws made it less necessary for whites and blacks to live far apart. Whites could live near blacks, for instance, knowing that their children would not attend the same schools.

Still, resistance to school desegregation policy in the post–Jim Crow era in the South was common, especially in the early years of the civil rights movement. All-white private schools, know as "segregation academies," became a popular option. In fact, four southern states supported these private schools by giving white parents tuition vouchers. Other efforts to prevent school desegregation included closing public schools in integrated neighborhoods, building new schools in racially isolated neighborhoods, and erecting interstate highways between neighborhoods to block student transfers (White, 1994).

By the 1970s these southern efforts to avoid school desegregation were somewhat minimized by federal court orders and government pressure. Current data show that because of these desegregation plans within large city-county districts, the South has the most racially integrated public schools of any region of the country (Orfield, 1993).

In St. Louis, with its history of southern segregation and northern geography, the cause and effect relation between segregated neighborhoods and schools has changed over the years. When St. Louis was de jure segregated, housing segregation existed, but black and white neighborhoods often butted up against each other. After the *Brown* ruling, the distance between white and black neighborhoods grew, exacerbating the color line. Whites fled to separate neighborhoods and separate school districts—safe, so they thought, from court orders to desegregate the city.

Thus, the history of race and public education in St. Louis, as in most northern and midwestern cities, is interwoven with the history of residential segregation discussed in Chapter 1. The demise of the St. Louis public schools, for instance, was both caused by and the cause of white flight from the city. Yet in St. Louis, where the racial history of North and South meet to make matters worse, a more comprehensive remedy was needed to remove the vestiges of Jim Crow. What happened in St. Louis was a political compromise between that comprehensive remedy and the demands of white suburbanites to maintain their separate school districts. The result is a unique metropolitanwide program that gingerly crosses school district boundaries without eliminating them.

This metropolitan desegregation plan intersects civil rights efforts and Missouri's political culture, which highly values the rights of small, locally controlled suburban communities. This quintessential American value of local control is reflected in Missouri's history of indifference to government-supported institutions, including schools. Thus, in keeping with its odd mixture of northern and southern influences, Missouri inherited from New England a township pattern of school organization; from the South it inherited a disregard for public schooling.

The former influence fostered a proliferation of small, inefficient school districts. In 1948 there were eighty-nine autonomous school districts in St. Louis County. By 1971, after massive consolidation efforts, the number declined to twenty-six and currently stands at twenty-three. The latter, southern influence, along with the strong preference of many European immigrants for Catholic education, brought support for private schools (Spitzer, 1971). In 1993, more then 20 percent of school-age children in the St. Louis metropolitan area enrolled in private schools, nearly double the national average of about 11 percent. Three-fourths of these private-school students, or one out of every seven children in the St. Louis area, attend Catholic schools (Savageau and Boyer, 1993).

The lack of support for public education, coupled with the need to create separate small and autonomous districts, is related to the elemental conservatism of Missouri and is the basis for its nickname, the Show Me State, which implies that Missourians demand proof, are slow to embrace change, and maintain an antitax sentiment. These attitudes, some historians claim, stem from a lack of state unity and from a failure to overcome local attachment in order to address statewide needs: "Thinking of oneself as an Ozarker, St. Louisian, Kansas Citian, or resident of the Bootheel instead of as a Missourian produces fragmentation rather than unity. . . . In this respect Missouri is just like the nation, and thus the most American of the midwestern states" (Christensen, 1988, p. 105). In fact, for many years Missouri's combination of political diversity and local parochialism have made it a political barometer in national elections. A *New York Times* article noted that Missouri has voted for the winning presidential candidate in every election this century except 1956, "when it somewhat inexplicably went for Adlai E. Stevenson" (Apple, 1992, p. A11).

The metaphor of Missouri as a political barometer is perhaps most obvious in the antitax sentiment that produced its Hancock Amendment in 1980. This amendment, like laws in at least ten other states, including California's Proposition 13, declares that taxes cannot be raised without voter approval (Christensen, 1988, p. 103). The antitax sentiment has left Missouri ranked last among the states in taxation per capita and forty-third in per-pupil education funding. In 1968 a report on social services in Missouri concluded that it offers a "very low level of social welfare services to its residents—not because the State is financially unable to remedy the situation, but because of the apparent unwillingness of the (more affluent) residents of the State to provide sufficient resources to the public sector" (cited in Human Development Corp., 1970, p. 20). According to Michael Fields, a lawyer in the Missouri attorney general's office, "Missouri has been a state that has resisted tax increases, and when you do that, you pay a price in state services."

Missouri's political fragmentation, reflected in strong resistance to state taxes and a kind of political localism, is manifested in rural residents' opposition to state spending on St. Louis and Kansas City school desegregation plans. These rural opponents of desegregation seem to forget their Missouri history, which clearly shows that it was their agrarian ancestors who brought African Americans to the state to begin with and who later sent blacks migrating to the cities, penniless, uneducated, and illiterate. It was also whites across the state who forbade the education of blacks and endorsed Jim Crow segregation in which blacks paid Missouri taxes but were denied access to state-supported educational institutions. They also forget that Missouri—governed by leaders they elected—was found guilty in federal court of violating the constitutional rights of blacks.

Yet perhaps more puzzling than rural residents' hostility toward metropolitan school desegregation is the general lack of political support for the inter-district desegregation program among suburbanites in St. Louis, even as their local schools benefit financially from the plan (Smith and Little, 1996). According to Missouri Department of Education data, the sixteen suburban districts participating in the inter-district plan received nearly $60 million in 1994, and more than $450 million total since the plan began in 1983, in "incentive payments," or their per-pupil cost for each black student who transfers in from the city. This extra funding has allowed the suburbs to hire teachers and create new programs—resources that benefit white suburban students as well as black city students. And if these suburban districts can prove that they need new buildings or classrooms because of desegregation-related growth in enrollment, they are entitled to additional state funding to help pay for construction. Between 1985 and 1995, suburban districts participating in the plan received more than $35 million from the state to help pay for their capital improvement programs (Bryant, 1995). Meanwhile, they have maintained their autonomous districts and thus their freedom to spend the extra money as they wish. In this way, the St. Louis inter-district desegregation plan is similar to school choice policies, or open enrollment plans, adopted by at least eleven states, including Missouri, since 1987. Under these popular open enrollment plans students can transfer from one school district to the next and take their public education dollars with them (Wells, 1993). In St. Louis, the transfer of students across districts has been going on for more than a decade, but because it is labeled a desegregation plan and because black students have more choices than white students do, it is not as politically popular.

We do not deny that some African-American students who transfer to suburban schools have brought with them problems of inner-city life, which result in fighting, theft, and in the occasional carrying of weapons. Reports of such incidents in suburban schools understandably concern white parents and taxpayers. But, as we discuss in later chapters, the number of such incidents is relatively low, given the scope of the desegregation plan. Students—both black and white—say they are tired of the media and others exaggerating the violence in suburban schools while ignoring the more positive aspects of the plan.

Certainly not all whites in St. Louis County are opposed to the inter-district desegregation plan, but few are strong and vocal supporters of it. White suburbanites' resignation and resistance toward the desegregation plan raises questions about racial politics. Time and again we heard whites in St. Louis County lament that "if they would just take all the money they are spending on busing and fix up the city schools . . ." Unlike their rural neighbors, the suburbanites generally do not say they are bothered by state spending per se, but they would rather have the money spent outside their districts. Their distaste for school buses carrying black inner-city students to their schools symbolizes their lack of understanding of the long legacy of racial discrimination, the vestiges of which are still with us. Thus their conception of who *deserves* what in this society is skewed in favor of hard-working white people like themselves. No one taught them how schools became so segregated and unequal in Missouri and elsewhere. No one ever demonstrated how they, as taxpaying, law-abiding citizens, have contributed, often indirectly, to the lived reality of present-day ghettos.

PUBLIC EDUCATION BEFORE *BROWN*

Despite Missouri's lack of commitment to public education, the state did, in a move reflecting its northern bent, establish free public schools years before most southern states (Anderson, 1988). The Geyer Act of 1839 created an elementary-through-postsecondary school system incorporating the Jeffersonian ideal of providing education to all white citizens according to their ability (Spitzer, 1971). African-American students were systematically denied access to free public schools, and in 1846, Missouri passed a law explicitly prohibiting the education of "Negroes" (Joiner, 1971; Troen, 1975).

The state legislature established the St. Louis school board in 1833 and charged it with serving the city's white students. According to the charter, only "free white males" could be officers of the Board of Education, which could not afford to build a school until 1838, when it opened a public school for boys and one for girls (Hyde and Conard, 1899; Troen, 1975; Faherty, 1976). By 1854 there were 27 public schools, 72 teachers, and 3,791 white students in St. Louis, and the following year the Board of Education opened the first public high school west of the Mississippi (Primm, 1990). Meanwhile, the statute forbidding the "instruction of free negroes and mulattoes" was strictly enforced, and the state imposed a $500 fine or six months in jail on anyone breaking this law (Troen, 1975, p. 80).

Several "underground" schools for black children were established in the basements of churches. The Reverend John Berry Meachum, a former Virginia slave, ran such a school in a Baptist church until the St. Louis sheriff closed it. Undaunted, Meachum built a steamboat and anchored it in the Mississippi River. Because the river is under federal jurisdiction, Missouri officials could not prevent Meachum from educating black children on his boat, which he named the Freedom School. For nearly two decades, black children rode rafts across the choppy Mississippi waters to the Freedom School, where they learned to read and write (Joiner, 1971; Primm, 1990).

While a small number of African-American students were attending underground or riverboat schools, many white students, including German immigrants, were well served in the St. Louis Public Schools. To accommodate German-speaking students, the Board of Education ordered that both English and German be taught. More important, however, the board integrated German and Anglo students, at the suggestion of Superintendent Ira Divoll, and offered bilingual education, unlike schools in other cities with large German populations. "It was the proclaimed policy to give the children of Germans a knowledge of English and the advantage of school association with Anglo-Americans, it being desirable that those two classes of the population should not grow up as two hostile castes, but, on the contrary, that they should grow up as fellow pupils and make a homogeneous population for St. Louis. It was assumed that German pupils should not lose their command of their native tongue while they learn English. . . . The study of German by Anglo-American students was encouraged" (Hyde and Conard, 1899, p. 2015). This policy was credited with helping to remove barriers between German and Anglo businessmen as well as with allowing inter-ethnic marriages, thus lessening the need for separatism (Hyde and Conard, 1899).

In contrast to the way it treated German-American students, the board did not open its first school for "colored" children until 1866, three years after the Missouri statute banning education for blacks was revoked and one year after the Missouri Constitution under Reconstruction required school boards to support black education. Years later, in its post-Reconstruction Constitution, Missouri ordered that schools for black and white students must be separate, but the St. Louis board had already ensured this would be the case (Adair, 1984).

By 1875, Superintendent Divoll and the St. Louis board had established twelve separate "colored schools," usually housed in dilapidated quarters and frequently moved to new locations. This meant that many black students were forced to walk long distances to school, "often passing several white schools en route" (Primm, 1990, p. 335). According to Troen (1975), "At best, blacks would inherit an old 'white' schoolhouse that had been abandoned for more modern facilities. More often, however, Negroes were educated in inadequate, inferior, and occasionally distant buildings, sometimes pursuing instruction at different locations each year" (p. 85).

Until 1890, most black schools were not named but had numbers—Colored School No. 1, Colored School No. 2. The teachers were paid about half of what teachers in white schools earned. In 1880 the average value of land, buildings, and furnishings for the sixty-eight white schools was $39,330. The average value of the colored schools was $14,600 (Primm, 1990). Still, many whites opposed any public funding for colored schools. Superintendent Divoll reminded his white constituents that blacks were contributing about $15,000 per year to the city's school revenues; he said he assumed that whites would not wish to benefit from such money, arguing that the "best way to dispose of it was to expend it on Negroes" (Troen, 1975, p. 83).

African-American parents were diligent in lobbying for better educational opportunities for their children. They built a school at their own expense and donated it to the Board of Education. They pressed the board to provide their children with kindergarten, trained teachers, and a high school. In response, the board designated an abandoned white elementary school in 1875 to house the High School for Colored Children, later named for Charles Sumner, a senator from Massachusetts and the first prominent politician to support emancipation (Primm, 1990; Wright, 1994). Sumner, the first black high school west of the Mississippi, became a source of pride for the black community, renowned for its caring teachers, who were among the lowest paid in the district. The long list of famous Sumner graduates includes Arthur Ashe, Chuck Berry, Grace Bumbry, U.S. Representative William L. Clay, and Dick Gregory (Wright, 1994).

For more than fifty years every black student in either St. Louis City or County who was able to attend high school went to Sumner. Tuition for students who lived outside the boundaries of the St. Louis public school system was $100, much more than most blacks could afford. But a 1918 Missouri Supreme Court ruling required every school district providing a high school education for white students to also provide one for black students. This prompted several suburban St. Louis districts to pay half of the out-of-district tuition for their resident black students to attend Sumner. The state paid the other half. Still, some suburban districts were reluctant to pay, and at least one district was often late with its tuition payments, causing the St. Louis board to dismiss the black students until their fees were paid (Dawson, 1981). In interviews, blacks from St. Louis County who had attended Sumner prior to 1954 said that they had given St. Louis public school officials a city home address—usually that of a friend or relative—to avoid having to get tuition from their home district in the suburbs (Dawson, 1981).

No transportation was provided for black county students who attended Sumner; they were forced to rely on city-suburban trolley cars, trains, or horses to get to school. James DeClue, former president of the St. Louis NAACP, recalled that until the *Brown* ruling in 1954, black students would come from miles away to attend Sumner: "There was a street car that came down Taylor and Cobb to drop students from the county to go to Sumner High School. Kids from all over the county would come."

Because of the difficulty of getting tuition and transportation into the city, many black students from the county who wanted to attend high school would either move in with relatives in the city or become urban "boarders." According to Kenneth Brostron, the attorney for the St. Louis School Board, "Eventually, the black families who wanted their kids to go to good schools would end up migrating to St. Louis because the suburbs did not have black schools. So the relationship of housing to schools is strong." Brostron noted that even new suburban school districts formed via consolidation in the 1940s and early 1950s did nothing to accommodate black high school students, whom they continued to send to Sumner, thereby forcing more blacks into the city in search of an education.

Furthermore, an 1865 Missouri law stated that local districts were not required to establish a new school for fewer than 20 students. Under this law, suburban districts reported they had too few black students to warrant the creation of a "colored school," whether they did or not. A 1922 state of Missouri report noted the ongoing "migration of blacks into urban areas, such as St. Louis, to get an education" (Missouri Population Report, 1922). The state's 1929 population report stated that "outside of St. Louis and Kansas City, high school opportunity for negro children is very limited. Although less than half the total negro population of the state lives in these two cities, 84 percent of all the high school education [for blacks] in the state is provided by them" (see Dawson, 1982).

Finally, in 1925, fifty years after the founding of Sumner High School, one of the suburban St. Louis districts with a significant number of blacks, Webster Groves, added a high school "department" to its colored school (Confluence, 1989; Wright, 1994). And in 1931, after lobbying by black leaders, the St. Louis school board converted Vashon Intermediate School into the city's second black high school. Vashon, named for George Boyer Vashon, the first black graduate of Oberlin College, and his son John Boyer Vashon, a teacher and principal in St. Louis, served the growing black population east of Sumner High in the Ville (Wright, 1994).

These efforts by black leaders and parents to force the all-white St. Louis school board to provide greater educational opportunities for black children were representative of the value that African-American families in St. Louis and throughout the South placed on education (Anderson, 1988). In fact, before Missouri passed a compulsory school attendance law in 1905, there were more black children in St. Louis enrolled in schools than there were whites of similar economic status (Primm, 1990).

Still, the separate black and white schools in the city were far from equal; the board continued to spend three times the money on white high school students as on their black counterparts (Troen, 1975). James DeClue of the NAACP and a pre-*Brown* graduate of Sumner, recalled the unequal treatment of black and white students: "We got the old books from the white high school—pages tattered and torn, answers marked in the book, and all that nonsense. You don't forget things like that."

Black students were also denied access to white universities. Of the twenty-one institutions of higher education in St. Louis, only Homer G. Phillips School of Nursing and Stowe Normal School served black students. Lincoln University, established in 1866 in Jefferson City to prepare blacks for teaching, eventually became the Missouri state university for blacks. Missouri was a leader among southern states both in providing higher education for blacks and in keeping the races separated (see Kluger, 1975; Confluence, 1989). This combination made the concept of separate but equal more difficult to fight.

In July 1936 the famous NAACP attorney Charles Houston went to Columbia, Missouri, to argue one of the three higher-education cases that would constitute his legacy as a civil rights lawyer. According to Kluger (1975), "From the Missouri case would stem a full-scale assault on segregation in all the nation's schools" (p. 202). The case, *Gaines v. Canada*, concerned Lloyd Lionel Gaines, a twenty-five-year-old from St. Louis who wanted to be a lawyer. But Lincoln, the only full-fledged university for blacks in Missouri, did not have a law school. Gaines, a Lincoln graduate, was denied admission to the University of Missouri's law school. At the time, Missouri had only forty-five black attorneys, fewer than it had ten years earlier (Confluence, 1989; Kluger, 1975).

The Missouri case was similar to *Murray v. Maryland,* a case the NAACP had won in January 1936, when the Maryland Court of Appeals ruled that a black man be admitted to the all-white University of Maryland Law School because the state had failed to provide him with a viable alternative—either a law school at its black college or funding for legal studies outside the state. Shortly after the Maryland ruling, the Missouri legislature allocated money for scholarships so that black students could attend out-of-state graduate schools (Kluger, 1975). Lloyd Gaines' case was different, therefore, because Missouri's out-of-state subsidy was a bona fide offer and because Lincoln University, unlike Maryland's black college, was a reputable institution that conceivably could create and sustain a law school. The state's attorneys argued that Gaines' remedy lay in the hands of Lincoln University officials, whom they said should provide for his legal education. The Missouri court agreed and ruled against his admission to the University of Missouri. The NAACP appealed.

When the case reached the U.S. Supreme Court in 1938, Charles Houston argued that he was not challenging the separate but equal doctrine of the landmark 1896 *Plessy v. Ferguson* ruling, but he insisted that the Court enforce the principle of "equal." He said that if Missouri offered its white citizens a law school, it had to offer its black citizens a law school every bit as good. The Supreme Court agreed with Houston, overturning the lower court's ruling: "The basic consideration is not as to what sort of opportunities other states provide, or whether they are as good as those in Missouri, but as to what opportunities Missouri itself furnishes to white students and denies to Negroes solely upon the ground of color." The Court ruled that Gaines was entitled to equal protection, and the state had to furnish him "facilities for legal education" (Kluger, 1975, p. 212–213).

But rather than admit Gaines to the University of Missouri Law School, the state legislature immediately appropriated $200,000 with which to establish a law school at Lincoln University. Similarly, in response to a black student's application to the University of Missouri's School of Journalism in 1939, the state established a journalism school at Lincoln, appropriating $64,000 in the first year for a program serving three students (Confluence, 1989).

The *Murray* and *Gaines* cases represented a legal if not an educational milestone because they became the basis for suits against other states and school districts and were the beginning of the NAACP's deliberate march toward *Brown* in 1954 (Kluger, 1975). The Missouri case helped to lay the legal groundwork for such cases as *Sweatt v. Painter* (1950), in which the NAACP argued that Herman Sweatt be admitted to the University of Texas Law School even though Texas had established a separate black law school with five professors, 23 students, a library of 16,000 books, a full-time staff, a practice court, and a legal aid association. The Supreme Court ruled in Sweatt's favor, stating the University of Texas Law School and the new law school for Negroes did not provide substantially equal educational opportunities because the university possessed "to a far greater degree those qualities which are incapable of objective measurement but which make for greatness in a law school." Such qualities, the Court wrote, include reputation of the faculty, position and influence of the alumni, standing in the community, traditions and prestige (Kluger, 1975, p. 282). Because judges are lawyers themselves, the Court understood the significance of these qualities and thus what black law students stood to benefit from their association with prestigious white law schools.

In a simultaneous ruling in *McLaurin v. Oklahoma State Regents for Higher Education,* the Supreme Court stated that this association principle applies to other graduate programs as well. Thus George McLaurin, a black doctoral student at the University of Oklahoma, could not be forced to sit in a room outside the regular classroom. Nor could he be assigned a segregated desk in the mezzanine of the library or forced to eat alone in the cafeteria. The Court ruled that such restrictions "impair and inhibit his ability to study, to engage in discussions and exchange views with other students, and in general, to learn his profession" (Kluger, 1975, p. 268).

The *Sweatt* and *McLaurin* decisions rested on the negative effect of black students' exclusion from white institutions not simply because of the resources or facilities in these institutions, but also because of the institutions' status in society as well as the social networks within them. The status of educational institutions continues to be exceedingly important in American society in determining graduates' access to other high-status institutions and positions of power.

Social science research has documented this theory. Research on employers, for instance, demonstrates that African-American graduates of a white suburban high school are more likely to be hired by a white-owned business than are similar graduates of all-black, inner-city schools. "Knowledge that a job candidate graduated from a suburban school with a good reputation rather than an inner-city school is likely to signal to employers that the quality of education is better in the suburban school" (Braddock, Crain, McPartland, and Dawkins, 1986, p. 13). Similarly, Zweigenhaft and Domhoff (1991) found that most African-American students from low-income neighborhoods who attended prestigious private prep schools through a program called A Better Chance (ABC) used their prep school credential to gain access to high-status universities and successful careers.

This access to high-status schools is an important component of the St. Louis inter-district desegregation plan, although opponents of the plan claim that money spent busing black students to suburban schools would be better spent "fixing up" the all-black schools in the city. Ironically, such a remedy—simply fixing up the segregated urban schools—was tried in Missouri's other large urban school district, Kansas City, where more than $1.1 billion was spent to make mostly black schools so good that whites from the suburbs would want to enroll their children there. The white students did not come and the achievement levels of the black students did not go up, and in the end the plan was dubbed a failure (see Kunen, 1996). Meanwhile, the students in St. Louis who ride the buses every day to the suburbs understand what Gaines, Sweatt, and McLaurin were fighting for nearly sixty years ago: access to schools with the best reputations and most influence in a predominantly white society (Jankowski, 1995).

AFTER *BROWN:* TRADING DE JURE FOR DE FACTO SEGREGATION

As the NAACP lawyers moved forward, initiating cases involving elementary and secondary schools, their legal theory began to rely increasingly on how segregation affected black children psychologically. Unlike many pre-*Brown* arguments based on black graduate students' access to prestigious institutions, the legal rationale for the five cases included in the *Brown* ruling focused more specifically on the "hearts and minds" of children.

Thus, in the early 1950s, arguments for school desegregation became more disparate. Psychologists and educators maintained that allowing black children to attend the white schools from which their parents had been excluded could lead to greater self-esteem, academic achievement, and educational attainment for black students, and improved race relations among all students. Since Kenneth B. and Mamie Clark's research on black children and their preference for white over black dolls, the rationale for desegregating students has been steeped more in psychological theory about feelings of inferiority than it has around broader issues about how institutions such as schools maintain different status in this country by virtue of the race and class of the students within them (Rosenberg, 1986; Jankowski, 1995). Although the differences between the two theories are subtle, they are important to understanding whites' resistance to school desegregation policy and the waning political support for desegregation on both sides of the color line.

The "hearts and minds" policy argument suggests that simply enrolling African-American students in white schools would increase their achievement. Thus, in the early years of desegregation, few policy makers or researchers asked *how* these policies were implemented but rather whether black students in racially mixed schools—any racially mixed schools—had higher test scores than did black students in segregated schools. Gary Orfield (1978b) argues that when researchers asked whether desegregation "worked," they turned to their most familiar instruments: standardized achievement tests. These tests set a standard for desegregation success or failure often *after only one year*, as researchers often ignored such important contextual variables as school climate and curriculum. Thus, much of the earliest and most influential research on school desegregation failed to examine *how* desegregation was being implemented—including whether schools resegregated students by tracks, whether there were differences in how black and white students were disciplined, or whose history and culture was reflected in the curriculum (Brown, 1990; Grant, 1990). As the success of school desegregation became defined by narrow and incomplete measures of its implementation and effects, political support for desegregation among whites also came to rest on the belief that these programs would help black students score higher on standardized tests. "Despite the very contradictory literature on school desegregation, the case for desegregation was seen as hinging *primarily* on whether it improves the achievement test scores of minority students" (Levin, 1975, p. 238).

In this way, school desegregation came to be perceived as more an act of charity to black students than a legal remedy for what whites had done wrong for so long. This benevolent rationale for school desegregation policy is politically palatable but greatly misguided. Although greater educational achievement for blacks is a significant goal, the argument that black students need to sit next to white ones to achieve it is weak. Although African-American students are more likely to have access to educational resources and rigorous curriculum in a predominantly white versus all-black school, their educational outcomes do not hinge on the racial makeup of the school. If researchers and policy makers focused solely on educational resources and curricular content, separate black and white schools could, in theory, be "equal."

But educational achievement alone does not solve economic inequality among different racial groups. School desegregation must do more than raise black students' test scores and close the black-white achievement gap; it must also break the cycle of segregation that leaves blacks and whites worlds apart. As the NAACP lawyers in the *Sweatt* and *McLaurin* cases argued, *who* you know and associate with is as important (or even more important) as *what* you know. Most black students in segregated urban schools lack the social networks and personal contacts with people in corporations, law firms, universities, and art museums—contacts who could help them get summer jobs, teach them about career paths, and introduce them to possibilities for life after high school. Cut off from powerful people and economically viable institutions, blacks in highly segregated schools receive the message that they are inferior. These students must then decide what to do with the anger that results when they confront segregation as a symbol of white racism (Crain, Peichart, Hawes, and Miller, 1993). Many become caught in a cycle of segregation and alienation, which repeats itself generation after generation.

Equally important, however, is the reality that when whites view school desegregation as a way to help blacks raise test scores, they disassociate themselves from racial inequality, as if the color line had been drawn without their involvement. Instead of seeing school desegregation as a way to remove vestiges of nearly 200 years of discriminatory acts, many Americans see it as punishment for whites—an effort to give undeserving blacks additional opportunities at the expense of white taxpayers. As we mentioned, the turning point in the civil rights movement occurred when whites began to believe that there were no more vestiges of discrimination, a misunderstanding that led to frustration in black communities and eventually to rioting (Stahura, 1986). Most whites fail to acknowledge society's broken promises to blacks, the most painful of which occurred between 1954 and 1964, when the promise of *Brown* faded into whites' resistance. Because they never clearly understood the subtle and not-so-subtle ways they created segregation, whites conveniently ignore the relation between white privilege and black deprivation, and they view policies like desegregation as benevolent gifts.

Blacks learned that de jure, or state-sanctioned, southern-style segregation could easily be replaced by northern-style de facto segregation, a more private, insidious form. The famous last stands of Jim Crow segregationists—Governor Orval E. Faubus on the steps of Little Rock's Central High School and Governor George Wallace at the University of Georgia—were decoys for the more silent revolution taking place behind the cameras (White, 1994). In St. Louis, the transition from de jure to de facto segregation was so smooth that the St. Louis Board of Education's halfhearted and largely unsuccessful efforts to desegregate schools managed to garner nation praise (Crain, 1969).

In fact, when riots broke out across the country, St. Louis remained deceptively tranquil. James Buford, president of the Urban League, argues that St. Louis was relatively calm because the frequent waves of poor, uneducated blacks from the South were both appreciative of the opportunities available in this more northern city and calmed by its genteel southern tone. They did not, according to Buford, "have a real sense of who the enemy was."

St. Louis offered black migrants more than did the rest of the South, especially in the area of education. The St. Louis public schools were touted as a premier school system, and the black schools, whose quality was lower than the white schools', were far superior to those of rural Mississippi. During the years of heavy black migration to St. Louis, several forward-looking leaders, including the St. Louis school board president, tried to accommodate the needs of the growing black community by constructing new segregated schools in black neighborhoods. By 1945, the 30,880 black students enrolled in the St. Louis public schools were assigned to forty-two all-black schools while the 58,600 white students attended ninety-one all-white schools (Horton, 1991).

One month after the Supreme Court's *Brown* ruling, the twelve-member, all-white St. Louis Board of Education abandoned mandatory segregation of black and white children, well ahead of school boards in most southern cities, and reassigned all students to "neighborhood schools" under a three-step plan:

1. By September 1954, junior and teachers colleges were desegregated, which led to the merger of Harris and Stowe teachers colleges.

2. By February 1955 all high schools, except for the technical high schools, and all adult education programs were to be desegregated.

3. By September 1955 the two technical high schools and all kindergarten through eighth grade schools were desegregated (Confluence, 1989; Horton, 1991).

With this policy in place, the St. Louis board reported that 6 of its 7 previously all-white high schools and 50 of the district's 123 elementary schools were desegregated. *Time* magazine hailed the St. Louis plan as a model. Still, the actual "integrative effects" of the plan were mild (Horton, 1991) because St. Louis, as so many border state cities, was slipping from de jure to de facto segregation with relative ease. White (1994) writes that the impact of *Brown* was fairly mild in most of the border states, "which had relatively small black populations that were for the most part concentrated in large, central, and overcrowded downtown sections of cities" (p. 16).

At the time of the *Brown* ruling, St. Louis was home to more than half of the 63,000 black school-age children in Missouri. The creation of a neighborhood school policy meant the St. Louis school board not only allowed the segregated housing to guarantee segregated schools, but in some instances the board drew attendance zones to excluded black neighborhoods. Behind the public praise of its 1954 plan, the St. Louis Board had made only minor adjustments to the attendance boundaries of sixteen of its eighty-four white elementary schools to include a small number of black students. No changes were made for forty-one white elementary schools, and in the remaining twelve, boundaries were redrawn to exclude black neighborhoods. The board also changed high school "feeder patterns" to ensure that students attending black elementary schools would enroll in either Sumner and Vashon. The boundaries of a white high school, Southwest, were redrawn to exclude blacks (Horton, 1991).

In addition, the St. Louis board allowed students to transfer from their newly assigned racially mixed neighborhood school to a school of their choice. Under this policy white students assigned to majority black schools were able to remain in the schools they attended under the segregated dual system (Horton, 1991). According to William Russell, lawyer for the black plaintiffs, the Board of Education's post-*Brown* transfer policy meant that "blacks who wanted to transfer had a difficult time doing it, but there was no problem for white families to transfer their children into schools that were practically all-white."

And despite the Board of Education's stated goal of desegregating teachers and administrators, educators were allowed to remain in schools they had been assigned to before 1954. By 1966, thirty-five of the district's forty-one all-black elementary schools had no white teachers, and in 1973, more than 90 percent of the black teachers were still teaching in all-black schools (see Horton, 1991; La Noue and Smith, 1973).

As these post-*Brown* policies led to few "integrated experiences" within the St. Louis public schools, continued black migration into the city caused overcrowding in black schools. At the same time, the rapid flight of white families from the city to the suburbs was thwarting meaningful desegregation efforts by the Board of Education. Between 1942 and 1967, the white student population of the St. Louis public schools dropped from 76,000 students, or 78 percent of the total enrollment, to 43,500 students, or only 37 percent.

In the 1950s, as black families were pushed north and west within the city by urban renewal, whites who lived in these area moved across the border to the county, leaving behind the city and its school system. The once-posh West End neighborhood changed from 98 percent white in 1950 to 64 percent black in 1960. Soldan High School, the reputable all-white high school serving this neighborhood, was close to the Ville, where many blacks who worked in West End houses lived. Soldan, one of the schools that began enrolling black students under the neighborhood schools plan, went from all-white prior to 1954 to 26 percent black in 1955. By 1964, Soldan was 90 percent black (Horton, 1991).

Public schools on the city's north side flipped almost overnight from white to black during the 1960s, when the first wave of black families moved north of Natural Bridge Avenue—a dividing line between black and white St. Louis for many years. On the south side of the city, where whites were more insulated, dramatic white flight did not occur until the 1970s. The Board of Education was redrawing school attendance boundaries almost as quickly as whites were leaving the city, gerrymandering to maintain predominantly white schools whenever possible. Meanwhile, black students in segregated schools faced increasingly crowded conditions. For instance, the ghetto expansion and ongoing migration of blacks into the West End area of the city overwhelmed the public schools. New schools and additions to old schools were built as student enrollment in this area soared from 2,760 to 6,186 between 1956 and 1962 (Orfield, 1981).

During the 1950s, one of the board's solutions to overcrowded black schools was to bus students to undersubscribed white schools on the city's south side. The process, known as intact busing, ensured that the black students would arrive at school after the white students were in class. The black students were kept in self-contained classrooms, given lunch and recess at different times from the white students, and loaded onto their buses for home after the white students had departed. "The white and black children never saw each other; they were on completely different schedules," said Brostron, the school board attorney.

By the early 1960s, nearly 5,000 black students were bused to southside schools under this policy. During the summer of 1963, black parents and civil rights leaders began to mobilize against the Board of Education, protesting the intact busing practice in particular. The board discontinued the intact busing that fall, but rather than integrate all the black and white students in southside schools, the board built, between 1962 and 1967, nine new elementary schools in virtually all-black attendance zones in the city's West End and north side. Funding for these schools came from successful city bond issues (Crain, 1968; Horton, 1991). According to Minnie Liddell, who had four small children at the time, these new schools were known as "containment schools—the result of bond issues that were approved based on a lot of racist statements in South St. Louis: 'Build some more schools so that you keep them [black students] all over there.'"

As in most cities, the St. Louis board conveniently avoided building schools in areas that could draw from both black and white neighborhoods, thus guaranteeing that segregation would continue in the schools and the housing market (White, 1994). In 1968 the board opened the Yeatman Elementary School, one of the so-called containment schools, on the north side. According to Liddell, the school was all black and overcrowded from the start. Despite the racial overtones of the bond election that financed it, Yeatman was a popular neighborhood school. Black parents liked that their children could walk to school and come home for lunch. Liddell and Beatrice Yarber, a mother of six who had three children enrolled in Yeatman at the time, recalled that there was a lot of parent involvement and a strong sense of community. "I was feeling kind of smug about Yeatman School, and we . . . felt that Yeatman had everything that we would want in an elementary school," said Yarber.

But in a few years the St. Louis Board of Education would turn the contentment of these black parents into a powerful political force. In the 1950s and 1960s the school board had walked a fine line, generally alienating neither whites or blacks. It had built new schools for black children, made a token commitment to desegregation, and kept the southside schools' classrooms segregated. But as black parents became more assertive the school board ran out of room to maneuver the racial politics, and its decision about one neighborhood school set off a firestorm. Little did the board know that the pent-up frustration of generations of black parents who had fought more than a century for decent education would give birth to a court case that would profoundly change public education in St. Louis City and County.

SCHOOL DESEGREGATION IN ST. LOUIS—THE FIRST PHASE

Minnie Liddell, who has lived in St. Louis since she was nine months old, attended racially segregated public schools in the city. She was enrolled in the all-black technical high school when the Supreme Court ruled that separate schools were inherently unequal. But from where she stood, no significant changes took place after the *Brown* ruling. She does remember, like James DeClue, that her textbooks were discards from the white schools. And like Buford at the Urban League, Liddell recalled that blacks in St. Louis did not demand bold changes in the early years of the civil rights movement: "If you were aware at all you knew that the educational delivery and the services to the black schools was much more limited than it was in the other parts of town. . . . But I am not sure that meant a lot to black people back in the '50s because they had always been [limited] anyway. So we just accepted it for what it was. I don't think a consciousness had really started taking place among black folk."

But by the time her own children were in school, Liddell was becoming more concerned about the unequal treatment of black children in the St. Louis public schools. When he was in first grade, her oldest son, Craton, was transported out of his neighborhood school because of overcrowding. Then, in 1968, Craton and his siblings were assigned to the new Yeatman School, which was within walking distance of their home. In August 1971 the Board of Education sent letters to parents in a three-block area near the school stating that their children were reassigned because of overcrowding at Yeatman. These children, including the Liddells and the Yarbers, were to attend the Bates School, located in a boarded-up building surrounded by deserted and burned buildings. "It just appeared to me to be a very frightening place for a youngster to have to attend school," recalled Beatrice Yarber.

The angry parents whose children were reassigned to Bates began meeting, first at a church and then nightly at the Yarber home, to plan their protest against the board. Liddell and Yarber remember that they were at first concerned only about their own children, and their goal was to get them back into Yeatman. Meanwhile, white parents from the city's south side protested a similar decision to reassign their children because of overcrowding. The board rescinded its decision for these parents, allowing the white students to return to the neighborhood school, but it refused to allow the black students to return to Yeatman.

This decision ignited a grassroots movement among the black parents whose children had been reassigned. According to Yarber, the protest took on greater significance: "I think at some point in time, in the middle of my living room floor . . . we began to realize that we were not as fortunate as those peo ple on the south side who were able to keep their youngsters in their own schools. We also realized that we could not do anything for our group of youngsters without making changes for all black youngsters. . . . We knew there were youngsters who had lived in the same house for all their lives and had attended six schools in six years. We were aware of that."

The core group of about fifteen parents, Concerned Parents of North St. Louis, organized a boycott of the Bates School and continued to protest. Their children were out of school for six weeks before the board allowed parents to choose an alternative school to Bates, as long as it was not Yeatman. Meanwhile, the school board did not provide transportation for black students who were reassigned because of school overcrowding, thus many students were forced to rely on the public bus system. When a black boy was killed by a public bus when trying to get to a school he had been reassigned to, the Concerned Parents became increasingly vocal in their school board protests. "We boycotted their meetings, we disrupted their meetings[,] . . . we picketed their meetings. We did everything at their meetings. . . . They took one of the most supportive groups of parents and turned them into their rebellious parents," said Yarber.

They organized community meetings of 200 parents to discuss educational issues. Despite their lack of resources and the initial lack of involvement by civil rights organizations, the Concerned Parents found an attorney, William Russell, to work with them. On February 18, 1972, they filed a class action lawsuit, *Liddell v. Board of Education of the City of St. Louis, Missouri*, in U.S. District Court, Eastern District of Missouri. The plaintiffs were seeking equal protection under the laws and equal treatment of black and white students by the St. Louis Board of Education. What had started as a movement by a few angry parents who wanted their children readmitted to an all-black school would become one of the most important school desegregation cases in the country.

According to Buford, the St. Louis case initially did not have the political urgency of other desegregation cases because the parents were not trying to get their children into schools with white children but rather wanted to return them to their all-black neighborhood school. The parents were passionate but lacked funding for experts and legal researchers. Yarber said she is not sure why Russell agreed to take their case, because they had no money. Lacking resources, Russell got the parents involved in researching the case. "This was not a case where the attorneys handled it; it was a case where the parents were actively involved," said Liddell.

This direct involvement of the parents is in part what led to the expansion of the case. Liddell, for instance, recalled reading school board documents and becoming more aware of the unequal treatment of black students. Because members of Concerned Parents had friends who worked for the St. Louis public schools, they had access to "mounds" of information. "We discovered we knew more about what was taking place in the St. Louis public school system than the school administrators," she said.

They collected data on student assignments, the physical condition of schools, distribution of resources, and student achievement. The more information the Concerned Parents received, the more aware they became of the racial isolation within the city schools and what that isolation meant for black students' access to quality educational programs. By 1975, 72 percent of the city schools were still segregated by race, and a 1978 Missouri Department of Education survey found that 90 percent of black students attended predominantly black schools, many of which were overcrowded (Confluence, 1989).

The parents began to see a pattern of the board treating black students like pawns on a chessboard. They learned about the intact busing program of the 1950s and '60s and the board's efforts to continually redraw attendance lines, repeatedly closing and reopening black schools. Yarber noted, "We in the black communities had never really had the opportunities to experience a full neighborhood school."

In spite of their fears of sending their children to southside schools, where whites were not known for their racial tolerance, the Concerned Parents finally decided to push for desegregation. As Yarber explained the decision, "People are more apt to take care of your children if you have some of their children to take care of."

Prior to a trial in the *Liddell* case, district court Judge James H. Meredith ordered a consent judgment and decree on December 24, 1975. The decree, agreed to by the school board and the black plaintiffs, stated that "segregation is present, as a matter of fact, in the Public School System of the City of St. Louis." Meredith ordered that the defendants—the St. Louis school board and its employees—were "required to take affirmative action to secure unto plaintiffs their right to attend racially nonsegregated and nondiscriminatory schools, and defendants will afford unto plaintiffs equal opportunities for an education in a nonsegregated and nondiscriminatory school district" (Confluence, 1989, p. 88).

The decree purposefully avoided mandating any student reassignments or busing, which was politically important for a school board rapidly losing white constituents to the suburbs. St. Louis' now-defunct *Globe-Democrat* newspaper on Christmas Day ran a front-page story headlined, "No-Busing School Desegregation Plan Will Go in Effect Next Fall." The article quoted Judge Meredith: "The agreement may be an alternative to the type of plan which is causing so much confusion in other parts of the country" (Waters, 1975a).

The decree required the board to reduce racial imbalance through various nonmandatory means, including specialty or magnet schools that would draw white and black students (*Liddell v. St. Louis Board of Education*, 1975). Yet the most controversial aspect of the decree was its requirement that the board increase the number of minority teachers in the system and balance the racial makeup of the teaching staff until no fewer than 10 percent of the staff at each school would be of a different race from the majority of students. The minimum percentage of black teachers in the system was to increase to 20 percent in 1977–78 and to 30 percent in 1978–79. The local teachers' union strongly protested these measures.

Meanwhile, the plaintiffs continued gathering evidence, for the trial to establish the liability of the St. Louis board was still pending. In 1976 the NAACP intervened on behalf of another group of black families, known as the Caldwell plaintiffs. And in 1977 the U.S. Justice Department intervened on behalf of all black plaintiffs. In addition, a group of white southside parents opposed to desegregation—Concerned Parents for Neighborhood Schools—

entered the case. They were referred to as the Adams plaintiffs after Janice Adams, the leader of the group. The state of Missouri, the state commissioner of education, and the Missouri Board of Education were also added as defendants.

The case proceeded to trial with the eight parties aligned into two principal groups: The Liddell and Caldwell plaintiffs, the NAACP, and the Justice Department argued that the St. Louis Board of Education had violated the U. S. Constitution in operating its public schools. These parties sought a desegregation remedy. The second group of parties included the St. Louis Board of Education, the state of Missouri (including the state Department of Education, the State Board of Education, and the state commissioner), the Adams plaintiffs, and the city of St. Louis, which had been added as a defendant in 1973. This second group denied that any constitutional violation had occurred. The Board of Education argued that it was not responsible for the racial segregation within the school system. Similarly, the state argued that it was not responsible for segregation in the city schools and therefore should not participate in any remedy imposed by the court.

The trial began in November 1977 and lasted until May 1978. On April 12, 1979, Judge Meredith ruled in favor of the defendants, finding no constitutional violations and concluding that the Board of Education had fulfilled its obligation to black students in the 1950s when it adopted the neighborhood school policy and that resegregation of the schools had occurred because of demographic shifts influenced by federal and state policies and individual choices, not school board actions. Meredith instructed the board to continue implementing the consent decree by hiring more black teachers and establishing magnet schools. The criteria for these schools was to be quality education and integration where feasible (*Liddell v. St. Louis Board of Education,* 1980).

The case was appealed to the Eighth Circuit Court, where, in March 1980, a panel of three judges reversed Meredith's ruling, holding that the St. Louis Board of Education and the state of Missouri were liable for maintaining a segregated school system and that the board's establishment of a neighborhood school attendance policy in the 1950s had not fulfilled its duty to eliminate racial discrimination "root and branch." Citing a 1968 Supreme Court decision, *Green v. New Kent County,* the circuit court judges ruled that it was the school district's responsibility, not the students' or their parents', to create a system without identifiable black or white schools because the Supreme Court has "consistently held that merely establishing a racially neutral school assignment system is not sufficient to eliminate the constitutional violation caused by past intentional discrimination" (*Liddell v. St. Louis Board of Edu-*

cation, 1980, p. 1286; Yudof, Kirp, and Levin, 1992). The Eighth Circuit also cited the Supreme Court's *Swann v. Charlotte-Mecklenburg* (1972) ruling, which stated that "racially neutral" student assignment plans proposed by school boards may be inadequate when such plans fail to counteract the continuing effects of past school segregation resulting from discriminatory location of school sites or the distortion of school sizes to maintain artificial racial separation" (*Liddell v. St. Louis Board of Education,* 1980, p. 1286).

In addition to the student assignment policies, the Eighth Circuit ruled that the board's prior actions to segregate teachers and administrators had contributed to segregation in the St. Louis system. The court also recognized that the actions of the state and federal governments had intensified racial segregation in St. Louis, and thus it ordered the defendants to "take those steps necessary" to bring about an integrated school system in accordance with specific guidelines:

1. The St. Louis Board of Education is principally responsible for developing and implementing a comprehensive plan to integrate the district no later than the beginning of the 1980–81 school year.

2. Voluntary techniques will not effectively desegregate the St. Louis school district.

3. In addition to desegregating, the board should develop compensatory and remedial education programs, part-time integrative programs, expanded transfers within the district, and a comprehensive program of student exchange with suburban school districts.

The case was remanded to district court Judge Meredith, who on May 21, 1980, issued an order approving the St. Louis Board of Education's plan for an "intra-district," or within-district, school desegregation plan. Meredith also ordered the state to pay half the cost of the approved program, which was nearly $18 million for the 1980–81 school year.

The intra-district plan included establishing middle schools for grades five through eight, thus transforming the old kindergarten through eighth-grade schools into kindergarten through fourth-grade schools; reassigning students to integrated schools on the south side and central corridor; and adding magnet schools, primarily in black neighborhoods. As a border state city that had convinced so many people that its school board had done the right thing after *Brown,* St. Louis was suddenly being treated by the federal courts like a guilty southern city that had continued to segregate students behind a facade of neighborhood schools. Yet because of its northern geography of separate city and suburbs, the solution to segregation in St. Louis was to be far more complex.

By the spring of 1980 it was clear to the court-appointed school desegregation expert Gary Orfield and to the board members and administrators of the St. Louis public schools that despite the good intentions of the courts, this isolated urban school district was no longer in a position to "desegregate" itself without assistance from the surrounding suburbs. By 1980, only 23 percent of the students enrolled in the St. Louis schools were white, and most of them were clustered on the south side.

Orfield wrote to the district court that the Board of Education's proposal had "resulted in a plan which integrated the white and black schools of the South Side and the largely black schools of the central corridor" but that the plan had "relatively little impact on the schools of North St. Louis. . . . Many of the most segregated parts of the city remain totally segregated" (Orfield, 1980a, p. 14). In fact, under this plan some 30,000 black students, or nearly two-thirds of all black students in the city schools, were to remain in virtually all-black schools (La Pierre, 1987). Orfield noted criticisms from African Americans, including the black plaintiffs, that the plan would leave untouched the "very ghetto schools where the violations were proved in the first place." Yet he defended the board's decision to integrate some of the city's schools—those in the southern and central areas—at 50 percent white and 50 percent black as opposed to trying to integrate all the schools in the district at 23 percent white and 77 percent black, which he noted would cause more white flight to the suburbs. "To integrate all city schools 77 percent black within the city would be to imply that there is a full solution within the city. There is not," wrote Orfield (1980a, p. 17).

SCHOOL DESEGREGATION IN ST. LOUIS—THE SECOND PHASE

In the section of his report entitled "Voluntary Metropolitan Desegregation," Orfield highlighted several reasons why the solution to segregation in St. Louis must extend beyond the city boundaries, why the St. Louis public schools alone could not remedy all the historic constitutional violations. He also noted that St. Louis County's twenty-three school districts, which ranged enormously in wealth, educational quality, and racial composition, had many empty seats after enrollment declined in 1970s. Student transfers across district boundaries would greatly increase the desegregative effects of the plan for the black children of North St. Louis, Orfield argued.

Judge Meredith had read Orfield's report when he ruled in May 1980 to implement the St. Louis Board's intra-district desegregation plan. The ruling included what was to become known as the "infamous" paragraph 12, in which he ordered the state, the United States, and the St. Louis board to:

a) make every "feasible effort to work out with the appropriate school districts in St. Louis County and develop, for 1980–81 implementation, a voluntary, cooperative plan of pupil exchanges which will assist in alleviating the school segregation in the City of St. Louis;

b) develop and submit a plan for the consolidation or merger and full desegregation of the vocational educational programs operated by the city and the county;

c) develop and submit a "suggested plan of inter-district desegregation necessary to eradicate the remaining vestiges of government-imposed school segregation in the City of St. Louis and St. Louis County";

d) develop and submit . . . a suggested plan for ensuring that the "operation of federally-assisted housing programs in the St. Louis metropolitan area will facilitate the school desegregation ordered herein"; and

e) develop and submit a plan which allows all the schools in the city of St. Louis to be eligible for Title 1 federal funding for the 1980–81 year.

Although much of paragraph 12 was alarming, it was section c that sent shock waves through many of the suburban school districts. The implication of this proposal was the creation of one large metropolitan school district, ending local control in St. Louis County.

Several appeals were filed in the Eighth Circuit Court regarding Judge Meredith's order. The Liddell and Caldwell plaintiffs requested that the intra-city mandatory reassignment plan be expanded so that all schools would reflect the racial balance of the district. The state and the Adams plaintiffs attempted to curtail the intra-city desegregation plan and the state's responsibility to pay for it. The state also argued to remove paragraph 12 of the Meredith order. The Eighth Circuit rejected these appeals, affirming the district court's ruling, which meant that the intra-district plan was implemented and that an inter-district student transfer plan was possible.

The 30,000 black students left in segregated schools on the city's north side as a result of the school board's intra-district plan, and section c of paragraph 12 of Meredith's ruling spurred the NAACP to request an expansion of the desegregation case on behalf of the black plaintiffs and the St. Louis Board of Education, and it named suburban school districts in St. Louis County and nearby St. Charles County and Jefferson County as defendants.

Meanwhile, in the summer of 1981, a new district court judge, William L. Hungate, was assigned to the case. He appointed Edward T. Foote—the dean of Washington University's Law School and the chair of Meredith's court-appointed desegregation monitoring committee—to draft a voluntary inter-district student transfer plan. In July the district court approved Foote's plan to allow students to transfer between city and county schools, with the state of Missouri paying for student transportation and providing a "fiscal incentive," or per-pupil tuition payment, for the receiving district. Five school districts in St. Louis County agreed to participate. Judge Hungate, a former Democratic congressman and a Carter appointee, ordered that the pilot transfer plan be implemented in these five districts, which were granted a temporary stay of litigation pending a trial between the city and the suburbs. During the 1981–82 school year, 125 black students from the city attended schools in the participating suburban school districts (La Pierre, 1987).

In a recent interview, Foote, who is now president of the University of Miami, noted that the creation of the pilot plan was the beginning of the effort to settle a case that was rife with important social, policy, quality of education, and "extremely complicated" constitutional issues. The question at the time, he said, was whether you can settle such a case in a way that is "acceptable legally and constitutionally."

In September, Hungate granted the motion by the NAACP and the St. Louis school board to expand the case, naming the suburban districts as defendants. At this point, the St. Louis board—the main defendant in the first phase of litigation—became a plaintiff along with the NAACP, the black families, and the U.S. Justice Department in suing the state and the suburban districts for an inter-district or a metropolitanwide remedy (Confluence, 1989). Still, the possibility of a remedy that would cross school district boundaries (or eliminate them altogether) seemed remote.

A February 1982 Eighth Circuit ruling, which defined the possible scope of an inter-district remedy in the event that the suburban districts lost at trial, stated that mandatory inter-district transfers and school district reorganization and consolidation—that is, the creation of one or two large urban-suburban districts—could be ordered only if the suburban school districts were found to have contributed to the racial isolation of the city schools, or that the state, through its control over suburban districts, created the segregated city schools (La Pierre, 1987). This ruling was consistent with the exceptions established by the U.S. Supreme Court in *Milliken v. Bradley*, which had all but shut the door on urban-suburban school desegregation in 1974. In that case the Supreme Court ruled that suburban Detroit school districts could not be consolidated with the nearly all-black Detroit public schools because the plaintiffs failed to prove that there had been a "constitutional violation" on the part of the suburban districts that created a segregative effect in another district. "Specifically, it must be shown that racially discriminatory acts of the state or local school districts, or of a single school district, have been a substantial cause of inter-district segregation" (*Milliken v. Bradley*, 1974, p. 717). In his dissenting opinion in *Milliken,* Thurgood Marshall wrote, "In the short run, it may be the easier course to allow our great metropolitan areas to be divided up into two cities—one white, and the other black—but it is a course, I predict, our people will ultimately regret" (p. 717). Since the Supreme Court's decision in *Milliken* there has been no significant improvement in the desegregation of African-American students nationwide, and there has been an increase in the segregation of Latino students (Feldmen et al., 1994).

Today the Detroit public school system is 94 percent black, more racially isolated than ever. Similarly, the eighteen largest northern metropolitan areas, which were left with segregated urban school systems after the *Milliken* ruling, are some of the most segregated in the country (Kunen, 1996). Rist (1976) notes that by deciding in favor of the Detroit suburbs the Supreme Court chose local communities' rights to autonomy over children's rights to "education not encumbered by segregationist practices." The Court wrote in *Milliken,* "No single tradition in public education is more deeply rooted than local autonomy over the operation of schools; local autonomy has long been thought essential both to the maintenance of community concern and support for public schools and to the quality of the educational process" (cited in Rist, 1976, p. 425).

Thus, by the time the St. Louis inter-district case was filed, efforts at city-suburban school desegregation had failed in Detroit, and only a handful of cities—including Wilmington, Delaware, and Louisville, Kentucky—had achieved real cross-district integration by blending city and suburban districts. Other cross-district desegregation plans, in Hartford, Boston, and Milwaukee, were small-scale voluntary transfer programs that maintained separate urban and suburban school districts. Meanwhile, in Detroit, the city schools had gone back to court in a case now known as *Milliken II,* in which the district sued the state to pay for quality education programs to remedy the harms of racial segregation. In 1977 the U.S. Supreme Court authorized the lower court to order the state of Michigan to pay for educational enrichment programs for the segregated schools in the city. Eventually, other segregated city school systems, including that of Kansas City, Missouri, would win similar *Milliken II* cases, in which they would strike Faustian bargains similar to those that their city housing authorities had struck with the federal government—more money in exchange for continued segregation.[1] The failure of such bar-

---

1. The Kansas City school desegregation case, *Jenkins v. Missouri,* and the resulting court order are distinct from the St. Louis plan in several ways. First of all, the Kansas City plan does not entail the massive transfer of students from the city to the suburbs. Instead, most of the state funding has been spent on magnet school programs within

gains to make meaningful change in the areas of housing, employment, or education is becoming increasingly obvious (see Feldmen et al., 1995; Kunen, 1996; Morantz, 1994; and Wilson, 1996).

Despite the legal precedents against inter-district desegregation, suburban school board members in St. Louis were afraid of losing their locally controlled districts, partly because their formerly de jure state had already been found guilty, and their districts were technically arms of the state. They were also concerned because of St. Louis' history as the site of two Supreme Court housing discrimination cases. But, perhaps most important, the suburban school districts were afraid of Judge Hungate himself.

Hungate had grown increasingly impatient with the suburban districts and the unwillingness of most of them to participate in the pilot city-to-county student transfer program. Furthermore, the Eighth Circuit had mandated that Hungate "proceed promptly" with the trial on the inter-district liability of the state and suburban districts. In the spring of 1982 Hungate caught suburban residents off guard by issuing an interim order warning the suburban districts

_____

the Kansas City Public Schools, with the goals of providing black students in the city with viable educational options and attracting white students from the suburbs. This form of remedy, known as a Milliken II program, is intended "to counter the educational impairments caused by segregation and to prepare students and faculty for a desegregated environment." The Kansas City program began in 1985, and since that time it has cost the state of Missouri $1.1 billion to fund fifty-seven magnet schools, including the infamous $33.5 million Central High School with its "Classical Greek" theme, which stresses a sound mind and a sound body and hosts an Olympic-sized swimming pool, racquetball courts, and an impressive weight room (Little, 1995; Mosley, 1992). Michael Fields, a lawyer in the Missouri attorney general's office, referred to Central High School as the "Taj Mahal" and said that it was a $30 million athletic facility in which students could play what he referred to, in mimicking Black English, as "bathetball." Most of the state officials we spoke to dislike the Kansas City desegregation plan even more than they do the St. Louis plan because it has been more expensive on an annual basis and includes very expensive urban school programs such as those at Central High School, which elected officials can use as political symbols on the campaign trail.

Despite the extra resources that flowed from the state to this segregated school district, student achievement did not increase. In its 1995 ruling in the Kansas City case, the Supreme Court stated that low achievement levels among African-American students was not reason enough to continue a court-ordered remedy (Savage, 1995). And by the summer of 1996, the state of Missouri and the Kansas City school district had entered into an agreement to phase out the state support of the desegregation plan (Hendric, 1996).

that if they were found liable in the inter-district case, the remedy could well include consolidation of all twenty-three suburban school districts and the St. Louis public schools into a single metropolitan district, with a uniform tax rate and a system of mandatory student reassignment, sending white students to schools in the city. He set the trial date for February 14, 1983 (La Pierre, 1987).

Hungate recalled his tactic of announcing the scope of an unpopular remedy for a case that had not yet gone to trial: "I said we've got two phases. We've got liability, and we've got remedy. And we are going to do the remedy first, and if you are not liable, don't worry about it because you will never need it." But Hungate knew that the odd mixture of northern-style suburbs and southern segregation laws had come together in St. Louis in a troublesome way for suburban schools. In the *Milliken* case in Michigan, which had not had legally mandated separate schools for black and white students, the plaintiffs had to prove that the districts had segregated their schools deliberately. Yet in Missouri, a former separate but equal state, the burden of proof was on the districts to demonstrate that they had attempted to desegregate after *Brown*. Hungate said that even the suburban school districts that were not yet incorporated prior to *Brown* were in danger because the former districts that were merged to create them were part of the state at the time of the violation.

Thirty years earlier these suburban districts would have violated state law if they had integrated their schools; in 1983, the same districts were allegedly breaking federal law by maintaining the separate and unequal system that segregation had created. Lawyers for the NAACP were keenly aware of how St. Louis differed from Detroit. According to William L. Taylor, an NAACP lawyer on the St. Louis case, the long history of legal segregation in Missouri allowed lawyers to "go back into the state codes in Missouri in a way you couldn't quite do in Michigan, to show how rigid segregation was."

Hungate's proposed remedy was well publicized, and white suburban residents feared that their districts—one of their main reasons for moving to the suburbs—were going to be abolished. Throughout St. Louis County, school board members, district officials, and lawyers met with parents and community members. According to a lawyer representing several of the suburban districts, "We had a district court judge who was rattling the saber at that time and was threatening the county districts and was indicating that if there was a finding that the county districts had committed a constitutional violation, that he was thinking seriously about making one large school district. And of course the school districts wanted to maintain their own identity."

In most cases the local leaders were urging the suburban districts to avoid a long and expensive trial by entering into a settlement agreement with the St.

Louis public schools, the black plaintiffs, and the NAACP to create a large-scale student transfer program that would leave the districts in place while enabling thousands of black students to attend suburban schools.[2]

Meanwhile, Judge Hungate, who pushed ahead with the pretrial discovery, was receiving death threats, and for two weeks federal marshals were guarding him. The local media also attacked Hungate, with the conservative *Globe-Democrat* calling him "Attila the Hungate" and demanding his impeachment. The attacks on Hungate by those opposed to desegregation were testimony to his central role in moving the negotiations forward. In an interview on the St. Louis desegregation case, Eighth Circuit Court Judge Gerald W. Heaney stated, "I think that Judge Hungate was the factor in the case that finally brought about in large measure the solution that our court [the Eighth Circuit] finally approved, because the suburban school districts were scared to death that he was going to order some kind of involuntary participation or consolidation, and they didn't know what he was going to do. So, at least in my judgment, he was the right man, in the right place, at the right time."

Amid this chaos, Hungate assigned a "special master"—Washington University law professor Bruce La Pierre—to work toward a settlement agreement. On Monday, February 14, 1983, the day the trial was to begin, La Pierre reported to Hungate that, after 250 hours of negotiations between the parties, "some promising developments" had occurred. He requested postponements to the trial to continue the negotiations. Hungate agreed, and during the following sixty hours—until the late afternoon of Wednesday, February 16— lawyers for the Liddell plaintiffs, the NAACP, the St. Louis public schools, and 20 of the 23 suburban school districts worked toward an agreement in principle (AIP) to take back to their clients. The state's attorneys refused to partici-

---

2. By this time, the U.S. Justice Department, under the leadership of the Reagan administration, was not actively involved in the case. Eventually, the Reagan Justice Department came to oppose all court-ordered school desegregation (see Orfield and Ashkinaze, 1991). William L. Taylor, one of the NAACP lawyers on this case, noted that under the Carter administration, the Civil Rights Division of the Justice Department was conducting its own preliminary investigation into the St. Louis case and thus was considering playing a major role in the case up until the 1980 presidential election. Taylor also commented that, given the large amount of evidence in favor of the plaintiffs, had the St. Louis case succeeded up through the courts, civil rights lawyers and black plaintiffs would have needed Justice Department involvement to bring similar cases in other metropolitan areas: "We recognized it was going to be an enormous effort, and that in part, by the way, is why it would have been very useful to have the Justice Department on our side because these cases really took an awful lot of person power."

pate in the negotiations, although Missouri was to bear the brunt of the cost of the resulting desegregation plan (La Pierre, 1987).

Lawyers on both sides like to take at least partial credit for creating a situation in which an agreement could be crafted. One lawyer recalled the long and difficult settlement process: "It was a unique combination of people and time that enabled this to be put together. I don't know if it could ever be done again." But according to La Pierre, Judge Hungate was the most important factor in bringing the parties to the table: "I think if you asked some of the county districts they would tell you that there was no way on God's green earth that they would be found liable [if the case had gone to trial], but they were saying that 'the judge [Hungate] is determined to hold a trial and determined to shove this massive remedy right down our throats. . . . So we face the risk of losing.' And what they stood to lose was a lot from their perspective—no local control of the school district, no local control of the tax rates and substantial busing of white students into all-black schools."

Several additional months of negotiation took place as the AIP was molded into a formal settlement agreement and approved by Judge Hungate, who ordered it implemented for the 1983–84 school year. The state of Missouri, after refusing to participate in the negotiations, appealed to the Eighth Circuit, which modified the plan to some degree but upheld the district court's order. The state, still refusing to cooperate, appealed to the U.S. Supreme Court to nullify the agreement and thereby relieve the state of its responsibility to pay for the programs. The Supreme Court denied certiorari.

The court order that grew out of the final settlement was composed of three main components: the city-to-county voluntary inter-district transfer program; a magnet school program for the St. Louis public schools that includes a county-to-city transfer program; and a quality education and capital improvements program for the St. Louis public schools.

The most visible component of the court order is the voluntary inter-district transfer plan, which offers black students in the city the opportunity to transfer to 122 schools in the 16 suburban districts with the smallest number of resident black students (less than 25 percent of their total) at the time the agreement was made. Ten of these districts had black enrollments of less than 4 percent in 1983. Under the terms of the settlement agreement, the 16 suburban districts were required to increase their black student enrollments to at least 15 percent but to no more than 25 percent.

The final court order was a long and complex compromise that sugarcoated the bitter pill of desegregation for the suburbs with a number of concessions, making it a more forward-looking desegregation policy—one that emphasizes student and parental choice while abandoning politically unpopular mandatory busing practices but also extends far beyond a faltering urban school system to include the wealthy, prestigious suburban schools. White suburban students, meanwhile, stay in their neighborhood schools unless they choose to transfer to a city magnet school. Black students who live in the city can choose to stay in their neighborhood school; enroll in a magnet school; or transfer to a suburban school, provided that there is space and that the student does not have a poor disciplinary record. Suburban districts cannot deny admission to African-American students from the city because of grades or test scores. The St. Louis inter-district plan represents gradual change that does not force individuals to attend schools they do not want to attend but still challenges the system of separate and unequal. In this way, the St. Louis case stands in direct contrast to Kansas City on the other side of the state. The main focus of the Kansas City court was on improving the quality of educational programs in the city, without any meaningful desegregation component. The strikingly different tales of these two cities are testimony to the contrasts between inter-district desegregation and well-funded segregation. St. Louis shows the promise of urban-suburban solutions to metropolitan-wide problems, while Kansas City shows the weakness of urban-only solutions (Morantz, 1994).

The state of Missouri, despite the reluctance of its attorneys to participate in the settlement negotiations, was ordered by the district court to pay the suburban school districts an incentive payment, which would equal their per-pupil cost, for each black city student who transfers to their schools. The state must also pay to transport black students from the city to any suburban school. The state provides each of the 12,700 city-to-county and the 1,500 county-to-city transfer students with one free round-trip from home to school each day. This round-trip includes drop-offs or pickups for students attending before- or after-school programs. During the 1990–91 school year, for instance, the state contracted with bus companies for 700 buses and 125 taxis traveling nearly 10 million miles.

Providing parents and students with virtually unlimited school choices is not the most cost-efficient program. During the 1995 fiscal year, the total state transportation cost for the desegregation plan was more than $28.7 million, which averages out to about $2,000 per student, including the cost for white suburban students who attend city magnet schools (Mannies and Little, 1996). According to the Missouri state commissioner of education, Robert Bartman, the problem with the St. Louis inter-district plan is the absolute free choice that black students in the city have: "One family in one residence could have five kids going to five different schools in five different parts of the county."

In reality, black students who transfer usually go to the same county schools as their siblings and friends, but even if they do not, the point of the inter-district transfer plan is to provide African-American students who live in racially isolated urban neighborhoods optimal choices in where they attend school. The idea is not to minimize the cost of the program for the state of Missouri, whose attorneys refused to participate in the settlement negotiations even after the state had been found guilty of denying African Americans their Fourteenth Amendment rights to equal protection for more than 100 years. Had the state's attorneys participated in the settlement negotiations, they in fact might have extracted some concessions, such as a limit on the number of suburban districts each student could choose, thus minimizing the cost of transportation considerably. But the state's attorneys did not—for very political but perhaps not very savvy reasons—participate. Instead, they fought every development in the case as it was shaped by the negotiations of other parties. In a highly unproductive manner, the attorneys have appealed district and appellate court rulings and been denied certiori to the Supreme Court a total of seven times in the history of this case.

Because the state's lawyers were missing from the table, the settlement agreement was designed to maximize black students' access to quality educational programs without the input of those who would have to pay the bills. In 1994, the St. Louis desegregation program cost the state $134 million. Yet it is important to remember that prior to 1954, thousands of blacks paid Missouri taxes to support public schools and universities that they could not legally attend. Now the state is paying for the descendants of these African Americans to have additional choices and options.

Regarding the cost of the St. Louis desegregation plan, Eighth Circuit Judge Heaney argued, "It is expensive because there are significant transportation costs, but really it isn't costing any more to educate those black kids out in the county than it would be if they were given a good education in the city. So I don't view that as a net increase in the overall cost to the larger community. . . . The burden may be distributed a little differently, but the only extra cost is transporting students from the city to the county, and that is costing $1,500 to $1,600 per pupil [in 1990], which is a lot of money to spend, but there would have been transportation costs half that much if we would have tried to integrate every school in the city to 80–20, and we really wouldn't have accomplished that much."

Perhaps the only real losers, from a fiscal perspective, in the inter-district desegregation plan are the seven suburban districts that were not included in the agreement because their resident student population is more than 25 percent black. These are mostly the inner-ring suburbs to which black migrants to the suburbs flocked as whites left. A few of these districts are virtually all-black and quite poor themselves. Despite their demographics, these suburban districts were brought into the case as defendants and did not bring any claims on their own behalf against the state or the other suburban districts. Thus, the federal court could not provide them with a remedy from the state in the form of funding for magnet schools or transfers for their racially isolated students. They have in essence been shut out of the inter-district transfer program because they were, in many ways, on the wrong side of the case.

Meanwhile, the St. Louis public schools receive state funding for their magnet schools, whose goal is to attract white students from the county. Under the court order, the state must bear the full capital and operating costs of the inter-district magnet schools created as part of the 1983 settlement agreement, but only half the cost of the intra-district magnet schools created in the 1970s as part of the initial consent decree.

And finally, the Court order also included quality education programs for the city schools. According to La Pierre, the drafters of the agreement recognized that even with the large inter-district transfer program, at least 15,000 black students would remain in all-black schools on the city's north side. Thus, the settlement agreement contains provisions for the all-black or "nonintegrated" city schools to receive state money to improve the quality of education provided by shrinking class sizes to a pupil-teacher ratio of 20 to 1 and adding instructional coordinators. Several remedial and enrichment programs were also added to the all-black schools, which were encouraged to develop a specialized "school of emphasis" program. In addition, the St. Louis public schools received funding for a capital improvements program for many of the older school buildings in the district.

In all, the settlement agreement was a hard-fought political compromise stemming from an emotional legal battle. The black plaintiffs, the St. Louis school board, and the NAACP succeeded in creating a desegregation plan that included the suburban districts—a plan that cuts across the color line. Although participation in the city-suburban transfer plan is completely voluntary for the transfer students, the sixteen suburban districts are required to participate. The advantage of the compromise for the suburbs is that they maintained their autonomous, locally controlled districts and avoided mandatory student busing.

David Tatel, now a federal circuit court judge, represented the St. Louis school board during the second phase of the case. He said that while Judge Hungate was very effective in pushing for a settlement, he wonders what might have happened had the case been tried, given the huge amount of evidence he had collected against the St. Louis suburbs and the state. "I think we could have won the case with a trial court, and I think in the early '80s we clearly could have won in the circuit and even the Supreme Court of the United States. . . . And I think in the long run, it might have been better for St. Louis."

William L. Taylor, lawyer for NAACP, added that sending the St. Louis case to trial would have tested the Supreme Court's *Milliken* ruling that inter-district remedies could be imposed if plaintiffs proved school districts were segregated because of deliberately imposed housing patterns. "If the [St. Louis] case had gone all the way through the courts and we had won, then we would have given content to that exception to *Milliken,* and we could have done the same thing in other cases."

Still, lawyers and educators on both sides of the St. Louis case found something in this unique settlement agreement to appreciate. George Bude, a lawyer for suburban districts, noted that had the case been litigated, it would have widened racial divisions between St. Louis City and County. "It would have caused people to feel more strongly. And if there was a finding of violation [on the part of the suburbs], and if there was an involuntary inter-district transfer plan, it would have been a real serious blow to the school systems in St. Louis County, and to the community overall."

More than ten years later, no one knows what would be different if the St. Louis case had gone to trial, but the settlement agreement has produced more than a trivial amount of desegregation. During the 1995–96 school year, more than 12,700 black students from the city were enrolled in suburban schools, and almost 1,500 white students from the suburbs attended magnet schools in the city of St. Louis. Thus, the public schools of the St. Louis metropolitan area are far more desegregated than those of Detroit, Atlanta, Chicago, or most any other city. In 1996, district court Judge Gunn, now overseeing the case, called a hearing to determine whether, how, and when the St. Louis desegregation case would end (see Chapter 3). Thus the history of what happened in St. Louis as a result of this unique case and settlement agreement must not be forgotten. The lessons to be gleaned from this story are many, and the implications for future educational policy making, particularly school choice, are great.

The St. Louis inter-district plan is a school choice program geared toward helping inner-city students who want to leave their neighborhood schools. The account, therefore, of who goes to the suburbs and who stays in the city school system has several implications for the larger policy debate on providing parents and students with greater school choice. The students left behind in the city schools are those who in many ways need the most from the educational system. Like all political compromises, the St. Louis desegregation plan has its share of casualties.

PART II

The City

3

Urban Education:
The Decline of the St. Louis Public Schools

Some school systems, of which St. Louis is one, have another complicating factor. They and others have been declared by the courts to be constitutional violators of the rights of minority students. Their programs and funds, therefore, must also be directed to solving the violations. Accordingly, the Board of Education for the City of St. Louis not only addresses the regular business of providing quality education for its students, but does so in an attempt to redress its constitutional violations as well. This case, then, is one of the mediums for the Board's endeavors.
—U.S. District Court Judge S. N. Limbaugh

When asked about the effect of the 1983 settlement agreement and the resulting urban-suburban desegregation plan on the St. Louis public schools, Jerome B. Jones, former superintendent of the urban district, shook his head, took a long, slow puff on his pipe, and explained that it is both a bane and a blessing. The agreement has been a bane on the beleaguered school system, said Jones, because thousands of black students have chosen to transfer out of the city to distant suburban schools, and when they leave, they carry with them some of the pride and morale of the teachers and students who remain behind. On the other hand, Jones knew all too well that the settlement agreement had blessed his district with millions of state dollars for quality education programs, capital improvements, and magnet schools. By the 1995–96 school year the St. Louis public schools were receiving nearly $60 million per year in state desegregation funds.

When the urban-suburban desegregation plan began, the St. Louis public schools were plagued by the same problems facing urban school districts across the country: many students from poor families, an ever-shrinking tax base, lack of political support among white voters for a majority "minority" system, and ancient buildings. The urban district was desperate for extra state resources. But the state's attorneys, who want nothing more than to end the program, and other observers voice ongoing concerns about how wisely the money has been spent in the city system and how much of it actually reaches the children it is supposed to serve.

Some say that the St. Louis public schools have made a slight turn for the better in recent years. School board elections in the early 1990s ushered in several "reform" candidates, who appear to be more focused on educational issues than many of their predecessors. Meanwhile, the man who replaced Jones in 1990, former superintendent David J. Mahan, cut more than 140 central office positions in an effort to get more money to the schools. Still, some worry that poor African-American students continue to be cheated by the St. Louis public schools and the politics of race that drives the system.

One thing is for sure: racial politics is alive and well in St. Louis, and the city's first black mayor, Freeman Bosley, Jr., has demonstrated that he knows how to play that game. Since his election in 1993, Bosley has come out in opposition to the most visible aspect of the settlement agreement: the inter-district transfer program allowing black students from the city to attend suburban schools. In a struggle that mirrors the intergenerational tug of war in black communities across the country over different civil rights approaches, the young mayor has angered many older blacks who fought hard for the school choices that African-American students in St. Louis now have. Even the mayor's father, a veteran city council member and former mayoral candidate, disagrees with his son's effort to end the urban-suburban transfer plan and argues that black students who want to go to suburban school should have that choice (Braun, 1993).

But the mayor says that the time for busing and desegregation has passed and that African Americans need to focus on improving schools in their own communities. While the black parents of the 12,700 students who transfer to suburban schools obviously believe that the transfer plan is worthwhile, there are many blacks in the city who concur with the mayor. Yet perhaps no one agrees with the mayor as wholeheartedly as the whites on the city's south side, who have firmly opposed school desegregation for three decades. This agreement between Mayor Bosley and southside whites has led some to fear that the mayor is using segregation in part to court white voters, who still comprise half of the city's electorate. Shortly after his election, Bosley addressed a gathering of white southside voters, and the *St. Louis Post-Dispatch* reported, "An area of the deep south St. Louis that voted against Mayor Freeman Bosley, Jr., in April gave him two standing ovations and cheers Tuesday night when he reaffirmed his call to end school busing here" (Mannies and Lindecke, 1993).

Meanwhile, in 1995 the two-thirds white St. Louis Board of Education presented district court Judge George F. Gunn, Jr., who has presided over the case since 1981, with a desegregation policy statement requesting a phaseout of his supervision over the city schools. Although the board's report stopped short of calling for an end to the urban-suburban voluntary transfer program, it did demand the return of local control for the city schools and thus an end to its intra-district student reassignment for racial balance. (About 2,500 students are bused within the city to 25 schools as part of the intra-district component of the desegregation plan.) The board also asked for continued state funding for quality education programs in its all-black or nonintegrated schools and for its magnet schools, although the board no longer wishes to give white county students priority for magnet school seats (St. Louis Board of Education, 1995).

The board members, like the mayor, are elected by citywide vote, so they too stand to gain the support of white antibusing voters on the south side and black separatists on the north. But the African-American children of St. Louis stand to lose because it is unlikely that state funding for the urban-suburban transfers or the city's magnet schools and quality education programs will continue if the settlement agreement ends.

Under the court order, every time a black student transfers from a city school to a suburban school, the suburban district receives a state incentive payment. It is unlikely that the suburban districts would continue to accept transfer students from the city if they did not receive these payments. At the same time, the St. Louis public schools continue to receive one-half of the state aid for that student (about $1,100 per student) even though he or she no longer attends a city school. Thus, in addition to the special magnet, quality education, and capital improvement funding from the state, the St. Louis public school system also receives half of its state aid for students who transferred to suburban schools.

If the court order is lifted, the St. Louis public schools would be owed only half of the per-pupil state aid for every black student who would eventually reenroll in the city schools. If the desegregation order is rescinded, as many as 12,700 African-American students eventually would return to the St. Louis public schools, and 1,500 white students who attend the city's magnet schools would return to the suburbs.[1] The city schools would receive an additional $15.5 million or less to cover the other half of the state aid payment for each student returning but would lose about $42 million in state payments for desegregation-related costs—a net loss of $26.5 million in state funding—while gaining a net student enrollment of 11,200 students.

Table 3.1 itemizes state payments to the city district for desegregation-related costs. Payments in categories 1 through 5 would most likely end with the court order, those in category 6 would probably continue until all students returned from suburban schools, and payments for category 7 would be added to the district's state funding formula as students returned to city schools. As the table illustrates, the most likely scenario if the court order ended is that state payments to the St. Louis public schools would drop by about $27 million as about $42 million would be cut from the nearly $58 million in annual state desegregation payments to the city, and at most an additional $15.5 million would replace it. Under this scenario the district enrollment would grow from about 41,500 to 52,700 as revenues declined from $290 million to about $264 million, dropping the per-pupil expenditure in the district from more than $7,000 to about $5,000.

Former board president Eddie Davis said the main goal of the board is to end the federal court's supervision of their district while assuring that the city schools continue to receive state money for their magnet schools and quality education programs. In words eerily reminiscent of white segregationists of a prior era, Davis said, "We want to go back to local control and to oversee student assignments and programs."

It seems a bit naive to assume that Judge Gunn would declare the St. Louis public schools "unitary," or no longer a dual, segregated system, and return local control to the district while still requiring the state to pay the city schools extra money for desegregation-related expenses. This scenario seems even less

1. Black students from the city who are currently enrolled in the suburban schools and the white suburban students in city magnet schools may be "grandfathered" if the desegregation plan ends, allowing them to continue transferring until they graduate from high school. Still, as the number of these grandfathered students dwindles, the St. Louis public schools would enroll several thousands of African-American students who would have gone to the suburbs if they had the chance, and at the same time, a thousand fewer white students from the county who would no longer be eligible for the district's magnet schools.

Table 3.1. State Desegregation Payments to the St. Louis Public Schools for 1994

Category of Payment	FY 1994 Expenditure
1. *Intra-city plan.* Programs and staffing for nonintegrated and integrated schools.	$5,541,000 (would end with court order)
2. *Settlement plan.* Quality education and part-time integration.	$11,225,000 (would end with court order)
3. *Magnet plan.* Start-up and operations of magnet schools.	$18,635,000 (would end with court order)
4. *City capital improvements.* Nonmagnet school renovations and asbestos abatement costs.	$4,705,000 (would end with court order)
5. *Incentive payments.* Includes state tuition payments to the St. Louis public schools for the cost of educating 1,100 white suburban students in city magnet schools.	$2,040,595 (would end with court order)
Total state desegregation funding likely to end with the removal of the court order	**$42,146,595**
6. *State aid credit.* State credit for students who transfer to suburbs.	$15,477,194 (would continue after the court order)
1994 total state desegregation funding for the St. Louis public schools	**$57,623,789**
7. *Additional state aid credit.* The other half of state credit that would be paid to the St. Louis public schools if all the city students attending suburban schools returned.	$15,477,194 (amount that would be phased in after the end of the court order as students returned to the city schools

Source: Missouri State Department of Education (1994 dollars and 1993–94 enrollments of about 13,000 city-to-county transfers and 1,200 county-to-city transfers)

likely given state politicians' history of efforts to end both the St. Louis and the Kansas City desegregation plans primarily because of their cost. The state attorney general, Jay Nixon, has stated repeatedly that he is on a mission to save Missouri taxpayers the cost of this desegregation program. In a 1993 motion to the federal district court, Nixon asked Gunn to declare the St. Louis public schools unitary, which would "shut down the flow of millions of dollars from the state for desegregation programs such as city magnet schools, quality enhancements in all-black city schools, and the voluntary city-county transfer plan" (Eardley, 1993a). In 1996, Nixon asked Judge Gunn to end the desegregation plan quickly by denying any new students the opportunity to transfer and allowing the almost 13,000 city black students currently in suburban schools to finish at the school they were attending but to then enroll in a city school. In exchange, Nixon said, the state would pay the St. Louis public schools 25 percent of what it will save from ending the plan for three years, after which the city schools will have no extra funding from the state—for magnet schools or any of its quality education programs (Little and Mannies, 1996).

Meanwhile, Mayor Bosley has argued that the state should give the city schools the more than $80 million that now go to the suburban schools and busing companies each year for the urban-suburban student transfers. Despite his pleas, it is unlikely that any money that the state no longer spends on the desegregation plan will be handed over to urban schools serving mostly poor and African-American children. The racial politics of Missouri, with its mostly white and rural constituents, makes it difficult for elected officials to fund urban education programs in the absence of court orders that say they must. As an editorial writer noted regarding Bosley's call to end the desegregation plan *and* keep state desegregation funds: "Not many things in life are certain, but count on this much: If the desegregation program ends, and the sun rises in the east, the state of Missouri will most assuredly *not* gratuitously pump into the city the . . . extra desegregation dollars it now spends under the court order. . . . Perhaps Bosley could cut a deal with the state officials for the short run, but there is no possibility of a serious ongoing state commitment of extra education money for St. Louis" (Hartman, 1993).

According to the former St. Louis public schools superintendent, David J. Mahan, if the state funding for the magnet schools, quality education programs, smaller class sizes, and so forth ends, the city schools will be forced to eliminate these programs because the district "cannot provide for all the services, and they cannot be picked up with local funds." Furthermore, if the court order ended and the transfer students returned, the city schools would have to pay teachers and find the space to educate these students (Braun, 1993; Corrigan, 1994).

St. Louis politicians might take a closer look at the options that black students have now and the reasons why so many choose to leave their neighborhood schools. Critics of the mayor and the school board have pointed out that the students who transfer from the city to the suburbs do so voluntarily. As Minnie Liddell said, "I don't think Bosley or Davis needs to be taking away opportunities from children and parents who have no faith in the St. Louis Board of Education. . . . If parents had faith in the school system, they would not be putting their kids on buses for an hour ride to the county" (Eardley, 1993b).

In December 1995 a group of elite St. Louis business leaders known as Civic Progress released a report written by a special task force that was convened by the organization to offer recommendations to Judge Gunn and the larger community about the future of the desegregation plan. The report strongly favored the continuation of the desegregation components of the urban-suburban plan and urged state officials to help create innovative ways to finance the cross-district school choice aspects of the program (Civic Progress, 1995). William H. Danforth, the former chancellor of Washington University and brother of the former U.S. senator, chaired the task force. The day the report was released Danforth commented, "The single most important thing we have said is that this is a community problem, and we are urging the community to come together for the benefit of the children and wrestle with these issues" (Freivogel, 1995).

To understand why so many African-American students choose to leave the city schools for distant suburban schools and why others stay behind, we examined the history and current conditions of the city schools. We identified a mixture of social, economic, and political factors that have contributed to the demise of a once innovative if not racially equal school district. We found that both the city of St. Louis and its school system have, over the decades, been both the victims and perpetrators of the racial politics that led to their decline.

We have come to believe that neither the city nor its school district, given their lack of resources and political support, can hope to adequately serve the educational needs of the African-American children who live within their boundaries. The burden of remedying past discrimination must continue to be shared across the metropolitan area and the state of Missouri, because residents of the state and the suburbs helped to make the St. Louis public schools what they are today.

THE ST. LOUIS PUBLIC SCHOOLS—FROM FAME TO INFAMY

Once considered a leading school system with more than 110,000 students, the St. Louis public school district has become one of the most disparaged in the nation, serving about 42,000 mostly poor students, nearly 80 percent of whom are black. Although the urban-suburban desegregation plan and the extra resources it has brought to the St. Louis public schools have in many ways lessened the city system's rate of decline, this is still a politically and economically bankrupt school district, serving many of the most needy students in the metro area.

In American society, the status of a school system, like that of each individual school, generally matches that of its students (Jankowsky, 1995; Wells and Crain, 1992). So it is no coincidence that the reputation of the St. Louis public schools plummeted along with the income of families whose children attend the district's schools. Nor is it a coincidence that the demise coincided with the massive white flight from the city and the influx of poor blacks from the South. Yet befitting St. Louis' mixed legacy, the decline of the city school system was faster and more dramatic than most because, as the northern-style suburban school districts lured whites and the tax base across the city-county line, the St. Louis public school system was forced to face its Jim Crow past.

At the turn of the century the St. Louis system was a model progressive public school district. By the 1870s, under the stewardship of Superintendent William Torrey Harris, the city's public schools were among the first to have libraries, art and music programs, teacher training programs, early childhood education, and scientific and manual arts curriculum (Spitzer, 1971; Faherty, 1976; Primm, 1990). In 1873, the St. Louis schools became the first public education system in the United States to offer kindergarten. Harris, who later became U.S. commissioner of education, advocated kindergarten as a way to save slum children from poverty (Troen, 1975; Spring, 1990).

In similarly bold fashion, the St. Louis public school system became a leader in vocational education. Under the tutelage of board president Calvin Woodward, a Washington University professor, the St. Louis system developed a model manual training school to foster both the "cultured mind" and the "skillful hand" (Troen, 1975, p. 169). And in 1868, the St. Louis Board of Education took over the O'Fallon Polytechnic Institute, a vocational evening high school established by Washington University and affiliated with the university's preparatory department. The institute was designed to teach something of "practical value," but its curriculum was made up of difficult courses in algebra, natural philosophy, and chemistry (p. 134).

The city's reputation for model vocational education programs would, more than a century later, become one of the greatest of all ironies, as a federal judge would rule that the district's vocational programs had "failed miserably" (Bryant, 1991). But in the intervening years, the face of the St. Louis public schools was to change color dramatically, making viable vocational education politically less practical.

As we noted in Chapter 2, progressive and innovative educational programs in St. Louis rarely benefited blacks. While white high school students enrolled in either a traditional academic program complete with Latin and Greek or in the new manual training schools, black students at Sumner High School were often assigned elementary schoolwork (Troen, 1975).

Until the 1954 Supreme Court ruling in *Brown vs. St. Louis Board of Education* and the post–World War II exodus of whites to the suburbs, the St. Louis school board pretty much ignored the demands of the black community. But as whites left the city, blacks gained more power. Today, St. Louis has an African-American mayor, an African-American school board president, and its second African-American superintendent. But in St. Louis, as in other cities, the urban system that these newly empowered leaders inherited reflects years of societal neglect. Thus, the political power of these leaders is a Pyrrhic victory of sorts—they now rule a city all but abandoned by the white and wealthy people with the resources it desperately needs (Wilson, 1987; Orfield and Ashkinaze, 1991; Fine, 1993). In time, these black leaders, and not the historical forces that preceded them, will most likely be blamed by white society for the further decline of urban America and its schools.

White Flight and Mismanagement

Whether abiding by state segregation laws or contributing to de facto segregation through its placement of new schools and design of school attendance zones, the St. Louis Board of Education has perpetrated the racial politics that led to its demise. On the other hand, the urban district was, like St. Louis itself, a casualty of federal housing and transportation policies that helped lure the white middle class and many employment opportunities to the suburbs. Amid these larger social forces the Board of Education has traditionally responded quickly to the demands of white constituents in the hopes of staving off their flight. The conflict between the demands of these constituents and the constitutional requirements of the district's federal court order has helped to fuel the school board's efforts to end the case and get out from under court supervision. White working-class voters on the south side of the city still influence citywide elections, although the black political voice has grown louder in the past thirty-five years.

John Hicks, elected to the St. Louis school board in 1959, was the first black official elected by citywide vote. Over the next ten years, three additional African-American board members were elected as part of the racially mixed reform slate, called the Citizens Association for the Public Schools

(CAPS), founded by community leader Daniel Schlafly. A wealthy white businessman and devout Catholic who sent his own children to parochial schools, Schlafly became an institution in St. Louis politics when he served on the St. Louis school board for twenty-eight years.

When Schlafly was first elected, in 1953, he and two other board members tried to clean up some of the corruption in the St. Louis public schools by filing criminal corruption and mismanagement charges against the board president and the district building commissioner, leading to their ouster ("Fletcher found guilty," 1958). By 1961 the reform slate had a majority of seats on the board, and Schlafly himself became board president. By 1973 the reform slate, renamed the Citizens Committee for Quality Education, controlled every seat on the board, with each member, including the three African Americans, essentially handpicked by Schlafly (La Noue and Smith, 1973).

In case studies of urban school leaders, La Noue and Smith described Schlafly: "It is said of Daniel Schlafly that while some rich men like to run horses or yachts, Mr. Schlafly likes to run a school system. Owner of a lucrative family beverage business, Schlafly estimates that he has spent half of his time for the last eighteen years on education. Even after all those hundreds of committee meetings, he maintains his enthusiasm for working on education problems, and St. Louis voters have not lost their enthusiasm for him and his slate" (p. 39).

Still, Schlafly and his coalition's efforts to reform the St. Louis schools were limited by larger political forces. For instance, when Schlafly was elected, the discriminatory practices of the city's powerful labor unions were condoned by the board, which, at the time, employed 150 union craftsmen, including painters, carpenters, and plumbers. In addition, the St. Louis public schools operated segregated union apprenticeship programs through the district's vocational education department, thus aiding and abetting the union practice of apprenticing only whites into their trades (Skocpol, 1988). According to a former board member, in unions requiring a test for admission, exam study guides were handed down from father to son and not made widely available.

Schlafly pressured the union leaders of the board-employed craftsmen to hire more blacks and allow black students into the vocational high school programs. In response, the unions withdrew support from the board's vocational schools. O'Fallon, the flagship vocational school in the city, quickly became predominantly black, and its training programs, no longer linked to the powerful unions, rapidly deteriorated. According to a 1967 St. Louis public schools report:

> When the vocational and technical schools like O'Fallon become predominantly or totally Negro, white youngsters who could profit from vocational training withdraw

and deprive themselves of it. The Trade and Industrial teachers, with long and familiar contacts with white employers, have shown that they can place white *and* Negro graduates in jobs, but they have much greater difficulty in placing exclusively Negro graduates. It is apparent that O'Fallon Technical High School can be successful only if it is a healthfully integrated institution. In the 1966–67 school year we had 629 white youngsters and 2,069 Negro youngsters enrolled in the technical high schools. The handwriting is on the O'Fallon wall. (St. Louis Public Schools, 1967, p. 5, emphasis in original)

There is little evidence that the vocational schools in St. Louis ever were extremely successful in placing black graduates in well-paying skilled trade jobs, making many African-American students and parents reluctant to choose vocational high schools over "academic" ones. According to the district's 1967 report, many "Negro youngsters" who could profit from the training in the vocational high schools are instead attending regular high schools and "emerging without marketable skills, swelling the numbers of the city's unemployment" (St. Louis Public Schools, 1967, p. 5). The report also states that businessmen who employ St. Louis high school graduates frequently criticize their reading, spelling, language, and arithmetic skills. "The traditional high school curriculum was designed for students who already had mastered these tools of learning. Yet at least a third of the human race apparently can achieve only a limited facility with them" (St. Louis Public Schools, 1967, p. 11). This passage illustrates the attitudes influencing decisions in the district during a period of tremendous racial and social change.

To make matters worse, the district was, according to Schlafly, full of incompetent employees hired because of the board's cronyism and corruption. Also, the city schools' influx of black students in the 1950s and '60s led to a severe teacher shortage that forced the board to hire and tenure many teachers in a short period of time. "We locked in teachers we never should have hired and never would have hired in other days," Schlafly said.

Meanwhile, the board was under intense political pressure from white parents who had not yet fled the city and who did not want their children in racially mixed schools. This resistance made desegregation decisions difficult for board members who faced citywide elections. In 1954, when the board adopted its neighborhood schools policy, many whites were outraged, despite the inability of the policy to promote true desegregation. Schlafly recalled that some of his white West End neighbors accused him of "ruining" the public schools and, worse yet, of "ruining the whole Goddamn neighborhood" when the board voted to send black students to nearby schools.

During the 1977 trial in the St. Louis desegregation case, a former principal testified that in 1958, the then-superintendent of St. Louis schools, William Kottmeyer, stated he would not force a white child to go to a school that had a black principal and teaching staff. Kottmeyer, a famous educator known for his nearly 200 reading textbooks, testified that he had never said such a thing. But a white parent later testified that when she tried to transfer her daughter to an all-black school she was told it was not the board's policy to put one black child in an all-white classroom or one white child in an all-black classroom (see Horton, 1991; La Noue and Smith, 1973).

As the board's racial policies became more evident, the racially mixed West End Community Conference, a group committed to integration, in 1963 issued a report claiming that West End schools, with their rapidly expanding enrollments, were too segregated given the housing patterns. The report accused the Board of Education of permitting white students to transfer out of schools in the area while refusing Negroes the same privilege (Crain, 1969, p. 17). The board held a public hearing at which the West End Community Conference and local branches of the NAACP and the Congress of Racial Equity (CORE) testified. The coalition of civil rights groups filed 136 allegations of discriminatory practices by the board, including allowing white students to transfer to all-white schools, moving the white teachers college out of an integrated neighborhood, and creating the intact busing program in which African-American students were contained in separate classrooms in otherwise all-white schools. The coalition had three central demands: an end to intact busing by fully integrating the transported students; integration of faculties at the schools to which students were bused; and redrawing of school district boundaries to assure maximum integration. The school board, under the leadership of Schlafly, appointed an interracial citizens committee led by the Reverend Trafford P. Maher, a St. Louis University professor, to evaluate the charges. Meanwhile, leaders of militant civil rights groups testified before the board on June 5 about the intact busing program and other issues. When the board failed to respond, they set up a blockade to prevent the school buses from picking up black students in the West End for the last two days of the school year (Crain, 1969).

The summer of 1963 was long and hot in St. Louis. Although it would be another decade before legal action would be taken against the Board of Education, it was that summer that black parents and civil rights activists first gained a voice in the St. Louis public schools. A July article in the *Times* of London ("Racialism creeps," 1963) noted, "The summer of discontent through which the American Negro minority passes reflects itself in St. Louis in widespread demands for a greater degree of actual desegregation of the city's schools." But the protests in St. Louis never mounted to the kinds of riots that would break out in other cities in the following summers. In fact, the tense but never explosive summer of 1963 in St. Louis was symbolic of the relative calm and less publicized manner in which civil rights demands were dealt with in this city. Minnie Liddell recalls the political climate in the early 1960s: "I was personally becoming very concerned about what was going on in St. Louis compared to some of the things that were happening in other parts of the country. But [we] never, ever had any desire to do anything about it. [We were] just complacent—that is just the way it was here."

At the same time, the Board of Education resisted meaningful decentralization of authority and power to community groups, a movement that was gaining national popularity. With federal funding for community action programs (CAPS), low-income communities in other cities were launching grassroots educational initiatives for every age group—from preschool students to the elderly (Jackson, 1993). But in St. Louis, Schlafly and his "progressive" board were not enthusiastic about sharing decision making: "Like other socially elite reformers who have struggled to overcome the evils of partisan interference in schools, he has less than complete faith in the will and wisdom of the 'people.' He has taken steps to see that parents and teachers have channels of communication for their problems and grievances, but he stops short of sharing power. Consequently, most school business is transacted in closed committee meetings. The agenda is not circulated" (La Noue and Smith, 1973, p. 42).

The closest St. Louis came to true decentralized and grassroots educational programs was in the late 1950s, when the board received federal and private foundation funding for ten community schools designed to empower members of low-income communities through education and political organization. Each school had its own community school advisory council, but the council members were appointed by the school board; there were no elections, and militant blacks were excluded (La Noue and Smith, 1973). With the school board's control over these councils, members rarely articulated community problems or advocated solutions: "In general, the community schools function much like suburban YMCA's—offering recreational and vocational opportunities to local residents on an individual basis. This is a worthwhile activity, but requires little in the way of community decision making. Consequently, the councils have had difficulty discovering their role" (La Noue and Smith, 1973, p. 44).

Further efforts to decentralize decision making in the St. Louis schools were also thwarted. In the 1970s, when two Missouri legislators representing poor districts of St. Louis—one white and one black—proposed a bill to change the school board election process from an at-large, citywide vote for each member to a system of subdistrict representation, Schlafly used his political connections in the legislature to kill the bill. He argued that this more decentralized form of representation on the board would lead to cleavages along political, religious, and ethnic lines (La Noue and Smith, 1973).

Later in the summer of 1963, the citizens committee led by Maher issued a report on the allegations against the board and urging the board members to adopt many of the measures that the West End Conference and civil rights groups had requested, including redrawing school boundaries, integrating black and white students within the "desegregated" schools, and integrating the teachers at all schools. The board argued that it would encounter "staggering administrative problems" in trying to carry out the recommendations and ultimately refused the requests related to all 136 original allegations ("Racialism creeps," 1963).

Schlafly still uses the "administrative burden" defense for the board's arguably indefensible actions, including the intact busing policy. In an interview Schlafly said that it was easier administratively to take a whole class of students from an overcrowded all-black school and send it, intact, to a white school with an empty classroom than it would be to ask the white school to "slot" the students into different classrooms. In an effort to recall the political pressure on the board to institute the intact busing policy, Schlafly said that, in addition to the administrative issues, "maybe there was some racial issue there."

As we noted, the board terminated the intact busing program in 1963 but only after the opening of several new elementary schools in black neighborhoods that fall conveniently diminished the need for busing anyway. When the new all-black schools opened, the busing program was cut back to 700 black students, and the receiving schools were desegregated. The second and third demands of the protesters were largely ignored until the *Liddell* lawsuit was filed.

According to Crain (1969), during that tense but nonviolent summer the St. Louis Board of Education decided to "walk the tightrope between the civil rights groups and the segregationists" by building the all-black "containment" schools while slowly integrating a small number of students in a program that it did not advertise more than necessary (p. 22). This was integration St. Louis style: incremental change designed more to stave off violent protests than to make meaningful reform in the system (Hochschild, 1984). Still, the St. Louis board's small steps toward desegregation in the 1950s and early 1960s looked progressive in comparison to most other cities (Crain, 1969). Paradoxically, these small steps bought time for St. Louis; a decade later, Minnie Liddell and the Concerned Parents were beginning to understand how little St. Louis had done to desegregate its schools and serve its African-American students.

The summer of 1963 and the protests it brought ended figuratively in August when the NAACP and CORE had a falling out over tactics. Members of CORE, who were unwilling to compromise on many of the unresolved issues, picketed the homes of black school board members and the superintendent. Finally, after failing to elicit a response from the school system, CORE members turned their attention to the Jefferson Bank and Trust Company and began a seven-month demonstration aimed at forcing the bank to hire black clerical workers (Wright, 1994). While these CORE demonstrations at the bank proved effective—five black clerical workers were hired—complaints registered with the St. Louis school board elicited a polite response and extremely slow, incremental changes at best.

By 1966, only 14 percent of the black elementary schoolchildren in St. Louis were attending a school with white students (Wyant, 1966). The residential segregation within the city and the white flight to the county did not, in all fairness, make the Board of Education's job any easier. For instance, when the federal government built Pruitt-Igoe, the St. Louis Board of Education built four new schools to serve the children in the project and surrounding neighborhoods. Initially, when Pruitt-Igoe was racially integrated, so were the schools. But as whites left the housing project, the schools quickly became all black, and the board was blamed for building the schools to contain the black children in the project and thus keep them out of white schools. According to Schlafly, it was unfair to blame the Board of Education for these segregated schools: "Look at what the federal government did to us. They pumped those children in there [to Pruitt-Igoe]. . . . They didn't give us a fighting chance to spread them around. Then we build the new schools, and we're going to say to the parents of those children, 'You can't go to that lovely new shiny school . . . because we're going to ship you down to an older school in south St. Louis.' . . . We would have had a first-class riot if we had said that to the parents."

Behind the board's racial politics, the steady march of whites out to the suburbs continued. Between 1953 and 1967 the number of white students in the St. Louis public schools decreased from 59,142 to 45,042, or by 24 percent; at the same time, the number of black students increased from 31,185 to 72,300, or by 132 percent (St. Louis Public Schools, 1967). In 1967, the St. Louis board sent letters to eight suburban school districts contiguous with the city, inviting them to "cooperate in joint efforts" to ameliorate the conditions of "de facto segregation and limited physical facilities within the St. Louis City boundary." The board suggested that the neighboring districts enroll "Negro" pupils from overcrowded St. Louis schools and was even so bold as to suggest that the suburban districts, whenever possible, provide transportation for the black students who had none. The board also suggested a teacher exchange program between inner-city and suburban schools. None of the suburban districts took up the board on its offer.

In 1968 a state legislator from St. Louis introduced a bill to merge the city and suburban school systems. The legislation would have divided the metropolitan area into ten districts, each with an elected local board to decide personnel and curriculum issues, and a Metropolitan School Board (MSB), whose members would be appointed by the governor and authorized to engage in collective bargaining; construct new buildings; and set, collect, and distribute taxes (La Noue and Smith, 1973, p. 41). The bill, referred to as the Kottmeyer Plan, after the St. Louis superintendent, was supported by the St. Louis school board but was not politically popular in the suburbs, nor was it well received by blacks in the city, who realized that it would reduce their small but growing political influence. The bill was quickly killed in the legislature (La Noue and Smith, 1973, p. 41).

With little chance of dissolving itself into a metropolitan-wide district, the St. Louis Board of Education was on its own to face its ugly history of discrimination. By 1975, when the consent decree between the St. Louis public schools and the original black plaintiffs was signed, 70 percent of the 88,500 students in the urban school district were African American. Three of the ten high schools in the district were all black and two additional high schools were more than 90 percent black. Of the 140 kindergarten through eighth-grade schools, 122 were either 90 percent black or 90 percent white ("St. Louis schools," 1975).

The 1975 consent decree was, as we mentioned, seen as a politically strategic agreement that gave black plaintiffs a sense of victory while averting a mandatory busing plan. And once again, as in 1954 and 1963, the St. Louis Board of Education appeared fairly progressive on race issues and successful at precluding riots while doing relatively little to achieve desegregation. A newspaper article on the consent decree noted, "The broad language in the agreement does not fence the city into any specific integration method, and a wide variety of new educational programs and concepts are expected to be examined" (Waters, 1975b). In typical fashion, the St. Louis board moved very slowly, promising to investigate lingering racial segregation and create a handful of magnet schools—but always, no matter what, avoiding conflict and thus meaningful change.

Racial Politics in Urban America

When white middle-class families with children left the city, so did much of the economic and political support for the St. Louis public schools. Meanwhile, these schools became increasingly burdened with the problems of the poor children who remained. Between 1950 and 1960, as the district's enrollment swelled with black students, the number of city residents older than sixty-five increased 16 percent while the number of people in the income-producing age range of twenty to sixty-five declined 25 percent (St. Louis Public Schools, 1967).

Most whites who had not left for the suburbs strongly opposed the 1980 intra-district school desegregation plan, which reassigned students, most of whom were black, to the southside and central corridor schools. The plan ensured there would no longer be all-white schools in the St. Louis system, which was at that point 79 percent African American, even though 30,000 African-American students would remain in segregated schools (Orfield, 1980a).

When buses of black children rolled southward in the fall of 1980, the private school enrollment of white children increased. By the 1991–92 school year, there were 67 private and parochial schools in St. Louis, enrolling 16,084 students, or nearly 23 percent of the city's estimated 71,500 school-age children. Almost 60 percent of the white school-age children who live in the city attend private schools. With 12,700 African-American students transferring to suburban schools, the St. Louis public schools are now serving only about 42,000, or 60 percent, of the city's school-age children, considerably lower than the already low rate of 73 percent in 1980 (see table 3.2).

The low percentage of children attending public schools, the aging population, and the racial polarization translate into little political support for the mostly black St. Louis school system, illustrated in a racial breakdown of city residents' voting patterns on a failed public school tax increase in 1988: In the city's all-black wards, nearly 13,000 voters favored the school tax while 1,400 were opposed. In the all-white wards, more than 12,000 people voted no while 5,700 voted yes (Confluence, 1989, p. 37).

Table 3.2.   School-Age Population in the City of St. Louis

Year	School-Age Population (5–17 years)	Public School Enrollment	Percentage of Blacks in Public Schools	Percentage of School-Age Children in Public Schools
1950	133,017	91,773	35	69
1960	155,801	107,742	55	69
1970	148,577	111,233	66	75
1980	86,075	62,759	79	73
1991–92	71,000	42,000	79	60

Source: St. Louis Public Schools and Missouri State Department of Education

Between 1962, when the bond to build the segregated northside schools passed, and 1991, city voters failed to pass a single school bond issue. La Noue and Smith (1973) note that after Schlafly removed patronage and corruption in the system, many city politicians no longer supported the board's bond issues because they offered no lucrative contracts for their constituents as payback. Also, a former state requirement that bond issues receive 66.66 percent of the votes to pass meant that several times between 1962 and 1991 a majority of St. Louis voters—59 percent in 1968, 64 percent in 1970, and 58 percent in 1984, for example—approved school bond issues that could not be passed (Community Advisory Committee, 1985).

But in 1991 the Missouri constitution was amended to help St. Louis pass bond issues with a lower majority—four-sevenths, or about 57 percent of the vote, instead of two-thirds (Lindecke and Hick, 1992). That spring, a $131 million bond issue to pay the St. Louis board's share of capital improvements ordered by the settlement agreement passed with 60 percent of the vote on the coattails of the racially mixed reform slate of school board candidates. The reform slate, called "4 Kids," was backed by Schlafly and members of Civic Progress, the organization of elite business leaders.

In 1993 Missouri passed the landmark Outstanding Schools Act, which was designed to equalize school funding throughout the state by requiring districts to have a minimum tax levy of $2.75 per $100 assessed valuation in order to continue to receive state funding (Pope, 1994). This new funding formula has not had a positive effect on the St. Louis public schools (Little, 1994). But in 1994 city voters supported the St. Louis school board's request to permanently waive a property tax rollback and thus maintain the district's property tax rate at $3.75 for each $100 of assessed valuation. The rollback would have cut the tax rate by 38 cents and cost the schools $12 million a year.

The constitutional change from two-thirds to 57 percent of the votes required to pass bond issues has allowed a coalition of blacks and liberal whites to overcome most white city voters' opposition to spending on the St. Louis public schools. "They don't like the public schools because they are perceived to be black," said one former school board member about whites who live on the south side of St. Louis. In the city's eleven predominantly white wards, the 1991 bond issue lost by almost 2 to 1, and an antibusing slate of school board candidates, which lost to the 4-Kids slate, received 75 percent of the vote.

Some perceive the 1991 election as a turning point for a mostly black urban school district that, until then, had five school board members who represented the southside antibusing contingent. Four of these five—none of whom had children in the public schools—were members of the Metro-South

Citizens' Council, a chapter of the national Citizens' Council, a less violent version of the Ku Klux Klan that organized to resist integration in the South during the 1950s and 1960s. The Citizens' Council logo, which bears the Confederate flag, proclaims "States' Rights; Racial Integrity" (Lowes, 1990). In St. Louis City and County, the Citizens' Council is known for its strong opposition to both the intra-district desegregation plan in the city and the urban-suburban transfer plan.

After the 1991 election, however, only three board members were outspoken antibusing politicians with links to the Metro-South Citizens' Council. One of them, Thomas S. Bugel, who was on the school board from 1987 to 1993, was the president of the council. In an interview, Bugel clearly stated that he believes the "whole idea of racial integration of students in schools is flawed." He advocated neighborhood schools and back-to-basics curriculum, arguing that school desegregation is too expensive and that court-ordered quality education programs, such as the smaller class sizes for the all-black schools, will not make a difference. Ironically, it was not until 1005, when Bugel and his Citizens' Council colleagues were no longer on the board, that it issued a report to Judge Gunn calling for the end of mandatory reassignment of students based on race within the St. Louis system. And, as we mentioned earlier, if this new reform-oriented board continues to push for an end to the court order, the quality education programs may soon be abolished as well.

In the late 1980s and early '90s, Bugel and his allies were a powerful force on the board, and divisive racial politics was the norm. In addition to opposing school desegregation they also strongly opposed efforts to include minority-owned contractors in the bidding on construction contracts for the city schools' capital improvement renovations called for in the settlement agreement and partly paid for by the state. Bugel also opposed former superintendent, Jerome Jones' decision to hire a woman as the district's deputy building commissioner. Bugel claimed that she was unqualified because she was not an architect or an engineer. Former board president John Mahoney defended Jones' decision, however: "She was hired because it was an old boys club over at buildings and grounds. Jerome Jones knew that with a $300 million renovation project we had to have somebody who could cut through all the featherbedding and the absenteeism and the abuse of workmen's comp, and that is where all that was coming from. Not withstanding the fact that it [the building and grounds] had been the most glaringly racially isolated unit in the whole division."

But according to Bugel, the woman was hired only because "there were enough liberal and black votes on the board to ratify her." Bugel also fought to get rid of Jones, the first black superintendent of St. Louis, and he eventually won.

Every summer, Bugel's Metro-South Citizens' Council, with an estimated membership of 1,000, holds a large picnic in a park on the city's south side (Lowes, 1990). The council and the racial attitudes it represents maintain a presence on the city's far south side and in the county's southernmost suburbs. The Knights of the Ku Klux Klan Realm of Missouri even applied to the state Highway and Transportation Department to "adopt" a stretch of highway I-55 on the city's south side (Schlinkmann, 1994).

The visibility of the Metro-South Citizens' Council for years fueled political resistance to desegregation in South St. Louis, resistance so strong that only the federal courts—not the state or locally elected officials—could effectively fight it. When the school board instituted the intact busing program southside whites were angry—not because black students were contained in separate classrooms within a single school but because black students were allowed into *their* neighborhood schools at all. A 1970 study of segregationist attitudes among whites in fifteen "northern" cities found that St. Louis whites scored the lowest on such measures as "desire for integration; belief in discrimination against blacks; and sympathy for black-led reform movements" (Human Development Corporation, 1970).

Throughout the 1980s, St. Louis school board elections were dominated by issues of race and the court-ordered intra-city desegregation plan, with antibusing slates opposing the more moderate Schlafly-backed slates. Both groups won seats, which left the board more divided, especially over racial issues (Confluence, 1989, p. 35). Even in the mid-1990s, finally rid of the antibusing politicians, the St. Louis Board of Education has been left to serve an increasingly poor student body with a greatly diminished tax base. If it were not for the extra desegregation funding from the state and the opportunity for thousands of black students to transfer out of the once-overcrowded northside schools and into the suburbs, this urban school system would be in even worse shape. While generous state and local tax abatement programs lured a handful of businesses to the city instead of the suburbs, increasing office tower construction in downtown St. Louis, they have also decreased by nearly $17 million per year the city's real estate tax income, which is the largest chunk of revenue for the public schools (Primm, 1990; Community Advisory Committee, 1985). Furthermore, St. Louis has traditionally fared poorly in competition for state resources. In 1970, the city produced 25 percent of the state revenues, mainly through sales tax, but it received in return only about 12 percent of state services and expenditures (La Noue and Smith, 1973). And the state's 1993 school funding equalization law has continued that pattern by bringing no increase in general state aid for St. Louis schools (Little, 1995).

Meanwhile, the concentration of public housing projects in the city has reduced local property tax revenues while concentrating low-income children in the city's schools (St. Louis Public Schools, 1968, p. 40). Between 1950 and 1969 the city school system grew by almost 20,000 students, but the total assessed property value was less than 1 percent greater than it was in 1950 (Human Development Corporation, 1970). The St. Louis public schools' operating revenue decreased, when adjusted for inflation, by $31.6 million, or 17.4 percent, between 1970 and 1985 (St. Louis Public Schools, 1985).

By the late 1970s the St. Louis public schools were in many ways politically and economically bankrupt, a discarded educational system serving the least powerful and most disenfranchised families in the metropolitan area. Yet it was a group of these families who, by suing the St. Louis public schools, allowed the district to obtain state funds to remedy its racially discriminatory acts. By 1984, as a result of the court orders for the intra- and inter-district desegregation plans, the state spent more than $72 million on desegregation in St. Louis city, up from about $35 million in 1975 (St. Louis Public Schools, 1985). This was only the beginning of the state's court-ordered investment in removing the vestiges of segregation in the St. Louis schools. Although the annual desegregation funding for the city schools has dropped in recent years as the capital improvements are near completion, state policy makers incessantly complain about the cost of the program.

THE COURT ORDER: BANE AND BLESSING

With dwindling resources and an increasingly black and segregated student population, the St. Louis public schools' participation in the 1983 settlement agreement came just in time. Although the resulting student transfer program has drained the city of a total of nearly 25,000 black students over the thirteen-year course of the plan, it continues to deliver millions of state dollars to the bankrupt urban school system. The state funds have paid for quality education programs in the city's remaining all-black or nonintegrated schools; magnet schools; extensive capital improvements of school buildings; and dozens of other, part-time integration programs, such as joint field trips with county schools. Also, unlike other urban school districts across the country that have continued to experience white flight from the public schools over the past fifteen years, the percentage of white students in the St. Louis district has remained the same—21 percent—since the court order.

The St. Louis public school system, in its current political and economical state, depends heavily on this additional state funding. Nevertheless board members say they want to regain greater control of their district from the court, which could mean the end or phaseout of the extra state support. Yet for court supervision to end, the St. Louis public schools must be declared unitary—or no longer operating a dual, black and white, system. In 1991 the U.S. Supreme Court ruled in *Board of Education of Oklahoma City Public Schools v. Dowell* that a district court could declare a school district unitary and dissolve a desegregation court order if the district proves that it has "complied in good faith with the desegregation decree since it was entered, and whether the vestiges of past discrimination ha[ve] been eliminated to the extent practicable" (Yudof, Kirp, and Levin, 1992).

We question whether the St. Louis public schools are unitary under this Supreme Court definition, because the distance between the court order and what has actually happened in the St. Louis public schools is fairly large, particularly in the all-black schools. In fact, the evidence suggests that over the past thirty years the St. Louis school board has taken better care of many of its employees than it has of the children whose life chances depend on the board's ability to lead. Schlafly's efforts to clean the St. Louis system of corruption more than thirty years ago may have come back to haunt him in a system rife with new forms of incompetence. A closer look at the St. Louis system, even with its new reform-oriented board, helps explain why so many black students choose to transfer to suburban schools, but it also raises serious concerns about those who do not.

Before the recent round of administrative job cuts by former Superintendent Mahan, the Board of Education during the late 1980s employed nearly the same number of central-office administrators—more than 200—as it had decades earlier. During that time the number of students had fallen from more than 100,000 to 43,000. A 1988 audit of the St. Louis system recommended that the board trim the number of administrators and close more schools. The report found one central-office administrator for every 194 pupils, a much higher ratio than in most urban school districts, and an average of only 411 pupils in each school building (Gayle, 1988).

Since the district's central office cuts in the early 1990s, the St. Louis public school system spends about 6 percent of its nearly $300 million budget on district-level administrative salaries. This figure is down from 7 percent in the late 1980s and is now the same as the average for all of the suburban school districts in St. Louis County. Meanwhile, the district spent about 14 percent of its 1993–94 budget on district- and building-level administrators' salaries combined; this figure compares with the 12 percent average for suburban school districts.

As part of the school board's effort to cut the central administration and devolve decision-making to the schools, it launched a school-based management (SBM) reform effort in 1994. Across the country, SBM reform has been a popular way to decentralize authority to the school site, thereby empowering parents and teachers. Six schools in the St. Louis system served as pilot sites for the SBM program, and twenty additional schools signed on for fall 1995. In an intensely negative report on the district's SBM reform, an outside team of evaluators (hired by the district) noted that the SBM pilot had not been successful: "Principals are unclear about which decisions can be made by the schools and which will be made by the central office. The lack of policy and guidance ... is considered the major stumbling block to implementing SBM in the pilot schools" (McKenzie Group, 1995). In 1996 a citizens' task force established by the incoming St. Louis superintendent, Cleveland Hammond, Jr., called for further decentralization of decision-making authority.

Thus, there is little evidence that most African-American students in city schools are reaping the rewards of the district's administrative cuts or efforts to decentralize decision-making. And despite the tendency of critics to point to oversized central office bureaucracies as the main cause of inefficiency in urban schools, our research suggests that in St. Louis the lack of political will among school leaders to serve their most disenfranchised constituents— mainly poor, black families—is the main cause of failure. This lack of political will trickles down to district employees at all levels, which means that truly dedicated and visionary urban educators become outliers in a field of low expectations; many are eventually swallowed up in the inertia. Yet we should not smugly point fingers at these educational leaders and their employees; their lack of will is derived from a society that has physically and morally abandoned poor inner-city children and chosen to assume that they created their own plight (Kozol, 1991). And in poor cities, where most of the decent-paying jobs for African Americans are in the public school system, we should not be surprised to find patronage and less-than-qualified employees. Furthermore, the story of the decline of the St. Louis public schools flies smack in the face of the argument that greater competition between schools will force them to either improve or go "out of business." For the last forty-some years, urban school districts like St. Louis have been in competition with private and suburban schools for the highest-achieving and easiest-to-educate students. In St. Louis the urban schools also compete with suburban schools through the desegregation plan and the student choices it provides. Despite all this competition, the St. Louis public schools are still fairly dreadful.

Perhaps there is no better illustration of the ill will in urban school systems than the ultimate demise of the once highly touted vocational education programs in St. Louis. In a sternly worded 1991 memo, the district court judge overseeing the case at the time, Stephen N. Limbaugh, chastised the St. Louis public school system for its poor vocational programs, stripped it of all vocational education, and ordered city students to attend vocational schools in the county. Limbaugh noted that the St. Louis school board was spending $8.6 million a year for 450 vocational students—a per-pupil cost exceeding $16,500. Despite these expenditures, the city's vocational education had "failed miserably." He described the programs as places where "chaos reigns each year.... Supplies, equipment and textbooks are not ordered until the last minute and often are not in place until well into that year." Limbaugh ordered the board to halt plans for new vocational programs and to "begin preparation for dismantling its secondary vocational education system" (Bryant, 1991).

But the accusations of mismanagement may not have been the only issues influencing the judge. As with most decisions concerning public education in St. Louis, the final blow to the city's vocational education program was, according to some, also related to racial politics. For instance, the Reverend Earl Nance, Jr., the St. Louis school board president, said that Judge Limbaugh had previously decided to close one of the county vocational education programs and move the students into a renovated O'Fallon Tech in the city until the white people of south county "had a fit." "They were out there writing letters and protesting and everything—things that black folk here don't do well enough until it's too late," said Nance. When Limbaugh ordered the city's vocational education programs closed, the south county residents were able to keep their vocational school. In 1995, Judge Gunn appointed a seven-member board to oversee the creation of a separate city-county school district for vocational and technical education. Part of the board's mission was to propose a new vocational high school to be located in the city of St. Louis but run by this separate district, not the St. Louis public schools (Little, 1995).

Still intertwined with the racial politics of St. Louis is the school board's failure to fulfill many of the requirements spelled out for it in the 1983 settlement agreement. In looking at the three main components of the court order that the St. Louis board was responsible for implementing—quality education programs in the all-black schools, magnet school programs, and the capital improvements program for urban schools—we found that the board has made significant strides in the last two areas but once again shortchanged those students who remain in the all-black and often most needy schools.

Quality Education Programs for the All-Black Schools

The 1983 settlement agreement, reflecting the demands of the black plaintiffs and the NAACP, included several quality education programs designed to enhance the educational opportunities of students who would remain in all-black schools on the city's north side. In examining the St. Louis board's implementation of these quality education programs, James D. Dixon II, executive director of the court-appointed Education Monitoring Committee, said he is often discouraged by the "lack of vision" on the part of many educators and board members in the city system and their "lack of commitment" to providing the educational services to all-black schools. "They do not think these kids can learn," he said. "How much effort are they going to put into something when they think these kids cannot learn?"

Four years after the settlement agreement, Bruce La Pierre wrote that the accomplishments in the implementation of the settlement agreement "appear to be concentrated in the district-wide programs, and most of the implementation problems are in the settlement programs designed for the all-black schools" (1987, p. 1031). Unfortunately, this early observation appears to have developed into a trend.

Reports from Dixon's monitoring committee and other evaluators, as well as our visits to the "nonintegrated," or all-black, schools in North St. Louis, suggest that not one of the four main quality education programs for the all-black schools—the 20-to-1 student-teacher ratios in elementary and middle schools, the school of emphasis programs, the enhancement or remedial programs, or the instructional coordinators—has been successfully implemented across the board in these schools. Furthermore, the distribution of resources across the district is highly uneven, and many of these segregated all-black schools lack even basic instructional tools.

At the time of the settlement agreement, there were sixty all-black schools in the city. By the 1994–95 school year, there were only forty-five left after the creation of twenty-seven magnet schools drawing black students and the departure of black students to the suburbs. The remaining all-black schools enroll more than 20,000 children.

The 20-to-1 Student-Teacher Ratio The settlement agreement spelled out that the students who would remain in the city's nonintegrated schools would benefit from smaller class sizes and thus more individual attention. At the time of the agreement the student-teacher ratio in these schools was "at best" 35 to 1, "and in many schools it was probably higher" (La Pierre, 1987, p. 1006). The court ordered a student-teacher ratio for elementary and middle schools of 20 to 1; the all-black high schools were not to exceed 28 students in a class. Reports on the implementation of this requirement suggest that class size in these nonintegrated schools has more to do with shifting enrollment patterns than with an active board effort to assure that those students who need the most individualized attention actually receive it. As La Pierre (1987) noted, the board has reduced the student-teacher ratio on a districtwide basis, but there has "been little or no effort to lower the pupil-teacher ratio in the all-black schools below the district-wide average" (p. 1031).

In the all-black high schools we visited, enrollments had declined so significantly, as thousands of black students chose suburban or magnet schools, that there were often fewer than twenty students in a class. Yet in the elementary and middle schools, classes sometimes had more than twenty students, and there appeared to be little difference between class size in the nonintegrated and the integrated schools. Faith Sandler, former member of a court-appointed Quality Education Committee, which was later merged into Dixon's committee, said, "Overall, the district-wide ratios had been reduced no further in nonintegrated schools than other types of schools in the school district." Sandler's committee proved to the court that the board had "misappropriated and misdirected funds for district-wide improvements at the expense of what the district was required to do in the all-black schools."

By 1988, five years after the settlement agreement, the student-teacher ratios were 23 to 1 in the all-black middle schools and 24 to 1 in the elementary schools (Gayle, 1988). And in 1993, even as district officials proclaimed that they had met the 20-to-1 ratios in the all-black schools, teachers in these schools were reporting that they had many more than 20 students in their classes but were told by district administrators to report fewer students. One teacher in an all-black elementary school said that although he has twenty-seven students in his class, "each day on my attendance roll I have to write down that I have 20 children in my class. Other teachers have to do that, too" (Little, 1993a).

School of Emphasis Programs Another court-ordered quality education program for the all-black or nonintegrated schools is the school of emphasis concept, designed to provide students in segregated schools with extra enrichment programs within their neighborhood schools. According to the settlement agreement, each all-black school was to choose a theme for a "special academic emphasis" through "alternative educational programs." The St. Louis public schools' guidelines state that the school of emphasis programs should not be strictly remedial, duplicate existing required programs, or focus on areas already receiving sufficient curricula attention (St. Louis Public Schools, Division of Evaluation and Research, 1990a). Yet more than ten years after the agreement was signed, few school of emphasis programs in St. Louis fully met these criteria.

Only one of the six all-black schools we visited had a viable school of emphasis program, which lasted only as long as the principal did. This was Williams Middle School, in a blighted neighborhood on the north side of the city. The former principal of Williams, Acme Price, established a sophisticated aerospace school of emphasis program built around a partnership with McDonnell Douglas. The school, decorated from floor to ceiling with Styrofoam models of the solar system and murals of the Final Frontier, had infused the curriculum with aerospace themes. McDonnell Douglas volunteers taught students about aviation and astronautical careers. Each classroom had an aerospace project developed by students, teachers, and a McDonnell Douglas volunteer. The school had a young astronauts club, and students built hot air balloons and conducted a simulated space shuttle launch. Federal aviation officers even brought a flight simulator to the school for the students to experience. This school of emphasis program is an example of what educators in the all-black schools could create with desegregation money, but most of them have not done so.

According to Faith Sandler, Williams Middle School was an anomaly because Price, who was abruptly removed from the school by the board, knew how to "work the system," having served on court-appointed committees. "He knew what this school was supposed to have, but a lot of principals don't. So he knew how to go down to 911 Locust [the District Office] and say, 'The settlement agreement says that my school will have a school was of emphasis program, and I want it.' He is political from the word go, but he was a real advocate for his school, so his students got five times the resources that other schools have."

The state and the city school system share the cost of the school of emphasis program 50–50. During the first year of the settlement agreement, 1984–85, the school of emphasis program budget was $1.57 million. In subsequent years, the annual budget included a $10,000 allotment per nonintegrated school, plus a reserve fund of about $30,000 allocated among the nonintegrated schools based on need. The court order guidelines stipulate that the funds be used for facility renovations, consultants, staff training, and equipment related to the program's theme.

In 1990 the St. Louis Public Schools Division of Evaluation and Research (1990c) reported that the district had spent only half the allocated money and that, especially early in the implementation process, the school of emphasis programs tended to get lost among the other federal, state, and private partnership programs in the schools. Thus, the scope and impact of the emphasis programs vary greatly across the all-black schools, but most seem to be feeble extensions of something already offered in the regular curriculum, mainly reading and writing. For instance, the second most promising school of emphasis program we found, in an all-black elementary school in a low-income area, focused on "language and thinking." The principal of this school said that even though language and thinking need to be taught in elementary school regardless of a school of emphasis program, "our children come to school unprepared, and that is why we have identified this emphasis. We tried to combine social studies and sciences, but now we are trying to go gung ho to get our children to speak correctly."

A teacher at the school said that the language and thinking emphasis has encouraged her to study children's writing processes and how they learn to create their own voice. She read from a poem by one of her students: "'I love my sweet summer. The blue sky is in my summer, the hot good days. Summer, sweet summer, my sweet summer.' . . . This is a second-grader, and he is writing like that on his own," she said.

But Dixon argues that the school of emphasis program should, in theory, go beyond regular learning and instruction to create mini-magnet schools within the nonintegrated schools. The existence of these programs, said Dixon, should not depend on the vision and commitment of one principal or group of teachers. They should be ongoing programs that enrich the educational experiences of those students in the all-black schools—the students who have traditionally received the least from the system.

Dixon blames the St. Louis Board of Education for its lack of commitment to the emphasis programs. One school official reportedly dismissed the program as "magnets on a shoestring" ("Separate and unequal," 1994). Dixon said that principals and teachers in the all-black schools find the district's central office hard to work with, thus they have had difficulty obtaining the extra state resources for the school of emphasis programs. He added that the board often does not approve budgets for school of emphasis programs until halfway through the school year, making it virtually impossible for schools to plan ahead.

According to Acme Price, most educators in the all-black schools are not taking full advantage of the school of emphasis resources, in part because the board and administration have not informed principals about the intent and the funding of the program. Price noted that when he was on the Quality Education Committee, some principals of all-black schools were requesting less than $1,000 for their school of emphasis, "and this is supposedly a motivational impact that gives kids in the community a message that says something is happening to you. . . . Nobody ever made it clear to them [the principals] what the intent was and what they should have done, and so they do nothing." Price collected about $50,000 a year in district and state funds for the aerospace program at Williams, and he wrote grants for outside funding. Similarly, in the 1995 report of the SBM reform in the St. Louis public schools, the

McKenzie Group notes that communication between the schools and the central office is often "poor" (p. 30).

James Dixon, director of the monitoring committee, concurs that the school of emphasis programs are highly dependent on the political savvy and efficacy of the principals. This means that once a principal leaves, as Price was forced to do, the emphasis program will most likely end. For instance, the next principal at Williams did not keep the aerospace program in part because it had been Price's pet project. Thus, since the early years of the court order the St. Louis Board of Education has underspent the state funds allocated by the court for emphasis programs in the all-black schools (La Pierre, 1987).

This fragmented approach to school reform leads to gross inequality across the all-black schools in St. Louis. The district's 1990 report pointed to "significant improvements" in school of emphasis programs, finding that nine out of twenty programs were "very good," which meant they had distinct themes, served all students, and offered quality educational experiences beyond the regular curriculum (St. Louis Public Schools, Division of Evaluation and Research, 1990c). Even if this evaluation were accurate, which seems unlikely given the lack of evidence that these viable programs exist, board members still cannot explain why the other eleven all-black schools did not have "very good" school of emphasis programs a full seven years and millions of dollars after the settlement agreement was signed.

In 1991, with few exemplary school of emphasis programs operating in the St. Louis schools, Judge Limbaugh ruled that the all-black high schools could substitute for their school of emphasis program a self-esteem-building program called Project Courage, which teaches students basic skills and how to "cope with life" (Volland, 1994b). Project Courage consisted of a mandatory daily course that gave students a half-credit each year. There was no standard curriculum, so teachers were free to teach whatever they wanted. In some classes students would play games, and in others they would talk about current events or teen issues and problems. "It was a bankrupt program in the first place," said Dixon. District evaluations of Project Courage concluded that it had little or no effect on student attendance or achievement, and in 1994 the board eliminated the program from the three remaining all-black high schools—Beaumont, Sumner, and Vashon—but did not propose a replacement program (Little, 1994b). Once again the students in the all-black schools were left with less than what the court order mandated for them.

Enrichment and Remedial Programs Under the settlement agreement the St. Louis board was also required to implement enrichment and remedial programs in the all-black schools. But, like the school of emphasis programs, these enrichment programs appear to be a low priority for the St. Louis public schools. According to Faith Sandler, "Part of the thinking spelled out in the settlement agreement and all the orders of the court was that students who remained in nonintegrated schools would have to be given the chance to make up for all those years of inequity and inferior education, and what would have to happen would be enrichment programs and remedial programs . . . to give kids a chance to get caught up. And as of year four or five into the settlement agreement they were to be entirely implemented. There were budgets allocated each year. There were state dollars sitting in the city school board accounts for a year, and nothing was being done."

One of the most significant enrichment programs for all-black schools is the College Preparatory Program (CPP), which provided a college-prep curriculum, tutoring, preparation for entrance exams, comprehensive college and financial aid counseling, and college visits (Education Monitoring and Advisory Committee, 1994). The college prep program began in 1976 as a pilot at two St. Louis high schools—Northwest and Sumner—as part of the original consent decree in the first phase of the desegregation case; it was supported with federal desegregation funds. In 1980, after the St. Louis public schools were found guilty of discrimination and ordered to implement an intra-district remedy, the college prep program was to be a cornerstone of the desegregation plan. The Board of Education consistently stated its intent to expand the program to additional schools, and in 1983 the board pledged to offer the program to all students in regular or nonmagnet high schools. But in the final approval of the 1983 settlement agreement, the court of appeals, while recognizing the college prep program as a "component" of quality education programs, did not order the state to pay for the program's expansion (Education Monitoring and Advisory Committee, 1994). In 1989 the St. Louis public schools filed a motion in the district court seeking to eliminate the college prep program, arguing that the district could not afford it. The judge denied the motion, but the board still cut the central office staff for the program.

As a result, the St. Louis school board never expanded the college prep program beyond the two pilot high schools and shared the cost with the state. Despite the state resources available for the two schools, the Board of Education has continually underfunded the program and thus underspent its court-approved budget. For the 1992–93 school year, the court approved $694,000 for the college prep program, but the board spent only $605,000. Between 1984 and 1993, the St. Louis public schools underspent the allocated state and district funds for college prep by $234,529. The college prep enrollment target is 650 students, or 325 per high school. In 1993–94, the program served only 159 students at Sumner and 209 students at Beaumont, which absorbed

Northwest's college prep program in 1991 when Northwest was converted to a middle school. Still, in 1995, the program was expanded to Vashon High School.

While the St. Louis Board of Education has consistently underutilized or tried to eliminate college prep, James Dixon's Education Monitoring and Advisory Committee (EMAC) has found that students who participate in the college prep program demonstrate improved school attendance and achievement rates and are better prepared for college than are their fellow students. The EMAC report (1994) argued that in a school district in which only 10 to 15 percent of the students who enter ninth grade will obtain any postsecondary education—college or vocational training—"this statistic clearly and strongly underscores the need for CPP expansion and effective implementation of prior recommendations for improvement in the regular high school curriculum as part of a comprehensive effort" (p. 15).

Furthermore, the benefits of the college prep program are relative to the low-quality curriculum generally available to students in the all-black high schools, which does not really compare with the college prep curriculum in the suburban schools. Freivogel (1994) found, for instance, that a student in the college prep program at Beaumont High School had no advanced math or English class to take during his senior year. These classes had been cut because there were not enough students prepared to take them. According to a spokesperson for the national advanced placement (AP) program of college-level courses for high school students, the St. Louis public schools lag far behind other urban school districts, including Chicago and Detroit, in the number of AP courses offered. During the 1993–94 school year only six St. Louis students, all from the Gateway Institute of Technology magnet school, took AP examinations in the spring. "St. Louis is my biggest disappointment," said the college board spokesperson (Bower, 1994b).

The underfunded, underdeveloped, and undersubscribed college prep program, coupled with Judge Limbaugh's 1991 order to pull all vocational education out of the city schools, leads us to conclude that students attending the all-black high schools in St. Louis are being prepared for little other than a hopeless and jobless future.

Instructional Coordinators Another court-ordered quality education program for the nonintegrated schools is the provision of instructional coordinators, experts in curriculum and instruction who help create educational programs to better serve the students. The 1983 settlement agreement spelled out the need for instructional coordinators as integral to the goal of improving instruction in the nonintegrated schools: "As a multitude of desegregation and instructional programs are implemented, each individual nonintegrated school will be asked or required to participate in a number of endeavors directed toward the improvement of instruction. Significant demands will be made on the administration and the instructional staff members of each building to alter, change or adopt specific educational strategies which are believed to assist in the provision of instruction to minority children. In order to maximize the results of this myriad of activities, it is proposed that an instructional coordinator be assigned to each nonintegrated school" (St. Louis Public Schools, Division of Evaluation and Research,1990b, p. 51).

The St. Louis public schools described an instructional coordinator as someone who "assists the principal in providing leadership and coordination of the instructional programs within the school [and] . . . serves as a catalyst for assuring effective implementation of the regular instructional program as well as for supplemental programs of enrichment and remediation" (St. Louis Public Schools, Division of Evaluation and Research, 1990b, p. 52). The duties that instructional coordinators are to perform include assisting instructional staff in lesson planning; demonstrating lessons for faculty; and coordinating curriculum development, adaptation, and implementation. In 1989 the St. Louis public schools distributed to all high school principals a document that further defined the curricular thrust of the instructional coordinator position (St. Louis Public Schools, Division of Evaluation and Research, 1990b). Clearly, the intent of the district court, echoed in the official policy of the St. Louis public schools, was for the coordinators to focus on improving *instruction* in the nonintegrated schools.

But the St. Louis public schools' evaluation report (1990b) on instructional coordinators and our own observations and interviews indicate that these coordinators spend much of their time performing administrative tasks for the principals, particularly in the many elementary and middle schools where assistant principal positions have been cut. We found little evidence at the all-black schools we visited that the instructional coordinators had the time or the latitude to work with teachers in developing comprehensive changes in the instructional programs.

According to the St. Louis public schools report (1990b), instructional coordinators in the all-black high schools spend only 15 percent of their time in such direct classroom and instructional assistance activities as classroom observations, demonstrations, or lesson plan reviews. The high school coordinators report spending 26 percent of their time working on desegregation-related programs, such as school of emphasis, after-school, or school partnership programs, and 8 percent of their time coordinating field trips and assemblies. Another 19 percent of their time is spent attending to "school management" responsibilities, such as processing purchase orders and completing administrative reports; 8 percent of their time is spent substituting for absent teachers (St. Louis Public Schools, Division of Evaluation and Research, 1990b).

In the nonintegrated elementary schools, instructional coordinators spend 21 percent of their time on direct classroom and instructional assistance activities, 21 percent of their time on desegregation-related programs, 6 percent arranging field trips and assemblies, 17 percent on school management tasks, and 4 percent as substitute teachers. In the all-black middle schools, only 12 percent of coordinators' time is spent on instructional tasks; 25 percent of their time is spent on desegregation-related programs, 10 percent coordinating field trips and assemblies, 15 percent on school management tasks, and 4 percent substitute teaching (St. Louis Public Schools, Division of Evaluation and Research, 1990b).

At all grade levels, instructional coordinators in the nonintegrated schools spend about 13 percent of their time supervising students on the playground (St. Louis Public Schools, Division of Evaluation and Research, 1990b). In other words, these extra educators, whose purpose is to improve classroom instruction in the all-black schools, spend at best only one-fourth of their time directly involved in curriculum and instruction. This may help explain why the pedagogy in the all-black schools we observed was generally far from innovative or exemplary, especially in the three high schools we studied, where most teachers appeared to have very low morale. For many, using mimeographed worksheets with fill-in-the-blank answers was a standard instruction strategy in most classrooms we observed.

But like most programs in the St. Louis public schools, the effectiveness of the instructional coordinators is highly dependent on the vision and commitment of the educators, particularly the principals, at each site. One middle school teacher we interviewed found the instruction coordinator at her all-black school helpful not only in arranging field trips and extracurricular activities but also in monitoring her lessons and giving constructive feedback. She only wished she could have more of the coordinator's time and attention. "She [the instructional coordinator] is really supposed to deal with nothing but instruction and helping out with the instruction. She probably has a lot of other things to do in the office, but really her main focus is supposed to be instruction," the teacher said.

A principal who had just moved from an all-black to an integrated elementary school, which did not receive an instructional coordinator under the settlement agreement, recalled how much she had appreciated the coordinator in her prior job. "I've just come from an all-black school . . . and the most important thing that we got after desegregation at the other school was the fact that we had another administrator on staff, we did have the instructional coordinator." This principal said the instructional coordinator had brought in innovative ideas for the teaching staff. "I just think an instructional coordinator is extremely important," she said.

Educational Resources   For the past several years the St. Louis public schools have faced massive budget cuts each fall. In 1992 the district had a $38 million shortfall, and Superintendent Mahan announced the elimination of 457 jobs, including those of 60 administrators, 107 teachers, and 248 other staff members, including teacher aides, custodians, and security guards. The district also eliminated soccer, wrestling, and tennis teams. The purchase of classroom and library supplies was postponed, and summer school programs were curtailed (Gillerman, 1992).

But James Dixon is concerned that these budget cuts clash with the district's obligation, under the court order, to improve its educational programs. In a report to the district court, Dixon's monitoring committee noted that the 1983 settlement agreement's quality education component included libraries and media centers in accordance with the states's highest (AAA) accreditation standards (Education Monitoring and Advisory Committee, 1995). During the 1993–94 school year EMAC assessed the library and media centers in the St. Louis public schools and found "no clear evidence of a formal process to ensure library/media services were an integral aspect of the overall instructional program at each school" (p. ii). The study also found that more than half of the schools' library collections were in dire need of "weeding, updating, and/or upgrading," and that many school libraries lacked materials on current issues.

Dixon concluded that the libraries in most city schools, especially the non-magnets, are far below an acceptable standard, which should prevent the district from receiving an AAA rating from the state. According to the court order, however, if the St. Louis public schools do not maintain AAA status, the state and district must accept joint responsibility for improving the city system. Thus, when the St. Louis public school system lost its AAA rating in the early '80s, the district court ordered the state to provide extra resources to help upgrade the district. Ever since, Dixon said, the state has made sure the St. Louis public schools receive an AAA rating, despite the poor condition of the libraries and the lack of resources in many schools. This way the state does not have to provide the district with any additional resources.

In this highly rated urban school district we found that teachers often go without basic classroom supplies and that, once again, the variation between schools is great. In an all-black elementary school we met a special education teacher working with severely physically and mentally disabled students who had to wait until January of the school year to receive the supplies and instructional materials she had ordered from the district's central office. As this teacher struggled to create lessons with no materials, she met teachers from other schools at a districtwide workshop who told her that they never have trouble getting resources. "This one woman was saying, 'You have no supplies? I have so many I don't know what to do, I can't use them all.' . . . I don't know where the inequality came from. I don't know how in one school district [supplies] can be dispersed so poorly."

Each fall, teachers in many of the city schools scramble for textbooks and basic supplies—items that were ordered the previous spring. During the 1993–94 school year the students of at least one of the all-black high schools were not able to take books home with them to do homework because there were not enough to go around. One of the teachers in a magnet school noted that she is able to get any supplies or textbooks she wants, but when she was in an all-black school she was constantly struggling to get the books she needed. "You could go almost the whole semester and not have enough books for each child. And here the books are here, ready from day one, and you're ready to start."

"The problem of getting textbooks to students is a perennial one in the St. Louis Public Schools," read a 1993 newspaper article, which reported that some classes may be short twenty to thirty books. The district administration blames the shortages on student mobility, which makes it difficult to calculate school enrollments. But reports show that it can take eight to nine months for schools to order furniture and equipment; it often takes two months for the orders to get to the district's purchasing department (Little, 1993d).

But as with everything else in the St. Louis public schools' rather oddly decentralized system of resource allocation, the general wealth or poverty of any given school depends on the ability of the principal to navigate the system. According to the city schools' budget director, Norm Walsh, discrepancies in schools' resources are primarily the result of different management styles on the part of principals. "I think there's a mind-set out there among some building principals that they don't have enough money to go around so they are not going to even worry about it, they're just going to try to get by the best they can," said Walsh. Yet he argues that the principals need to determine their budget requests and then justify what they need. The central administration is much more flexible, Walsh said, about allocating extra supplies and resources to principals who demonstrate the programmatic need for the expenditure.

The "integrated" schools—those that are neither all-black or magnet schools—on the south side of the city were desegregated in 1980 as part of the intra-city desegregation plan. They were supposed to be 50 percent white and 50 percent black, plus or minus 5 percentage points. Most of the schools are now closer to 70 percent black, but under the court order they receive few of the extra resources—smaller class sizes, instructional coordinators, school of emphasis programs—that the nonintegrated schools theoretically receive, nor do they have the extra funding of the magnet schools. The Patrick Henry Elementary School, one of the integrated schools that we visited several times, did have larger classes—generally between twenty-six and thirty students—than the all-black schools. But one veteran teacher we interviewed noted that these classes were much smaller than when she began her teaching career in St. Louis in 1950, when she had fifty-five to sixty students in a class.

We did find, however, that in this integrated elementary school—the category of school that should receive the fewest extra resources under the settlement agreement—the teachers had adequate resources. They would like to have another film projector or some extra televisions with VCRs, but they were not lacking basic classroom supplies. One teacher at Patrick Henry who had taught in other city schools noted that the availability of supplies in individual schools is heavily dependent on the person doing the ordering from the central office. Patrick Henry had a dynamic principal who knew how to work the system and get what she needed for her students—black and white—most of whom are from very low-income families.

Meanwhile, in two of the three all-black high schools we studied, science teachers did not have the equipment or supplies to conduct basic lab experiments. One biology teacher said that he had not had adequate lab supplies in the eight years he had been at this all-black high school, where the principal was at the time doubling as the head basketball coach. At this school, the state championship basketball team was decked out in expensive sweatsuits and sneakers bought through "fund-raising efforts" while the science classrooms were bare. But even after the basketball coach became the assistant principal, the classrooms still lacked basic instructional supplies. But the young and still fairly idealistic biology teacher has tried to maintain his commitment to his students: "I fill out an order every year for the biology equipment, and they don't give me anything I ordered for the last eight years. So you see, like I say, I don't know where it is going or who it's going to. . . . I'm not trying to point fingers any which way, but the fact [is] that it might be a slow process downtown as far as these things go, or we might turn our requisition in late—it could be a number of factors."

He added that when he was teaching in an integrated school in the 1980s he had all the equipment and supplies he needed. Now, at in his all-black high school, he has no frogs to dissect with his class. "In biology, you definitely need to dissect," he said. "And I can count, out of eight years, I've had one frog."

The uneven distribution of resources in the St. Louis public schools is alarming. With the exception of the magnet schools, which automatically receive a larger per-pupil stipend, the schools—nonintegrated or integrated—seem to be fairly unequal, with their "wealth" at least partially dependent on the political savvy of the principal. Thus, despite the court order requiring the nonintegrated or all-black schools to have extra resources and educational programs, the St. Louis Board of Education has failed to assure that this happens. Sandler noted that the political forces within the district make it difficult for the board to lavish extra resources on the least politically powerful schools and students in the district. But the point of the court order, after all, was to force the board to ignore these political forces and follow the direction of the court. Unfortunately, the political forces often prevail, and, according to Sandler, the clout of the all-black schools has diminished as many of the more vocal and involved black parents have put their children in magnet or county schools. "When the school board meets on a Tuesday night to discuss the budget or a program in an all-black school, you see very little of the kind of voter and parent and community push that you need to put pressure on the school board to make the right decisions."

Many of these all-black schools are perceived to be schools of last resort by students, parents, and even teachers. A sixth-grade teacher in an all-black school echoed a common sentiment among educators in these nonintegrated schools: "The desegregation program only takes the better students—academically and in terms of parental support. They don't take those with problems."

A teacher in an integrated school had a slightly different perception of the students who transfer out to a county school: "They are better in their work possibly, a little better in behavior, but they are not our most well-behaved kids. Yeah, they aren't the underachievers, they are doing average or above." Still, this teacher, as most of the city teachers we spoke with, said that students who transfer to county schools often have the most involved parents.

Magnet Schools

The magnet schools are, in many ways, the bright spots in this urban school district. The 1983 settlement agreement called for the creation of twenty-seven magnet schools in the district. These specialized schools, with themes ranging from visual and performing arts to Montessori, are to serve a total of

14,000 students—at least 1,600 of whom should be white students who would transfer in from suburban county districts. By the beginning of the 1996–97 school year, all of the twenty-seven magnet schools were operating, and most were quite successful at attracting students—from other city and many county schools.

The number of white suburban students who choose to attend magnet schools in the city has risen steadily—from 800 in 1990 to more than 1,400 in 1995—as many of the most innovative magnet schools have opened in the past few years (Voluntary Interdistrict Coordinating Council, 1995b). In 1993, for instance, a new elementary magnet school—the Mullanphy/Botanical Garden Investigative Learning Center—opened in cooperation with the Missouri Botanical Garden. Students enrolled in this school will benefit from frequent visits and class projects in the large garden, where their teachers will receive assistance with the development of the science curriculum (Little, 1993b). In the fall of 1995, the Gateway Elementary and Middle School complex opened in a spectacular state-of-the-art facility on a corner of the vacant lot where Pruitt-Igo once stood. These modern, high-tech schools focus on the sciences, mathematics, and technologies of the future. The two schools are connected by a courtyard with a weather station and several garden areas in which students grow plants indigenous to Missouri. The elementary school has its own greenhouse for winter growing, and in the science classroom there are as many small animals as there are students. In fall 1996, a $9.5 million middle school magnet opened adjacent to the St. Louis Science Center, and scientists work with magnet school teachers and students on special projects (see Prost, 1994). Under the settlement agreement the state pays the start-up of the magnet schools as well as most of the extra costs of maintaining the specialized programs within the schools.

Because the city's magnet schools are perceived to be superior to the all-black or integrated schools, many black and white parents are eager to enroll their children in the magnet schools. Waiting lists for the most popular magnet schools are long. The racial balance in most of the schools is between 50 and 60 percent black and 40 and 50 percent white. Since 1988 the St. Louis public schools have operated a lottery system for admission to the magnets, which eliminated the long lines and the need for parents to camp out overnight in order to get their children into magnet schools.

The magnet schools enroll only about 23 percent of the students in the St. Louis system, and, as in most urban districts, African-American students are proportionately underrepresented in these more elite schools (see Moore and Davenport, 1990; Wells, 1993). For instance, although only 21 percent of the students who live in the city and attend the St. Louis public schools are white,

35 percent of the students who live in the city and attend magnet schools are white (not including the white county students who attend city magnet schools). This means that while 79 percent of the students in the city schools are black, only 65 percent of the students who live in the city and are enrolled in magnet schools are black. Thus, only 19 percent of the black students overall who attend city schools are enrolled in magnet schools (Little and Todd, 1994). Still, it is the white parents who live in the city who complain most loudly about the lack of access to magnet schools because, under the court order, the St. Louis public schools are obligated to recruit and admit white students from the county until the district reaches its 1,600-student goal (Lhotka, 1988). This means the number of magnet school seats available to white students who live in the city are limited.

Meanwhile, magnet schools receive extra resources for start-up costs and maintenance of their specialized program. Table 3.3 presents the different per-pupil expenditures for magnet and regular nonintegrated and integrated—schools in St. Louis.

According to Dixon, the magnet schools get extra resources for two reasons: to attract students from suburban school districts and because they are considered "path finder schools," which means that what is learned in magnets about teaching and instruction should spread to the nonmagnet schools. But teachers in the nonmagnets wonder how they might duplicate magnet school programs and techniques when they lack the extra resources of the magnet schools.

In addition, educators in nonmagnet schools complain that the magnets "cream" the highest achieving or most motivated students. This creaming phenomenon occurs across the country in school district that have both magnet and nonmagnet schools (see Moore and Davenport, 1990). In St. Louis, achievement data demonstrates that African-American students who attend magnet schools have higher initial test scores than do students who transfer to

Table 3.3. *Per-Pupil Expenditures in St. Louis Magnet and Nonmagnet Schools, 1992–1993*

	Elementary Schools	Middle Schools	High Schools
Magnet Schools	$7,191	$8,187	$9,137
Regular Schools (nonintegrated and integrated)	$5,600	$6,236	$6,944

Source: St. Louis Public Schools (cited in Little and Todd, 1994)

suburban schools or attend integrated or all-black schools in the city. Yet the data suggest that scoring higher on tests in magnet schools is not simply a creaming process because the achievement gains on Stanford reading and mathematics tests hold, even when controlling for "pretransfer" scores, as the magnet school students progress through the system until high school. Between eighth and tenth grade, the reading scores of black students attending magnet schools level off, and their math scores begin to decline. Meanwhile, black students who transfer to suburban schools start off in elementary and middle school performing at a lower level than black students in city magnet schools but at a slightly higher level than black students in nonmagnet city schools. But these transfer students then show a consistent increase in performance from eighth to tenth grade, leaving behind students in all of the city schools, magnet or not (see Chapter 5). Consistently, black students in the regular—integrated or nonintegrated schools—remain far behind the magnet and transfer students in achievement gains (Lissitz, 1993 and 1994).

Capital Improvements

Nearly all of the St. Louis public school buildings have benefited from the capital improvements portion of the settlement agreement. The total cost of the capital improvements plan will be about $355 million—half from the state and half raised from the city. The capital improvements portion of the court order was designed to assist the city school system in renovating its aging school buildings, some of which are more than 100 years old. At the time of the settlement agreement the newest schools in the district were those built to relieve overcrowding after the 1962 bond issue. The capital improvements were to bring the city schools up to state health and safety standards and make them more comparable with county schools.

While the capital improvements program has been fairly successful, its implementation has taken far longer than anticipated in most cases. Many of the projects have run a year or more behind schedule as the St. Louis school board and the state of Missouri argued over the specifics of each plan, backing up the renovation process. According to Dixon, during the 1990–91 school year, 37 of the district's 110 buildings were undergoing some form of renovation and construction. Meanwhile, in many of these schools, students and faculty were temporarily reassigned to other school buildings, leading to tremendous relocation of people and programs.

By fall 1993, a full ten years after the settlement agreement, 60 of the district's school buildings had been renovated. But the battles between the state and the St. Louis Board of Education continued, and in the spring of 1994, when the board proposed to use capital improvement funds to construct a new building to house Metro High School, a small magnet school for gifted students, the state objected on two grounds. First, the St. Louis board proposed to spend $5.1 million on the new building, which the state argued was an exorbitant amount for a school with an enrollment of only 240. Second, the St. Louis board proposed to build the school on the site of an existing middle school. The state objected to tearing down the middle school building because the board had recently spent $2 million in capital improvement funds to renovate it. The board responded that the capital improvements to the middle school building had "complicated access to the school for the disabled" and that the basement of the school was substandard (Little, 1994).

Future Directions

During the 1993–94 school year the St. Louis public schools, with desegregation money from the state, had the fifth highest average per-pupil expenditure ($7,019) of the twenty-four districts in the metropolitan area. This figure is inflated because the city school system incorporates an expensive special education program, which can cost more than $15,000 a year for a severely handicapped student, whereas the suburban districts maintain a separately funded countywide special education district. But the St. Louis public school's budget per pupil is still significantly higher than all but the wealthiest suburban districts and nearly double that of the poor all-black districts on the other side of the city-county line.

Despite the extra resources, the graduation and college-going rates for students in the St. Louis public schools are not increasing. According to reports from the St. Louis district's Division of Evaluation and Research, only 26 percent of the students in the high school class of 1988 graduated in four years. Another 3.6 percent graduated in five years. Another 13 percent of the class of 1988 had transferred to suburban schools, 5 percent had moved out of the district or gone to a private school, 27 percent had "officially" dropped out of school, and 21 percent were "missing in action" or in the "did not return" (DNR) category. The author of the report estimated that at least half of the "did not return" students dropped out (St. Louis Public Schools, Division of Evaluation and Research, 1990a). No one knows where the other half went.

A postgraduation study of the class of 1989 by the same office showed that of the one in four students who had graduated in four years, 31 percent were attending four-year colleges one year after graduation from high school. Another 17 percent were attending two-year colleges. Missouri Department of Education data show that only 27 percent of the St. Louis public school students who were ninth-graders in 1989–90 graduated four years later. Each year in between, the city schools lost an average of 18 percent of the 4,200 students in the class of 1994. And those who stayed on to graduate were, for the most part, prepared for neither college nor work.

Caught between the departure of some of their more motivated students to the suburbs and a system that thwarts their attempts to help the children who stay behind, many of the teachers and principals in the city's all-black schools are counting the days to retirement. Morale is at an all-time low, according to several veteran teachers. The desegregation plan, they say, has promoted the suburban schools and the city's magnet schools while sending a message that the neighborhood schools are the schools of last resort.

As with any system of competition between prestigious and nonprestigious educational institutions, the schools of last resort are left with the highest percentage of fragile constituents—the students whose parents are overwhelmed with day-to-day survival, students who are denied transfers to suburban schools because of bad disciplinary records, and students who are "pushed out" of suburban schools. All of these factors add up to the self-fulfilling prophecy of the inferior inner-city school system with a fistful of fancy magnet schools that could disappear with the thud of a judge's gavel. But the question remains: Are the city schools better off today than they would have been without the 1983 settlement agreement? The answer to that question is clearly yes. The magnet schools, the capital improvements program, and some of the quality education components have helped to keep this urban system from falling into greater disgrace. Thus, while inner-city school systems across the country have become more racially segregated and isolated—for example, Detroit and many other urban districts are now 95 percent or more African American—the St. Louis public schools system has maintained the same racial balance for the past sixteen years.

Still, the St. Louis system is far from what it ought to be. If the board had, over the past decade, put aside its racial politics and followed the spirit of the court order, more of the nonintegrated schools on the north side of the city might have become the type of neighborhood institutions that the mayor and board members like to pretend they are, instead of the kind of schools that 12,700 black students choose to leave behind every day on their way to the whiter and wealthier suburbs.

4

Consumers of Urban Education

Our valedictorian, a very nice young man, chose to go to St. Louis University. And when the woman from there came here, I said, "How is he doing?" and she said, "Well, he went into remedial this summer and I kept him in remedial until January" because, she said, there are a lot skills people from the all-black city schools have to learn. There are social skills, too, you know, and it's sad because [she was] saying how could we have better prepared him. . . . But it is just very, very discouraging because they have a very hard time making it. It's just a handful, you know.
—English teacher from an all-black high school in St. Louis

The more we learned about the St. Louis public schools and the racial politics that drives the system, the more curious we became about the students who attend the all-black schools in North St. Louis. Who are these "consumers" of urban education, and why do they stay in racially segregated urban schools as their friends and neighbors leave for suburban and magnet schools? Too often policy makers and researchers oversimplify the process by which students and parents make school choices, as though it were similar to shopping for a car or a household appliance (Chubb and Moe, 1990). But the African-American students and parents of St. Louis, who, because of a voluntary metropolitan-wide desegregation plan, have more than 100 schools in 17 school districts to choose from, explain that the process is not that simple. When the choice is between a nearby and familiar all-black school in a low-income neighborhood and a faraway, mostly white suburban school, the decision is never easy nor is it necessarily based on "objective" standards of school quality. Race, social class, segregation, and alienation all play a significant and interconnected role in where students "choose" to go to school.

This chapter is about the experiences of the "city students" who have chosen not to choose a suburban school.[1] The first author, accompanied by an African-American woman researcher from St. Louis, got to know the families of twelve tenth-grade city students, interviewing them and their parents about why they attend all-black urban high schools as opposed to suburban or magnet schools. In addition, we have drawn on other studies of African-American city and transfer students in St. Louis to better understand who chooses to step over the color line, who does not, and what the consequences are for each. In listening to the stories of students and their parents, we have come to a clearer under-standing of the inherent possibilities and shortcomings of this inter-district transfer plan and how school choice and school desegregation policies might be improved to provide greater opportunities for all urban students.

In order to select the city students we would interview, we obtained the home addresses of tenth-graders attending three all-black high schools—Northwest, Sumner, and Vashon—from the St. Louis public schools. Focusing on the three neighborhoods surrounding these city high schools, we obtained from the Voluntary Interdistrict Coordinating Council (VICC), which manages the city-to-county student transfer process, the addresses of transfer students who attend suburban schools and return students who had attended a subur-ban school but had since returned to a city school or had dropped out of school altogether. We selected twelve students—four city, four transfer, and four re-turn—from each of the three neighborhoods by locating students who lived within a few blocks of the all-black city high schools (pseudonyms are used for all teachers and students quoted in this book; see appendix on methodology).

1. Throughout the next three chapters we refer to the African-American students who remain in the all-black city schools as "city students." The African-American stu-dents who have transferred out of the city to one of the suburban school districts and remained enrolled in those schools are referred to as "transfer students." The African-American students who have attended a suburban school at some point but who are no longer participating in the transfer program are referred to as "return students."

This process ensured that the city students we interviewed were indeed attending their neighborhood schools and that the neighborhoods in which they lived varied in terms of the average income of the nearby families, as well as the degree of deterioration of the social fabric of these neighborhoods. For instance, the middle-class neighborhood where Northwest High School (now a middle school) is located hugs the northwestern city-county border in one of the more middle-class areas of the city's all-black north side. Housing in this neighborhood consists of mainly single-family homes perched on small, neat lots. The median household income in this neighborhood is about $18,000 (in 1990 dollars).

Twenty years ago this neighborhood of single-family homes was white and middle class. The blacks who moved in as whites fled are, for the most part less affluent, and some of the two- and three-bedroom homes in this neighborhood are in need of repairs and general upkeep. Many of the parents we interviewed from this neighborhood expressed concern that their community had more gangs and violence than before. But for the most part, this remains a relatively middle-class black neighborhood in which most families own at least one car and have at least one employed family member.

Northwest High School sits on a hill overlooking this northern city neighborhood. Built in the 1960s to serve the white students on the city's north side, Northwest is the newest high school building in the St. Louis public school system, and its relatively modern architecture gives it a more suburban feel than most city schools. Northwest was once known for its championship wrestling teams, and several team pictures that decorate the waiting room outside the principal's office attest to the community's rapid white flight. Each year, beginning in the late 1960s, the pictures frame one or two more black faces and one or two fewer white ones. By the late 1970s there were no more white Bulldog wrestlers. When we visited, the school's enrollment had shrunk to 600 students, down from its peak enrollment of 2,400 in the 1970s. There were no longer enough students to field a football team, and soon the Board of Education would not only eliminate the wrestling team because of budget cuts but also close Northwest High School, converting it into a middle school as part of a districtwide school consolidation plan.

Sumner High School is located in the heart of the Ville, the "cradle of black culture" in St. Louis. According to residents and historians, this working-class neighborhood has always been fairly socioeconomically diverse, and before the flight of many black professionals to the suburbs, prominent black lawyers, judges, businessmen, and educators lived side by side with uneducated maids and custodians. Public schools, the black hospital, a shopping area with restaurants, and several churches helped to hold this community together before the more affluent blacks moved out, leaving the working-class and poor families to make ends meet. The hospital and many shops, restaurants, and churches are closed. The majority of houses are in disrepair, and on some streets close to one in five is completely abandoned—either boarded up or burned out. Most of the houses are two-family duplexes and at least fifty years old. By North St. Louis standards, this is a working-class to low-income neighborhood, with a median household income of about $11,000. The focal point of the neighborhood is the 120-year-old Sumner High School, a stately Georgian structure now registered as U.S. historical landmark. Enrollment has declined considerably at Sumner as well, in part because of the transfer plan and the choice of magnet schools. When we visited, the enrollment was at about 1,000 students, down from 3,000 students thirty years ago.

The neighborhood surrounding Vashon High School is, according to Census data, one of the lowest-income areas of the city. it includes the site of the former Pruitt-Igoe public housing complex, where the new Gateway Magnet Schools have been constructed. The median household income in this neighborhood is less than $9,000.

Three large public housing complexes are within walking distance of the school, as are many old brick two-family homes and acres of empty lots and abandoned buildings with boarded-up windows and graffiti-stained walls. There are also several newer duplex houses built for residents with federal Section 8 vouchers. The cheap aluminum siding on many of these homes is painted yellow and blue. But bright, cheery colors are not the rule in this neighborhood, where about a third of the land is vacant and a fourth holds empty, hollowed-out buildings.

Vashon High School enrolls many of the students from this neighborhood. The school, currently housed in a run-down, dingy building that resembles an old ammunitions factory, is known outside of the black community mostly for its excellent basketball team and outspoken coach. At the time we were conducting our research, the basketball coach was serving as the interim principal. He bemoaned the creaming effect of the transfer program and the magnet schools. "When you are losing your cream, you are dying a slow death," he said. Enrollment was down to 600 students in the early 1990s.

The three neighborhoods and their high schools differ dramatically in many respects. For instance, the percentage of residents in the Northwest high neighborhood who own their homes is 55 percent, one of the highest home ownership rates among all the neighborhoods on the city's north side. By comparison, near Sumner, about 30 percent of families own their homes, as opposed to about 2 percent of families who live near Vashon. Poverty rates for the three neighborhoods also show that Vashon High School draws from the lowest-income households in the city, with more than 50 percent of all families living below the poverty line. Near Sumner, Census data show that 40 percent of all families live below the poverty line. For families in the northernmost part of the city, near Northwest High School, the poverty rate is less than 20 percent.

We wanted to talk with city, transfer, and return students in each of these neighborhoods to better understand how African-American students and their parents living in very different inner city neighborhoods make sense of the inter-district desegregation plan and thus their school choices.

CITY PARENTS: THE BEAT DOWN

To know these city students and their families is to gain a deeper understanding of how alienation and powerlessness, which grow out of the poverty and isolation experienced by many inner-city black families, shape their view of the larger social structure and where they fit into it (Bourdieu and Passeron, 1979). This view shapes their achievement ideology, their racial attitudes, and their hopes for the future. In short, we found many of these students and their parents to be living under what West (1993b) calls nihilism: "the lived experience of coping with a life of horrifying meaninglessness, hopelessness, and (most important) lovelessness" (p. 14). Many of these parents and students were "beat down" by the burden of racism and severe poverty in a society that understands the weight of neither.

Perhaps the most striking finding from our interviews with the city students and their parents is that the key factor influencing the decision of an African-American student from the north side of St. Louis to transfer to a county school or to remain in an all-black neighborhood school appears to be the degree of parental involvement in the decision. In general, parents who were most involved in their children's educational decisions—indeed, those who *made* the decisions for their children—were those who insisted that their children attend county schools. Only one of the city parents felt strongly about her son remaining in a city school. The others were willing to let their children decide.

Our interviews reveal that students, for the most part, have to be pushed onto a bus heading for the county by a parent who is convinced that the benefits of going to a county school will, in the long run, outweigh the inconvenience, discomfort, and prejudice that the transfer entails. While there are a few exceptions, overall parental involvement in the students' education and the degree to which parents direct and control their children's educational decisions varied greatly between city and transfer students, and, to a lesser degree, between city and return students, with the city parents almost always leaving the school-choice decision to their children.

The city parents' lack of involvement echoes what teachers and principals in the all-black schools told us. Most of these educators insisted that the desegregation plan had resulted less in a "brain drain" of the highest achieving students from the city schools than in a drain of students with the most active and involved parents. One teacher referred to the phenomenon as the "motivation drain." Of course the correlation between student achievement and parental involvement has traditionally been quite high (see Epstein, 1990), so involved parents and high-achieving students often go hand in hand. But what these urban educators notice first is that many of the efficacious parents who provided a spark of momentum in their neighborhood schools and a more critical voice in the city school system have transferred their children to the suburbs in search of a better opportunity (see Witte, Baily, and Thorn, 1993).

A teacher in one of the city's all-black high schools said that she was "doing good" if she has five parents show up to open house to talk about their children's progress. "And we are here from 12:30 to 7:00 all day and have five people show up. If you ever get ten you have the record; people will say you are kidding. That's sad if you think about how many youngsters you have, and you get such a small percentage of parents involved."

In all but one case, "powerless" best describes the parents we interviewed whose children remain in the all-black city schools. They were generally shy and withdrawn, typifying, much more so than either the parents of transfer or return students, what Comer (1980) describes as alienated inner-city parents with deep distrust of educators and an inability to act on their child's behalf in the world of the school. Eight of the eleven city parents we spent time with said the decision that their son or daughter remain in a city school was made by the student alone.[2] Half of these parents said that they did not discuss this decision with their child.

The powerlessness and alienation that city parents experience in their own lives seems to preclude them from helping their children to make educational decisions. We know, for instance, from the demographic information we collected from the families we studied that city parents in any of the three neighborhoods are less educated and hold lower-status jobs than the transfer parents in all three neighborhoods. Furthermore, unlike the transfer or return parents, none of the city parents works in the county or goes to the county on a regular basis. In fact, many of these city parents have never been to the

2. Nearly all of the African-American parents and students we interviewed refer to the St. Louis public schools as simply "public" schools—as opposed to city schools— and the schools in the suburbs as "county" schools, as though the urban schools were public and the suburban schools were not.

predominantly white areas of St. Louis County, where the suburban schools that their children could choose to attend are located. The different educational backgrounds and lack of exposure to the suburbs seem to affect their perceptions of the transfer program.

Minnie Liddell, in an interview about the impact of the court case that bears her son's name, said that many African-American parents who keep their children in the all-black schools in the city are overwhelmed by just trying to survive in the impoverished north side of St. Louis: "You know, day-to-day living is their number one priority. . . . They don't have any hope for themselves so they don't have a lot of hope that Johnny or Mary is going to be a scientist anyway. So you know, he just goes to school where the law says he has to go to school. [So] you got that group too, where just living is a chore with them 'cause things are so hard for them."

What becomes more apparent as one gets to know these city parents is that all of them want what is best for their children, they all want their children to make it and be more successful than they have been. Like most parents, they care deeply about their children. But the degree to which they feel they can help their child attain the best—the best education, the best job after graduation, and so on—depends on their own self-concept and experiences in integrated settings.

The teenagers who are left to choose a school on their own are likely to choose city over county, familiar over unfamiliar—the path of least resistance. Meanwhile, the way that familiar versus unfamiliar is defined has much to do with geography and race—the result of living in a highly segregated society in which African Americans have been systematically denied opportunities to live in whiter and wealthier neighborhoods. The frustration of generations of African Americans who have been told by a predominantly white society that they are inferior reverberate in the voices of city students as they tell us they are afraid of not being accepted in a suburban school or of not being able to compete with the white students in these schools. In a survey of African-American tenth-graders from the city of St. Louis attending nonintegrated, integrated, magnet, and suburban schools, Lissitz (1994) found that students in the nonintegrated or all-black city schools are much less likely to agree with the following statements than are students who transfer to a suburban school:

1. Going to school with members of another race will help prepare me for life.
2. A student of another race could be my friend.
3. All racial groups are equally worthwhile.

These racial attitudes, coupled with the alienation of city students and their parents from the county and its suburban school districts, play a significant role in the school choice processes of these families and their decision not to cross the color line.

Troy's Mother

The Vaughn public housing project is a high-rise complex on the edge of a vast open space on the city's near north side. Less than three miles from the city's downtown business center and the famous Gateway Arch, the weedy vacant lots surrounding the project resemble a prairie. This barren stretch of urban St. Louis, symbolizes the leveled aspirations of many of the people who grow up looking down on the vacant land from their cramped quarters in the Vaughn (MacLeod, 1995).

This is where Troy grew up, living with his mother and older brother in a meager two-bedroom apartment. From here he can walk, through the vacant lots, less than two miles to Vashon, his neighborhood high school. And that is what Troy chooses to do. "He just wanted to go to Vashon, so we never discussed it," said Troy's mother, an attractive middle-aged woman who has not held a job in several years and receives Aid to Families with Dependent Children (AFDC). She has lived in Vaughn for most of her adult life with her two sons. Troy's twenty-five-year-old brother also went to Vashon until he dropped out. Troy's mother said that she was aware of the inter-district transfer plan; she heard about it on television, received information in the mail, and has friends whose children participate in the program. But when we asked if she ever had considered sending Troy to a county school, she turned toward her younger son, who was watching television on the other side of the room, and called out, "Did you ever want to go to a county school?"

Troy, without removing his eyes from the twenty-inch television screen, uttered an unenthusiastic no. His mother smiled, seemingly relieved by his answer, and then explained: "He is mostly conservative and all to himself. . . . You see those boys down there shooting dice and stuff, he don't even mess with the kids around here. And I am so blessed that he is like that. He doesn't smoke, he doesn't drink—nothing. He gets up and goes to school every morning—I don't even have to wake him up. He washes and irons his own clothes. He knows how to cook and everything. I am so blessed and thank the lord that he don't fool, that he's not bad or nothing, you know."

That Troy's mother is thankful that her son takes care of himself and makes his own decisions says something about her belief in her ability to help him make those decisions. And in saying that she is blessed to have such a good son she appears to take little credit for having raised him that way. The powerlessness that pervades her life—her inability to find a job or afford an apartment outside the decrepit project—no doubt affects her relationship with her sons.

Despite Troy's supposed ability and willingness to clean up after himself, the main room of the apartment, which serves as the dining and living rooms and opens into a tiny kitchen, was in disarray. Dirty dishes overflowed from the sink and covered an already cluttered coffee table. Clothes were strewn across the furniture and on the floor. And as if to block out the world beyond, drab green curtains remained drawn even on a sunny Saturday morning. The dark room was bathed in the fluttering light projected from the television screen.

Troy's mother went on to cite several aspects of Vashon High School that she disliked. She said, for instance, that she wished Vashon had a technical education program, like the one at the city's now-defunct vocational high school, which she attended, to prepare Troy for a job. Yet as we discussed in Chapter 3, the district court judge ordered all vocational education removed from the St. Louis public schools because of mismanagement and the ineffectiveness of those programs.

Troy's mother said she had not discussed with Troy or anyone else the impact of the desegregation plan on the city schools, but she said she knew that all the vocational education programs were gone. With all of those programs shipped out to the county schools, students who attend an all-black city high school are being prepared for neither work nor college. Meanwhile, Troy's mother has heard from relatives and friends with children in county schools that "some of those schools have better opportunities, and they offer classes in the career that they [the students] are striving for."

She also worries about gangs and weapons in Vashon. "It's not too safe. 'Cause nowadays they have guns and stuff," she said, adding that she wished the school would install metal detectors, which it finally did during the 1994–95 school year (Little, 1994c). Troy's mother noted that many black parents transfer their children to suburban schools because "they don't want their kids to be around a lot of fighting, you know, stuff like that." She told us about her cousin's son, who "had too much fighting or something" in his city school, so his mother put him in a county school, which he liked. "So that's where he graduated from. . . . It was way out." She turned toward Troy again and yelled so as to be heard above the television: "Do you remember the school that Manny went to?" No response.

In terms of how black students are treated in the county schools, Troy's mother said she had only heard of a "little prejudice—favoritism and stuff like that—you know. . . . I guess if they wanted to get on the football team or something like that they couldn't get on." The small irony behind this statement is that Troy had told us, in a separate interview, that he had tried out for the football team at Vashon two years in a row but was not picked for the squad. He accused the coach of having favorites but would not explain who the favorites were. Yet another student we interviewed who is currently enrolled in Vashon—a return student—told us that the football and basketball coaches at the school discriminate against students who live in the housing projects. He said that unless they are clearly outstanding players, boys who live in the Vaughn and other nearby projects are less likely to get on the popular teams at Vashon.

When we visited Troy and his mother, he was nineteen years old and still had a year and a half of course work to complete before graduating. While Troy's mother said that the teachers at Vashon are okay and that she likes the fact that Troy takes care of himself and makes his own school choice, she and her son are not the type of educational consumers who will force schools to improve through their choices. The lack of vocational education courses, the perceived need for metal detectors, the favoritism of the coaches, and so forth are all aspects of Vashon that either Troy or his mother would like to change. Yet they remain the silent consumers who do not consider the other educational options.

Salina's Grandmother

Salina, like Troy, was nineteen years old and in the eleventh grade when we visited. She lives with her grandmother, a diabetic woman in her late sixties who is raising five of her nineteen grandchildren. Salina never talked with her grandmother about transferring to a county school, although she said she thought about going to one of the suburban high schools when she was a freshman. When we asked her grandmother whether she had ever considered sending Salina to a suburban school, she replied, "Well, I haven't gotten around to that yet because all my kids went to Sumner and Turner Middle School [the neighborhood schools]. I like the idea that she's close . . . and she never said anything about it."

Interestingly enough, because Sumner High School was undergoing capital improvement renovations at the time we interviewed Salina's grandmother, students who attended Sumner were being bused to another high school about four and half miles away. Thus, Salina was leaving home at 6:30 each morning to catch a bus to her "neighborhood" high school. This was half an hour earlier than her neighbor, who attended a county school far away, had to be at his bus stop.

Salina, her grandmother, and four cousins live on the second floor of a two-family home. The grandmother, who recently suffered a heart attack, said she does not leave her home very often because the only entrance or exit to the apartment is a steep, dark, and narrow stairway leading from the front door. The two-bedroom apartment is crammed full; two of the grandchildren use the living room as their bedroom, thus twin beds with slipcovers serve as couches during the day. It is dark and dreary inside, as the windows are small and opaque.

In the middle of a weekday morning, sixteen-year-old Thomas, one of Salina's cousins, saunters from room to room. He hasn't been to school since his father was arrested for armed robbery and murder in the holdup of a local supermarket. The grandmother explained that Thomas is "just kind of waiting for the trial." Meanwhile, he has been in trouble himself with the police for a few minor offenses. "That's because he was being with other bad kids; he was just trying to do what they do. Now his mother has got him down here with me."

Another of the grandmother's children is in a mental hospital, and a third, Salina's mother, died when Salina was a baby. The grandmother sighed heavily and shook her head in embarrassment about her lack of knowledge of the transfer program and the county schools. "I don't know what to think," she said. "I haven't been keeping up with the schools and things." She said that the information on the transfer program comes in the mail, "but I never read it."

Her own education ended in the eighth grade in an all-black school in Arkansas. Sumner High School symbolizes the prosperity and upward mobility that she and her family moved to St. Louis fifty years ago to find. Sumner, the school that all five of her own children attended, still holds a warm spot in her heart. Her favorite aspect of Sumner is that "it's been here so long." And, she added, "I know all the teachers." But since she had her heart attack, she has been "real sick" and has not been going to parent conferences or any other events or meetings at the school. Despite her detachment from Sumner and the educational system, Salina's grandmother said she thought the school had changed: "It used to be real nice, but from 1975, it's gone downhill—ooooh, the fights. Just so many fights over there."

Salina's grandmother is one of what Hirschman (1970) calls the loyalists: "Those who stay [with an organization] out of 'loyalty' that is, in a less rational, though far from wholly irrational, fashion. Many of these 'loyalists' will actively participate in action designed to change [the organization's] policies and practices, but some may simply refuse to exit and suffer in silence, confident that things will soon get better."

Manny's Father

Manny and his parents live a few blocks from Salina and her grandmother in a similar brick two-family home with a large front porch. Manny lives with his mother upstairs, and his father lives in the downstairs flat. Although Manny's parents have split up, they cannot afford a formal divorce or the cost of two separate residences.

Manny, like Salina, attends Sumner, his neighborhood school; at nineteen he is also overage for his class. Although the St. Louis public schools' records show that he was a junior, he told us that he was a senior. He is the youngest of five children; his two older brothers attended city public schools, and his two older sisters attended Catholic schools. Manny was the only child living at home at the time of our visit, and he seemed to drift between the upstairs, where his mother was bedridden, and the downstairs, where his father spent much of his time on the porch with friends and neighbors. Because Manny's mother was very sick, we interviewed the father about Manny's choice of a city school.

Manny's father, a retired security guard in his early sixties, moved to St. Louis from the rural South when he was a young man. Like Salina's grandmother, he never went to high school, and he attended grammar school in Arkansas only when it rained and he could not be out working in the fields with his father, a sharecropper. "That's why I was so serious about my family's education," he said. St. Louis and its once-prominent Sumner High School were symbols of a promised land for him and his family. But times have changed, said Manny's father, and the city schools have not kept pace. Thus, he said he likes the idea of the urban-suburban student transfer program because the "world is integrated . . . and the city has not done a lot of improvements to their schools. . . . The city is behind. The county is more advanced."

Manny's father said he is "very aware" of the city-to-county transfer program because he "pays close attention to education," and he read about the program in the newspaper. And yet when asked what he likes most about Sumner High School, which is only half a mile from his doorstep, he said, "I don't know a heck of a lot about it." He also told us that the decision for Manny to stay in his neighborhood was made entirely by his son and that they did not discuss it. According to the father, "He never obeyed my rules and regulations. . . . He doesn't respect me, so we never discussed it. He never said he wanted to go to a county school."

It turns out that Manny was attending Sumner after leaving one of the city's magnet schools, where he went for ninth grade and most of tenth grade. Manny said that he left the magnet school because he didn't really like it, but his father said that Manny was "terminated" from the magnet, which had a junior Reserve Officer Training Corps (ROTC) theme and focus. Manny's father called the ROTC program "tremendous" and said that had Manny not been kicked out for misbehaving he would have graduated from high school already. "He wouldn't wake up; he should have graduated last June," said Manny's father.

The lack of parental control over the school choice process—and indeed over the lives of their children altogether—exemplified in this response is the rule among city parents. Two of these parents said that they had strongly disagreed with their child's decision to attend a city high school but had not done anything about it. For instance, Chandra's mother said, "I thought about sending them [to a county school] when they were in grade school, but they never wanted to go, so I didn't send them. . . . Instead of forcing my children to go to a county school, I said, 'If you want to go, go. If you don't want to, then stay.'"

Then, as if in direct contradiction to her initial desire to send her children to suburban schools, Chandra's mother stated that she disagrees with her daughter-in-law, who sends one of her sons to a county school because she believes he will get a better education there. Later Chandra's mother said, "I don't even know anything about the county schools."

Casey's mother told us that she thought about sending her son to a county school, "and he wanted to go too—thought he could do better. But then he never said anything more, and I didn't pressure him." Casey is the youngest of her fourteen children, and until the time of our interview with her she had assumed that he was enrolling in a county school for the following fall. This was not so, according to Casey, because by the time he got around to turning in the application to transfer he was already eighteen and almost a senior at his neighborhood high school. The county schools generally do not accept city students who want to transfer in their last two years of high school.

Despite this lack of parental involvement in their children's educational decisions, city parents are far from pleased with the all-black neighborhood schools their children attend. Nine of the eleven city parents interviewed had little positive to say about their child's high school. When asked what they liked most about these all-black schools, most of the parents cited familiarity and proximity factors ("It's close to home," "She just walks from here to school," "I like that I know everybody") instead of school quality factors.

The strongest critique of the city schools came from Kally's stepmother, who said that Northwest High School had done nothing for her mentally handicapped stepdaughter. "I don't like it at all," she said, adding that she would send Kally to a county school if there were a program there for handicapped students, but "I can't find it."

In fact, the transfer program does allow handicapped students to attend special education courses in the county. Meanwhile, Kally's stepmother's relentless condemnation of the city schools—"No one wants their children to go to city schools," and so on—conflicts with her decision to send her own six-year-old son (Kally's half brother), who is not handicapped, to the neighborhood city school.

The stepmother, who was pregnant with her second child at the time of the interview, was most concerned that eighteen-year-old Kally, who suffers from fetal alcohol poisoning, will never be self-sufficient. "She can't do the time, she can't count," the stepmother said, and her reading is on the first- or second-grade level.

"The teachers don't really care about the pupils," she said. Yet, sadly enough, one gets the impression that Kally, with her clubbed fingers and shrunken body (defects related to fetal alcohol poisoning), has no one to serve as her advocate. According to the stepmother, Kally's father works most evenings, and with the new baby due any day, the amount of time the stepmother can spend with Kally is even more limited. She also said that she worries about what will happen when her own son surpasses Kally in reading and other intellectual capabilities. "When I was 18, I wasn't at home anymore. . . . She should get out and get a job. I want her to be able to learn how to read so she could learn how to drive . . . because I am not going to do for her for the rest of her life. I have two of my own. She's grown."

Although Kally's stepmother criticized the educators in the St. Louis public schools, many of the parents we spoke to focused on the students and their behavior, not on the teachers, principals, or politicians who run them. For instance, most of the parents who stated strong dislikes of their neighborhood high school blamed the behavior of the students—"Nothing wrong with the school; kids just don't take the opportunity to learn" and "There are so many fights over there." Only two parents offered any critique of the educators and academic programs and the way that the schools are run: Kally's stepmother and Troy's mother, who bemoans the lack of vocational education.

The most positive reviews of the educators in the city schools came from two mothers with little in common except that they both live in the middle-class neighborhood. Leo's mother, a teacher at Northwest High School, where her son was enrolled, is definitely the most knowledgeable and informed of the city parents we met. She knows first-hand about the transfer program and its effect on the city schools. She is a thin, energetic woman with a strong opinion about the importance of neighborhood schools. What she liked most about Northwest High School is that it was right down the street from her house and that she knew all of the students and they knew her. She also stated that the teachers in the city schools are far more concerned about the well-being and success of black students than are teachers in the county schools. And while she is angry with the St. Louis Board of Education for not providing the all-black schools with the resources that the magnet schools have, it is her strong distrust of the mostly white teachers in the suburban schools that fuels her objection to the inter-district transfer plan.

The other parent with something positive to say about her daughter's city high school is Venicia's mother, who rated Northwest as "pretty fair" and said that the "learning skills are good there." Venicia's mother, who grew up in the rural South and did not attend high school, works in a local bread factory. She allowed her daughter to choose her own high school and reported that she never discussed the decision with her. "It ain't really never came up." She has a cousin who sends her daughter to a county school and reports that the suburban schools are better, "that some of the things they have in the county they don't have in the city." Despite this feedback, Venicia's mother stated that the city schools have everything they are supposed to have, except computers. In the next breath she emphasizes the importance of computer training for young people: "Within the next two years that's what they are going to be graded on—computers."

The city parents' sometimes contradictory responses to questions of likes and dislikes about the city schools and the lack of involvement in their children's choice of schools suggest a high level of alienation or powerlessness, which Seeman (1959, 1972) has described as the "expectancy or probability held by an individual that his own behavior cannot determine the occurrence of the outcomes, or reinforcements, he seeks" (1959; p. 784). Like West's (1993b) more recent conception of nihilism in the isolated inner-city neighborhoods, notions of alienation and powerlessness help to explain why city parents, with the exception of Leo's mother, do not view themselves as important actors in shaping the educational outcomes of their children.

Expressions of these parents' beliefs in their own powerlessness are sprinkled throughout their responses to questions concerning the city's schools and their children's education: "I don't know a heck of a lot about it," "I don't know what to say; I can't think about it," "I don't know; I can't speak to that." These are juxtaposed with several positive comments that these parents have heard about the county schools from parents who send their children there: "Better curriculum and more attention," "Children learn more and better in the county than in the city," and "They don't want their kids to be around a lot of fighting." Only two city parents—Chandra's mother and Leo's mother—even suggested that such positive appraisals of the county schools are false or exaggerated. When asked how the city schools compare to the county schools, seven of the eleven city parents stated that they did not know enough about the county schools to draw a comparison.

Another example of the level of alienation experienced by these parents is their eager adoption of a can-achieve-anywhere philosophy—the notion that the particular school does not matter and that academic success is entirely up to the student. Seven of the city parents we interviewed expressed some form of this philosophy, which helps to explain their lack of involvement in the school-choice process and their lack of information about the transfer program: "If the child wants to learn he can do it anywhere," "It's up to the child, not the school," and "I left it up to her to succeed. . . . [She] can achieve in city schools as well as county."

While this ideology is supposed to motivate children to try harder in school, it also allows parents to absolve themselves of the weighty responsibility of helping their son or daughter choose the "best" school. The process of gathering information, evaluating one school against another, and making an active decision about the educational options available is one that these parents have not engaged in since the transfer plan created greater school choices for them and their children. Ignoring the transfer program and leaving school choice decisions to their children is one way of dealing with the feeling of powerlessness. Except for Leo's mother, who is determined that her son will not be subjected to the racism and unfair treatment that she is certain exists in the suburban schools, these parents are too beat down to take an active stance. Meanwhile, their children are choosing to remain in the schools in which they feel most comfortable and familiar.

Another sign of the city parents' powerlessness and seeming helplessness is found in their responses to questions concerning their expectations for their children. For instance, when asked what they would like for their son or daughter to be doing in five years, four parents stated that they either "didn't know" or would leave that entirely up to the student to decide—"I can't pick for her." Three additional parents gave such general answers as "Working— on her own," "See him stand on his own two feet," and "To be an upstanding young man—get ahead."

The remaining parents were slightly more specific, with all four speaking of college. Leo's mother stated that she "knew" what her son would be doing in five years: "He will be graduating from college with an engineering degree." Chandra's mother said that she hopes her daughter will be "coming out of college." Casey's mother said her son will need to go into the service to "get that college" because she cannot afford to send him. And Erin's father wanted his daughter to be finished with college and "on her own" in five years.

Yet when asked whether their child's city high school was preparing their son or daughter for that future, only two of the parents—Venicia's mother and Erin's father—answered with an affirmative yes. Troy's mother said, "Yeah, they have nice teachers." Six parents said, "I think so," "I don't know," "It's hard to tell," or "I can't answer that." Leo's mother and Kally's stepmother said that the city high school was not preparing their son or daughter for the future. Leo's mother said that she and her husband were paying to send their son to a special blueprint class because it was not offered at his school. According to her, Northwest High School is not preparing Leo for his career as an engineer, "his parents are."

City Parents and Racial Attitudes

Related to the powerlessness expressed by the city parents were their racial attitudes, reflected in their opinions of city-versus-county schools. Many of these parents told us they thought mostly white schools are better than all-black schools and that white students are generally smarter than black students. School desegregation is a good thing, according to these parents, but it will work only for the very "smart" black students. For the rest of the African-American students the city schools are perceived to be good enough.

Salina's grandmother said she worries about what will happen to Salina, who has been classified as a high school junior for three years in a row and is receiving no guidance from the school about her future. Meanwhile, one of her daughters sends her son, Salina's cousin, to a county school because "he's real smart." The grandmother says he likes the county school and has excelled there academically and athletically. When asked whether she thought it was better for African-American students from the city to attend county schools, she nodded. "I just think it's not as loud in the county schools—it's more like Catholic schools. There's more time for learning." But for Salina, who loves babies and likes to take care of them at her church each Sunday, the grandmother never considered a county school—"Never thought about it," she said, "because of her not being real smart."

Manny's father expressed a similar sentiment toward the county schools and his son's ability to succeed there. He said he would not have dared send Manny to a county school because his grades in the city schools were not strong enough. He also said that Sumner High School would be a lot better if it were "mixed" or integrated. He said that is why he sent two of his children to private schools when they were younger: "The teachers were Caucasian and the board was mixed." He adds that "most Caucasian people I have been around are very serious about family," and he wishes more blacks were that way.

This deprecation of their own children or grandchildren and of blacks in general is also accounted for in research on poor people and members of oppressed racial groups; it is a perspective that grows out of years of being treated as the other or as less than wealthier people or members of higher-status racial or religious groups (see, for instance, Bourdieu and Passeron, 1979, and West, 1993c). In other words, this deprecation is part of the self-fulfilling prophecy of racial prejudice, which indicates that blacks have been told overtly and covertly for so many years that they are inferior to whites that some have come to believe it and even accommodate society's expectations by playing the part (Snyder, 1988).

When asked about the benefits of an all-black school, seven of the city parents said that they either did not know or did not think there would be any benefits. "It's just a school," said Venicia's mother. "All black, that's about the size of it," said Manny's father. Mildly positive reactions came from Casey's mother, who said that being in an all-black school could keep her son out of trouble, and Paulette's mother, who said that the benefit of an all-black school is that her daughter is "adjusted to her color, her race." Yet when asked about the benefits of an integrated school, Paulette's mother said her daughter "would learn to adjust herself to black and white." A cost-benefit analysis of an all-black versus an integrated school and the ramifications of each choice had clearly not been conducted by any of the city parents except Leo's mother.

As the one parent who stands out from the rest when it comes to the impact of racial attitudes on school choices, Leo's mother maintains a firm separatist attitude that reflects her resistance to African-American assimilation into a white world. The benefit of an all-black school, she states emphatically, is that "my baby will know who he is." She adds that black people are "crazy to ship" their children out to the county. "Black folk used to get educated in a dark shack. Why do they have to sit next to white folk to get an education? . . . Many of the people who moved out there [to the county] did so because they did not want to live next to blacks." Why, Leo's mother wants to know, would black parents send their children out to schools full of white students whose parents fled the city and the African Americans who live there. "If this were true integration," she adds, "for every black student who goes out there [to a suburban school], they should have a white student come in here."

Because she taught at Northwest High School, Leo's mother was fully aware of the school's shortcomings. Yet, instead of blaming the black students for the decline of the city schools, she faults the racial politics of the St. Louis Board of Education for allowing the county schools and the city's magnet schools to cream off the best students or those with the most involved parents, leaving the all-black schools on the city's north side with few resources and many of the hardest to educate students. "All of the problems I have with this school are the result of Board of Ed policy." She noted, for instance, that many of the long fluorescent light bulbs in her classroom were burned out for as long as five years before she got them changed. The Board of Education has hired only twelve electricians to service the more than 100 school buildings in the district. "The all-black schools are deliberately allowed to fall down while the magnet schools look gorgeous," she said. Leo's mother has a clear vision of the causes of decline in the black community: racial discrimination and the politics that endorse it.

CITY STUDENTS: COMFORT AND HOPELESSNESS

The city students, while perhaps not as shy as their parents, were more defensive than either the transfer or return students when talking to a white interviewer about their neighborhood high school and the transfer program. This is probably to be expected in a discussion of black versus predominantly white schools between a white researcher and black students who chose to remain in all-black schools, but some of these students appeared very uneasy and uncertain. Others seemed swallowed up in hopelessness. They, like many of their parents, argued that it didn't really matter where they went to school. Yet what is most striking about the city students and their discussions of why they choose to stay in their neighborhood schools is the degree to which they are attracted to that which is familiar and comfortable.

Erin

In one of the least dismal sections of the low-income community surrounding Vashon High School, Erin lives in a small, dilapidated single-family house with her father, stepmother, six stepbrothers and sisters, and twenty-year-old brother. The stepsiblings range in age from seven to sixteen, and Erin, who is seventeen, is burdened with many of the parenting responsibilities for these children.

On our weekday afternoon visit, the tiny living room, which serves more as a roadway between the kitchen and the flimsy screen door at the front of the house than as a place to sit and talk, was in constant turmoil as Erin's stepsiblings ran through, sending the screen door banging. The furniture in the cramped room was springless and threadbare. Erin's thin and timid father, who works at night as a machine operator at an electric company, was dozing on one of the couches.

Erin, meanwhile, was excited to have visitors and eager to talk about her experiences at Vashon. Despite her warmth and friendliness, Erin is not bold or outgoing. She exudes a strong desire to fit in, to follow but not to lead. She said that her favorite aspect of her high school is that she "knows a lot of people up there ... and I don't feel lost." She said that she never considered transferring to a county school, and when asked why not, she replied, "Well, first, with the school I go to, it's a lot of people I know." Her second reason for not transferring is that she hears "about all the accidents they have with the busing."

Erin knows several black students who have transferred to county schools; in fact, she rattled off the names of three friends and a cousin who attend suburban schools. And when asked if she thought they are doing the right thing, she said, "I don't think there is a right or wrong." But Erin has heard of black students being treated differently from white students in the county schools. One of her friends told her that "there is prejudice out there. Several incidents like that happened to her out there."

Still, Erin knows that life at Vashon High School is not easy. Both she and her father spoke of the "rowdiness" among gang members there. And when asked whether she thinks the transfer plan is a good idea, Erin said yes, because maybe the black students from the city who go to the county are "more comfortable" being out there because they think city schools are "too rowdy." Her immediate response to the question of how her school would be different if there weren't a transfer program and all the black students who attend county schools from her neighborhood would return to Vashon was that "there would be more trouble—more gangs."

When asked what she liked the least about Vashon, she said the crowded lunch room, which is on the fifth floor and takes too long to get to. She also noted, as did other Vashon students, that students who are on the basketball team are favored. "They're easy on the basketball team." This is, after all, the high school with a state championship basketball team. Only when asked direct questions concerning her courses or plans for postsecondary education did Erin mention academics. She was less than enthusiastic about a special internship program in which she was selected to participate during her upcoming senior year because it would take her away from the campus and her friends for half of each school day to do clerical work in a downtown corporation. Luckily, she said, the program allows her to miss work for such school events as Colors Day, when the seniors dress up and "you vote for the best couple, class clown, best dressed, athletes, and stuff."

The social construct of the school and the adolescent society—with its own definition of success and failure (see Coleman, 1961, and Peshkin, 1991)—are paramount to Erin's school preferences. It is clear that in her school choice, Erin's strong desire to fit in and be well liked superseded any objective school quality characteristics, such as the courses offered or number of graduates who get into colleges and receive scholarships.

The strong social attachment to the neighborhood schools that Erin and other students cited as their primary reason for not transferring to a suburban school also showed up in the attitudinal survey of African-American students in St. Louis conducted by Lissitz (1994). The survey shows that elementary and tenth-grade students enrolled in the nonintegrated or all-black schools were much more likely to agree with the statement that "old friends are better than new ones" than were same-grade students who attended magnet schools or those who transferred to suburban schools.

Furthermore, in a focus group study of student and parent perceptions of the inter-district transfer program, researchers at the University of Missouri–St. Louis (Public Policy Research Centers, 1993c) found that African-American high school students who remain in city schools talked about their strong social attachment to their schools and teachers and a desire to stay in their own neighborhood. Despite this attachment, these students also expressed fear of violence in city schools. One student stated, "Whether it be in school, it could be after school, on the school premises, there's always going to be a fight somewhere. If you get stabbed, then you get stabbed. You go home, recuperate, and you come back to school" (p. 30).

Although Erin became defensive during the interview when she was asked several questions about her knowledge of the transfer program and the students who participate in it, she did not defend her decision to remain in a city school on the basis of the academic quality of Vashon or the opportunities that could arise as a result of her attendance there. Her father, meanwhile, stated that he had left the school choice up to Erin: "It's her decision where she wants to go," he said.

Venicia

Venicia, one of the most assertive of the city students we interviewed, saw her decision to stay in a city school as more or less a nondecision—the result of difficult circumstances and missed opportunities. She had a baby at age seventeen, and now as a nineteen-year-old high school junior, she reflected back on the time when she almost went to a county school. Although Venicia, her mother, three brothers, two nieces, two nephews, and her own eighteen-month-old daughter live in a middle-class neighborhood, their living conditions and the mother's employment status as a bun bagger in the bread factory are somewhat below the neighborhood average.

Their single-family home, while in far better condition than most of those in the working-class or low-income neighborhoods, was in serious need of paint and repairs. The spacious living room off the front porch was only partially furnished, which left plenty of room for the toys belonging to Venicia's nieces, nephews, and daughter, all of whom were younger than five. Venicia's daughter wore her hair neatly braided and fastened with pink and yellow hair clips that matched her jumpsuit. Venicia, meanwhile, wore an old T-shirt and a pair of cut-off sweatpants; her hair was brushed down over one side of her face. She tried to keep her daughter at her side, away from her older and more rambunctious nieces and nephews.

Venicia is a perceptive young woman who seemed slightly frustrated with her situation and prospects for the future. She blamed herself for her mistakes, though she apparently received little guidance from her mother in making important educational and life decisions. When asked if she had ever spoken to her mother about remaining in nearby Northwest High School as opposed to transferring to the suburbs, Venicia stated that her mother wanted her to go to a county school, "but she knew I didn't want to go that far." She then went on to explain about the negative peer pressure at Northwest: "There are a lot of problems—not the teachers, just the environment, the people I hung out with . . . all of my friends. I wanted to impress them and I got into a lot of trouble."

But Venicia said she occasionally was able to escape this peer pressure at Northwest because she was on the pompon squad and had practice every day after school. "My friends would get mad because I didn't want to skip practice to fight or whatever," she said. Yet the paradox of Venicia's story is that the one activity that kept her out of trouble in her neighborhood high school became one of the overriding factors that prevented her from transferring to a county school, which she said would have allowed her to escape the peer pressure completely. "I was thinking of going to Pattonville [one of the suburban high schools], but I just never made it out there. I didn't go. I don't know why. . . . I didn't want to leave the pom squad. . . . I didn't want to go that far," she said.

The peer pressure that Venicia faced is symbolic of a form of resistance to academic achievement that other studies of African-American students have found (see Fordham, 1988, and Fordham and Ogbu, 1986). This research argues that because African-American students are aware that educational attainment is not easily translated into well-paying employment, they shun the "achievement ideology," or the idea that those who work hard and achieve in school will be rewarded with good jobs and a bright future. Fordham and Ogbu have both argued that many African-American students do not believe that this ideology works for people of color and thus they say that black students who achieve in school are "acting white" by buying into an achievement ideology that will not work for them. But there is evidence from our interviews and the Lissitz (1994) survey that the degree of resistance toward the achievement ideology varies with the type of high school the students were attending—all-black, magnet, or suburban—and with their reasons for attending these schools. Lissitz found that those students attending the all-black city high schools are more likely to agree with the statements that students who appear smart and those who do well on their homework assignments are more likely to be disliked by other students. Certainly there are many black students in city schools, such as Venicia, who do not buy into the "acting white" critique of academic achievement, just as there are some black students in the county schools who do, but the students in the city talk a great deal about classmates who have given up on the educational system and the American Dream.

For instance, the city students who stated what they dislike about their high schools were focused on factors that make their daily school experience less pleasant, especially the actions of their fellow students. Three students—Venicia, Kally, and Paulette, all of whom attended Northwest High School and live in the same middle-class neighborhood—cited the fighting and the juvenile behavior of students as the aspect they disliked the most about their school. "They act like they was eleven years old," said Paulette of her classmates. Several city students mentioned that the students at their schools do not respect the teachers.

Still, students such as Venicia defend their decisions not to transfer with the can-achieve-anywhere philosophy voiced by many of the city parents. "There are a lot of honors students at Northwest; if you want to learn—you got the ability, you will," she said. Yet when asked why some black students from the city choose to transfer to county schools, Venicia explained, "Maybe it's more advanced to them than the public [city] schools. Maybe they think there are more computers or they can learn a little more . . . , maybe they don't think the public school teachers will teach them enough. . . . I wouldn't want to teach them either."

The sad ending to Venicia's school choice story is that she eventually had to quit the pompon squad when she became pregnant, but she said she no longer hangs around with the group of friends who used to get her in trouble. When we interviewed her she was hoping to transfer to O'Fallon Technical High School, the city's last vocational school—the one that the district court judge would order closed only a few months later. "It didn't really matter where I went," said Venicia, who would like to go into cosmetology and maybe open her own salon someday. Still, she said she does not "really want to do hair or nails all my life, it's just something to fall back on."

Erin's emphasis on fitting in and feeling accepted in her school and Venicia's lack of an explanation for the choices she had made sum up the majority of reasons city students give for staying in their neighborhood high school. Of the twelve responses to what students like most about their city high schools, nine clearly have nothing to do with learning, the quality of the school, or the long-term goals of the students. Dominating the list of things that students like most about their high schools are "comfort factors"—those having to do with their familiarity with students or teachers, tradition and pride associated with certain extracurricular activities, or closeness to home. This seems slightly contradictory given that many of these students were also disillusioned with several aspects of their schools' environment. These students, like their parents, strongly resemble Hirschman's (1970) loyalists: "Loyalist behavior . . . can be understood in terms of a generalized concept of penalty for exit. The penalty may be directly imposed, but in most cases it is internalized. The individual feels that leaving a certain group carries a high price with it, even though no specific sanction is imposed by the group. In both cases, the decision to remain a member and not exit in the face of a superior alternative would thus appear to follow from a perfectly rational balancing act of prospective private benefits against private costs" (p. 98).

Only two of the students—Angie and Gwenn, both from the lowest-income neighborhood and both students at Vashon—related their decision to remain in city schools to issues of school quality or achievement. Angie noted that before she went to high school, people would put down Vashon and say that bad things happened there. But, she said, "it's not that bad." She went on to explain that while she greatly dislikes several aspects of Vashon—"that the students don't respect the teachers or the school, and they smoke reefer, and [that] there were all kinds of gangs bringing trouble and having shoot-ups"— she feels that the school is helping her learn. As long as it helps her get an education, she said, she will continue to go there.

Gwenn, whose family moved to St. Louis from Arkansas when she was in eighth grade, said that what she liked most about Vashon was that the teachers "want to see us make it somewhere when we get out of high school. They care about us." Later in the interview, however, Gwenn told us that she would prefer a county high school to Vashon because a county school "has more privileges and you get more out of it. County school requires a lot."

The University of Missouri–St. Louis focus group study (Public Policy Research Centers, 1993a) found that students in the city schools had "great affection for their teachers." Only two city students we interviewed had complaints about the educators at their schools. Leo, the son of the math teacher at Northwest, said that the "teachers aren't always doing what they should. They don't always spend enough time with the students." Chandra, who said she was going to transfer from Sumner High School to the Health Careers Magnet School when we interviewed her, told us that what she liked least about Sumner was that the counselors are "too slow" to help students plan their high school program and their postsecondary school options.

Still, "school environment" issues dominated city students' evaluations of their high schools. And not surprisingly, these same environmental or comfort factors appear to strongly shape their perceptions of the schools they did not choose and their reasons for not choosing them. We could see this when we asked city students whether they ever had considered attending a county school and, if so, why they did not transfer. Several students gave more than one answer; some gave rambling answers that were scattered throughout responses to other questions. This lack of coherence suggests that remaining in an all-black neighborhood school was for many city students less a conscious decision than a subconscious avoidance. Only Leo and Paulette defended their choice to remain in a city school by insisting that the quality of the education in their school is comparable to that of a county school.

Four of the city students' responses were laden with insecurity and fear of the unknown: Chandra said she did not want to meet new people; Manny said he did not want to go far away from the city to school; Salina told us she worried about not understanding what is *not* [emphasis added] taught in county schools; and Erin said she wanted to stay where "I know a lot of people." None of these students discussed his or her decision to remain in a city school in terms of the academic opportunities in either the city or county schools. Again, the comfort of the familiar was a deciding factor in the school choices of many city students.

Meanwhile, Venicia, Kally, Angie, and Casey all said that they once had been interested in attending a county school, but in each case, intervening circumstances, such as lack of parental involvement, prevented them from transferring. During their interviews each of these students, with the exception of Kally, tried to down play any differences between city and county schools by stating that the school does not matter, that students' ability and desire is what is important. In fact, the most often stated response by city students to any question concerning the comparison between city and county schools is one that reflects this "learn anywhere" attitude that schools don't matter.

Six of the city students, including three from the low-income neighborhood, referred to such a belief during their interviews. According to Erin, there is no difference between the city and the county schools: "If you're going to learn something, you do your best anywhere you go." Paulette, who lives in the more middle-class neighborhood and attends Northwest, told us that her next-door neighbors attend county schools because their mother did not want them to go to a city school. "She thinks the county schools are better than the city schools as far as teaching. I don't think that is true because a teacher is a teacher. . . . You have to want to learn, then you're gonna learn. It doesn't matter who might be teaching."

In the focus group study (Public Policy Research Centers, 1993c) of students enrolled in city schools, the researchers found students saying similar things. For instance, one student stated, "I think it's the person. If you want to go to school and become somebody, you can, no matter what school you go to" (p. 31).

This attitude relates to what Jay MacLeod (1995) found in his study of "the Brothers," a group of African-American boys growing up in a low-income housing project. These students had internalized an achievement ideology and had come to blame themselves—not the larger, white-dominated society that affords them fewer opportunities—for their failures in school and eventually in the job market.

In terms of their own career expectations, city students tended to respond to the question of what they would like to be doing in five years with vague, wishful answers. Seven of the twelve city students stated things that they "hoped," "wished," or "probably" thought they could be doing in five years.

Six said they would be in a school of some sort in five years, with five of these students stating that they would be in college. Of the six who did not want to be in school five years after the interview, two of them—Venicia and Angie—said they wanted to be cosmetologists; Manny said he would be in the Navy; Troy said he would be "working—fixing or building things"; Chandra said she wanted to be a pediatrician "doctoring someone's baby"; and Salina said her goal was "to have ten kids."

Troy said that after high school he would like to work in construction or electrical appliance repair. He said he has had one course at Vashon, metal matching, that will help prepare him for that future. When asked whether he planned to attend a trade school or community college to receive additional training, he said, "I don't think of nothing like that." Troy said he has met with his high school counselor but that he did not speak with her about his goals:

> *Troy:* I be laughing at her because of the questions she'd be asking.
> *Q:* Like what?
> *Troy:* Like she say would I like to do that, and I'd say no; she say why, why, why I be saying no to everything?
> *Q:* What kind of things was she asking you if you wanted to do?
> *Troy:* I don't remember that.
> *Q:* Did you tell her you wanted to be a carpenter?
> *Troy:* I don't stay in there long. I just talk to her and then I leave.

Most of the city students' long-term goals followed logically from their five-year goals, except for Chandra, who hopes to be a doctor in five years, and Salina, who wants to have ten kids and wants a "good job," a house, no husband, and to go to college. With two pediatricians, two engineers, two cosmetologists, a mechanic, and an electrician, these city students cover a wide range of anticipated careers. Still, while they appear to maintain fairly high expectations for themselves, they have less information than do students in the other two groups about how they receive the training and credentials they need to reach these goals. Furthermore, comparisons of test score data demonstrate that the students who remain in the nonintegrated, all-black schools have, in general, the lowest achievement levels of all the groups of black students examined—those in magnet, city, and county schools (Lissitz, 1994). During the 1992–93 school year, students enrolled in Vashon High School did extremely poorly on the Missouri Mastery Achievement Tests. In mathematics, for instance, Vashon students had on average mastered only 7 percent of the math skills; the state average was 47 percent (Little and Todd, 1994).

City Students and Racial Attitudes

Leo, like his mother, stands out among the city students for his black separatist attitude. His assertion that the county schools are just taking city students to "tear them down" and "keep people under control" poignantly expressed his views on white dominance in American society. In fact, Leo's critique of black-white relations—a separatist ideology that strongly resembles that of his mother—shapes his perspective of the transfer program. When asked what he thinks of black students who go to county schools, he said that the transfer students are "confused. . . . They let themselves be programmed by people."

Meanwhile, most of the city students we interviewed said that black students who want to go to county schools are doing the right thing by transferring. "I have no disagreement with kids who go to the county," said Salina. "They should have the freedom to go wherever they want to." Other responses to the question of whether transfer students are doing the right thing contained hints of defensiveness and insecurity on the part of city students. "If they think they can handle it, they should go," said Venicia. According to Chandra, "They're just trying to show off. They are not better."

The extent to which racial attitudes and a fear of competing with whites affect the city students' perceptions of comfortable and uncomfortable territory is obvious in Salina's fear of not being able to understand what is *not* taught in a county school. This suggests that she feels less knowledgeable than the mostly white students in county schools. As Bourdieu and Passeron (1979) might posit, Salina fears she does not have the "cultural capital" needed to succeed in an upper-middle-class, predominantly white school.

When asked the more general questions of "What are the benefits of going to an all-black school?" and "What are the benefits of going to an integrated school?" city students revealed their racial attitudes. Seven responded by either criticizing all-black schools or blacks in general:

> *Venicia:* There isn't any benefit—any benefit at all; it's just an all-black school.
> *Kally:* It's good because when they [black students] get around other people—white persons—they pick on white kids. When they get around white persons, they get worse. . . . I'm a good person, the rest are like animals.
> *Chandra:* The teachers teach real well—just students, they don't want to learn—they be carrying on and partying too much.
> *Gwenn:* None. When us black people get together, we don't know how to act. We try to appear more than ourselves when with our own kind.

Only two of the city students had anything remotely positive to say about all-black schools. Leo said that at all-black schools there are fewer problems with racial tension. Manny noted that in all-black schools students have a good chance of getting into a nice college because they have a better opportunities for receiving financial aid. The remaining three city students made rather benign comments about the "benefits" of an all-black school, such as, "It's close to home" and "All-black or all-white, it shouldn't matter."

Furthermore, two of the city students' responses to the question concerning the benefits of going to a racially mixed school indicate a sense of racial inferiority and insecurity. Salina, for instance, said the benefit of going to an integrated school is that "whites are more mature. Black students play in the halls, skip class." Angie stated that she would like to go to a "mixed" school but added, "I don't know how they would react to me."

Meanwhile, four of the city students referred to the importance of integration and improved race relations as a benefit of attending an integrated school:

> *Venicia:* Maybe you could learn more about each other's culture. How they grew up, the things they know—how we grew up, the things we know.
> *Leo:* You learn to relate with other races better.
> *Casey:* Being able to interact with different races and know kids from suburbs.
> *Gwenn:* Be better dealing with many different types of people—that's about it.

These responses to questions pertaining to race and school choice suggest that many of these students who remain in all-black schools buy into the notion that white schools in general are superior to all-black ones. But they have chosen for themselves the schools that are more safe, comfortable, and perhaps less challenging. This finding causes us to wonder whether the level of alienation from the larger, whiter world that was exhibited by their parents has been passed down to the next generation.

Choosing Not To Choose

The evidence cited here paints a portrait of twelve black students who end up in all-black inner-city schools for several reasons that have nothing to do with the quality of education offered. Many are the children of tired, beat down parents who have not actively investigated the educational options. They often come from homes where day-to-day survival taps so much energy that little is left for gathering information on schools of choice. They attend city schools because the schools are close to their homes and host many familiar faces.

In other words, most of these city students attend their neighborhood schools because their parents never said they could not. Their parents, for the most part, do not feel capable of making major educational decisions for their children. And the result is the choice not to choose. When parents left the choice to the students, the students followed the path of least resistance. This is not the story of self-maximizing families who have evaluated their options and their long-term goals and decided that a city school would serve their needs better than a county school. Empowerment did not result from a voluntary transfer plan, because the lack of power that these families experience is embedded in several aspects of their social and economic lives. Offering these students the choice of higher-status schools will not free them from the fear and insecurity they face in a world that places them at the bottom of the social structure.

5

The Upwardly Mobile:
Black Students Who Succeed in the
Suburban Schools

*Merely a concrete test of the underlying principles of the great republic is the Negro
Problem, and the spiritual striving of the freedman's sons is the travail of souls whose
burden is almost beyond the measure of their strength, but who bear the name of an
historic race, in the name of this the land of their fathers' fathers, and in the name of
human opportunity.*
—W. E. B. Du Bois, *The Souls of Black Folk*

On the hot and sticky June morning after his high school graduation, Will
awoke in one of the cramped apartments in the Peabody housing project in
the city of St. Louis—the place he has called home since he was twelve years
old. Outside his window a garbage dump overflowed with beer and wine bottles; crack vials and broken glass littered the sidewalks. Every third or fourth
apartment in the two-story red-brick project was boarded with rotting sheets
of plywood. Half a block up the street is the middle school where Will graduated from the eighth grade. An aging brick fortress with thick bars on the windows and with graffiti-stained steel doors, the school stands between the
project and an unkempt vacant lot.

In the tiny living room of the apartment where Will, his mother, and youngest brother live, a frail window fan blew almost cool air over the faded couch and piles of graduation presents for Will, an aspiring artist. There was a sleek leather portfolio from a group of his former teachers at the middle school. Tubes of acrylic paint and charcoal pencils were from relatives, along with a plastic tube to carry rolled-up sketches. Graduation cards were propped upright on the coffee table amid family photos in silver frames.

Next to the stairway leading up from the door and the dismal scene outside, a wobbly bookshelf prominently displayed the newest, most coveted addition to the family memorabilia: a stiff leatherbound high school diploma. Etched ever so lightly behind Will's name on the diploma was a drawing of his alma mater—a sprawling modern campus stretched out across several bucolic acres of green suburban grass. The drawing of Parkway West Senior High School stood as a symbol of the mid-twentieth-century American Dream: life in suburbia and a good public school.

Will was up relatively early. The party he had gone to the night before was broken up by the police before 1:00 a.m. It was not a rowdy party, according to Will, but the police came because they did not want black students partying in white neighborhoods late at night. "It's like they're saying, 'You know you ain't nothing but a nigger. I don't care if you just got your diploma or not. Get the hell out of this neighborhood.' That's what they're there for—those white cops."

It wasn't the first time Will had felt unwelcome in the suburban neighborhood where he attended high school. There was the mathematics teacher who grabbed him by the arm and shouted, "You're on your way out of here, boy," because he was helping a friend to the nurse's office without a hall pass. There was the history teacher who decided to skip over the units on Africa and Asia so that she could spend three extra weeks covering the Soviet Union. There was the suburban police officer who accused Will and his friend Richie of dealing drugs when they greeted each with a high five and a "brotherly" handshake. They were searched and taken to the office of the assistant principal, who told Will that he should not be upset about the accusation and that he and his friends should watch how they shake hands.

Such occurrences are common in the suburban St. Louis schools that enroll black students from the city. Help from caring, understanding white teachers is also common—and becoming more so. But Will and other transfer students who stick it out until graduation do not endure the long bus rides from places like the Peabody projects to white and wealthy suburbia because they expect everyone there to like them. These students know, better than any group of people in metropolitan America, that taking the giant step over the color line is often painful and lonely. But they are drawn to the suburbs by their long-term goals and dreams of the good life.

The stories of the black inner-city students who succeed academically and socially in the suburban schools reflect much of the triumph and a bit of the tragedy of the political compromise that created the St. Louis inter-district student transfer plan. The triumph is that for this group of black students who choose white and wealthy suburban schools and are able to take advantage of what they offer, the program works. Although many of these students would probably be somewhat successful no matter which school they attended, moving away from the violence and hopelessness of their neighborhoods leads them toward a significantly brighter future. These students are nearly twice as likely as their peers in city schools to complete high school, and those who graduate from suburban schools are much more likely to go on to two- or four-year colleges than St. Louis Public School graduates (Voluntary Interdistrict Coordinating Council, 1995; Missouri State Department of Education, 1995).

This chapter is based on data from several sources, including our lengthy interviews with twenty transfer students—twelve from the same neighborhoods as the city students discussed in Chapter 4 and eight whom we met by spending time in the suburban schools—eleven parents of transfer students, and more than sixty suburban teachers and principals who work daily with transfer students. We also draw on the Lissitz (1994) achievement study; a survey of 2,500 parents and students conducted by Dean Jones at the University of Missouri–St. Louis for the *St. Louis Post-Dispatch* (Jones, 1988); and the focus group research conducted by UMSL's Public Policy Research Center (1993c, 1993d) to help us better understand the lives and experiences of transfer students in their predominantly white suburban schools. Based on this data and our own observations, we believe that while not all African-American students who transfer to the suburbs thrive there, the vast majority of transfer students who graduate from suburban high schools benefit greatly from the inter-district program. These successful transfer students talk about the new worlds that have been opened up to them—about scholarship programs, internships, and jobs they say they never would have heard of in their city schools. They are exposed to significantly more challenging curriculum, learn how to get along in a "white world," and befriend white students and teachers, dispelling some of the stereotypes that whites have of blacks so that those who come behind them might be more easily accepted.

Then there are those who do not succeed in the county schools. These students—most of whom either return to a city school or simply drop out altogether (see Chapter 6)—often come to their suburban campuses full of rage.

These are often the students with a strong critique of racial inequality in America (Fine, 1993). They are almost always the students who will not put up with suburban whites who treat them unfairly (or who they perceive to treat them unfairly), and they either act out their impatience with violent behavior or they silently go away.

Thus, the less optimistic aspect of the St. Louis inter-district transfer plan is the large number of African-American students who remain in the city schools, in an environment of low expectations and despair, and those who do transfer to the suburbs but who end up back in city schools or on the streets. The differences between city, transfer, and return students become more pronounced in the portraits of successful transfer students. Their aspirations, talents, outgoing personalities, parental support, ability to deal with prejudice, and reasons for leaving the city schools speak to their vision of the future and their understanding of opportunities available to them through desegregation.

Yet even the successful transfer students occasionally act out and demand extra support and attention from suburban teachers and administrators. But most of these students also must endure the racial and cultural insensitivity of whites in the suburbs in order to thrive there. Many of the suburban white teachers, administrators, and students regularly make the transfer students feel unwanted and unwelcome. They fail to consider the perspective of black students, who travel many miles each day in search of a better education. Although the degree of racial insensitivity appears to be diminishing somewhat, the prejudice found in the white suburbs forces transfer students who persevere until graduation to either suppress their anger and frustration, re-create their own racial attitudes in a way that leads them to dislike people of their own color, or try to balance their critique of white racism with their need to survive in a predominantly white society.

PORTRAITS OF SUBURBAN SUCCESS

The teachers in the city neighborhood schools complain of a brain drain of their highest achieving black students to the suburbs and the magnet schools, and pretransfer test score data on African-American students who go to suburban, magnet, and "regular"—integrated or nonintegrated—city schools mildly support this assertion, though the differences are not great. African-American students who attend city magnet schools have the highest pretransfer test scores. Transfer students who attend suburban schools generally have lower pretransfer test scores than do magnet students, but they score higher than African-American students who remain in nonintegrated or integrated schools in the city (Lissitz, 1994). But perhaps the most interesting aspect of the Lissitz study is that the transfer students consistently outperform African-American students in magnet and regular city schools in the eighth- to tenth-grade growth in test scores. Furthermore, our in-depth interviews with black students—those in nonintegrated city schools, successful transfer students, and return students—showed that by the time the students were in tenth or eleventh grade, half of those who had remained in or returned to city schools were at least one year behind in school. Only one of the transfer students was behind.

But interviews with successful transfer students and their parents reveal that the long-term impact of the transfer program on the city system is probably more accurately measured by the attitudes and efficacy of the African-American students who choose suburban schools and succeed there. For instance, a black student's belief that he or she can make it in a white world— that is, achieve a high level of self-esteem vis à vis white students—is probably a more accurate barometer of potential success in the suburbs than are standardized test scores. And while there is no doubt an overlap between students with high self-esteem and those with high test scores, the correlation is not perfect. We believe, based on our interviews, that athletes and musicians or very outgoing students with good-to-adequate test scores and grades are more likely to succeed in the suburbs than are the more introverted but high-achieving students. For the most part, the black students who remain in the suburban schools until graduation do so because of sustained parental support and encouragement or because they have a special talent—academic, athletic, or artistic—that is recognized and valued by whites. The most successful transfer students have both of these factors working in their favor.

In the way they speak to a white interviewer, in the way they carry themselves, and in the way they explain why they get up at 5:00 A.M. to get to school every day, the transfer students, as a group, are by far more confident and goal-oriented than their counterparts in the city schools. They are, for the most part, steeped in an achievement ideology that defines their rationale for going to a suburban school. Successful transfer students draw heavily on reassurance from teachers and fellow students and on parental support to propel themselves forward. Because of security and achievement in other aspects of their lives, they are better able to deal with the culture shock and racial prejudice of life in suburban schools. Most enter the suburbs with a positive view of themselves—something that many of the students who remain in the city schools lack—and with a more positive outlook on their chances of success in American society. Those who are admired for their talents usually encounter less blatant prejudice. But transfer students are quite perceptive of the realities of race and education in America—they have a clear sense of why a diploma from a white and wealthy school is more valuable than one from an inner-city school—and thus why the transfer program will help them attain their long-term goals.

Transfer Students

The Lissitz (1994) data on eighth- to tenth-grade test score gains in the suburbs, our interviews with transfer and other students, and our knowledge of what is taking place in the city schools—no vocational education and very little college prep—leads us to believe that attending a suburban school positively affects the aspirations and expectations of transfer students. They have confirmed their belief that they can make it in a white world, and that does wonders for their self-esteem (Braddock, 1980; McPartland and Braddock, 1981).

Will Will wants to be a graphic artist. He would also like to be a photographer and work on films: "Since I was a kid, I was real good in art. I started drawing when I was three. The first picture that I drew—it was a cowboy on a horse. It was on display at the preschool."

Will's high school portfolio is decidedly more sophisticated; his four self-portraits speak of life in the ghetto. In one, his angry eyes peer through iron bars. In another he appears frightened and apprehensive—his hands raised above his face, pinkish palms pushing outward. A row of green beer bottles teeter above his head. "That's what we do quick with our hands when the cops come near us to show them we don't have a gun," he said. The beer bottles serve as a reminder of what he doesn't want to become: "I see these old men who just hang out on the street corner down here all day drinking beer and leaving the bottles all over—not me."

His pride and joy is a prizewinning graphic design of the African continent. Superimposed along the eastern shore is the profile of a black man. The horn of Africa is his nose; South Africa is his scruffy chin. The red, yellow, and green background accentuates the powerful image of the man and the continent as one. Will plans to make T-shirts bearing the design and marketing them in his spare time between his two summer jobs—one picking up trash after the St. Louis Cardinals baseball games and the other as a bellhop at a downtown hotel. At the end of the summer Will will head to Chicago to a competitive college of art on a full presidential scholarship—a scholarship he said he never would have gotten if he had gone to high school in the city. "The county schools," said Will, "that is where the money is at. You figure, the people with the most money got the most connections. You've got to put those together: money and connections."

Because of his artistic talent, Will made friends relatively easy in his suburban high school. He was popular and friendly with a number of white students. "Through my art work—that's how I made friends. Kids saw my art, and they liked it. I thought, 'Cool, they like my art work.' From day one, it was like, 'Whew, look at that boy.' And the teachers caught on like wildfire—the art teachers. That's how it all started off for me. I started making friends through my art."

People believed in Will and in his future as an artist, hence the graduation gifts from his former teachers and relatives. He was not a straight-A student—he got mostly C's with a few B's in everything but art—but his gift was obvious to anyone who looked through his portfolio.

Will credits his mother for much of his success thus far because he says that she taught him right from wrong at an early age. Although Will ultimately made the decision to transfer to the suburban school on his own, he discussed it with his mother, who remains an important influence in his life. She moved her three sons from St. Louis to a small town in Indiana when Will was in elementary school because she wanted to get them away from their father and uncles, who were involved with two ganglike groups in the city.

"If you want to come to St. Louis and sell drugs, you go to the Bays and make sure that it's okay with them first," said Will, who grew up hearing stories of people shot in his grandmother's living room. "My mother did not want us to grow up around all that—she didn't want me to grow up to be like my father or her brothers, so she moved us away."

But when Will was twelve his mother moved the family back to St. Louis because she was homesick and wanted a better job. She ended up in the projects with no steady work and health problems. Meanwhile, her second son began getting into trouble. Will's younger brother had stayed in the city schools and continued to "hang" with his friends from the neighborhood—a little robbery, a little drug dealing—and ended up in a juvenile detention center. He missed Will's high school graduation.

When he was fourteen Will lied about his age so that he could get a job with Operation Bright Side, a city run program that paid teenagers minimum wage to pick up trash along the highways. He has held at least one part-time job ever since. "My brother never wanted to do any of those jobs. He said he was not gonna wear a bright red T-shirt and pick up trash. He was afraid of what his friends would think. He said he could do better selling drugs. He did better until he was caught."

Will said that being in a suburban school, removed from many of the temptations in his neighborhood, provided a safe space in which he could focus on his art and his education. This does not mean that suburban St. Louis welcomed him with open arms or that he did not have to deal with racial issues at Parkway West. But it did provide Will the opportunity to succeed in his efforts to be different from his brother.

Cathy With her picture-perfect smile, fifteen-year-old Cathy looks like a model on the cover of a teen magazine. She is energetic, positive, and outgoing. Cathy, like Will, is generally well liked by the white students at Parkway West High School and admired for her talent. She is an exceptional dancer and was one of the first black students selected for the school's prestigious pompon squad.

Because her mother moved out to one of the poor, all-black suburbs, Cathy lives with her grandparents in a small, quaint house on the northwestern edge of the city so that she qualifies for the transfer program. Her grandmother, a driver for one of the bus companies that transports black students to the suburban districts, knows more about the desegregation program and the suburban schools than most blacks in the city. Cathy's grandmother is attending classes to earn her general equivalency diploma. "I'm going back to school after all these years," she said. "I got pregnant at an early age, you know, and now it's so important for me to show my grandchildren the right road to take because I experienced a lot of disappointments when I was young."

Cathy first transferred to the Parkway School District when she was in the fifth grade. The original decision for her to go to a suburban school was made by her mother and grandmother. "My mother told me that it might offer me much more than I would regularly get in the city schools, and this is what I wanted to do ever since."

At first, however, it was difficult for Cathy in the county school: "I used to always come home and tell my mom that my teacher does not pay enough attention to me. She said, 'All you have to do is to go there and do what you have to do and try to get the best out there you can—just ask questions and keep on asking until she lets you know it. . . . If she doesn't give you a response, then ask again.' And I came back home and my mother saw that I was different because I was just trying to get the best I can."

During her sophomore year of high school, Cathy's average school day looked something like this: She woke up just before 5 A.M. to catch a 5:50 bus to school, where she had a 7 A.M. "zero hour" Spanish course (zero hour is for those students who can't fit in all the courses they want or need to take during the regular school day). She attended regular classes until 3 P.M., when she headed for two and a half hours of pompon practice. On a good day she would get home at 6:30 and have a couple hours for dinner and homework before falling into bed. According to data compiled by the Voluntary Interdistrict Coordinating Council, about two-thirds of the city-to-county transfer students have a daily commute of sixty minutes or less each way. Nineteen percent of these transfer students commute sixty-one to seventy minutes each way to school, and about 4 percent spend seventy-one to eighty minutes on the bus each morning and afternoon (1995a).

Cathy said she regrets not having enough time to spend on her homework and her social life: "I have no time to do anything," she said, adding that she strives for B's but often earns C's because of the lack of study time. Still, the thought of leaving Parkway West to attend an all-black city school—Northwest High School was approximately a quarter-mile from her grandparents' house—causes Cathy to wrinkle up her nose and shake her head. "Well, I would have more time to do my homework and study, and it would not take so much time to get home," she said. But she added that if she had one wish, it would not be to transfer to a city high school but rather to stay in the county school and "make more hours in a day and do everything I need to do."

Her favorite aspect of the suburban elementary school she attended was the variety of subjects available, especially art and music. Cathy is a flutist as well as a dancer. And her suburban high school offers students more freedom, "so we can make our own decisions—I love high school." She said she enjoys the large, well-equipped marching band, in which she played before she joined the pom squad, and the drama department that puts on at least one major play a year in the school's high-tech theater.

Their Parents

The control that most transfer parents have over their children's lives and educational decisions is exemplified in a comment from one mother who participated in the focus group study at the University of Missouri–St. Louis: "And I told her, you're going out there, so that's it, you might as well do what you can do to resolve your problem, because you're going" (Public Policy Research Centers, 1993c, p. 11).

Gerald's Mother Gerald wants to be a scientist—either a physicist or a biologist; he's not sure which. Outgoing and articulate, fifteen-year-old Gerald seems to be well on his way. He held a B-plus/A-minus grade point average at Lafayette High School, a highly respected suburban school about thirty-five miles southwest of his lower-middle-class neighborhood in the city. Gerald lives with his mother and her husband in a small, well-cared-for house. He is the youngest of three children.

What surprised Gerald most about the suburban schools was the equipment—computers, televisions, well-stocked science labs, and so on. He wants to take advanced placement physics for college credit during his senior year even though few black students enroll in the college-level or honors courses at his school. But short and husky Gerald, who answers almost every question with "Yes, ma'am" or "No, ma'am," said he gets along fine with everybody— black and white—at his school.

Gerald's mother is a vibrant and forthright woman. She fills the house with excitement, talking nonstop in a booming voice. Her tone is firm but not threatening toward her son. Gerald jumps up to help her with her packages when she entered the room. The two seemed very close. Gerald's mother often said "we," meaning she and Gerald, when discussing specific experiences: "It was a choice we made ourselves," "We have not come across any pettiness [in the county school]," "We understand that some people are not satisfied with who they are."

She said she heard about the transfer program through her involvement in the city schools when she was helping to organize magnet schools. "Because I had been in on school planning from the beginning, I knew what was available to the children. . . . I had a direct line to this program," she said.

With her assertiveness, Gerald's mother typifies the parents of the successful transfer students we interviewed—they are, in general, better educated and more securely employed than the parents of the city or return students. Although transfer students were not more likely than city students to be living with both parents, they were twice as likely to be living with a parent who holds a high school diploma and half as likely to be living with an unemployed parent. The parents of successful transfer students tend to have a different outlook on life and education; they have not eliminated themselves or their children from the competition for greater success and status and they see a diploma from a white and wealthy high school as a source of upward mobility for their children. These parents tend to be more optimistic and in control of their own lives as well as those of their children. Furthermore, most seem to relish involvement with their children and view themselves as instrumental in their children's development. Half of the transfer students interviewed had been attending suburban schools since elementary school, and most of the rest began transferring during junior high school, which says a great deal about their parents' involvement in the transfer decision.

Tina's Mother In one of the powder-blue rowhouses recently built in the low-income neighborhood next to Vashon High School, fifteen-year-old Tina lives with her mother, two teenage cousins, and her sixteen-year-old brother. Tina's mother learned of the transfer program through her work as a volunteer in the city schools. She said she immediately liked the idea of sending her daughter to a county school because she "felt there were more advanced classes and a lot of opportunities that weren't in the city schools."

Tina's mother works as an assistant director of a homeless shelter, and her leadership abilities are evident in the stories of her interaction with educators. What Tina's mother likes most about the Affton High School in the tiny middle-class and suburban Affton School District is that the principal and teachers contact her often: "They call when they feel the child is not doing well; you know, when their grades start slipping. They really try to work with you."

In contrast, she said, the teachers and administrators in the city schools have little contact with the parents. She said one of her older sons cut class twenty-four times at nearby Vashon High School, but nobody called to inform her. "They had both my work and home phone numbers." Finally, she said, the principal called her to say that they were holding her son back a year, that he couldn't graduate because he had missed so much school. That was when Tina's mother marched to the high school to confront the principal: "I told [the principal] that he was not to hold my son back or I would go to the Board of Education and tell them what had happened—how he didn't call me."

Tina's mother said she also threatened to request that the principal, who also served as the basketball coach, be removed from his job. She said that, among other things, he used in-school suspension time to conduct basketball practice. Once, she said, when her son was supposed to be suspended, she went to the school to check on him, and "they were up there playing basketball in the gym!" She said that the principal favors the athletes and is more interested in sports than academics. She said that it is easy for the basketball players to get their grades changed and that they graduate without knowing how to read.

Her younger son also attended a county school until he had to return to the city "because of health reasons." But instead of sending him to nearby Vashon, Tina's mother petitioned the Board of Education to place him in high school in a more middle-class neighborhood on the south side of the city.

Urma's Mother A few miles north of Tina's house and two blocks away from Sumner High School stands a small one-story gray home surrounded by a neat wire-link fence. The front porch is covered in bright green Astroturf, and shrubs and hedges line the front yard. Next door are the remains of a burned-out house; across the street is a community center with a large Head Start program. This is where Urma, a fifteen-year-old sophomore at Lafayette High School in Rockwood at the time of our visit, lived with her mother, stepfather, grandmother, and eleven-year-old brother. The neat little rooms are crammed with worn furniture. Urma's mother is savvy, and sophisticated. She works as an executive secretary at Ralston Purina, and she dresses for her role in corporate America, wearing stylish suits accented with fashionable jewelry.

Urma's mother began sending her children to the Rockwood district when her son was in first grade and Urma was in sixth grade. She said that she and her husband had made the decision "to try it and see how it worked out—basically we enrolled them on a trial basis." Before she transferred to the suburbs Urma was enrolled in an all-black Catholic school in the city. Neither she nor her brother has ever attended a St. Louis public school. Across the city, about 12 percent of the transfer students who enroll in the inter-district desegregation program come from nonpublic schools (Voluntary Interdistrict Coordinating Council, 1993).

When asked whether she thought her children were treated fairly in the suburban schools, Urma's mother was quick to reply: "Pretty much so, but then that is because of me—I make it a point of taking a part in their education and keeping abreast of what is happening—having my face known. I have dealt more with her counselor, so the counselor knows that I am concerned with what's happening. Something that may happen with another student may not happen to Urma because they know her mother is in touch, her mother will say something."

Urma's mother exudes assertiveness and self-assuredness, which she said were prerequisites for her high-profile job. The extra hassle of sending her children to a county school and monitoring their treatment presents less of a problem for her than it might for other black urban parents with less experience in powerful institutions.

WHY THEY TRANSFER

For black students in the city of St. Louis, the decision to transfer to a county school reflects the realization that separate will never be equal. In our interviews and in focus groups conducted by researchers at the Public Policy Research Centers, transfer students cite the same two central reasons for transferring to predominantly white suburban schools. First, they and their parents perceive the county schools to be better than the city schools (although the vast differences between the county school districts or within the city school system are rarely acknowledged or discussed). The 1988 Jones survey also found that 70 percent of the transfer students "strongly agreed" that "I was looking for a better education when I decided to go to school in St. Louis County." Second, they want to escape negative peer pressure and violence in the city schools. Escape to the suburbs means freedom from the daily pressure to join a gang—to wear the colors, sell drugs, and fight rival gang members—a factor that has little to do with the academic quality of suburban schools per se.

Other reasons include transferring to play on sports teams.[1] In fact, some suburban schools actively recruit talented athletes out of city schools—a practice that has become more common and more obtrusive as the transfer program continues. Some transfer students go to the suburbs because their friends do; others go because their parents tell them they must.

But all the black students who transfer do so because they believe that somehow the suburban schools will better help them attain certain goals. The extent to which the whiter and wealthier schools are objectively "better" than the city schools is immeasurable. Every variable used to assess school quality in the United States—test scores, dropout rates, attendance, college-going rates, and so on—is contaminated by the fallout from racial and class discrimination and segregation in America. "School effects," as a distinct and separate variable from student background, does not exist. School quality, therefore, is strongly related to the educational needs of the students and the meaning that educators make of those needs, which will vary according to the students' and the educators' social class, race, gender, and personal experiences. Educational research has shown repeatedly that educators hold higher expectations of and demand more from white or wealthy students than they do from poor or African-American and Latino students (see Oakes, 1990, and Rosenberg, 1986).

Thus, we should not be surprised to find that most of the transfer students said that the teachers and the curriculum move much more quickly in the county than in the city schools. A transfer student participating in a focus group provided a typical description of the comparison of city and county schools: "The work was harder. You know in city schools I got by with a lot of stuff. I got out there [in the county school], and I fell behind. . . . They knew a lot of things I didn't even know." Another transfer student noted, "I kind of had to jump up a step; it was a change. . . . If I was still in the city and in the seventh grade, it seems like out in the county that would be sixth grade work" (Public Policy Research Centers, 1993d, p. 13).

It is also true that most of the whiter and wealthier suburban schools have greater resources, including newer buildings, more computers per student, and an abundance of textbooks. The suburban districts, even those that have a

---

1. The required grade-point-averages to play on a team in most suburban districts, were, until recently, lower than that of the St. Louis public school system, which requires a 2.0.

lower per-pupil expenditure than the St. Louis public schools, have more real income than the city to expend on rigorous educational programs. They do not, for instance, have to provide special education services for disabled students in their districts because the Special School District educates all handicapped students in the county. Nor do most of these districts have to maintain 100-year-old buildings or provide social services for large numbers of students from extremely poor families.

Research by Gary Orfield and others has shown that intensely segregated African-American and Latino schools are fourteen times more likely to be predominantly poor. "Disadvantaged students in such schools score far worse on standardized measures than their counterparts in schools that are not predominantly poor. High-poverty schools have more dropouts, less success in college preparation, fewer well-prepared teachers and less-advanced curriculums" (Orfield, 1994). Furthermore, segregated urban schools are not as effective in helping to raise even high-achieving African-American students out of poverty, because a diploma from an inner-city school will never get them as far in the college admissions process or job search as one from a wealthy suburban school (Braddock et al., 1986).

Educational institutions acquire their status from their students, and those that serve only high-status students will be better connected to the high-status colleges and well-paying employers (Jankowski, 1995). This reality contributes to a vicious cycle of poverty and despair for those in low-status urban schools. It leads to the anger and violence of teenagers who consciously and subconsciously know they have been excommunicated from opportunity. It leads to the self-fulfilling prophecy of inner-city schools as a place where failure is virtually assured.

Student Flight

To listen to the transfer students talk about their decision to attend a suburban school is to better understand how they have come to interpret "school quality" and reconcile their need to flee the all-black neighborhood schools.

Will When Will moved into the housing project with his mother and brothers, he went to neighborhood schools in the city. But by the end of eighth grade, he was thinking about his "little plan of how I was going to get out of the ghetto." His options for ninth grade were either a nearby "zoned" high school, a magnet school for the arts in the city, or a suburban high school in St. Louis County. "I figured that if I went to high school in the city—any city school—I wouldn't do the work 'cause we got too many other things we have to tend to, you know, as far as dealing with kids from other neighborhoods who like to fight and gang bang or just hustle you in the hallways and things like that. So I figured . . . in order for me to follow my little plan, I had to get away from my friends."

In fact, Will said, the main reason he chose Parkway West over other county schools he had heard about was that he didn't know any other black students from the city who went there. "I went to see Parkway South [a newer, slightly larger high school in the same district], but a lot of other kids I knew were transferring out there. So I decided to go to a different school."

The desire to escape the peer pressure of the inner-city adolescent world is one of the most prominent themes in the narratives of the black transfer students we interviewed. For eight hours a day county schools help remove these teenagers from the pressure to choose between joining a gang or becoming the victims of one.

Arlene The vivacious and outgoing Arlene was one of the few successful transfer students who had little parental support in the decision to transfer. Her quiet mother, who has no high school education, knew little about the transfer program or the suburban schools. But Arlene's street smarts and an older sister, who transferred to a county school first, steered her toward the suburbs.

Arlene has always been a good student. In fact, she said she found out about the transfer program from her elementary school teachers who told her she was "too bright" to stay in the city schools: "Well, I heard about it when I was in the fourth grade, and everyone told me I had done real good on a CAT [California Achievement Test] or something, and they thought that I should go to a county school rather than a city school." But at the time Arlene said she wasn't ready to go to a faraway school. Then her sister, her cousin, and her good friend from next door all transferred to suburban schools, and she began to reconsider. Then in eighth grade something happened that sealed her decision not to go to the city school: "One day, some guys who go to Vashon—you know, that's the high school you go to here—and they were saying, you know, 'God, you're kinda cute. Oh, you're gonna be a freshman this year at Vashon? Okay, we're going to be waiting for you up on the balcony.' And the balcony is like a place—in the theater or whatever and there's a balcony up at the top, and from down on the bottom you can't see what's going on up there—that's where they take girls and do things to them [she giggled nervously]. . . . And I got kind of scared to go there."

For Arlene, the choice to transfer to a suburban school was not based on school quality per se but on the need to remove herself from the threats in her neighborhood school. Directly and indirectly, all of the transfer students interviewed spoke of the benefits of getting away from the poverty, crime, and racial isolation in the city schools. Whether talking about specific student behavior or a characteristic of a city school that results from disruptive behavior—that is, less student freedom and lower teacher expectations—these students are clearly looking for a different social environment.

"Flight" from an undesirable situation is more often undertaken because of the negative aspects of what is abandoned than because of the specific benefits derived from where one is going. Although virtually all of the transfer students and their parents interviewed said that the county schools the students were attending were "better" than the city schools, they also said they did not have any specific information on how the sixteen predominantly white suburban districts differed when they chose to transfer to one of them. Many went by name recognition and hearsay—"I heard about Parkway from my cousin" and "All my friends go there."

All the transfer families said they had received the information booklet on the suburban districts that came with the inter-district transfer application. And despite the range of differences in district size, school size, per-pupil funding, specific courses, and even instructional philosophies offered by these suburban districts, the black families said they did not choose schools based on such measures. The primary assumption was that a predominantly white suburban school—*any* predominantly white suburban school—was better than a city school. The important decision, therefore, was not which suburban district to attend but rather whether to attend one at all. The real choice was between urban and suburban, black and white, poor and nonpoor.

In choosing Parkway over other county districts and Parkway South in particular, Arlene said that she wanted to go with her best friend. "He was saying it was fun, and I should just go ahead . . . and we were real close . . . and my sister said go out there with him since she didn't want me to go to school with her."

Like Will, Arlene avoided one suburban school, Mehlville High School, because she did not want to be around the black students from the city who had transferred there. "I would have gotten into trouble there 'cause they had a lot of city people, city kids who went out there who like to start stuff with you," she said. Academic variables—such as class sizes, courses offered, or number of guidance counselors—did not affect her decision between mostly middle- to working-class Mehlville and more upper-middle-class Parkway School District.

Maurice Half of the transfer students interviewed told us that if they had not left their city schools they would probably have dropped out or been arrested. Tall and handsome Maurice is one such student. His mother insisted that he transfer to the Parkway District when he was in fifth grade. After a few rocky years in a Parkway middle school, when he was getting in trouble for going to class late and not doing his work, Maurice pulled up his grades to a C-plus average in high school. He said he got a lot of individual attention from several teachers and counselors in both the middle school and the high school. At Parkway North High School, Maurice said that the principal "told me how they were going to let me control my own actions, and how they trusted me. I appreciated them for trusting me."

By his sophomore year, Maurice was playing on the varsity basketball team and planning to go to college and become a school counselor. "I think I wouldn't even be in school right now if I had gone to school in my neighborhood. I would have dropped out by now." Maurice said there were too many things going on in the city schools—the students fight a lot and try to act tough, and the teachers don't have the time and energy to give the kind of one-on-one attention that he found in the suburban schools. He said that his friends who go to city schools make fun of him when he comes home and does his homework instead of hanging out with them.

The transfer program has placed Maurice and most transfer students into a state of social limbo; they do not fit comfortably in either the white and non-poor world or the black and nonwealthy world (see Zweigenhaft and Domhoff, 1991). "I have to act one way in school and another way in my neighborhood," said Maurice, who said he spends his weekends with his friends in the city, not at suburban parties.

Cliquishness, racism, logistics, and lack of transportation make it difficult for transfer students to become an integral part of the suburban social scene. So they teeter between the complex social environment of their neighborhoods, which they leave for only eight hours a day five days a week, and the elusive more white and middle-class party circuit that they are far removed from on the weekends. "The only thing I do out in the county after school is basketball," said Maurice. "I wish I could be more involved out there because sometimes they talk about stuff they do, but I don't have nothing to say because I do my partying in the city. When they talk about that, I just go in another room, that's all."

The parents of transfer students also talk about what their children are transferring away from when they leave the city schools. Gerald's mother, for example, said the decision that her son transfer to a county school was one she and Gerald made together: "The kind of child he is, he was not used to pettiness. And he was being confronted with a lot of pettiness [in the city schools], and I thought it was time to make a change. Sometimes you have to make sacrifices to keep your children good."

Gerald's mother explained that she picked the Rockwood district for her son after reading the short descriptions of the sixteen suburban districts in the brochures. "I read about it [Rockwood]. And I heard about the program there, and it was most suitable for Gerald. They are all about education and no mess," she said with an air of complete satisfaction. She said she went to visit the junior high school Gerald was assigned to before he started there. She took a tour of the school and sat in on the classes.

Although Gerald's mother was one of the most informed transfer parents, she said she did not visit any other county schools before choosing the Rockwood district. And when she was asked about the advantages of having her son attend Lafayette High School, she spoke of general county-city, suburban-urban, black school–white school comparisons: "City schools have a lot of distractions—distracting educators as well as students. Teachers in the county get the full amount of sleep, and they don't bring their problems to school. They keep it away from the children. . . . In the county, they're into more wholesome fun—they just do what they have to do. City people just aren't like that. I prefer county schools."

Urma's mother said the best aspect of enrolling her children in suburban schools is the valuable interaction they have with different people. But she explained that when she made her choice she knew very little about the differences between the various large and small, wealthy and not-as-wealthy suburban districts. "They send you a breakdown of different districts and you have like three choices. And I chose . . . I think . . . I really don't remember, but it wasn't Rockwood—whichever one I chose was filled. So I had one alternate school district, and Rockwood was one of them. So my husband and I just chose Rockwood. I really didn't know because I wasn't really that familiar with any of the school districts, so it was just a blind choice—I'll take this one and see how it works."

Carl's mother, a softspoken but stern single mother of two, said, "I sure did not want them in city schools—there's a lot of fighting and drugs. I though it would be nice to try something different." When asked to compare her son's suburban high school to all-black Northwest High, less than one mile from her house, Carl's mother said that although she didn't know "a lot about the teachers," she thought that Northwest was a bad school because of the students "always fighting and acting up."

The Rewards

While the desire to escape the social ills of the inner city provides much of the impetus for black students to transfer to schools twenty to thirty miles from their homes, they also know that going to school with white and wealthy students has a lot of added advantages. It is not that these African-American students need to sit next to white students to learn, but because if they do they are more likely to be admitted to social institutions that confer status and prestige (Zweigenhaft and Domhoff, 1991). For instance, white suburban schools—unlike schools that serve poor and black students—are much more likely to be focused on preparing students for college and white-collar lives; they are generally more intricately linked to the admissions offices of top universities.

As we mentioned in Chapter 3, the graduation rate for students enrolled in the St. Louis public schools—black and white—was only 27 percent for the class of 1994. The graduation rate for the mostly white students who live in the sixteen county school districts that accept transfer students averages about 75 percent. The graduation rate of the transfer students from the city who attend these suburban schools is nearly 50 percent. (This rate could actually be higher because some of the students who do not graduate from suburban schools may return to city schools and graduate there.) Thus, despite the hassle of going to a school far from their neighborhood, nearly twice as many of these transfer students are graduating from their suburban high schools in four years as are students in city high schools, many or whom take five or more years to graduate. Between 1983 and 1995, 5,330 African-American students who live in the segregated city of St. Louis graduated from suburban high schools (Voluntary Interdistrict Coordinating Council, 1995).

As we noted, the St. Louis public schools have a 48 percent college-going rate for those students who do graduate—31 percent go to four-year colleges and 17 percent attend two-year colleges. This means that for every 100 ninth-graders in the St. Louis public schools, about 74 fail to graduate from a city school four years later, and of the 26 who do, about 13 go on to receive postsecondary education. Chances are that only about 8 of the 100 freshmen will find themselves in a four-year university five years after they enter high school. Given that these numbers are not broken down by race, and given that enrollment in the St. Louis public schools is about 21 percent white, even if the racial balance of college-going graduates was distributed equally across the two racial group (which it probably is not), out of every group of 100 ninth grade students in the city schools, only 6 black students will graduate in four years and go on to attend a four-year college.

The average college-going rate for graduates of the sixteen predominantly white suburban districts is about 75 percent. The more affluent of these districts have college-going rates of more than 90 percent. About 68 percent of the transfer students who graduate from suburban schools are college bound: 44 percent go on to four-year colleges, including Yale, Brown, the University of Michigan, Washington University, and Purdue. Another 24 percent enroll in two-year colleges. This college-going rate is nearly three times the national average for black high school graduates. So, for every 100 transfer students who are enrolled in suburban schools *by the ninth grade*, about sixty graduate from the suburbs, and forty of these graduates go on to college (Voluntary Interdistrict Coordinating Council, 1994). These are much better odds than those of the students who remain in the city schools.

An eleventh-grade transfer student who participated in a focus group explained the high school-college connection this way: "A city school person and a county school person—let's say they apply for some college. Let's say they both have the same grades, but more than likely the college is going to choose that county school person because everybody knows county schools give better education than city schools" (Public Policy Research Centers, 1993d, p. 7).

For students who want to go to college, the suburban schools are a better choice than city schools. These data suggest that simply ending the desegregation plan and putting the money spent on busing into the city schools (even if the state would agree to do such a thing, which it probably would not) is not the solution.

In addition to having more money for college, white suburban students are generally shielded from the social ills that often hurt inner-city black students' learning and motivation—that is, poverty, crime, violence, discrimination, isolation from the labor market, and transiency. Thus, white suburban students have more time to dedicate to school and a better understanding of the direct link between school and work than their counterparts in the ghettos. Their parents demand schools that prepare children for college and high-paying jobs. Parents who hold college degrees and high-paying jobs can make these demands of the teachers and administrators in their suburban public schools, but they rarely need to verbalize them. The suburban educators expect as much for their white and wealthy students (Lareau, 1989).

The separate and unequal missions of the urban and suburban schools result from—and contribute to—the lack of opportunity for inner-city teenagers. Students from families with no money for college tuition are less likely to demand precollege courses. Parents who have not been to college themselves or have few friends or relatives who have been to college have less information about what to demand. Schools that serve students from such families are generally less connected to college admissions offices and scholarship programs. Educators who see so few students go on to higher education do not emphasize college preparation.

When asked how Parkway South was different from what she had expected, Arlene said, "They have a lot of different classes that I wouldn't expect in a high school—like law and accounting." She said what she likes most about her high school is that it has this variety of classes—"a lot of classes that will help you as far as college goes."

These different urban-suburban school cultures and institutional expectations may help explain why the longitudinal studies of African-American student achievement rates in the county versus the city schools have found that the transfer students who participate in the inter-district school desegregation program show a "consistent, continued increase in performance on Stanford Reading and Mathematics from the eighth to the tenth grades." No other group of African-American students in the study—those attending magnet schools or all-black or integrated schools in the city—showed improved performance on standardized tests between the eighth and tenth grades (Lissitz, 1993 and 1994).

Furthermore, the Lissitz study shows that between the eighth and tenth grade the transfer students also improve their attitudes and feelings about themselves and their future. A possible explanation for this attitudinal finding is located in the stories of Will, Cathy, Gerald, and other transfer students. These students have learned that they can make it in a white-dominated society because their futures are highlighted by real job opportunities and college preparation. They no longer have to fear leaving the north side of St. Louis and trying to compete with whites in educational institutions or the job market. They have been there, and they know they can succeed. They are not afraid to integrate into a predominantly white social structure (Braddock, 1980). This finding in St. Louis is supported by a growing body of research on the long-term effects of desegregation on African-American students and how experiences in racially mixed schools lessen black students' fears that they cannot be successful in a racially mixed world (see Wells and Crain, 1994).

Tara   The day that Tara finished her junior year at Parkway West High School she stopped by the main office to say good-bye for the summer to Martha Irving—a warm, loving ex-nun who counsels the transfer students and runs a program to promote racial harmony in the school. Tara, energetic and full of life, was visibly pleased with herself. "I'm officially a senior now," she shrieked, holding her arms up in the air and stomping her feet at a quick pace. She told Irving how she was getting B's in all but one of her classes, having pulled her grades up from mostly D's and F's in only two semesters at Parkway West. "I've learned a lot since I've been here—just this year I've learned so much. Ask me anything about history," she said with a huge smile. "At Roosevelt [her city high school], I didn't learn anything I didn't already know. When I was in Roosevelt, I was a strong C student, but I wasn't really trying. I came out here, and I could not do what I was doing back there—just getting by. I had to do my work or I was going to get F's. . . . It's a lot harder, this school is a lot harder. I mean you really have to apply yourself."

Tara said that the biggest difference between her city high school and Parkway West is that the teachers and counselors "really push" students toward college. "I've always said that I'm going to go college, but I never knew what colleges were good. I never thought about it—I never knew what Spelman and Morehouse were. I didn't know what any of that was until I came out here. . . . But I never made the effort—yeah, I'm going to make good grades so that I can go to a good school. I didn't try 'til I got our here—cause the counselors are real concerned. In the city they don't push it. I mean they PUSH it out here—they be on you, like, 'What are you going to do when you graduate?' They bug you. In the city they may ask you once, like when you're getting ready to graduate or something dumb like that. At Roosevelt, I never saw a college fair. But they did have a black college fair out here—I was surprised."

The tradeoff for all this extra nudging toward college and higher teacher expectations, according to Tara, is that black students have to give up almost all of the social clout they have in city schools. "It's a lot harder to be in groups or to be on cheerleading here—they're working on it—but I mean it's hard because it's a white-run school. It's more white kids; you have to do things their way. You know it's harder to fit in." Like Maurice and Cathy, Tara often feels caught between separate worlds: "It's not cool to be totally 'city,' but then it's not cool to be like the white kids because you'll be labeled a sellout or an Oreo—you know, it's hard to be yourself."

Will Will, sitting pretty with his full college scholarship, likes to articulate his money-connections theme. He said that his artwork won more awards and garnered more attention because he was a Parkway student and not from a city school. In one high school art contest at a local university, nearly two-thirds of the winners were from the Parkway District. Yet in Will's opinion the judging was subjective, and the work of students from other districts was often as good. You can get a lot of mileage out of the name of your school, he said. "I ain't no fool. I know money talks."

But Will, like Tara, also said that being in a school where more than 80 percent of the students are planning for college makes a big difference. The workload is different and the expectations are definitely different. "When I first came out here I came with the goal in mind that there were better facilities to help me become what I wanted to be—more money, more connections, more prestige. So I came out here. But college wasn't necessarily real for me. But the longer I stayed and the more I learned—now I know that college is what I need. I visited two colleges that paid for me to come. I got the Presidential Scholarship."

Other talented transfer students garner more attention when they attend county schools. Black athletes, for example, benefit from large, well-funded sports programs in suburban schools. Wealthy districts, many with fancy football stadiums, huge gymnasiums, and Olympic-size swimming pools, field more teams than the St. Louis public schools, especially since the 1992 round of budget cuts in the city schools ("Yes for city schools," 1992). Because athletic skill is often a poor black student's only ticket to a college scholarship and life outside of poverty, many transfer students take their sports seriously. They often outshine suburban white students on the playing fields and please suburban coaches who are associated with college scouts.

Richie Will's good friend Richie ended up with a college scholarship in a sport that most city schools no longer offer—cross-country. The slight, soft-spoken Richie was an unlikely candidate for a high school success story and an athletic scholarship. He was born with a hole in his heart in a small Mississippi town to a teenage mother with a drug and alcohol problem. Richie's father left the family after the migration to St. Louis, when Richie was still a little boy. As a child Richie was shuttled from apartment to apartment as his mother moved from boyfriend to boyfriend. "She was involved with drugs, and she was like a party animal—she didn't have time for her kids. She had lots of boyfriends. . . . I think she probably needed some psychiatric help—she was drinking real bad. And she would just disappear. I mean she left me with some guy that I didn't know. She did not come back for a month and a week. . . . So I started disliking her because she didn't care about me."

When Richie was five he began living on and off with his "guardian mother," a woman who had been a close friend of his grandmother back in Mississippi. In addition to the emotional trauma of being bounced between his mother and guardian mother, Richie had a speech impediment—"I was bad with slurring everything together"—and had difficulty concentrating. In elementary school in the city, Richie's speech teacher, Ms. Taylor, would pay for him to go on field trips or participate in school activities when his mother would not provide the money.

Richie said that by the fifth grade he had persuaded the family's social worker to place him permanently in the custody of his guardian mother. "Every time the social worker would come to my mother's house, I'd act crazy just so she would know that I disliked it there." Richie said that his mother and her boyfriend at the time wanted Richie to live to with them so that his mother could get an AFDC check. Finally, a judge placed Richie in the custody of his guardian mother, who lived in the Peabody projects, one building over from Will's apartment. He started doing better in school, and while he had always been good in math, he began to move further ahead of his classmates. He was making all A's in math and finishing his assignments so quickly that he got into trouble for playing around while the rest of the class was working. His fifth-grade math teacher, Mrs. Langford, told him that he needed a bigger challenge and that he should transfer to a county school. Mrs. Langford, knowing Richie's home situation, took matters into her own hands and signed up Richie for the transfer program.

Beginning in the sixth grade, Richie rode the bus every day from the dismal housing project to the pastoral suburban neighborhoods. It was for him a greater escape than for most of the transfer students. It was a chance for him to leave his family problems thirty miles behind. "One thing the county schools helped me with, they helped me get away from the environment—into something new and fresh. Because I was really tired of seeing what I left behind," said Richie.

During junior high school, after an operation on his heart, Richie began running for relaxation. In ninth grade, his first year at Parkway West High School, Richie joined the cross-country team. "Imagine this—the first day of cross-country. I'm the only black person there. There's forty-five white people on the team. I walked in, and I wasn't sure if I was in the right place 'cause I thought there would be brothers running cross-country. There was none. I didn't want to speak to anyone cause I didn't know what to say to them—I didn't know anybody. So I just ran. I said I'll make the best of it. I'll just run to my fullest. I'll do the best that I can."

Richie's cross-country career took off. In his freshman year he was promoted to the varsity team, and by sophomore year he had dethroned the school's star runner. He started to develop a name for himself as a top runner and became confident. In his senior year Richie ranked second in the state in cross-country, and he was recruited by colleges from Boston to Wyoming. He said that although he had always wanted to be an accountant, he was never sure how he would get into college and pay for it. But at Parkway West he saw other distance runners get scholarships, and there were coaches and counselors to help him find a school that would pay his way. "I realized that I could get there if I kept running. I kept running and running; I kept training so that I could get a scholarship," he said.

Richie accepted a scholarship to a small college in Illinois, planning to transfer to the University of Missouri or the University of Illinois for his junior and senior years. Richie noted that he would not have had the opportunity to go to college had he stayed in the city schools. First, there is the ubiquitous negative peer pressure: "In the city they call you a nerd and tease you if you try hard in school and want to learn." But, more important, few urban high schools have cross-country teams.

Richie said that because he graduated from a school known for cross-country and acknowledged in general as offering a superior education, he could get the recognition he deserved. One of the local newspapers ran an article about him and his running career. "It helps to go to one of those schools that is always in the news, always recognized," he said. Success after high school, he has concluded, "all depends on what school you graduate from."

While the parents of students in city schools tend to talk about familiarity or convenience as their favorite aspects of the all-black neighborhood high schools, transfer parents spoke of school quality in discussions of what they like about the suburban high schools: "County schools have more to offer," "They teach kids more," "He'll be more advanced," and "[There are] smaller classes in the county."

But these perceptions, most of which were stated as city-versus-county school comparisons, are not always accurate. For instance, a mother who cited the computer classes offered in her daughter's county school as an important reason for transferring lives less than a mile from an all-black city high school that also has computers and computer courses. Furthermore, many of the county school districts have larger class sizes than the all-black city schools, especially at the high school level, because of declining enrollments in the city high schools. Although the average high school student-teacher ratio for the suburban districts participating in the plan is 18-to-1, some of the larger suburban districts, including Parkway, have ratios as high as 22.5-to-1 (Missouri State Department of Education, 1995).

The argument that county schools teach more and that black students who attend these schools are more advanced than their counterparts in the city schools is undoubtedly true on average, given all the social factors mentioned above and the differences in teacher expectations that come with them. Nationwide, test scores in the white and wealthy suburbs are significantly higher than those in urban schools. Many of the suburban high schools we visited in St. Louis offered several advanced placement courses, allowing students to earn college credit while they are still in high school. Ten of the suburban high schools provide advanced placement courses in virtually every subject. Only one city high school—Metro High, the magnet for gifted students—offers several of these courses (Frievogel, 1994).

Urma's mother said that her daughter is exposed to a variety of different programs in her county school that she would not be exposed to in a city school—public or private: "The curriculum is set up to help prepare students to continue after high school." She said that the urban parochial schools that her daughter attended were not as advanced and that Urma's transition to the county was difficult. As for the city's public schools, Urma's mother, a graduate of Sumner High School, confessed to having little firsthand knowledge— "There's a big difference since I graduated from high school in 1972," she said, speaking of the social decline of the Ville area around Sumner and of the school itself. But she added that some of her friends' children go to city public schools, and they appear to be "on the same level" as Urma and her brother.

In addition to resource and achievement factors, four of the eleven transfer parents[2] we interviewed in depth said that the dedication and concern of the teachers and staff are what they like most about their child's county school—"These people bend over backwards for my child," "Teachers seem more concerned [than in city schools]," and "County schools are more interested in what students are learning." While these generalizations would no doubt sadden dedicated St. Louis schoolteachers, the city school system, as we mentioned in Chapter 3, also has its share of teachers and administrators who are incompetent but cannot be fired because of tenure, the politics of the system, or inertia. And because teaching in a county school carries more clout, the suburban districts—half of which pay higher salaries than the city system—can recruit top educators more easily.

Still, not all county teachers are wonderful. White, middle-class teachers who work with black students from an inner-city world often perceive some students' coping mechanisms—a tough persona, for example—as indicating a lack of motivation and concern. Three-fourths of the black students interviewed who had spent at least one year in suburban schools (including students who returned to city schools or dropped out) stated that some of the white teachers and administrators treat black students less fairly than they treat white students. Yet all but two of the transfer parents—those whose children remain in suburban schools—were convinced that their children were treated fairly at school.

This discontinuity between the perceptions of the transfer students and their parents regarding fair treatment in the suburban schools was discussed in focus groups with eleventh-grade transfer students (Public Policy Research Centers, 1993a). Several of the students spoke of negative incidents in their county schools when teachers or administrators treated them differently than the white students. When asked whether they spoke to their parents about a

2. One of the twelve transfer parents in our original sample was in the hospital at the time of the data collection and unable to meet with us.

particular incident, the students often said no, that they needed to deal with it themselves. For instance, one eleventh-grader was not selected by his choir teacher to go to Chicago for a concert because the teacher assumed his family did not have the money to pay for the trip. When asked whether he told his mother about this incident, he said, "That was a long time ago, but I did tell her about it. But a lot of times I kind of take that into my own hands. . . . I can take care of myself, I don't even tell her. Because I know how my mother is, she'd be like well . . ." Another transfer student finished the thought: "Yeah, most parents are like that, 'Well, I'll go over there and talk to her.' You know what I'm saying, you don't want that to happen, that's everyday life. I mean, people are prejudiced, you gonna have to learn it" (pp. 26–27).

We can better understand these responses when we hear the transfer parents emphasize the importance of exposure to people of other races as a primary reason for sending their children to suburban schools. These parents say the transfer program allows their children to learn more about people of different races and backgrounds. The benefit of attending integrated schools, these parents said, is that their sons and daughters will "learn how the other half lives." According to Tina's mother, her daughter will learn about different cultures in the suburbs: "It will make her a better person." Urma's mother noted, "The exposure [to nonblacks] helps a lot so that she is not paranoid around different people."

The Jones (1988) survey of black parents found that 59 percent of transfer parents agree with the following statement: "Going to school in the county has helped [my] child learn to understand and get along with white kids a lot." Another 30 percent said it had helped somewhat, and only 7 percent said not at all. The survey also found that the vast majority of transfer parents are so supportive of the desegregation plan that they advocated expanding it; 74 percent of the 352 black transfer parents said they would favor enlarging the program to let more black students attend county schools. Another 13 percent said "It depends" or "Don't know."

Whether these parents and guardians are completely accurate in their assessment of the quality of the county schools, the fact that they cited resources and achievement-oriented factors, as opposed to the proximity and familiarity factors cited by the parents of students in the city schools, makes an important statement about their view of the role of the school in shaping their children's lives. While city parents are likely to say that it does not matter where their children go to school—they can learn anywhere if they want to—the transfer parents see a more complex and competitive opportunity structure in which more demanding curriculum and better networks are available in some schools but not in others. Their role then as parents is to get their children into the "better" schools, and the transfer program does indeed empower them to do that.

The degree to which better is defined by "wealth" (students from privileged backgrounds) and "whiteness" (educators who offer college-prep curriculum because their white constituents have the power to demand it) is obvious in the comparisons of city and suburban, black and white schools. Access and exposure to white and wealthy schools and students are the central criteria for black parents trying to help their children move up in the world. Although these parents know that their children do not need to sit next to white children to learn, they also know that schools with many white and wealthy students are more likely to offer challenging curriculum and be linked to social networks in which high-status curriculum matters.

The transfer parents are, for instance, much more confident that the county high schools are preparing their children for the future. Ten of eleven transfer parents as opposed to only two city parents agreed that their child's high school was preparing him or her for higher education or the job market. When asked in the Jones (1988) survey whether they agreed that the money spent on the transfer program would be better spent fixing up the city schools, 42 percent of the 352 black transfer parents "strongly agreed." Twenty-two percent partly agreed and 31 percent disagreed, and 5 percent said they did not know. It seems that if it were simply a matter of unequal school resources between city and suburban schools, more of these black parents should have strongly agreed with spending the money in their own neighborhood schools. But interestingly enough, their children were less certain about the desirability of "attending school in my own neighborhood if the schools there were better." According the survey, only 31 percent of the transfer students strongly agree with this statement, 21 percent partially agree, and 47 percent disagree (Jones, 1988).

In response to questions concerning what they liked least about their children's county schools, four of the transfer parents we interviewed said that the schools have no faults. Three cited the distance of the school from their home. Not one of the transfer parents criticized the academic programs in the county schools. This is similar to the responses of city parents when asked what they like least about city high schools. To the extent that parents in either group has a criticism of their children's schools other than the inconvenience of a school's location, it is more likely to be a criticism of the social climate and attitudes of students in those schools—the prejudiced students in the suburbs or the disruptive students in the city.

Still, the transfer parents' dislikes of the county schools clearly suggest that the transfer process is a tradeoff. In order to get what they consider a better education, their children will have to experience some inconveniences, like long bus rides, and the discomfort of feeling like an outsider and being exposed to racial prejudice. But these parents think that the benefits of a suburban school diploma will outweigh the costs in the long run. Meanwhile, the city parents, with little positive to say about their local schools, seem to take the good, the bad, and the ugly in stride, as though there were no options available to them.

DEALING WITH RACIAL ISSUES—ASSIMILATIONISTS AND VISIONARIES

That transfer parents knew little about the specific county district they and their children were choosing says something about the role of race in their decision to transfer. But at some point in the process of attending and believing in the suburban schools, black students and their parents must reconcile themselves with all the reasons why white and wealthy schools are "better" than the urban schools staffed and attended by African Americans—why they offer more advanced classes and more opportunities to learn about college, and why white suburban students seem to be more focused on school achievement than do the students in the mostly or all-black city schools.

In a racially polarized society the pro-suburban stance of the transfer families sound like a "white-is-right," antiblack attitude, which West (1993a, p. 27) calls the "narrow assimilationist position." And for many this is the case. But others have a sophisticated, visionary critique of the color line—how it was created, how it is perpetuated, and why they must cross it, even if it means leaving their own community behind.

The Assimilationists

We saw a profound difference between the visionary transfer students and parents and those who appear to buy into the assimilationist perspective. The assimilationists tended to put whiteness on a pedestal and blame blacks for the social and economic problems in the inner-city ghettos. To hear these black parents and students criticize members of their race with little mention of the larger issues that deprive blacks of opportunities is disheartening. From their perspective, the transfer plan is a way for upwardly mobile blacks to remove themselves from undeserving blacks. They say that only the best black students should be allowed to go to the suburban schools.

Maurice's Mother If ever there were a mother who was supportive, encouraging, and a real cheerleader for her son, it has to be Maurice's mother, a loud and energetic woman who squealed with excitement at the sight of her sixteen-year-old son walking toward their home in a lower-middle-class neigh-borhood: "That's my baby! Here he comes—that's my Maurice," she said, jumping up and down and waving both arms in the air as if she hadn't seen him in months. Her high-pitched voice carried down the street, and Maurice looked up at her with a smile charged by both embarrassment and flattery.

"I sent Maurice to the county school for me. I thought it was neat," said Maurice's mother after the excitement of her son's coming home from school for the day had died down. "I really wanted to put Maurice in a Catholic school because I wasn't satisfied with the education that was given in the public [city] schools. When Maurice was going to the city schools he was like a beast."

She explained that Maurice was skeptical about going to a county school: "He said, 'I don't know if I am smart enough to be out there.' And I said give it a year. If you drop out we'll just bring you back to the city."

Maurice's mother said that the teachers and counselors in the county schools helped Maurice get through some of his more rebellious periods as an adolescent, including his ninety-day bus suspension when he and a girlfriend were caught committing a "moving violation" on the back of the bus. "They have more things available to help children in trouble—qualified people, so-cial workers, tutors, people to sit and go over homework," she said when asked what she liked most about her son's county school.

Despite her adulation of the county schools and her condemnation of the city schools—"The teachers in the city don't care; they just there"—she has chosen not to send Maurice's little sister to a county school. "I wanted to put her out there, too, but it would be too stressful for her. She is not as quick as Maurice. He is very quick; he just memorizes—has an excellent memory. She is very active—won't sit still to grasp it. If I put her out in Parkway, it would be very stressful. She can't deal with it."

Throughout the interview Maurice's mother talked of how proud she is of her son for "making it" in the county school: "It's good to know that your child can handle it—makes me feel good." Her negative opinion of the city schools and the inability of the city teachers to educate the children was reiterated in several statements, including one concerning her daughter's education. "My daughter . . . is in the city school, and her reading comprehension is very bad. So if I want my daughter to know how to read, I can't depend on the reading teacher. . . . I have to spend money to send her to Evelyn Woods or somebody who can help her," said Maurice's mother. "I'm not happy with the city schools. They tell people to keep their children in public schools—for what? I'm not happy with them."

Nonetheless, Maurice's mother is convinced that her daughter should not go to a suburban school. She did place her daughter in one of the city's magnet schools, which she said is superior to the neighborhood all-black schools, but nearly every comment comparing the city and county schools communicated her belief that only the "best and brightest" black students should compete in the predominantly white schools. In other words, her son should go but her daughter, no matter how poor an education she may be receiving in a city school, should stay. This thought was reiterated when she was asked whether she ever had considered sending Maurice to a magnet school: "Well, that's where I put my daughter, in the magnet school. . . . Magnet school is fine for some children. A lot of them [black parents] want their children in magnet schools. But I want him in a county school. That's what I want, and he's happy there. So it all worked out fine. I'm happy with my decision."

Further evidence of Maurice's mother's belief that only certain black students should venture out to the suburbs is found in her discussion of how she would change the interdistrict transfer program. She replied matter-of-factly that the number of black students allowed to transfer should be limited because having too many black students was having a negative impact on county schools.

"Something about when you get a lot of blacks together—it causes friction. I don't want to sound that I am putting my people down, because I'm not. But sometimes you have to say things that are realistic. It's unfortunate, but sometimes it's right," said Maurice's mother. "I don't know what it is about our people, but many times . . . when you get too many blacks in school or shopping in a clothes store or in the neighborhood, then all the whites they had would leave. They would say, 'Fine, let all the blacks come into this program, and my child will be in a private school.'"

The solution to this potential decline of the county schools, according to Maurice's mother, is to "throw out the bad" black transfer students from the county schools and begin screening new students who want to transfer.

Throughout her interview, Maurice's mother never criticized a suburban teacher, administrator, or student. Nor did she offer any critique of the St. Louis Board of Education and the racial politics that had kept the all-black schools inferior for so many years. She displayed the type of symbolic politics that Sears, Hensler, and Speer (1979) and McConahay (1982) found in their research on white attitudes toward busing: the degree to which a school desegregation plan affected whites personally mattered less than their racial attitudes when it came to accepting or rejecting the plan. While it clearly seemed as though it would be in her, and certainly her daughter's, best interest to send her daughter to a county school, Maurice's mother chose not to do this because she believed her daughter could not "handle it." It is not surprising that members of an oppressed minority group buy into the dominant perceptions of the larger society that they are intellectually and socially inferior and then internalize the blame for their inferiority (West, 1993a). A broader critique of a political and social system that keeps blacks down—such as the one offered by Leo's mother in the last chapter—is rare among blacks in St. Louis.

While Maurice's mother represents an extreme viewpoint, other transfer parents also expressed a similar sentiment. Not one of these parents could think of a true "benefit" of an all-black school: "No benefits," "I don't see any," and "There aren't any—that's why we changed . . . just don't hold the same magic." This echoes the Sobel and Beck (1980) finding that the race of the students in a school does more to shape parents' perception of the school than does any objective information about the curriculum or the teaching.

Thus, it appears as though some parents of both the transfer students and students remaining in city schools tend to buy into an assimilationists ideology, yet the way that this belief affects their school choices is mediated by their sense of their children's ability to survive in the superior white schools. If they view their children to be among the most able black students, as Maurice's mother views her son, then they should go to a high-quality county school. If they are seen as average or worse—the way Maurice's mother views her daughter—they should stay behind in the inferior schools. These statements are similar to those of some of the city parents cited in Chapter 3.

Still, the out-and-out fear of whites evident in comments made by city parents is practically nonexistent in the responses of transfer parents. The transfer students also tended to be much less fearful of whites and less likely than city students to suggest that they themselves feel inferior to whites. But this does not mean that all transfer students possess a greater sense of black pride or offer a critique of racial segregation. A few more visionary students do, but they are the exception. In fact, many of the transfer students who garnered more of an assimilationist's perspective found fault with the behavior of other blacks—either those in the city schools or their fellow black transfer students. Still, they were inclined to be more critical of the county schools' white teachers, principals, and students than their parents were.

Cathy   Cathy, the dancer and pompon team member, is probably the best example of a transfer student with this attitude. When asked whether the principal and teachers in the county schools treat black students the same as white students, Cathy gave an answer that suggested some inner conflict between her desire to relate to and bond with black students in the mostly white school and her even stronger desire to play the part of a suburban student who is adored by the faculty and white students for being, as she put it: "a great dancer and really cute." "Well . . . it depends on how you carry yourself, I feel.

If you see a person walking down the hall and you see that they don't care about themselves you might stereotype them right there—you'll probably not treat them the same as you would if you saw somebody dressed nicely. But they try to not show the difference between the two."

This conflict appears to be exacerbated by the fact that Cathy does not fit perfectly into either of the social groups in the school: the black city group or the white suburban group. Of course there are several subgroups within these two groups—the jocks, burnouts, and "soches," or socialites—and some overlapping as well. But the resegregation along racial lines within the desegregated school—in the lunchroom, after school, and so forth—is real, and Cathy teeters between the two worlds.

By her own account, Cathy dresses and acts "whiter" than most of the transfer students. And she says that more of the black students give her trouble than the whites. "Most of the white people might look up at certain people. 'Cause of my being on the pom squad—they really notice my dance and they really look up to me . . . you know how they compliment me all the time. But it seems to me that I have more problems with the black kids than I do with the white because of the fact that I think the blacks think that I'm so much because other people compliment me—it's mainly the black people who give each other trouble. So I just stay away."

The pompon tryouts seemed to signify a break between Cathy and many of the other black students in her school. The black girls who did not make it onto the squad went to the principal and complained. Cathy said that many of the black girls thought she was the token black dancer for the squad, because very few blacks had ever been selected for the squad. "Even some of the people I consider as my friends asked, 'How did she make it?'—but I think I had the ability," said Cathy, adding that the judges also consider students' grades when choosing the pompon girls, as well as "if you smile and enjoy yourself and knew what you were doing. Most of them [the black students] knew what they were doing, but they got up there and they forgot," said Cathy.

When asked what she considered the benefits of going to an integrated school, Cathy explained that "white kids can offer you more." She then cited the example of a white girl who had let a close friend use her car when she went off to college. "If it was a black person they would probably let the car sit there. I think mainly we have trouble with blacks because we go against each other instead of trying to stick with each other. But I see that a white person will never go against another white person. . . . That's because blacks try to fit in so badly that they just totally turned the whole situation around. I think that's bad."

Cathy then explained several of the reasons why she did not want to go to an all-black school in the city. She said that black people are always trying to prove a point by saying something that they know they could have kept to themselves. She said that blacks stereotype each other because of the way they look or dress. When questioned whether whites do the same thing—as she had mentioned earlier in the interview when talking about the white teachers and principal in the county school—she said: "They do not make it so obvious. They look you in the face and smile and keep walking. . . . But I noticed a difference with the blacks."

By and large, the transfer students, like many of the black students remaining in the city schools, appeared to have internalized much of white society's negative attitude toward blacks. But as Cathy's comments illustrate, the transfer students also have to deal with the embarrassment of being associated with other transfer students whose behavior displeased whites in their schools.

Another portrayal of transfer students' racial attitudes is found in their responses to the question concerning the benefits of going to an all-black school. All but a few of the transfer students responded negatively. In other words, when asked about the benefits—any benefit—of an all-black school, they stated drawbacks. Their answers included: "There'd be more trouble" and "I would not learn as much." Maurice, after some thought, simply said, "I don't know—can't answer that."

The Visionaries

Still other transfer students and parents looked far beyond the white-is-right attitude when discussing the differences between the city and suburban schools. They maintained a deeper sense of pride in their own racial and cultural heritage and offered a more complicated and critical view of black-white relations. They stated that whites have cut off blacks from economic opportunities for centuries and that the student transfer plan is a payback—a way to finally give inner-city blacks a shot at the good life that whites have monopolized. They were not afraid to criticize the white educators or students in the county schools. Arlene, for instance, said that the biggest benefit of going to all-black schools is that a student is able to learn more about black people and their history. She believes that the suburban schools should incorporate a more Afrocentric perspective into their history and social studies courses.

While these transfer students and parents do not try to glorify what is taking place in their all-black neighborhoods—black-on-black violence, drug dealing, teenage pregnancy, and so on—they believe that these activities grow out of a larger social context, a long history of racist policies and practices embedded in the current global market that is creating a greater economic divide between the haves and the have-nots. This larger-picture perspective forces some transfer students to walk the line between buying in to (or selling out to) the white middle-class ideology that says everyone has a fair chance—an attitude that will serve them well as they try to get into colleges and corporations—and maintaining and respecting their own cultural heritage. This is the balancing act of any upwardly mobile immigrants or people of color, but it tends to be most difficult for those who have good reason to resent the way that their people have been treated by the white majority. Transfer students like Will seem to be teetering between the sophisticated critique of white society, which can result in a great deal of anger, and his understanding of how he is going to "make it."

Will The day after graduation Will hitched a ride to the St. Louis Art Museum to see an exhibition of works by black photographers. He had worked at the museum during his senior year as part of a special internship program for high school students to teach young children about art and the museum. He learned about the program from his high school art teacher. Will said he never would have learned about the program in a city school.

He walked through the grand museum with an air of confidence and familiarity. He knew where almost everything was, and he knew that most of the museum is dedicated to the works of European artists. He stopped to chat with several museum employees on his way up to the small, narrow room housing the photo exhibition—a powerful showing of hope and despair in African-American life. There were uplifting shots of Martin Luther King, Jr., and the marchers in Selma, Alabama, as well as a striking photo of Elijah Muhammad addressing a crowd. But Will's favorite piece was a blow-up of a photograph from *Life* magazine, circa 1960, showing a black man chained to a tree and being whipped mercilessly by white men. The battered man leaned heavily against the thick tree trunk and appeared unconscious; his back glistened with the blood of freshly opened wounds. The artist had cut the photo reproduction into several large pieces and patched them together imperfectly. The caption read "Who took this picture?"

Will stood shaking his head. "How could someone stand there and take that picture?" For him the art symbolized too many years of too many people standing by and watching racial oppression without doing a "damn thing about it."

There is a parallel to what Will went through in his suburban high school. He said that the biggest problem with the county schools is that many of the teachers are racist. "Some of them cover it up better than others. But the ones that are—nothing is being done about it."

Thus, Will's greatest disappointment the day after his high school graduation was that Parkway West had not changed enough while he went there—

that too few of the white, middle-class teachers had learned any lessons from their interaction with the black students. Even the most, basic understanding of where the black students were "coming from" was too much for many suburban teachers to comprehend.

The math teacher who grabbed Will by the arm and called him "boy" when he was helping a friend to the nurse's office particularly irritated Will. He said it was almost all he could do not to "kick his ass. But I was still trying to handle myself. I mean, I got to go through all this trying to adjust to them, and they make no adjustments to me."

If there is anything that teachers in the county school should know about, said Will, it's "don't put your hands on me if I'm a city student. That's number one. You're not supposed to put your hands on any kid—but not on no city students because we are taught from day one, from birth on this planet, that if someone touches you, you crack 'em—anybody—black, white, Oriental, your uncle, your father. The second thing is don't call me 'boy'—they know that. Any teacher knows that. Don't put your hands on kids, and never, ever call a black man—*Man*—a boy."

Will still remembers when he first read the *Autobiography of Malcolm X*—the summer between his freshman and sophomore years at Parkway West—and how it changed his way of thinking about race in America. "It was like, 'You can't tell me nothing—I'm too black.' Ya know what I'm saying?"

Malcolm X might not have approved of Will's exit from the neighborhood city schools to whiter and wealthier suburbia, and Will knows this. But he has tried, in the face of what he considers unjust treatment by white teachers, to reconcile his anger toward "white society" with his appreciation of the individual whites who believed in him and helped him achieve his goals. He said he has also come to realize how important integration is—not just because it connects black students to the clout that comes with a suburban school diploma, but also because the white teachers and students who are open to reevaluating their beliefs really benefit as well. "They need us. They need us out there bad. . . . I mean, when you think about it, the United States needs integration bad, 'cause white people stereotype black people bad. And white people don't realize that they have the history of killing blacks, not vice versa. . . . Of course, we get the experience of dealing with white people, but you're also gonna eliminate a lot of ignorance—and get rid of a lot of prejudices, too. A lot of benefits for everyone—for mankind as a whole—but, see, people don't want to hear that."

Will talks about his transfer to the suburbs as if it were a mission of sorts—one that has allowed him to reach for his dream while changing the way a few white teachers and students think about blacks. "I let them see things my way—'Just as you show me what things look like from your eyes, I'm gonna show you what they look like from my eyes.' I got a card from . . . my junior English teacher. At graduation, she was waiting to give it to me. And I read it—she said she really enjoyed having me in her American literature class because of the views I expressed. 'From the eyes of a black man'—I put it to her like that—and she said that opened up a lot of doors for her."

Will said that for the most part, the white suburban students are not "that racist." He said that main reason the black and white students are not more integrated is the different cliques they "hang" with, including the "street-hard brothers: baseball cap wearing, tennis shoes on all the time, blue jeans pulled up 'til the crack of your butt showin'." Still, he said, on the whole, white kids seem to be "real cool." "Now, we aren't always going to get along with one another, but that's the way it is—I'm not talking about black and white, white and white, black and black—but on the whole, a lot of people just want to stick with their group of friends."

As for the incessant black-on-black fighting in the suburban schools, Will said it is the natural outcome of a program that brings black students from different neighborhoods and different gangs together under one roof.

> Cause, I mean what you gonna fight the white kids for? A lot of stuff that starts things you got to have in common—neighborhoods, girls, something that happened outside of school. 'Cause a lot of fights don't deal about racial things, they're about things that they got in common with each other. We share a lot of things in common with brothers, but we share a lot of conflicts with each other too. Maybe they got the same group of friends, maybe their friends jumped this boy that don't even go to this school—his cousin had a fight with him—they happen to go to the same school—they live in the same neighborhood—he got into an argument with his friend—it could be anything.

Val Seventeen-year-old Val is tall, lanky, and polite. The only child of his widowed mother—"I'm not a bastard; my parents got married before I was born, but my father was killed," he made a point of saying—was living in a Catholic Boys Home his sophomore year of high school because his mother was hospitalized. Val, like seven of the transfer students interviewed, was one of the first black students from the city to transfer to a county school. He started in the wealthy, prestigious Clayton District when he was in elementary school. The decision for him to transfer was made entirely by his mother. "She thought it would be a good education and a good chance for me to get to know more different people, where I could just not work with all blacks."

When asked how he or his mother chose the Clayton District from the sixteen possible districts, Val explained that his mother investigated the history of racial prejudice at all of the county schools, "and she said Clayton had the less prejudice that she could see." Nevertheless, Val said that he had experienced prejudice in the Clayton schools he has attended, and that at first he was somewhat surprised by it. There was the sixth grade teacher who was "doing a little pushing along"—or giving him a higher grade than he felt he deserved because she thought he couldn't do any better.

> I was getting up giving these book reports, and all I was seeing was all these fours— a four was like a B-plus. And I was talking to my friend, and he said, to tell you the truth, you shouldn't be getting all these fours. . . . And so I tried something, did it on purpose—you know, mess around with my grade. I took this tape by Michael Jackson and this Wham! tape . . . and I was doing this book report on tapes—about the different kinds of music. And I gave the worst speech I ever gave. My information was totally wrong, my sources and everything. I should have at least got a negative zero 'cause it was really bad. And I said, well, that should have done it. I get back my sheet, and she gives me a four. . . . And that's when I started thinking, she must have thought that I couldn't do any better. . . . And if a teacher has that attitude that's what you are going to expect from yourself. I could have just sat in the class and didn't do anything, and I still would have made it—if I was that kind of person.

But Val's mother ingrained in him a drive to challenge himself that serves as his central motivating force. Despite other examples of racial prejudice—the coach at Clayton High School who said to him that white people learn quicker than black people, county students who "stereotype all blacks as street people"—Val remains bent on sticking it out in the county school because to go back to a city school now would be "the easy way out." He added that by attending schools in the Clayton District he now has skills that he would not have acquired until he was twenty-five years old had he gone to a city school.

"It's just the different stereotypes that I don't like. And you know this is something that still goes on at schools, and I hate it. I hate it so much," said Val. He described a scene in Clayton where he and a black friend wanted to join a basketball game with some white students, who had no idea whether they were any good at hoops. The white students assumed because Val and his friend are black they would be good. "And they said, 'Aw, you all going to come and take the game.' I mean, you see all these black pro basketball players, they had to work hard, they had to dedicate their lives to basketball and become that good to make it as far as they did. It's not just because they are black."

Yet for all the skepticism of Will, Val, and others, the transfer students and parents, as a group, are far less critical of whites and the white suburban schools than are the return students, those who did not complete their education in the suburban schools. In addition to the other benefits derived from court-ordered access to a high-status suburban school—a more conducive learning environment, college counseling, prestige—the black students who succeed in suburbia also learn something they could never come to understand in an all-black school: they can make it in a predominantly white society. Some of them, like Will, make it while maintaining their critique.

With or without a critique, these courageous transfer students rise very early in the morning, stand outside in the cold and dark waiting for their school buses, and travel many miles each day because they and their parents believe that separate is not, and never has been, equal in St. Louis. They are the spiritual descendents of black students from the early twentieth century who rode trolleys and horses for miles to go to Sumner High when it was the only secondary school that would teach them. When asked by an interviewer in the focus group study (Public Policy Research Centers, 1993a) why he endured a the long bus ride, one eleventh-grade transfer student answered matter-of-factly: "To get to school."

6

Suburban Refugees

What struck me about this little girl was the depths of her pain and rage. She was an-
gry. And yet her anger had no voice. It could not say, "Mommy, I am upset that all
these years from babyhood on, I thought I was a marvelous, beautiful gifted girl, only
to discover that the world does not see me this way." Often she was "acting out."
—bell hooks, *Black Looks: Race and Representation*

In any given year, about one in five of the African-American students from the city who transfer to suburban schools through the inter-district transfer plan leaves those schools for various reasons. According to the eleventh annual report on the student transfer program submitted to the district court by the Voluntary Interdistrict Coordinating Council (1995), in September 1993, about 940, or 7 percent, of the transfer students did not return to their suburban schools. These students are classified as DNRs, but there is really no data on why they did not return to their suburban schools, where they are, or what they are doing.

Furthermore, during the 1993–94 school year, 1,510, or 11 percent, of the 13,500 African-American students who were participating in program at the time withdrew from their suburban schools before summer. When the transfer students leave their suburban schools, some return to city schools and others move out of the city of St. Louis, making them ineligible to transfer to a predominantly white county school through the desegregation plan. Others simply drop out and end up back in the segregated north side of the city, with no diploma and no future.

When transfer students withdraw from their suburban schools during the school year, most fill out an exit survey, listing the reasons for their departure. The Voluntary Interdistrict Coordinating Council report (1995) includes the tabulations of these surveys, which show that during the 1993–94 school year 453, or 30 percent, of the city-to-county transfer students who withdrew did so because they no longer were eligible to participate (see table 6.1). This means that either their families moved out of the city or, in the case of fifty-one students, they have been placed in special education programs in the suburban Special School District, which means that they are still technically participating in the urban-suburban transfer program but have left their regular suburban schools. The second highest percentage of students, 25 percent, who withdrew from the transfer program report that they are enrolling in "alternative education"—magnet schools in the city, vocational education programs in the county's Special School District, or private schools. Another 25 percent listed "other" as the reason for withdrawing. The fourth most popular explanation for leaving the suburban schools—reported by about 19 percent of the students—was "personal," which includes an illness in the family, student difficulties in adjusting to their suburban school, and chronic nonattendance (p. 65).

In studying the information on the students who withdrew from the program for personal reasons, we found that about one-third said their parents requested they leave their suburban school. Another third stated that they either chose to drop out of the program due to lack of interest or they were dropped by the school due to lack of attendance. This is an interesting finding given that returning transfer students are rarely out-and-out expelled from their county schools. More frequently they receive a number of suspensions of increasing length—a ten-day suspension followed by a thirty-day suspension followed by a ninety-day suspension—until they have missed so much schoolwork that they cannot catch up. This is what the students often refer to as being "put out" of a county school.

Yet aside from these general statistics, little is known about the African-American students who leave the suburban schools—those whom we refer to as return students. We spent some time with thirteen return students and parents from the same three neighborhoods as the city students and most of the

Table 6.1. City-to-County Transfer Students' Reasons for Withdrawal, 1993–1994

	Eligibility	Personal	School-Related	Transportation	Alternative Education	Other	No Report	Multiple	Total Withdrawal	Total Transfers	Withdrawal Rate
Number of students	453	281	69	25	374	34	50	224	1510	13,500	
Percentage of students	30%	18 6%	4.6%	1.7%	25%	25%	3.3%	15%			11%

Source: Voluntary Interdistrict Coordinating Council (1995)
Eligibility: Students moved into districts from which they cannot transfer; they moved out of town; they became full-time special-education students.
Personal: Family or student-centered problems, such as illness in the family, adjustment difficulties, or chronic nonattendance.
School-Related: Reasons that could be traced to the student's experience in the host district—either academic or disciplinary concerns.
Transportation: Frustration with the distance between home and school.
Alternative Education: Students who transferred to magnet schools, vocational-technical programs, or private schools.
Other: No particular reason cited.
No Report: The student failed to fill out a report when withdrawing.
Multiple: Students gave multiple reasons for withdrawal.

transfer students we interviewed.[1] In fact many of these students lived on the same block or in the same housing project as a city or transfer student we had met.

Tammy   Tammy was sixteen years old with a three-month-old baby when we visited. She lived with her mother and her sister a few blocks from Vashon High School in the low-income neighborhood, but on the summer day that we met with her she was staying at her grandmother's house in the more working-class neighborhood near Sumner High School. Tammy was still enrolled in Parkway West High School in suburban west county, but within a matter of weeks she would become a DNR statistic in a year-end report. It was not just the demands of single motherhood that had caused Tammy to persuade her mother to take her out of the suburban school, it was also her negative experience with white teachers and students that had led her to give up on the transfer program. "I feel like I am getting treated wrong," she said. "So I give them as many problems as I can, 'cause I feel like they are giving me problems. I deserve to be treated better than that."

This angry young woman with a round, cherubic face had been told by her mother and older sister, who graduated from the same county high school, that the transfer program would provide her with a better opportunity. But Tammy is not afraid to tell a white administrator, teacher, or student in her suburban school what she thinks. She is not inhibited from acting out the anger she feels toward white students who say to her, "this is *our* school," or toward teachers who make it clear to transfer students that they do not want black teenagers in their school. "You can find a few teachers that will try to help out as much as they can, but mostly it's like a put on. They don't like us. Like sometimes you can even catch 'em talking, you know how they don't think you're listening, saying all negative stuff about the program." And then there are the little, seemingly benign, things that occur that make the transfer students feel like outsiders in their suburban schools: "They call a meeting, and they always go [on the loudspeaker], 'All voluntary transfer students please come to the gym.' And we *hate* that. I mean, I don't know, I don't know really what they were trying to say except, 'all black students please come here.'"

1. We ended up with an "extra" return student because one of the transfer students we had set up an interview with turned out to have left his suburban school to return to his neighborhood high school. Also, Tammy, originally part of the transfer student sample, is described in this chapter because she was in the process of returning to the city schools when we interviewed her.

Tammy's reaction to this treatment—her surly expressions and her self-professed tendency to pick fights with white students or teachers in order to scare them—is exactly the type of behavior that suburban educators and students abhor. It is the kind of sometimes violent behavior that makes whites in suburbia despise the desegregation program. It is the kind of behavior that results in transfer students like Tammy ending up back in their neighborhood schools in the city or out of school altogether. And yet, paradoxically, it is often behavior that whites unwittingly provoke through their insensitivity to racial issues in mostly white schools.

The return students we spoke to were one step ahead of Tammy in the process of checking out of a suburban school, and we wanted to know more about how they made meaning of that decision.

WHY THEY RETURN

While the circumstances and attitudes of the separate city and transfer families were consistent and distinct from each other, the return parents and students represented a more diffuse blend of experiences and perspectives. A few of the parents in this group were assertive and demanding—more similar to the transfer parents who had pushed their children out to the county schools. Others were as withdrawn and alienated as many of the city parents. The return students also varied widely from bold and outspoken to meek and soft-spoken. Yet, what is most interesting about this group of students is that who they are and how they view themselves in relation to the rest of the society—their "habitus," as Bourdieu (1984) would explain it—has everything to do with why return students return to a city school or drop out of school completely.

The return students and parents we spoke to offered an array of reasons for quitting the transfer program. Based on the students' responses and their parents' confirmation of these experiences, at least eight of the thirteen return students' reasons for dropping out of the transfer program were related to racial issues and the discrimination they perceived in the county schools. But these race-related issues overlap with four distinct categories of responses to the question of why students returned to a city school.

The first such category, stated by four of the return students, was that they were put out or pushed out of their schools as a result of disciplinary actions by white administrators. All four of these students (three boys and a girl) felt that these actions were the result of racial bias on the part of the administrators. These students were generally bolder than the other return students; they were the resistors who were not always willing to abide by the rules of the suburban schools—similar in many respects to the rebellious "lads" described in

Willis' (1977) book on working-class boys in England or the rebellious "hall-way hangers" described by MacLeod (1987). These students, sent to county schools by domineering parents, saw within the suburban schools' disciplinary codes an effort on the part of white educators to play into the racial attitudes of white suburban communities. The goal, according to these resistant students, is to keep the black students from the city under control.

The second category of responses came from five of the return students, who said that they left the county schools for comfort and convenience reasons that included everything from not liking the bus ride to finding the white county students to be unfriendly. Four of these students cited racial uneasiness and perceived prejudice in the county schools. These students, with one exception, tended to be the quieter return students, the ones who did not resist the oppression they felt by causing a lot of trouble, but rather the ones who wanted to return to a social environment in which they felt more comfortable. Four of these five students strongly resembled many of the withdrawn city students who liked their neighborhood high schools because they were nearby and full of familiar people. The parents of these particular students, meanwhile, like many of the city parents, seemed to play a much smaller role in helping their children make school choices.

Yet another category of responses came from three of the return students who said they left the county schools for academic reasons—one said she was skipping class too much in the county school, and the other two said that they came back to the admittedly less difficult city schools so that they could improve their grades. The latter two of these students appeared to be going through a cooling-off process in which they set their sights lower and removed themselves from the competition for achievement in a high-status school (Bowles and Gintis, 1976). The parents of these three students were concerned. Two had pushed their children to go to the county in the first place, and all three said they wished their children had not returned from county schools. But they were unable to give enough parental support, guidance, or encouragement to keep their children from returning to the city schools. While the initial decision for these students to go to the county, get a better education, and escape the violence in the urban schools had been made by the student, the parent, or both, the strength or willingness to sustain that decision under difficult circumstances was not there.

The remaining return student said he had no choice but to return from his county school after he had missed several months of classes to take care of his ailing stepfather. He said that after his stepfather died, he wanted to continue in the county school and make up what he had missed. But the principal had strongly discouraged him and told him he should seek out a vocationally oriented program elsewhere. This extremely timid student had let himself be pushed out of his county school by an insensitive school administrator.

Given these varied reasons for leaving county schools, a clearer picture of the return parents and students needs to be painted so that the complexity of this group of respondents can be fully appreciated.

Return Parents: The Bold and the Beat Down

The return students we interviewed were more likely to have begun transferring to a county school at an older age than the transfer students. For instance, only two return students as compared to six of the transfer students had attended even one year of elementary school in the county. Meanwhile, seven return students, compared to only one transfer student, had not transferred to a county school until they were in high school. These vast differences in the ages of return and transfer students when they first began attending county schools suggest different levels of parental involvement in the city-versus-county school decisionmaking process.

Compared to almost all of the city parents and one of the transfer parents who left the school-choice decision up to their children, five of the twelve return parents said they did so. Meanwhile, four of these return parents—as opposed to two city parents and six transfer parents—took full credit for the original transfer decision, with one woman saying she sent her son against his wishes.

Ronald's Mother On a deserted side street in the working-class neighborhood, Ronald lives with his mother and an older sister in a small gray single-family house greatly in need of repair. The rooms are dark and musty behind thick, faded curtains. Quiet despair hangs heavy over the house and the people inside.

At first, Ronald's mother was highly suspicious of the researchers who were asking her son about his experience in the county schools and his reasons for returning to the neighborhood school. But it was not apparent why. Finally, after she had interrupted our interview with Ronald several times by wandering in and out of the living room, smoking cigarettes, Ronald's mother sat down in a worn armchair and began to talk about her sense of guilt. She told of how she had pushed Ronald—a quiet seventeen-year-old who was wary of strangers—to transfer to a county school against his wishes. She said that the experience changed him, and now, even though he is back in a city school, he doesn't do his schoolwork—he doesn't try. She said she blames herself for everything; she feels as though she "messed up."

Ronald's mother learned of the transfer program through the brochures that came in the mail and from some of her friends and relatives who have children in county schools. She said she thought of sending Ronald's older sister to a county school first but changed her mind because her daughter needed some "special courses," remedial or special education classes that she did not think were offered in the county districts. She added that her daughter was a determined student but that she "didn't learn as easy as Ronald."

The pushing on her part came not at the point of deciding that Ronald would go to a county school but rather at choosing which district he would attend. According to his mother, Ronald wanted to go to the Hazelwood School District, where his cousin was enrolled. But that district, which has a relatively large resident black population and therefore takes only a limited number of transfer students, did not have room for him.

Meanwhile, Ronald's mother had heard a lot about the Parkway School District. "I heard Parkway West was a very good school. Of course my friend had a son that finished there and he got a scholarship and he is going to college now, you know. . . . He got a scholarship at that school."

When Ronald did not get into the Hazelwood School District, his mother went to a county school recruitment meeting for parents and students and learned that Parkway was taking more black students that year. So she signed up her son, and he grudgingly left for Parkway West the next morning to enroll in ninth grade. But he lasted only one year.

Although Ronald refused to answer much more than "yes" and "no" to questions about his experience at Parkway West, he did say that black and white students were treated equally there. The problem was that Ronald did not do well in his classes because "I didn't want to go in the first place." He said he came back to the city high school so he could get better grades.

Although she was trying to do the right thing by her son—sending him to a school she thought was better, a school that offered a better chance for scholarships—Ronald's mother now feels incredibly guilty about making her son do something that she thought would help him in the long run. "I just feel like I messed up when I put him out in the county and he didn't want to go. It's like it just changed his whole attitude, period. Because he always did care and try to learn—even in grade school he had better grades, he cared and studied, you know. And when I changed him and he didn't want to go it just changed his whole attitude."

When asked what she liked about the county school her son had attended, Ronald's mother said that it was a "nice, clean school. . . . I just felt like he had more to work with out there. I wanted him to go somewhere where he would really learn, you know. . . . If you wanted to make something of yourself, I thought it was the place to go."

She said that ultimately the decision for Ronald to return to a city school was hers—"I had to get him out because I felt he wasn't learning anything, and when the teachers told me his grades, he wasn't doing good. I felt the best thing for me to do was get him out and hope he would do better."

As of our interviews, Ronald was not doing better, though he had promised his mother that he would improve if he came back to a city school. In response to the question concerning what she likes about her son's city high school, Ronald's mother stumbled over her answer, trying to think of positive things to say. "Well, I guess I feel like they have teachers that care—but crowded, it's very crowded." She also said that, unfortunately, the school had cut back on some of the "special classes, tutoring and stuff" that her daughter had been enrolled in—classes that she suspected Ronald might now need.

Denise's Mother One of only a few mothers in the total sample who did not want her child interviewed unless she were present, Denise's mother seemingly plays an important part in almost every aspect of her children's lives. She and Denise live with Denise's father on a particularly pastoral street in the middle-class neighborhood. Her job as a medical technologist in a hospital in the county puts her in touch with people from all over the metropolitan area. She is a confident, aggressive woman who stands up for her children and pushes to get what she wants for them. She has three sons, the youngest of whom had recently graduated from Mehlville High School in the county and was enrolled in college at the time of the interview, and one daughter, Denise. She said that she first heard of the transfer program through some "city educators I associate with."

She said that the idea to send Denise and her brother to a county school first occurred to her when her money began running out for the private Lutheran schools they had been attending. "Being the product of St. Louis public schools, I wanted my children to have better than what I had—not that I turned out so bad," said Denise's mother of her decision not to enroll her children in the city schools.

Her youngest son transferred to a county school first, but there was no room for him in any of the three suburban districts that he and his mother selected as their first choices. Their choices at that point were either Mehlville in the county or one of two city schools—Beaumont or Northwest—and they did not want a city school. Denise followed her brother to the Mehlville District a year later, when she was in the seventh grade. "She had no choice," according to her mother who did not want Denise in a city school.

Yet while Denise's brother was successful and popular in the county school—an outcome their mother suspects had as much to do with his athletic abilities as anything else—Denise did not get along with the staff or the students, especially when she got to the high school. According to Denise's mother, there was a serious double standard for black versus white students in the county schools regarding discipline and achievement. She said that this double standard was applied more to black girls, who were usually less valuable assets to the school's athletic program. "I think the only reason my son and his friends graduated from Mehlville without a lot of pressure is because they were in sports. And Mehlville for the first time in history won the district championship [in basketball] with these boys on their team," she said.

Denise's mother also said that when her son was still enrolled in the high school, the principal and teachers tried to help make her more involved, encouraged her to join the athletic mothers' club, for instance. "They were so phony," she said of the way they treated her, "but they gave a real appearance." Nonetheless, Denise's mother would faithfully drive the 30-some miles to watch her son play on the basketball team.

After her brother graduated, things became more difficult for Denise, who said that her favorite aspect of the county school had been that her brother "was there to watch me." Denise said that some of the white students were racist—calling the black students "niggers" as they walked down the halls. She said she was involved in two racially motivated fights between black and white students, one while in junior high school and one in senior high. After the fight at the high school, Denise reported, the administrators tried to expel several of the black students, while giving the white students only a detention.

Denise's mother was aware of the racial issues: "I'm not saying that my daughter was an angel, but blacks were suspended when whites got detention. And a couple of remarks he [the former principal] made to me personally about my daughter let me know that he was a complete bigot—he said my daughter was ignorant, and she would never learn anything."

At first, Denise's mother said she fought with the administrator to keep her daughter in the school. She told Denise to try to stick it out until graduation. But after several phone calls and a visit to the school to talk with the principal, "I decided it was time to bring her back—it was either that or she and I would have both ended up in jail by the time it was finished. I think I had enough of this principal and his remarks."

Despite all she had been through with Mehlville High School, Denise's mother decided to place her daughter in another county school. She had heard about the Parkway District from people she works with and teachers in the city. But because transfer students are not allowed to transfer from one county district to another under the rules of the court order, Denise's mother could not place her daughter in Parkway. Denise would have to go back to a city school for at least a year before enrolling in another county district. So Denise ended up at nearby Northwest High School, much to her mother's chagrin. When asked what she liked about this neighborhood high school, Denise's mother said, "Nothing. I'm not saying the teachers don't care in the city schools, but they're less effective." And when asked why she thinks they are less effective, she said, "I don't know."

Denise's mother was insistent that a county school would be better for her daughter—that county schools were better connected. She said that Mehlville had helped her son get a job at McDonnell Douglas and a scholarship to St. Louis University. "This all stems from being in an integrated school," she said. "The curriculums are higher and they do a little bit more to help their students." But then she added that "if it wasn't for the sports, I think they wouldn't have done all that."

At the time of our interview with Denise and her mother, Denise was transferring back to the county, this time to the Parkway District. Her mother said that after a "lot of phone calls" to the Voluntary Interdistrict Coordinating Council office and the schools, she had finally managed to get her daughter into the county district of her choice. Unfortunately, at that point Denise was nineteen and starting her senior year.

Penny's Mother Just a block away from the high-rise Vaughn public housing project in the low-income neighborhood, is the sprawling two-story brick Carr Lane public housing project, considered one of the most dangerous communities on the ravaged North Side of St. Louis. Wars between drug dealers and teenage gang members are fought here, and their battles are played out on the evening news. Children are rarely seen playing outside the heavy gray steel doors that barricade their apartments.

Carr Lane is home to Penny, her baby daughter, her mother, and her two brothers. A narrow stairway framed by two cement walls leads to their chilly and damp apartment. The sparsely furnished living room is dark and gloomy. Ten- and fifteen-year-old portraits of smiling children stand dusty and disorganized on a wobbly coffee table.

In the middle of a weekday morning, when all is quiet in the neighborhood, Penny and her family are also inactive. Even her five-month-old baby made little noise in the time we spent there. Although we had set up an appointment, both Penny and her mother said they had forgotten. But it didn't seem to matter because they said they had no immediate plans. After we had interviewed Penny, a soft-spoken girl who seemed more tired than anything else, she went upstairs to call her mother.

Several minutes later, Penny's mother came slowly down the stairs. She wore a faded bandanna on her head, and she acted groggy. Throughout the interview Penny's mother rocked slowly on a plastic-covered chair, hugging herself with one arm and chain-smoking with the other. She was only thirty-seven years old but could have easily passed for fifty. Her oldest child was twenty-two. She was unemployed and seemingly overwhelmed.

But her mood seemed to lift slightly as she remembered the details of how Penny first transferred to a county school. "I got some letters through the mail, and it looked like she'd learn more out there," she said. "It was mostly my decision. She was only in the third grade when I sent her, but she was so far behind."

According to Penny's mother, she did not choose a specific county district for her daughter. "I just filled out the papers, and they just told you where she would go." Penny ended up in the Lindbergh School District, where, according to both her and her mother, she was learning a lot more than in the city schools.

Then when Penny was in middle school, two black transfer students got into a violent fight at the high school. One of the girls stabbed the other in the arm and the leg, and the fight became well publicized throughout the metropolitan area when the media showed up at the school. "They made a real big deal of it," according to Penny, who was accustomed to much more severe violence taking place outside her front door.

Meanwhile, the white students began protesting and holding rallies in front of the high school, saying that they did not want the black city students in their school. Penny and the other transfer students in the middle school watched all of this from their school bus windows as they were heading home. It was then that Penny decided that she did not want to go to Lindbergh High School, and she started getting into fights of her own. "I was considered a bad kid who used to get in fights all the time—with city kids and county kids," she explained. "I didn't want to go Lindbergh because I knew I would be fighting every day."

"She wanted to go to Parkway, but they—the people at the transfer office—said that Parkway was out of her [suburban school] district. They said she would have to go to Lindbergh," said Penny's mother. "I didn't like that."

Neither did Penny, who opted to transfer back to her neighborhood high school, Vashon. Both mother and daughter cited several aspects of the neighborhood school they did not like, including teachers who "cuss back at you and hit you—sometimes you don't even touch them and if you say something smart, they hit you," said Penny.

"I don't like anything about Vashon," said Penny's mother, who never attended high school herself. "It's hard for a girl up there with all that fighting."

But seventeen-year-old Penny has not been back to school since the birth of her baby. "She just got to the point that she just doesn't care; she got it in her mind that she just doesn't want to go," said her mother in a tone of utter hopelessness.

This story of Penny's experience in a mostly white suburban school meshes with that of Denise. But unlike Denise's mother, who persisted in getting her daughter placed into the Parkway District, Penny's mother gave up. "I would let the kids go where they wanted to go, and that might keep them in school for a long time," said Penny's mother, responding to a question of how she would change the transfer program if she could.

Despite their vast differences, the return parents all agreed on one point: that county schools were better than city schools. For instance, when asked what they liked most about their child's county school, only two of the return parents—Walter's and Gail's mothers—did not respond enthusiastically. Most of the return parents talked about the learning, curricular, or general achievement factors as their favorite aspect of their children's former county schools, including "They had more to offer," "They were up on a lot of things" (teaching techniques, and so forth), and "If you want to make something of yourself, county school's the place to go." Four of the return parents cited the caring and concern of the educators in the county schools as their favorite aspect— "Principals and teachers worked together . . . go the extra mile," and "They act like they care."

These responses mirror those of the transfer parents in their discussions of what they like about the county schools their children still attend. As with the transfer parents, the return parents' responses to the question of what they liked about county schools contrasts them to city parents who cited mostly proximity and familiarity factors as what they liked most about their children's schools of choice in the city.

In response to questions concerning what they liked least about their sons' and daughters' county schools, seven of the twelve return parents said they had no complaints against the county schools. Two return parents stated convenience factors—the school was "too far" and the "kids get up so early, makes them cranky"—and the remaining three return parents cited prejudice on the part of the county school administrators and teachers as what they liked least.

In contrast to the transfer parents, therefore, return parents are less likely to be critical of the county schools, with almost twice as many return as transfer parents saying they had no complaints about the county schools. Furthermore, return parents were even less likely than transfer parents to say that what they liked least about the county schools was prejudice on the part of the educators. This is somewhat surprising considering that transfer parents still have children enrolled in these schools and return parents have children who left these schools—most of them because of perceived prejudice.

In fact, of the eight return students who said that their decision to return to a city school had something to do with perceived racial prejudice in the county—either its impact on disciplinary actions or its impact on the level of social discomfort they felt—half had parents or guardians who said they had no complaints at all toward the county schools. It appears as though return parents we spoke to are even less aware of the prejudice their children experience in the county schools than the transfer parents, such as Gerald's or Urma's mothers, who said they stayed on top of such things and made sure that their children were treated fairly in the county schools. Similarly, according to the transfer students, six of the transfer parents talked to their children about prejudice and what to expect from whites in the county before they transferred, whereas only three of the return students said their parents had talked to them about these topics. Although, as we noted in Chapter 5, the transfer students do not always tell their parents about their negative experiences in their suburban schools, they had learned from their parents that prejudice exists in the suburbs and in most of society and that they were going to have to deal with it. Yet among the return parents we interviewed, Denise's mother—the parent who kept close tabs on her daughter in the county school, went out to the school to argue with the principal in Denise's defense, and provided a strong critique of the school and the administrators—is an exception. These findings suggest that less support on the part of return parents than transfer parents may have been a factor in their children's lack of success in the suburbs.

Furthermore, when asked whose decision it was for their son or daughter to come back to a city school, half of the return parents said their children made the choice on their own. Three return parents said that they themselves had taken their children out of county schools—one because she thought her daughter was not being treated fairly, one because her son was not doing well academically, and one because her daughter was skipping too many classes at her open-campus county school. Three of the return parents said that the decision for the student to quit the transfer program was made by an administrator in a county school. Although none of those students was told that he (they were all boys) could absolutely not remain in the county school, two were, according to their parents' recollection, faced with an ultimatum: if you come back you'll be watched very closely, and the first thing you do wrong will result in yet another, longer suspension. For instance, Robert's grandmother said, "Robert wanted to go back [to the county schools], but the way the principal was talking, he did not want Robert there anymore. . . . So we agreed that he didn't really have a choice."

The third student whose mother said that the county school had "decided" for her son was Barrett, the boy who had missed several months of school to take care of his stepfather. Barrett's mother said she was not involved in the process: "It was mostly the school's decision. The principal dissuaded him from going back." She said that she still would like for her nineteen-year-old son to go back to the county school someday.

Thus, most return parents we interviewed clearly did not choose to have their children leave the county schools. Half of them responded negatively when asked what they liked about the city schools their children enrolled in after returning from the county, including Denise's mother, who had taken her daughter out of the county school, and Robert's grandmother and Barrett's mother, who said that the county school had made the return decision for them. The negative comments toward the city schools from return parents included: "Teachers not act like they are interested," "[The school] has a lot of gangsters . . . used to be a good school until the students took it over," and "Don't have the equipment—they are in terrible shape."

Meanwhile, only three of the return parents stated something positive when asked what they like about their son's or daughter's city school: "Famous graduates . . . good football team," "He keeps his grades up," and "Teachers are dedicated." This last comment was made by Dee Ann's mother, a teacher in her daughter's city high school. Other return parents gave fairly neutral or convenience-oriented responses when questioned about what they like about the neighborhood school: "It's close—it's convenient for us," "They have teachers that care—but [it's] crowded," and "Principal and teachers are trying—it's hard in the city . . . guns."

When they compared the city schools to the county schools, the return parents' dissatisfaction with the city schools became even more evident. Nine of the twelve said they felt that county schools were clearly better—that is, county schools have more computers, broader advantage, stricter teachers, and so forth. Two return parents gave more neutral responses: one said that the "physical environment in the county is much better, but in terms of dedication—teachers in the city are very dedicated," and the other noted that "learning" was the same in both city and county schools. Only one return parent had anything remotely positive to say about the city school in comparison with the county school: "Easy to get to in case of emergency." Clearly return parents are not satisfied educational consumers. With their children enrolled in city schools or out of school altogether, they, often for reasons beyond their control, have not maximized their options in the school-choice market.

This evidence depicts return parents as individuals who for the most part fit between the transfer and city parents in terms of their parental involvement and aggressiveness. Four of them said that they pushed their children to attend county schools, but as the story of Ronald's mother reveals, even forceful parents back down under pressure from their children or the county schools. Their lack of a critique of county schools also suggests that they, unlike their children, believed that the problems faced by the transfer students are minimal.

Their lack of awareness regarding their children's school experiences matches their less-specific expectations for their children. Nearly all of the return parents gave vague responses to the question of what they would like their son or daughter to be doing in five years—"Good job," "decent job," "in some trade." The return parents, many of whom seem beat down and overwhelmed by the educational system, were more likely to give such answers than were city or transfer parents.

Denise's mother and Keenya's mother, however, had specific expectations. Denise's mother said that she would like for her daughter to be getting her master's degree in engineering, and Keenya's mother said that she wanted her daughter to become a teacher. Another return parent with specific answers to this question was Ronald's mother, who hoped that her son, who is doing very poorly academically in his city high school, would become a doctor, a nurse, or a basketball player. "He loves basketball," she said, "but he didn't get on the [high school] team."

When asked whether their children's all-black city high schools were preparing them for the future, four of the return parents said yes, as compared with only two city parents. Two return parents said that they did not know whether the high school was preparing their son or daughter for the future. One said no, and five of the return parents gave conditional responses, such as "They try" and "I hope so."

Return Parents and Racial Attitudes

What is perhaps most startling about the responses from return parents is how little they addressed race and racial issues. Denise's mother's commentary on bigotry in the suburbs and the way that county schools exploit black athletes stands out as an exception here. Indeed, Charles's mother, who said there was nothing she disliked about the county school, explained that her son had returned to the neighborhood high school because white students and administrators in the county schools try to blame black students for all the problems in the school. Blacks also try to blame the whites, she added, but because there were more whites than blacks in the county school, chances were that he would be more likely to be blamed for something. She has accepted her son's decision to return to the city school. "I just want to have peace of mind.

There's been too many people gone to jail for things they didn't do," she said wearily. Her recognition that such violations happen all the time to black people in a predominantly white society seemed to make her cautious.

Like the transfer parents, return parents show little sign of fear of contact with whites, but their responses to questions concerning the benefits of all-black and integrated schools suggest that many of them lean toward an assimilationist philosophy. Perhaps the most disapproving comment regarding the "benefits" of an all-black school came from Robert's grandmother—one of four return parents who responded very negatively to this question. She said, "In the city you just meet one class of people, and I hate to say it but it's a bad class. . . . In the county, everybody seems so nice—not talking about fighting and breaking into things—just better people in the county."

That this statement comes from Robert's grandmother is somewhat surprising considering that her grandson was put out of a county school for fighting with a white student whom he said told him to "sit with his own type" in the lunchroom. And yet Robert's grandmother said she "didn't find any problem" with the county school. This is also the grandmother who said that the principal of the county school just did not want Robert in his school anymore. While Robert is indignant about his experience in the county school, his grandmother seems resigned to the fact that a white principal pushed her grandson out of the county school because of a racial fight that was started by a white student.

Even Denise's mother, with her critique of the way that some black students are treated in county schools, said that she "can't see any benefits" to an all-black school. Positive responses to this question, however, came from four return parents, including Charles' mother, who said that her son could "get along with people better" in an all-black school. Then, as we mentioned earlier, she wouldn't have to worry about him being thrown into jail for something he did not do. Dee Ann's mother, the teacher in the neighborhood high school, gave the most affirmative response concerning the all-black school by defending the quality of education in the city schools and stating that many students receive scholarships through their inner-city schools.

The other return parents offered neutral or contradictory responses to the question concerning an all-black school. Donald's mother, for instance, said that if her son were the "kind of student I want him to be—it would make a real difference. If he had the leadership abilities, he could inspire other kids." Yet Donald's mother also berated the teachers and administrators in Sumner High School for not calling her when her son missed seventeen days of school. "Then they wanted to withdraw him—they had not called me once!" she said. When she went to talk to the principal about Donald's situation, she said he was "too busy dealing with gang fights and drug sales—it kept him from dealing with reason."

Walter's mother, frail and soft-spoken, said that if her son felt more comfortable in an all-black school, "that's where he will benefit." She stated rather proudly several times throughout the interview that she had nothing to do with her son's initial decision to transfer to a county school or with his subsequent decision to return to Vashon High School in their low-income neighborhood. "You have to let them go where they feel most comfortable," she said. She did not use the words "black" or "white" throughout the entire interview, even when asked direct questions about race.

When asked about the benefits of an integrated school, most of the return parents had positive things to say. For instance, three cited the benefits of meeting "different" people or of being exposed to racial and cultural diversity in general. Keenya's mother, however, said that in an integrated school her daughter would "get to be with white kids, and that makes it more competitive." Robert's grandmother said that integrated schools offer "better education" and the opportunity to "meet better people." Only Walter's mother said she saw no benefits to an integrated school.

Although the racial attitudes of the return parents were clearly not as pronounced as those of the assimilationist transfer parents or as telling as those of the city parents, they also suggested a belief that white schools are generally better than black schools. As is the case with other parents in the sample, this perception often seems to have as much to do with parents' understanding of the race and social class of the students who attend the white schools versus the all-black schools as the course offerings or curricular focus. That the return parents can make such statements in light of what many of their children have experienced in county schools suggests that the parents and students in this group either don't communicate or do not trust and accept each other's judgment on racial issues. While this behavior is similar in some ways to that of transfer students who did not tell their parents about their bad experiences in the suburban schools, the transfer parents were open with their children about racial issues and were more likely to have advised them before they transferred to a county school that they would face prejudice. On the other hand, the return parents' almost sedate outlook on racial issues sharply contrasts with their children's more poignant racial attitudes—angry resistance toward or timid insecurity among whites.

The Return Students: Resisting and Resigning

The city students were tied to their familiar neighborhood school and the transfer students were pushed toward the "better" schools by their parents.

The return students, however, were caught between their need for comfort, positive reinforcement, and someone to believe in them, and their own realization that the county schools represented something they once thought they could attain.

Gail In the few hours we spent with Gail and her almost two-year-old son, she never removed the oversized blue windbreaker that flapped against her thin frame. Although she told us that her second baby was "on the way," she seemed to want to mask any evidence of it.

Gail lived with her mother and her son, Conrad, in the Vaughn public housing project, in the high-rise building next to the one where Troy and his mother live. From the front of the Vaughn she can see the Carr Lane public housing project where Penny and her baby live. We went with Gail to pick up Conrad from the Head Start program housed on the ground floor of the apartment building. Conrad was thin and sickly looking. He walked hand-in-hand with his mother, letting her pull him up the four flights of stairs to their apartment. Gail said that it is too dangerous to use the elevators in the projects. "People will jam them so you're stuck, then drop in through the roof and rob you . . . or whatever." But the stairwell, covered with graffiti and smelling of urine, hardly seemed safe. In certain spots the lights had been knocked off the walls, and it was too dark to see the steps.

Their apartment was small and crammed with furniture. The kitchen was an alcove that also served as a walkway from the front door to the living room. A tiny Formica kitchen table and red plastic chairs took up nearly every inch of space in the kitchen, leaving no room for a high chair. Gail fixed Conrad a plate of bright orange macaroni and cheese and placed him on one of the red kitchen chairs to eat. He sat eye level with the top of the table, which made eating very difficult. While trying to help Conrad eat his dinner, Gail told us why she first went to a county school.

She said when she was in junior high school she would hear people talking about going to the county schools. When she was in eighth grade she decided to transfer because she did not want to go to her neighborhood school, Vashon. She said it was completely her decision, though her mother agreed that it was a good idea.

Gail transferred to Hazelwood West High School when she was in ninth grade. She said she picked that district because students had told her it was good, though she said she did not know anyone going there at the time. In speaking of Hazelwood West and what she liked about it, Gail mentioned both the pep rallies ("They had one every week") and the cafeteria food two or three times each. She said the teachers were "okay" and that the counselors were helpful. In discussing what she liked least about her county high school, which she attended for only one year, Gail began to explain some of the reasons she returned to the city schools: "The classes, they was kinda boring. . . . I really didn't have any fun. They weren't really no fun at all. I disliked it because you know how they break down the work for you, they don't really explain it to you. Some teachers they explain and others let you go on your own. . . . I didn't do no good—walked out with a 1-point grade average and I went back to public [city] school and my grades went back up to normal. I'm a B student but I was between a C and a D [in the county], and I didn't like that. I knew I was better than that. I knew I could function better than that. . . . It's just that . . . your mind had to be real wise to be out there."

Gail never mentioned her first pregnancy as a factor that brought her back to the city schools, but she did say that in her first year back she was enrolled in a special high school for pregnant students.

At the time of the interview, Gail, who was nineteen, still had a year to go before graduating from Vashon. Her view of her high school was that "It'll do, it ain't so hot, but it'll do. . . . It's trouble. . . . You're around a lot of blacks, and they're just fighting."

Gail emphasized that she tries to steer clear of most of the students in her high school and in her neighborhood, going only as far as her apartment and the school, and sometimes she takes her son to the park—"That's it," she said. She laughs at the thought of going to college, though she says she would like to. Her career goal is to "take up child care, child development—anything to do with children."

Robert   Robert lives with his grandmother and a cousin in the Carr Lane public housing project, a few blocks from Gail and Conrad and across the street from Penny's apartment. By the age of fifteen he already had been enrolled in and put out of three high schools—one in the county and two in the city.

On a weekday morning we found Robert and two friends sauntering down the street that runs through the center of the project. Robert had forgotten our appointment but said that he had nothing else to do, so he and his friends headed back into his apartment for the interview. All three of the boys wore the garb that was popular among gang bangers in the city at that time: bibbed overalls worn with one strap hanging down, thick, gold-link chains around their necks, gold bar rings that encompassed three fingers, and heavy ski parkas with fur-lined hoods.

Recounting his school history as if he were ticking off a win-loss record, Robert spoke in the passive tense: "Got put out of Webster [a county school].

Put me in Vashon, then put me out of there. Put me in Beaumont, and then put me out of there. . . . Now, don't go to school."

A careful look at Robert's reasons for being asked to leave each of the high schools reveals a pattern of increasing resistance toward schools and their achievement ideology. He first went to a county school in the fourth grade. He said he learned of the transfer program through the information that came in the mail, and though he did not know anyone transferring at the time, he said, "I just decided I wanted to go."

He reported that he was popular in all the county schools he attended—an elementary school, a junior high school, and a high school (for one semester). He was the quarterback of the freshman football team and had made it onto the basketball team when he and his friend started getting into trouble. According to Robert, "The principals were prejudiced to two people in the school—me and my best friend. Every time something happened, they came and got us. They don't like us. I feel like they didn't want us in their school."

He said that he and his friend were accused of stealing a leather jacket out of a locker—an accusation he denied. And finally, he got put out for fighting with a white student. "They [the white students] gave me trouble for a while until I tried to kill one of them," he said with a sheepish smile.

In Vashon, his neighborhood high school, he said he made "straight F's"—down from a C-minus average in the county schools—because he "knew everybody there and so I didn't get anything done for five months." Eventually, however, Robert was asked to leave Vashon as well. "The principal told me he just didn't want me there. Thought I was in the gang. I wasn't in a gang. So they transfer me over to Beaumont, and me and a teacher got into an argument and almost got into a fight. It was silly. I asked him if I could go to the principal's office, and he said don't return without a pass. But no one was there. He said I lied to him because I didn't have a pass. He told me to get out. I said, 'Put me out.' He called security guards. Told him he better move out of the door before I punched him in the face."

In less than a year Robert had gone from being a "popular" football quarterback to a seemingly very angry dropout. His two best friends were also out of school. His first child was due in a few months.

Once Robert felt that he was being treated unfairly by the administrators in the county school, he began to resist the educational system as a whole. His only method of communication with the people who legitimate the schools as institutions was through violence. This type of conflict between educators and students was common in the desegregated secondary schools studied by Metz (1978). Robert's final comment on the transfer program: "They need to change their attitude. Principals' attitudes gonna get them into trouble. Just a whole lot of brothers like to punch them clean in the face."

Charles Sixteen-year-old Charles looks and acts like a teenage version of Spike Lee—opinionated and forthright. He comes from a more privileged background than most of the students in the sample. His two-parent, one-sibling family resides in what was one of the newest and finest single-family homes in the middle-class neighborhood.

He transferred to the Pattonville School District when he was in seventh grade at his parents' suggestion: "They wanted me to try both sides." He said that what he liked most about the two county schools he attended—a junior high school and Pattonville High School for one year—was that "both had weight rooms." Throughout the interview he compiled a lengthy list of what he did not like about going to a county school, including the need to get up early, the bus ride, and more important, the curriculum and teaching style. "I thought I could hang tough with it. You know, going to bed early and getting up. . . . But I didn't expect all those science projects and reading all this history. Work on top of work on top of work. . . . In the city they give you more lectures. . . . They go too fast [in the county]. . . . I didn't do what she wanted me to. They only have so much time to explain stuff."

Charles' fear of failing in the county school was juxtaposed to his resistance to the way that black students are expected to act in county schools: "They brainwash you to go out there—that they teach you more. Then you get there. Oh, you're integrated. You're not yourself no more. Your voice changes like you are a little nerd or something. I felt like I was not myself anymore."

The transfer students' struggle to succeed in county schools while maintaining their identity, especially in their speech, was a central issue raised in the focus groups with transfer students (Public Policy Research Center, 1993a). For instance, the eleventh-grade transfer students participating in the focus group described how they "hate it" when African-American students talk and act "all white" when they are at their county schools and then get on the bus and start talking "black" again. According to one transfer student, "There's some . . . black people that, in our school, they try to act white. I mean I don't understand how they can dress like that" (p. 11). Another student noted: "There's some black people in my school that are worse, well, they talk worse, the way white people talk. Because . . . there's this one girl there . . . she talks like a white person would, I mean she just talks, she just changes it, I mean when she get around black people she can talk a little black" (p. 11).

As we mentioned in Chapter 4, the research on African-American students' "oppositional attitudes" toward academic achievement shows that some black students equate working hard in school and getting good grades with "acting white"—buying into an achievement ideology that has been carved out of white culture (see Fordham, 1988, and Fordham and Ogbu, 1986). Yet the transfer and return students in St. Louis tell us that while there is strong opposition to "acting white" as it relates to the way students talk or dress, that academic achievement is considered "acting white" only within a setting that completely devalues the intellectual contributions of African Americans—when it is a form of what Charles would call brainwashing. What these students seem to be saying, however, is that academic achievement in a school with a curriculum that looks more critically at race relations in America and at the oppression of blacks over the years is not at all "acting white" but a form of empowerment.

Charles' opposition to the academic push in the county schools has fueled his rejection of these schools and the predominantly white society that they represent. He demonstrated his anger by refusing to buy in to the legitimation of this more difficult curriculum and what black students could derive from it. He said that he had no discipline problems in the county school: "I was totally brainwashed. You think you're smart. I went with the system and I thought, 'I go to a county school.' You just think you are better than everybody else. Then you find out you are not."

Yet the push and pull between Charles' two separate and distinct views—that he had "failed" in the county school but that what he had failed in was illegitimate and false—represents the complexity of Charles' situation. When asked about the benefits of attending an integrated school, Charles stated that in county schools you learn about how whites try to brainwash blacks into thinking white is right. After leaving the county school Charles became involved with the Black Muslims in St. Louis. He is a racial separatist, one who believes that blacks are better off living separate lives—in separate schools, neighborhoods, and businesses—from whites. On the day we interviewed him he was going to hear Louis Farrakhan speak downtown. Charles talked directly to and made eye contact with the black interviewer, virtually ignoring the white interviewer.

Gail's resignation to her supposed inability to make it in a county school, based on her beliefs and expectations—or the "bounded rationality" through which she views her educational options (see Simon, 1987)—and Robert's and Charles' resistance to the county school and the achievement ideology on which they are based were two prevalent themes in the stories of the return students. That Gail took herself out of the more competitive county school so that she could earn better grades in a city school that she considers inferior says a great deal about the way she views herself and her chances of succeeding in other competitive situations, including admission to higher education and job searches. Robert's anger, similar in many ways to that of the hallway hangers whom MacLeod (1995) writes about in his book on students who live in a public housing project, may be directed at the schools and the educators, but it also encompasses a form of anger aimed at the larger society, especially now that he has lost his ticket to upward mobility: a seat in a high-status suburban school. Charles, on the other hand, shared Gail's motivation for leaving the county—getting out of a situation in which he thought he was failing—but he overlaps with Robert in how he responded to that situation: if you can't join them, fight them.

As mentioned above, the return students' reasons for coming back to city schools had much to do with how they viewed themselves in relation to the larger social structure. The two distinct reactions of Gail and Robert as well as the overlapping response of Charles illustrate this point. For instance, the eight return students who cited either comfort and convenience or academic reasons (with the partial exception of Charles) for returning tended to be more like Gail in terms of feeling inferior to whites and incapable of or unwilling to compete with suburban white students either socially or academically. Robert better typifies the resistance of the four return students who were put out of their county schools and who now reject the legitimacy of the reward system that they feel offers them no chance of success—either in high school or beyond.

Return students' commitment to academic achievement in the predominantly white schools and within these schools' reward structures was indeed much more tentative than that of the transfer students. The latter students clearly stated that better educational opportunities and removal from a negative environment were their central reasons for transferring. In fact, when return students were asked what they had liked most about their county school, only two stated anything remotely related to academic achievement—Dee Ann, who said that county schools had more classes and activities to choose from, and Donald, who liked how the school operated, how the days went by. One of the students just thought that the county schools were "fine." The remaining ten students cited facilities and amenities—the gym, the weight rooms, the variety of activities and sports programs. Meanwhile, practically everything that these students liked least about their county schools pertained to their discomfort there, with four of them directly related to perceived racial prejudice and unfair treatment.

In discussions of their likes and dislikes of the county schools, return students, as a group, more closely resembled the city than the transfer students in terms of what they looked for in a school. They sought schools where it was not a struggle to feel good about themselves. They sought reaffirmation that they could enjoy at least limited success in an academic setting. This is the kind of encouragement that many transfer students seemed to receive from their parents, allowing them to enter a predominantly white school environment without having to derive their entire sense of accomplishment and worth from the people within these institutions. For some of the transfer students, this support allowed them to put their negative experiences of racial prejudice into a larger perspective. Prejudice and discomfort then became part of what they had to put up with in order to succeed in a predominantly white school. But the result is that the transfer students, mostly because of their parents, have legitimized and internalized a reward structure that values making it in white society more than the comfort of remaining in a segregated world. The most successful of all—transfer students like Will, for instance—learned to walk the thin line between achieving according to white people's ideology while maintaining his own identity and standards of achievement, which include an informed critique of racial inequality in American society.

But the return students drew different conclusions, and many ended up either lowering their own expectations or rejecting the legitimacy of an achievement ideology as defined by the white educators and students. In either case, returning to an all-black inner-city high school appears not to be a self-maximizing solution but rather a choice of the lesser of two evils.

When asked to compare the city schools with the county high schools, all thirteen return students stated that the county high schools were more difficult and aimed at preparing students for a more challenging future. Meanwhile, only two of these students stated that their city school was less "fair" than the county schools they had attended. Realizing, at least subconsciously, that city schools are not preparing them as well for entry into a whiter, high-status society as the county schools did, these students' decisions to return to neighborhood all-black schools are a profound statement of their perceived long-term chances of success in competing for places in higher-status postsecondary educational institutions and adult employment.

Return Students and Racial Attitudes

The more resigned return students like Gail tended to report more fear of whites—or at least fear of competition with whites—than did transfer students, and in this regard, they more closely resemble the city students. Yet their explanation of their anxiety about attending a predominantly white county school was more sophisticated than was that of the city students, owing to their first-hand experiences.

Keenya Only a few blocks from Sumner High School in the working-class neighborhood, Keenya, her mother, and her three siblings live in a slightly run-down two-family duplex. Shy but perceptive, Keenya told the story of the prejudice she experienced in her county high school, Parkway West, in a calm manner that communicated her deep understanding of the reality of racial dominance. Her story also communicated her desire to buffer herself from that reality as much as possible.

Keenya decided to transfer to a county school while in eighth grade based mostly on the influence of her friends: "You know like how you be talking about like when I get into high school this was the particular high school I wanted to go to. . . . Everybody decided that they wanted to go out to a county high school, because they wanted to learn."

She reported that her mother had said that it was all right for Keenya to go, though her mother did not play an active role in the decision making. Keenya said she went out to Parkway West High School with high expectations predicated on what she had heard about the transfer program and the county schools in general. "Like before you hear all good things about the school, how people are friendly," she said.

Keenya said that what surprised her the most about her first week in the county school was the coldness of the white county students and their ability to make her feel unwelcome. "I thought it would be like—people would be easier to get along with out there. More friendlier, but they weren't. If you asked them where was the classroom, they act like they did not want to tell you," she said.

When questioned about the teachers and whether they treated black and white students equally, Keenya at first said, "Sort of, in a way, I guess." But when pressed, she explained the subtle ways that the teachers made her feel uncomfortable in the county school. "So basically, when the teacher was teaching and they would make an example about something . . . like they would say something like that was out in the county, and I wouldn't know what they are talking about. But the white students would, because they are out there . . . you know, like a shopping mall or something, and I wouldn't know what they were talking about."

Keenya's lack of knowledge of places and events familiar only to those students and teachers who live in the county relates to Bourdieu's (1984) and Bourdieu and Passeron's (1979) discussion of "cultural capital," or the valued cultural knowledge that some students have simply by virtue of being born to a middle- or upper-middle-class family. The highly valued cultural capital is that which the schools reward, while lower-status cultural capital—derived from growing up in a low-income, inner-city family—is not rewarded by the schools, particularly suburban schools. When applied to American suburban teenagers, the knowledge of shopping malls or retail outlets is considered valuable shared knowledge, a form of cultural capital. Similarly, teachers' use of this shared knowledge to make a point in class parallels Bourdieu's discussion of the French teacher's validation of the wealthy student's cultural capital, which leads to higher-status students gaining more self-confidence and to lower-status students feeling excluded.

Keenya recalled other classroom situations in which she felt uncomfortable, such as when her English teacher showed a film that "was like putting blacks down. And it made me feel real uncomfortable, seeing how they was treating the blacks in the movie."

Yet the most uncomfortable experience that Keenya described was when she had to give a speech in her public-speaking class. "I guess it was hard because I was the only black, and it was a public-speaking class. You know, you had to get up and speak in front of the class. And I got so I felt real uncomfortable because of my speech. All the white kids, you know, just stared at me. And when, like the speech was over, you try to be nice and applaud for somebody—they would not applaud for me."

This feeling of rejection was reason enough for Keenya to remove herself from the higher-status school. Interestingly, her mother said that she did not agree with Keenya's decision. In fact, Keenya's mother spoke as though she did not fully believe what her daughter had told her concerning the prejudice toward black students in county schools. When asked what she liked about Keenya's county high school, her mother replied, "I liked everything really, but she didn't like it—thought it was racist—but I think she couldn't put up with it." In reference to other transfer students who have remained in their county schools, Keenya's mother said, "As far as I know they are hanging tough. I think she would have made it, but she didn't want to be strong enough to hang." This distrust of her daughter's experience, or at least of the impact of that experience, typifies what was pointed out earlier in this chapter. The return parents appear to be unaware or unconcerned with what their children are reporting about the treatment of blacks in the county schools.

Students' decisions to remove themselves from the competition in high-status schools or to resist the legitimacy of those schools because of feelings of inferiority toward and distrust of whites is not surprising. But the fact that they sometimes receive little support or understanding from their parents is.

Furthermore, as with the two other groups of students, the fear, distrust, and even resistance toward whites experienced by the return students do not always lead to a strong pro-black stance. Only four return students saw any sort of benefit in attending an all-black school, and three of these cited factors that had to do with the familiarity of the people who went to the school. Only Charles, perhaps the most adamant resistor of the group, stated a benefit of an all-black school that dealt with black culture: "You're around your own culture, your own people—you can keep up with things and the trends in your neighborhood."

Meanwhile, six return students made negative comments when asked about the benefits of an all-black school. Three of these students, including two whose parents said the decision for the return to a city school had been made by the educators in the county school, made extremely negative statements about all-black schools:

> *Barrett:* I hate black schools. . . . I don't hate them, just don't like being with [the] same people—acting out and getting written up by teachers.
>
> *Donald:* None [no benefits]. . . . It's a downfall. Classes with black students and white teachers don't want to learn. White students try to work—motivates black students.
>
> *Robert:* Nothing challenging—I'm not saying black people are dumb, but most don't know shit. They all want to go sell drugs all their life.

This deprecation of other blacks by three students who left their county schools under less than ideal circumstances—Barrett because he could not go back after missing school to take care of his stepfather and Donald and Robert because of disciplinary problems—indicates that their anger and resistance toward the white educators who rejected them has not translated into a broader critique but rather into anger toward those they left behind when they made the first school choice to go to the suburbs. It may be that the city schools and the students within them serve as reminders of their own failure to succeed in the mostly white county schools and the higher status they did not attain.

Meanwhile, nine of the thirteen return students responded positively to the question concerning the benefit of an integrated school. Of these nine return students who spoke of positive aspects of integrated schools, four addressed the teaching or the quality of the education in the county schools, three referred to meeting different people in the integrated schools, one said there was more freedom in the integrated schools, and one simply said she enjoyed it. Of the return students who did not cite a benefit to attending an integrated school, none offered a critique of these schools.

The racial attitudes of the return students, like every aspect of this diverse group, are thus difficult to define. They appear to be somewhere between those of city and transfer students—some students are more fearful of or intimidated by whites, as were the city students, but others were more likely to put down members of their own race and want to separate themselves from blacks who signify the lower status of their group.

Whereas both the city parents and students and the transfer parents and students seemed to demonstrate several similarities—the same attitudes or degrees of shyness, and so on—the return group is more of a mishmash of different families and different views within the same family. The variation of these responses makes it impossible to draw definitive conclusions concerning the return students. Still, the lack of communication between return parents and their children concerning the prejudice that the students were often experiencing in the county schools is an important finding. It indicates a lack of vision or direction within the family—as if each parent had one set of beliefs or views concerning education and racial integration and each student had another. With little or no discussion between the two, the return students' decisions, driven by their own understanding of racial inequality in suburban schools, usually won out in the long run. This then makes the return families more similar to the city than the transfer families, who seemed to demonstrate a stronger mutual understanding between parent and student and certainly a stronger degree of parental control over the entire educational decision-making process. Once again, the efficacy of the transfer parents distinguishes them from the city and return parents in ways that will no doubt have a lasting impact on the lives of their children. When we look at the voluntary transfer program from the perspective of those whites who live and work in St. Louis County we will better appreciate the importance of this extra parental support.

PART III

The Suburbs

7

Saving Face in the Suburbs:
Local Control and Status Quo

No single tradition in public education is more deeply rooted than local control over the operation of schools; local autonomy has long been thought essential both to the maintenance of community concern and support for public schools and to quality of the educational process.
—U.S. Supreme Court, *Milliken v. Bradley*

Perhaps the most important aspect of the St. Louis metropolitan school desegregation program from the perspective of white educators and parents in the suburbs is the involuntary nature of this voluntary transfer plan. The sixteen predominantly white school districts that participate under the terms of the 1983 settlement agreement were not actively seeking to invite hundreds—thousands, in some cases—of African-American students from the city into their schools. Fear among the suburbanites that they would lose their locally controlled school districts and that white students would be forcibly bused into the city inspired the political compromise that became the settlement agreement. Thus, few whites in St. Louis County have shown any strong political support for the program, which they entered in an effort to avoid a more severe fate.

Our interviews with lawyers, school board members, educators, and parents in the suburbs demonstrate that what was most important to them in 1983 was the sovereignty of their districts. And yet the suburbanites' demand for local control is exactly what has made the implementation of the desegregation program so challenging. Local control has often meant the privilege to stay the same, to not change the school culture, climate, and traditions, or to challenge white suburbanites' understanding of America's racially separate and unequal society. When asked what new programs, staff, or resources he had implemented as a result of the desegregation program and the influx of nearly 300 black students into his all-white school, the principal of a suburban high school in South County responded, "I don't think we have changed that much. I think the school has remained pretty much in line or consistent. We are doing the same things that we did ten years ago."

From the perspective of many whites in St. Louis County, that is exactly how suburban educators should deal with the desegregation program. The general attitude in suburbia toward the cross-district desegregation program is at times hostile and often condescending and magnanimous. While conservative and resistant suburbanites call the plan a waste of state tax dollars, more liberal or sympathetic suburbanites view it as an act of charity from the suburbs to the poor black children of the city. From their ahistorical perspectives, the suburbanites in both camps are sometimes well meaning but almost always unaware of how things came to be the way they are in our segregated society. And from both points of view, it is the black transfer students, not the white suburbs, who need to change.

This section of the book is about the suburbs. In this chapter we describe the more resistant educators in the suburban districts, those who have attempted to maintain the status quo in their schools despite dramatic change in the composition of the students they serve and their districts' increasing dependence on state desegregation funding. In Chapter 8, we highlight those suburban educators who have used the desegregation plan as a lever for dramatic educational reform in their districts, schools, and classrooms—reforms that end up benefiting white as well as African-American students. These educators, sprinkled across several districts and sometimes isolated from one another, are, like the transfer students in Chapter 5, truly visionary. In Chapter 9 we focus on resistant and sympathetic white parents and students in St. Louis County and highlight some of the intergenerational and statewide political issues that shape their reactions to the city-county desegregation plan. These perspectives from the suburbs help explain the anxieties, experiences, and choices of the city, transfer, and return students discussed in the last three chapters. The suburban viewpoints shape and are shaped by the experiences of the African-American students who enroll in these locally controlled county schools.

DIVERSITY IN THE SUBURBS

The twenty-three school districts in St. Louis County—the sixteen predominantly white districts that receive black transfer students and the seven districts that do not—are distinct in size, demographics, and local politics. Given these differences, conclusions regarding the overall picture of the desegregation plan in the suburbs would be too simplistic. But distinct regions of the county lend themselves to some broad generalizations .

The lopsided, quarter-moon-shaped St. Louis County wraps three quarters of the way around the city of St. Louis, encircling it except on its eastern edge, which runs to the shore of the Mississippi River. The county is bordered on the north and west by the Missouri River, and it protrudes to the southwest to include the large Rockwood School District.

According to the 1990 Census, nearly 1 million people live in St. Louis County, more than double the city population of about 400,000. Less than 6 percent of the people living in St. Louis County are poor, as opposed to 25 percent of the people who live in the city. Not surprisingly, there is a strong correlation between race and poverty, as the county population is 86 percent white, whereas the city population is nearly 50 percent black. Despite the smaller percentage of African Americans in the county, the pattern of racial segregation and isolation there is nearly a mirror image of the city, reflecting the migration patterns of whites, and later blacks, out of the city into suburbia. North St. Louis County includes most of the predominantly black suburbs along the northwestern city border. The color line between these black suburbs and the Irish or Italian Catholic white suburbs to the north continues to move outward, as it did in the city just decades ago. This leaves the north county school districts, including Normandy, Jennings, and Hazelwood, with larger black resident student populations than most of the other county districts. In fact, the only north county school district that receives African-American transfer students through the inter-district plan is Hazelwood, because all of the other districts were at least 25 percent black in 1983, when the program began.

Central-west county, on the other hand, is an extension of the metro area's more affluent and more Protestant and Jewish central corridor, which began in the city's central west end. These central corridor suburban school districts,

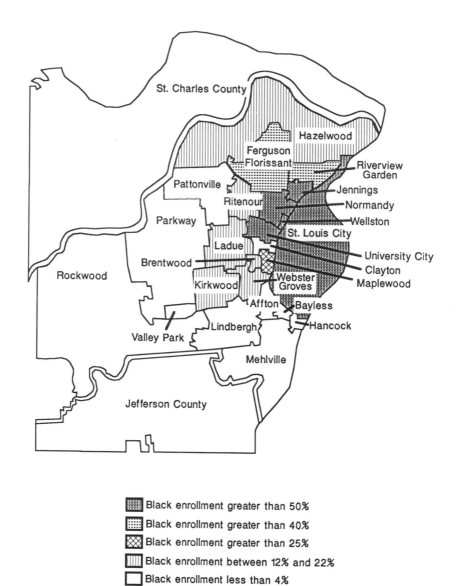

Figure 7.1 School Districts in St. Louis County and Percentage of Black Enrollment as of September 30, 1982
Source: Wisconsin Law Review 1987:971, 988. Reprinted by permission.

including Ladue, Clayton, and most of Parkway and Rockwood, are known as
some of the most desirable. Parents and voters in these districts are, on average, the wealthiest and most highly educated in the metro area. The political
climate in these districts is generally fiscally conservative but more liberal regarding social policies. This central corridor is also home to the most prestigious and selective private schools in the region. Thus, many parents who live
here can afford to be more liberal on such issues as school desegregation as
they send their children to private schools.

South St. Louis County is home to many white working- to middle-class
families who migrated from the city's south side and to the school districts of
Affton, Bayless, Hancock Park, Lindbergh, and Mehlville. The south county
residents who send their children to these schools are more likely to be Catholic or fundamentalist Protestant and more conservative on social issues than
are the central-west county residents. As the principal of an elementary
school in a south county district said, "St. Louis generally is pretty conservative, but this certainly is an ultra-conservative area."

South county residents are also more politically united with whites on the
city's south side through family ties and such groups as the antibusing Metro-
South Citizens' Council described in Chapter 3. Many south county communities consist of relatively recently developed suburban areas with no real
social structure or traditions of their own. As one Mehlville school board
member explained it, practically everyone in Mehlville is from somewhere
else—mostly the city's south side.

In addition, there are several suburban school districts that straddle west
and south county—Kirkwood and Webster Groves—and those that straddle
west and north county—University City, Ritenour, and Pattonville—and thus
represent an odd demographic mixture. The University City School District,
for instance, does not participate in the voluntary transfer plan because its student population is 83 percent African American. Its resident population, however, is only about 63 percent black. The southern edge of University City is
part of the affluent central corridor and adjacent to Washington University.
This area includes some of the largest, most beautiful homes in the metro
area. Most of the white, wealthy, and well-educated families that live there,
however, do not send their children to public schools. Meanwhile, the northern half of University City comprises low-income housing, where many poor,
African-American families reside (Bower, 1993).

Thus, when looking at the effect of the inter-district transfer program on
the entire metropolitan area, it is important to consider the similarities and
differences among the twenty-three county school districts, especially the sixteen predominantly white districts accepting transfer students from the city.

The similarities were perhaps most pronounced between 1981 and 1983, when these twenty-three school districts were codefendants in the inter-district desegregation case and county residents were challenged to reexamine the role that their suburbs played in creating the color line. Constituents in each of these districts were concerned about the consequences of a long, expensive trial; they were also equally committed to maintaining local control of their districts. They were united in their opposition to creating a large, metrowide school district, and in their efforts to distinguish themselves from the city schools. As an African-American administrator at Parkway West High School, noted: "Let's face it, the county districts didn't get involved out of a feeling of humanity. I mean, they went kicking and screaming the whole way."

But for all their similarities in 1983, the differences among these St. Louis County school districts have become far more pronounced in the years since the settlement agreement. In that time the sixteen predominantly white county districts, particularly the wealthiest ones, have received large amounts of state resources in return for accepting black transfer students from the city, while the poorer and less-white districts have been passed by. Furthermore, there are wide variations among the participating districts in how much money each receives from the state, how thoughtfully the program has been implemented, and what impact the plan has had on white or black students.

The Lawyers and the Autonomous School Districts

In August 1981, when Judge Hungate asked suburban school districts to volunteer to participate in the pilot city-county student transfer program, he offered in return a temporary stay of litigation from the pending trial between the black plaintiffs, the NAACP, and the St. Louis school board on the one hand and the twenty-three suburban school districts in St. Louis County and the state of Missouri on the other. The five districts that volunteered for the pilot program—Clayton, Kirkwood, Pattonville, Ritenour, University City—were all fairly centrally located in the county, with a range from the near north county (Ritenour and Pattonville)—to the near south side in Kirkwood. With the exception of Pattonville, these were some of the oldest districts in St. Louis County, thus they had the longest pre-*Brown* history of sending black students into the city schools. The lawyers for these districts knew there was a great deal of evidence that these suburban districts had contributed to segregation in the city schools by not providing educational opportunities for blacks in the suburbs.

With these five districts signing on in fall 1981 and information spreading about the pending inter-district desegregation trial, nine additional suburban districts decided in spring 1982 to begin accepting a small number of African-

American transfer students from the city in the coming fall. By the start of the second semester of the 1982–83 school year, fourteen suburban school districts were participating in the voluntary pilot program, 856 black students from the city were attending predominantly white suburban schools, and 350 white county students were attending magnet schools in the city. The state of Missouri paid to transport these students and provided the suburban districts with an additional $1,600 in state education aid for each nonresident student they accepted. The number of students that the suburban districts were required to enroll under the plan was quite small, less than 100 students per year for even the largest districts; the reward—a stay of litigation from the interdistrict trial—was great (La Pierre, 1987, pp. 993–994).

But a stay of litigation is a temporary solution. Meanwhile, the trial of the interdistrict case, with the state of Missouri and the nonparticipating county school districts, was to commence on February 14, 1983. Eventually, all twenty-three suburban school districts would be forced to either enter into the settlement agreement with the plaintiffs or face a long and expensive trial. The lawyers, policy makers, and some of the suburban constituents knew that the Eighth Circuit Court had in 1980 found the state guilty of violating the constitutional rights of African Americans; they also knew that school districts were considered arms of the state. But, more important, they knew what was likely to happen if they lost. Judge Hungate's rather unorthodox move to announced a proposed remedy before the trial began gave suburban lawyers and school board members the leverage needed to persuade their clients to sign on to the 1983 settlement agreement.

Frank Hackman, who was at the time the school board president in the Clayton District, "distinctly" remembered, more than ten years later, when Judge Hungate ordered experts to prepare proposals for a large metropolitan-wide school district in the event that the autonomous suburban districts lost the case. He remembers a map of the proposed school district as it was printed in the newspaper. "When you're the president of the school board and somebody puts a map in the paper that shows your district doesn't exist anymore, it's easy to remember," he said. According to Hackman, the proposed consolidation of districts and mandatory reassignment of white and black students to integrated schools—"the two [components] kind of blended together"—raised a great deal of anxiety in Hackman's small and affluent community and convinced his constituents of the necessity to be part of a compromise.

Washington University law professor Bruce La Pierre, who served as the Special Master to Judge Hungate, wrote that as he began meeting with the involved parties in the case there was broad agreement that three components of the voluntary pilot plan must be incorporated into any settlement. There should be no mandatory interdistrict student transfers and no school district consolidations, and the cost of any program that grew out of the settlement should be borne primarily by the state of Missouri (La Pierre, 1987, p. 995).

Hackman recalled that as his district entered into the settlement negotiations there were two additional factors on which his board and its constituents would not compromise: that any inter-district plan to be implemented would be "educationally sound," by which he meant that the legal negotiations should remain focused on the educational needs of the children involved; and that the Clayton School District must be allowed to maintain local control. "We wanted, as much as we could, to preserve our autonomy as a district and our ability to hire and fire teachers, to do teacher assignments, to control curricula and class size."

Similar stories echoed across St. Louis County as school board members and district administrators met with groups of parents and community members after the district court's remedy proposals were made public. According to one suburban superintendent: "Those who came to the meetings understood that we wanted to keep our school district. At the meetings we made it very clear that we were joining this plan so that our district could stay intact."

One of the small ironies of the St. Louis interdistrict desegregation plan is that it, in some instances, actually helped suburban districts maintain autonomy by staving off additional consolidation of small districts with shrinking enrollments. For instance, the superintendent of the tiny Brentwood School District noted, "With declining enrollments in most districts, empty classrooms probably affected decisions. . . . We needed some students and this [the transfer program] was the perfect way."

Still, a few of the suburban school districts—those more politically conservative, further from the city, and more recently established than the others—moved more slowly toward the 1983 settlement agreement. Some of these districts argued that they were not incorporated at the time of the worst constitutional violations (pre-1954) and therefore could not be liable for the damage done to African Americans. The lawyers for these districts knew that such an argument would not stand up in court, since these younger suburban districts were created via the consolidation of several smaller, rural districts that had existed before *Brown* and had sent black students into the city to attend school. Furthermore, these districts were part of a state-supported system of public education that had been, by law, segregated by race.

As we mentioned in Chapter 2, the St. Louis case was taking place in a former de jure state, which made it distinct from Detroit's *Milliken* case, in which the Supreme Court ruled that neither the state nor the suburbs contributed to the racial segregation in the city. In fact, as was noted in the evidence against the state of Missouri in the first phase of the *Liddell* case, state policy makers had not bothered to remove the "separate but equal" provision from the Constitution until 1976, even though such a provision was nullified by the Supreme Court's 1954 ruling (Confluence, 1989). Such an "oversight" was symbolic of the inattentiveness of the state of Missouri to equal educational opportunities for students of all races.

Despite the evidence against Missouri and its implications for suburban St. Louis school districts, in 1982, five of these St. Louis County districts—Affton, Hancock Place, Hazelwood, Mehlville, and Valley Park—hired James P. Groton of a prestigious Atlanta law firm to assist their local attorneys in the case. Groton and his firm had successfully defended ten predominantly white suburban Atlanta school districts against the 90 percent black, 80,000-student Atlanta public school system in the 1970s when it attempted to draw them into a desegregation lawsuit. Groton was quoted in a St. Louis newspaper as saying that he and his colleagues in Atlanta had proved that "people live in specific school districts and urban areas based on job needs, personal preference, and other factors—and not because of race" (Vespereny, 1982).

Groton said that he could help the suburban districts in St. Louis show that schools and government entities have had no major impact on housing patterns, adding that there is plenty of data, such as migration studies of the St. Louis area, "which can be used in this case very readily" (Pfeifer-Harms, 1982). (Groton did not mention why the St. Louis metro area was the home of not one but three Supreme Court cases on housing discrimination.) His "expertise" inspired the five St. Louis suburbs to pay thousands of dollars to hire his firm (Pfeifer-Harms, 1982; Vespereny, 1982). But the cost of an out-of-town attorney to litigate a case in which most of the other codefendant school districts were prepared to enter a settlement agreement proved unfeasible for these five districts. They too signed on to the agreement in spring 1983.

The last suburban district to sign the agreement was University City, a mostly black suburban district that had been one of the five districts participating in the pilot program. University City held out because, under the terms of the agreement, the districts that stood to gain the least were the seven suburban school districts with student enrollments that were more than 25 percent black—Ferguson-Florissant, Jennings, Normandy, Maplewood, Riverview Gardens, University City, and Wellston. These districts were essentially excluded from the inter-district program; they could not accept black transfer students from the city, nor could black students in their schools choose to attend another suburban district. And, in the final version of the settlement agreement, these seven districts were denied state funding for magnet programs to draw white students from other suburban districts. Three of the seven districts—those with a resident student population that was more than 50 percent white—were allowed, however, to send white students into the city to attend magnet schools there (La Pierre, 1987).

Under the final agreement, these seven school districts—three of which are virtually all black and extremely poor—have virtually no role in the desegregation program and thus have been shut out of the millions of dollars in state desegregation funds that go to the St. Louis public schools and the predominantly white suburban districts. Noting that many of these suburban school districts are quite poor relative to their neighboring suburban districts, an administrator in one of these districts said that the state funding going to the city schools and the predominantly white suburbs through the interdistrict transfer plan is like money "floating over the heads" of the black suburban districts. "As the students move from the city to the county, there are all these dollars from the state, and they [the black suburban districts] cannot grab any of them; that's the metaphor."

As the settlement agreement inched through the court approval process, University City eventually signed on in June 1983, after an amendment was added to give the district three state-funded magnet schools. Although district court Judge Hungate approved the agreement with this amendment, the Eighth Circuit later struck down the amendment, ruling that the state of Missouri was not obligated to fund magnet schools in any of the suburban districts nor did it need to fund student transfers between suburban school districts because these "county-to-county transfers were not designed to remedy the intra-district violation in the City of St. Louis" (La Pierre, 1987, p. 1019). This ruling was consistent with the court's determination that the state's intra-district violation in the city schools "is not a basis for imposing responsibility to reduce racial isolation in black county school districts" (p. 1020). In other words, because these seven suburban school districts, many of which were more racially segregated at the time than even the St. Louis public schools, were not plaintiffs in the case, they could not benefit from an agreement designed to address the needs of the African Americans represented in the suit—those who lived in the city of St. Louis and attended the St. Louis public schools.

Why these racially isolated and poor suburban districts did not join the city schools and the black plaintiffs in suing the other suburban districts for relief—a move that would have opened the door for suburban magnet schools and suburban-to-suburban district transfers—is not clear. These districts had been the victims of such discriminatory housing practices as racial steering and redlining in the same way as the St. Louis public schools, and the construction of their district boundaries also were circumscribed by the politics of race and class. But the answer to this question posed to district administrators and lawyers is simply that these districts have traditionally seen themselves as "other than" the city schools. The superintendent of a 97 percent African-American school district in St. Louis County said, "There wasn't any broad-scale consensus [to become a plaintiff]. I don't remember any kind of structured meeting about that." He noted, however, that under the current plan, with the state desegregation money going to whiter and wealthier suburban districts, "The rich get richer and the poor get poorer."

The identity of these districts is so vested in being suburban that even when it may have served them legally and economically to have shed their suburban label and all of the race and social class connotations that go along with it, they could not do it. David Tatel, one of the attorneys for the St. Louis public schools during the inter-district negotiation process, said that he urged the black suburban school districts to join the case. "I can't tell you how many times we told them and their lawyers that what they should do is join us. But they wouldn't do it. . . I told them again and again. I said, 'You guys are on the wrong side of this case.'"

In the end, only sixteen of the twenty-three suburban St. Louis school districts—those with a less than 25 percent black student population—were to participate in the student transfer program. The final settlement agreement stipulated that all student transfers would be voluntary, and while suburban districts are not allowed to deny prospective transfer students admission on the basis of prior academic achievement, they can refuse to admit a student because of previous disciplinary problems. The "plan goal" for the sixteen suburban districts is a racial balance of 25 percent black and 75 percent white. The districts' "plan ratio," on the other hand, is to increase their black student population by at least 15 percent from what it was in 1983. At the time, the racial breakdown of the student populations in these districts ranged from less than 1 to 24 percent African American (see table 7.1).

Under the agreement, the suburban school districts that were able to reach their plan ratios within five years received a stay of litigation in the inter-district case. The settlement stipulated that if any of the sixteen districts does not meet its plan ratio within five years, the plaintiffs and that particular district were to negotiate an agreement regarding future goals of these districts to meet their ratios. As of the 1994–95 school year, all but one of the sixteen suburban districts had reached its plan ratio, and the exception, Rockwood, a large and rapidly growing district on the far western edge of the county, was within a single percentage point of achieving its ratio. Meanwhile, two of the suburban districts that had reached their ratios at some point over the prior twelve years had since 1983 fallen behind.

Table 7.1. St. Louis County School Districts' Black Enrollment Ratios/Goals

Participating County Districts	Percentage Black, 1982–83	Plan Ratio	Plan Goal	Percentage Black, 1994–95
Affton	1.6	15.15	25	15.78
Bayless	0.1	15.15	25	13.15°
Brentwood	23.9	25.00	25	26.35
Clayton	6.0	16.27	25	19.45
Hancock Place	3.0	15.34	25	20.44
Hazelwood	17.4	25.00	25	32.51
Kirkwood	19.3	25.00	25	25.05
Ladue	15.6	25.00	25	25.09
Lindbergh	1.6	15.79	25	19.50
Mehlville	0.3	15.32	25	13.19°
Parkway	2.5	16.98	25	18.90
Pattonville	5.3	18.72	25	23.50
Ritenour	14.5	25.00	25	27.20
Rockwood	0.9	15.95	25	15.04†
Valley Park	0.4	15.48	25	24.13
Webster Groves	19.9	25.00	25	26.01

Source: Voluntary Interdistrict Coordinating Council (1995)
Note: °Reached plan ratio but fell behind. †Recruited large numbers of transfer students, but the all-white resident population continued to increase in large numbers, which increased the number of transfer students required for the ratio.

SAVING FACE—DESEGREGATION ASSIMILATION STYLE

When the student transfer program first brought African-American students from the city to the county, the strategy of most of the suburban educators was to resist change—to prove to their fearful constituents that an influx of inner-city students would not affect their beloved suburban schools. After all, the constituents in these districts had moved to suburbia specifically to avoid urban schools. The last thing they wanted was for their suburban schools to become what they had left behind.

Thus the consensus in the nervous suburbs was that the black students would simply have to conform to the districts' way of doing things—from the academic standards and disciplinary codes to the teaching styles and curriculum, from the way the cheerleaders cheered and the pompon girls performed to the music played at the football games and school dances. Every cherished intellectual and cultural tradition that makes predominantly white suburban schools places where middle-class parents want to send their children had to remain the same. The suburban schools were not going to change to accommodate the transfer students; the transfer students would have to change to accommodate the suburban schools. This was the only way that suburban educators could abide by the court order and still save face.

As one suburban superintendent explained, "You have to understand that children who live in the ghetto, grow up in the ghetto, have different sets of standards and behaviors. Therefore, you have to take that into consideration and help them understand why the mode of behavior in the school they are coming to is different than the mode of behavior where they live."

Never mind the gross generalizations about who the transfer students are and what kind of background they bring with them. The pressure was on to assimilate them to the suburban world. Thomas Pettigrew, a social psychologist who studies race relations and school desegregation, once said, "School desegregation was never meant to mean assimilation until white people got a hold of it" (1988). This thought comes to mind often when we listen to suburban educators in St. Louis County who saw little or no value in the inter-district transfer program and the black students it brings to their schools. As one suburban high school principal explained, "The main goal is to homogenize the populations you are dealing with to make them fit in better. That is the only way it will work."

An administrator in the Parkway School District reflected back on the first ten years of the desegregation plan and said, "We tried to make the black students into perfect little west county kids with Izod T-shirts. We did not appreciate the black students for who they were. . . . We kept thinking this program was going to go away."

Strongly related to this assimilationist view is something known as the color-blind perspective. Schofield (1989) writes about teachers in a desegregated middle school who say they do not see race or color, who treat all students exactly the same. The problem with this attitude, she writes, is that it denies the degree to which race is salient in desegregated schools and how students experience race. "Our data suggest," writes Schofield, "that, contrary to the teacher's view, race was indeed very salient to [the middle school] students" (p. 52). When these racial differences are excluded from the teachers' understanding, there is likely to be little meaningful discourse about racial issues, thereby limiting the kinds of inter-racial educational experiences that can happen only in desegregated schools. In St. Louis, where black students travel many miles to attend suburban schools in communities that are so different from their own, the color-blind perspective is particularly dangerous because it ignores the large political and social forces that created the separate city and suburbs and the color line between them, thus it denies the urban-suburban differences that the transfer students experience each day. When schools fail to teach this history, they perpetuate white suburbanites' attitudes and belief that African Americans are lazy, unmotivated, or content with their separate and unequal plight.

Still, we met many color-blind teachers and administrators in suburban schools. When asked how his school addressed the needs of transfer students, one suburban principal noted, "We just kind of feel like they moved in next door, and we just treat them like the rest of the kids." But of course the transfer students do not live next door, and the reasons they have been denied the opportunity to live in the suburbs is not discussed much in county schools, which means that white students, parents, and educators continually lose sight of the goals of the desegregation program. They also have a hard time understanding the logistical and social reasons why the parents of the transfer students are not as involved in the county schools as the parents who do live next door, as well as how the disjuncture between their school and their communities can affect the transfer students in profound ways. When we asked a suburban elementary school teacher whether having African-American students from the city in her classroom had caused her to reevaluate her teaching in any way, she said, "No. I mean, if you close your eyes, you really wouldn't know. In fact, people say, 'How many [transfer students] do you have?' and I really couldn't tell you without stopping to think."

Obviously there is significant variation across St. Louis County in the degree of assimilationist or color-blind ideology in a given district, school, or classroom. One suburban high school principal, for instance, noted that the norms regarding classroom dialogues about race and black males in particular vary widely: "What the kids tell me is that half of the faculty, who are from the South, don't want to talk about racial issues. About half of them are willing and 10 percent or 15 percent are really anxious to facilitate discussions on those matters. So it is interesting to kids to talk about that. It's sort of a schizophrenic world you've got: in one class race never gets mentioned, in another class it's discussed all the time."

But life in suburbia is schizophrenic in a multitude of ways. We learned of several distinctions in our district-level interviews with school board members and fifteen of the sixteen superintendents in districts accepting transfer students. In our interviews with principals we focused on one or more schools in eight of the sixteen districts. And for teacher responses we interviewed several in each of twelve schools within four suburban districts—Clayton, Kirkwood, Mehlville, and Parkway. These four districts represented an interesting cross-section of geographic, demographic, and political standpoints. Within each of the twelve schools—five high schools, two junior highs/middle schools, and five elementary schools—we interviewed the principals, often one or more assistant principal or counselor, and at least three teachers. These divergent views helped us understand that the educational and racial philosophies within the sixteen county school districts that accept transfer students vary greatly and are often reflected in the attitudes and beliefs of the board members and the district administrators. Their attitudes and beliefs are, in turn, shaped by the particular characteristics and demographics of these distinct suburban school districts.

The tiny Clayton School District in the central corridor of the county encompasses the business and government center of St. Louis County as well as a prestigious private university. It enrolls many children of professors and graduate students and those of the well-paid professionals and executives who can afford the mostly high-cost housing. Clayton High School is constantly ranked as one of the best high schools in the country, with low ratios of students to college counselors and a large number of advanced placement courses (Bower, 1994).

Parkway School District, further west of Clayton, is much larger—four regular high schools and one alternative high school as opposed to Clayton's one—and more middle class. Parents and homeowners in this district are more likely to be salaried white-collar workers and mid-level managers. Yet in some ways the diversity within the Parkway District is as significant as its distinction from other districts. Because it is so geographically large and stretches out in several directions, each of its high school zones is demographically and somewhat politically different, with the Parkway Central and West high schools, generally serving the wealthiest, central corridor families within the district, and Parkway North and South high schools, serving the more middle-class families.

Wedged between the central corridor and south county is the old and established Kirkwood School District. Kirkwood is unique within this group of districts because it is the only one of the four that had a substantial number of black students enrolled before the desegregation program began. This one-high-school district has a residential population that is bifurcated along race and social-class lines. About 85 percent of Kirkwood residents are white and from the upper middle class, and about 15 percent are African American and poor. Nearly all of the African-American families live in one small neighborhood within Kirkwood, known as Meachum Park (see Chapter 1).

The residential population in the midsized Mehlville School District, with its two high schools, is composed of more blue-collar, working-class families living in small, single-family homes and apartments. This district, like its neighboring district, Lindbergh, has a reputation for being resistant to desegregation. In fact, these two districts have had transfer student suspension rates that are significantly higher than those of other suburban districts. In 1993, for example, Mehlville and Lindbergh each suspended nearly one in four transfer students while Clayton and Kirkwood suspended fewer than one in fifty (see Eardley, 1993). Most of the residents of these south county school districts are fairly recent white refugees from the south side of the city.

The "central corridor" districts, especially Clayton, with the wealthiest and best-educated residential population in the county, tend to be more accepting of the desegregation program and more flexible in their approach to working with African-American transfer students. In these districts, a large portion of the parents and constituents embrace the concept of racial diversity within their previously all-white schools even if they are less open to curricular changes to accommodate that diversity. The south county districts, especially Mehlville, have been far more resistant to the desegregation plan and to the African-American students. Educators in such districts as Mehlville are in part responding to the demands of parents and constituents who are hostile toward desegregation in general and black students specifically.

At the school level the principals frequently reflected the district's political attitudes—evidence that district administrators seek out principals who "fit in" with the prevailing political climate within the community. But we did find, as does much of the literature on school administration, that principals can set an overall tone for the school, and that this tone can differ in subtle ways from community norms. Furthermore, the tone may vary from an open and accepting attitude to a resistant stance. As Al Burr, former principal at both Parkway West and Clayton high schools explained, "I think that the principal has got to be one of the mainstays. I think the principal's attitudes, I think the principal's vision, I think the principal's expectations, I think the principal's perceptiveness, and I think the principal's sensitivity sets the tone for the whole program in the school. And I think that the principal has a lot to do with how the community—both communities [black and white]—will feel about it [the desegregation plan] . . . and how the faculty approaches it."

But this setting of a school tone does not preclude some variation at the classroom level. We found, for instance, a great deal of diversity and a range of attitudes among teachers at every school in each district—from those who oppose the desegregation plan and strongly dislike the African-American students to those who believe that the plan is the best thing that has ever happened to their schools.

This divergence of views is reflected in the University of Missouri at St. Louis survey (Jones, 1988), which found that, on average, about 58 percent of the suburban teachers agree with the statement "Working with the transfer students has made me a better teacher." Meanwhile, 25 percent strongly disagree. Similarly, 25 percent of surveyed suburban teachers said that the quality of education in their schools had "gotten worse" since the beginning of the voluntary transfer program, 56 percent said that it had stayed the same, 12 percent said it had gotten better, and 7 percent said they did not know. This range in teachers' attitudes, which was also displayed in our interview transcripts, means that while the balance of opinions varies from school to school, there is often a broad mixture of views about the desegregation plan within each school building. The following sections focus on the more negative views of the resistors.

Glory Days

Instead of embracing diversity and appreciating the history, experiences, and culture that African-American students bring to the suburban schools, some of the teachers we interviewed spoke of the "glory days"—those good old days when their students were all white and all above average. Lloyd Moore, a math teacher at Parkway West High School, reflected on the years before 1983: "I look back on those days and, depending on my mood, I want to cry or I want to rejoice just thinking about how wonderful it was here; it was an absolutely fabulous place. A college—it was a small college, and kids were maturing and being exposed to things, and it was just beautiful coming here."

But according to an African-American administrator at Parkway West, teachers like Moore are basically perpetuating myths about what the school was like before the inter-district desegregation plan began—including the idea that virtually all of the students were in honors classes. "That's not true. It's not true now, and it wasn't true in the glory days." He added that when suburban teachers become fixated on the honors students, the National Merit finalists, and their memories of the glory days, they tend to ignore the potential of the other 90 percent of the students, both white and black.

Constant talk about the glory days supports the assimilationists' view that the black city students need to conform to the suburban way of life—that suburbia was utopia until the transfer students showed up. The tension between many of the suburban educators and transfer students led to, as it did in the schools that Metz (1978) studied in the 1970s, greater pressure on educators to get the situation under control. Yet efforts to rigidly control transfer students often backfired, as the students sensed that the educators distrusted them and reacted angrily. According to a teacher at Mehlville High School, "I sometimes think that we have a school out of control, personally, being an old teacher and used to the old way [when] we had, you know, total control."

By the fifth year of the program, when the total number of transfer students enrolled in suburban schools swelled to more than 10,000, it had become evident to a growing number of suburban educators that attempts to convert the black students into white, middle-class clones were not panning out. At that point, few of the districts had provided any special training for teachers or principals to sensitize them to the different educational and emotional needs of the low-income black students. Almost all of the suburban educators are white and middle-class, and most had taught only in suburban, middle-class schools. They had limited experience relating to black students, and few could fathom what it is like to grow up in a neighborhood where drive-by shootings are common. Few if any had been trained to create good race relations in a desegregated school, and there was little dialogue taking place within these schools about the problems or the possibilities of the desegregation plan.

Because of overcrowding, the Bierbaum Elementary School in the Mehlville School District did not begin enrolling African-American transfer students until several years after the desegregation plan had begun. Meanwhile, the principal of that school noted that rumors about the program and its negative impact had spread throughout this south county district, creating great fear among his teachers: "I think the teachers were more afraid of the kids than the kids were of the teachers because they had three years to hear the 'horror stories' about what happened in other districts. I mean they never got to hear any of the good stuff about how kids would come in ... and actually prosper."

The glory days sentiment often has been perpetuated by resistant educators who cannot separate the impact of the desegregation plan from other changes taking place in their suburban schools. For instance, the residential population at Bierbaum Elementary School was undergoing major changes while the desegregation plan was being implemented there. The construction of an apartment building near the school meant that the white resident students who enrolled there were likely to be more transient and lower-income than the traditional Bierbaum student.

Also, the desegregation program in Mehlville and in other districts began at about the same time as a major push for mainstreaming special education students into regular county schools and classrooms instead of keeping the students in separate buildings. The impact of mainstreaming special education students—a challenging process even in schools that are not also undergoing major changes in their racial composition—has often been conflated with the impact of the desegregation plan.

The Bierbaum principal explained that the district first mainstreamed the behavior disordered and learning disabled students during the same year the transfer students arrived from the city. There were many more "violent kinds of incidents" during that school year. But, according to the principal, "these were not racial in nature, although the teachers would say that the city [transfer] kids coming out reinforced that kind of behavior. But most of our problems were white-on-white and black-on-black."

In the same school year that the desegregation plan was implemented, the Parkway School District, as part of the restructuring effort, moved all ninth-graders from six junior high schools up to what had been four tenth- through twelfth-grade senior high schools. In the process the district closed one of its junior high schools and converted the others into middle schools serving seventh- and eighth-graders. This meant that the three-year high schools became four-year schools, with a younger, more immature group of ninth-graders added to the mix. Some teachers and administrators believe that many of the perceived problems with the inter-district plan in the Parkway high schools are related more to the fact that these schools now enroll hundreds of fourteen- and fifteen-year-old students who were not there in the so-called glory days.

We do not intend to portray the transfer students as angels. Compared with the suburban children these schools had been catering to for several decades, the transfer students tend to be much more challenging. They do not fit easily into the suburban model of a "good" school. In part because their parents are less likely to be well educated and because the students are less likely to have been in challenging schools or preschool programs before they come to suburbs, the transfer students are often behind the white and wealthier suburban students in some academic areas. They generally have far lower test scores and are far less optimistic about their futures than the suburban students. They are more likely to come to school tired, hungry, and at times homeless. Transfer students are often noisier in the hallways and more likely to get into physical fights at school. They are also more likely to carry weapons to school, though many who do contend that they do so for protection at their bus stops.

According to the Voluntary Interdistrict Coordinating Council (1995), during the 1993–94 school year 2,287, or about 15 percent, of the then 13,500 city-to-county transfer students were suspended at least once. The main reason for more than half of all suspensions (1,267) was fighting. The second most common cause for suspensions (624) was insubordination, and disruptive behavior was the reason for 519 suspensions. Failure to attend detention ranked fourth, and profanity was fifth. The sixth ranked reason for suspension, theft, accounted for 160 suspensions, and possession of a weapon ranked seventh, resulting in 132 suspensions.

As we demonstrated in Chapter 6, black students who attend suburban schools through the transfer plan frequently do not succeed there because they resist the attempts to assimilate them or they act out against an administrator or teacher whom they think is not treating them fairly. When focusing on just these students and their negative behavior, it is easy to see why some county school educators do not like the desegregation plan. But educators often fail to examine the transfer experience from the standpoint of the students who leave their families and neighborhoods behind to try to succeed in suburbia, only to find that they are frequently underprepared and unwanted.

A science teacher at Parkway South High School, for instance, noted that transfer students often come to school tired and hungry and will fall asleep in his class. He said some of these students tell him about shootings and stabbings that took place in their neighborhood the night before. Despite this information on the lives of his African-American students, he said that they fall asleep in class because they were up late watching television. As for their hunger, he said, "I hear kids tell me that they did not get breakfast or they have no money for lunch, sure. But we have state and federal programs to feed the kids, so I am sure that a lot of them sign up for that." But when questioned whether the school offered a breakfast program, he said, "No, we don't. We just have the lunch. Federal aid will provide for them if their families earn X number of dollars. But there's no breakfast program."

As the goal of complete and quiet assimilation faded, the response of many suburban administrators and teachers has been to tighten up on discipline and focus on specific problems as they arise. This response also allows for resistant suburban educators to continue avoiding discussions of the larger meaning of the social experiment they have been a part of for nearly a decade—why it exists, what its goals are, whether it is working. These resistant educators do not see the program as something that in the long run and in the larger sense will help their "community" but as something that makes their individual jobs more difficult and their individual schools less desirable places to work. Most do not, therefore, discuss the program with their students—black or white. Race is rarely mentioned, because it has become for many suburban St. Louis teachers, as it was for many of the middle school teachers in Schofield's (1989) study, a taboo subject in the so-called color-blind classrooms. It is as if the teachers pretend it doesn't matter; but of course it does.

Unfortunately, the assimilationist, color-blind, and glory days perspectives can too easily mesh into one large sense of inertia in the suburban schools. This inertia could have been easily predicted given how poorly the suburban educators were trained regarding racial diversity or desegregation before the transfer students showed up. Looking back on the lack of preparation that his staff had for the desegregation plan, a former principal of Parkway Central High School noted, "Those teachers—especially those outstanding teachers who were in the middle of their careers—never were prepared for that cultural change that they ran into [with the desegregation plan]. They weren't prepared for kids who were so far below grade level. They were used to taking kids from A to Z, and suddenly they were finding that they didn't know how to get from A to B with a lot of these kids. So we had several years of widespread faculty frustration. They felt as though they were failures."

By the late 1980s and early 1990s, the test scores and grade point averages of many transfer students remained far below those of the white suburban students, whose test scores have remained the same or have increased since the desegregation program began (see, for instance, Levy, 1995, and Shapiro, 1994). The more forward-looking administrators had become convinced that sensitivity and diversity training for their teachers was needed. By the mid-'00s this kind of training had become a feature of staff development programs in suburban schools. Many districts turned to outside specialists in the area of race relations and racially mixed schools. Kirkwood, for instance, encouraged all teachers and administrators to participate in special workshops designed by a Massachusetts scholar, Jeff Howard, to help educators enhance students', particularly African-American students', efficacy and self-esteem.

Some suburban teachers have been far more open to these special programs than others. At Parkway West High School, the administration brought in Jane Elliot, who conducts the famous "brown eyes/blue eyes" simulations in which participants take turns being labeled the inferior group based on their eye color. Whichever group is labeled inferior is treated as though they are less intelligent and are given fewer privileges. According to one administrator, "What this did was to foster lots of discussion about the topic of integration and what it means to live together and what it means to be multiculturally sensitive and insensitive." Yet he noted that the program created a "fairly traumatic situation," with about half of the teachers and staff coming out of the workshop "profoundly affected in a positive direction." A fourth of the faculty, he said, were profoundly affected and disturbed by the simulation, "but they could begin to see that there are some things that they have not necessarily been doing right." The last fourth of the faculty dug in their heals and became "very resentful in that situation."

Moore, the math teacher, fit into the last category. Moore, who is white, grew up on a farm in Tennessee in a very poor family. His parents' house did not have indoor plumbing until he was eight, and for as long as he can remember he has had to work to help support his family. "When I was 11, I was at least half breadwinner for my family," he recalled. He worked his way through college in the 1960s and became, in his words, "a little radical and leftist and liberal." But today Moore is disenchanted with the desegregation program and is having difficulty understanding why so many of the transfer students are so angry. He can't understand why his black students are not more motivated to pull themselves up by their own bootstraps, as he did. He said he is trying to understand how race affects his black students, making them distrustful of most whites, including him, but he said "it still does not jibe with me."

Moore said that he resented the workshop because Elliot was "so far in left field that it wasn't meaningful or helpful to me." He also said that the workshop polarized the school between those who favor the desegregation plan and those who oppose it. What Moore says is missing at Parkway West is an open and honest dialogue about the merits of the desegregation plan. "If you say the wrong thing—however that's determined—but if you say it even though you may be searching and thinking and arguing perhaps, then you're branded a racist or something worse."

Down the hall from the math department, the principal who strongly supported the Elliot workshop sat at his desk reflecting on the outcome of the brown eyes/blue eyes simulation. He noted that "there was a lot of subsequent dialogue. I think the more you can do with your faculty in terms of fostering that kind of dialogue and that kind of conversation, feeding them articles, then all of these kinds of things will create change."

Moore and his principal have different perspectives on not only the degree of open dialogue and discourse taking place, but also on how the suburban schools might help the transfer students become more successful. For instance, Moore focuses on the math content of his courses and whether he has covered all the material he is supposed to get through in a year. In talking about algebra B, a low-track course with many transfer students in it, he noted, "If you look at the content of what we do in the course, the content is there—it's been piecemealed and compartmentalized and digitized and all kinds of '-ized' to try to let kids get little bits of it. Yes, that has happened, but that notwithstanding, I and the rest of this department can speak for having provided solid instruction for the kids. I certainly wouldn't say it has been well received. I am not making that claim. . . . But the content that we put out there is solid. Our frustration is to try to get the kids to learn the content."

The principal, on the other hand, believes that if teachers focus first on their relations with students, the learning will follow more easily: "We all think we can stand back and say, I'm here to teach and they're here to learn. Sometimes you find that unless you build the trust, no learning will ever take place." He contends that educators will make little progress if they maintain an aloof, almost condescending attitude toward students—particularly the transfer students, who enter suburban schools with all kinds of insecurities about their abilities and how well they will be accepted. "Kids don't care how much you know, they want to know how much you care. If they sense caring and willingness to help, then you'll begin to make some gains."

Reading, Writing and Resegregation

The most resistant educators in the suburban schools are strongly focused on "curriculum content" as a sacred and non-negotiable truth. They talk about "coverage" and about "watering down" the content of the curriculum. The content taught in the glory days, imparted from their heads to students' notebooks and measured mainly by standardized tests, is the only knowledge these teachers seem to feel comfortable teaching and assessing. The reality is that many of the transfer students arrive in suburbia fairly deficient in this content and thus years behind the suburban students in everything from basic skills to mathematical theorems. Their knowledge and experience seldom match the suburban school curriculum. The resistant suburban teachers, meanwhile, do not recognize that while the transfer students' knowledge and experience may not perfectly match the curriculum, they may be valuable in their own right. Instead, the resistant teachers' focus is always on the deficit.

As one district administrator in Kirkwood explained it, the county schools have "damaged" many of the transfer students because the educators in these schools were not prepared: "The success stories are to the credit of the child, not the school or the district. . . . The reality is we've been taking the approach that they've come to learn from us so we're going to teach them how to be, and we've never bothered to dedicate any time to learning from them. We don't think they have anything to offer us."

There are definitely basic skills areas—especially reading and writing—in which many of the transfer students have not received the kind of training that they needed. This makes the suburban teachers' jobs that much more difficult, particularly in the wealthiest of the suburban districts, where many white students come to elementary school already knowing how to read. But suburban educators often conflate the needs of transfer students in these areas with their low estimation of the students' "intelligence" or "ability" to comprehend difficult material and grasp complex concepts. In reality, the day-to-day lives of the transfer students—negotiating the cultural divide between their homes and their suburban schools, for instance—are often far more complex than the curricula of most suburban high schools. Meanwhile, what suburban teachers often describe as intelligence among their white suburban students is little more than the "cultural capital" that students acquire at home from their college-educated and professional parents. It has little to do with innate ability or intelligence (see Oakes, Lipton, and Jones, 1995). In reality, perhaps the greatest challenge for a racially mixed school and a diverse society is to value the different ways of knowing the world.

But the strong focus on the deficits of the transfer students has served to legitimize rigid tracking, or so-called ability group practices. As long as content, knowledge, intelligence, and ability are all narrowly defined by a standard of white, middle-class norms, then those students who are not as adept in these normative dimensions must be placed in separate and unequal classes (Oakes, 1990). Racially identifiable tracking or "resegregation" of the black and white students within the desegregated suburban schools is the norm in nearly all the secondary schools we visited. Some of the schools added remedial courses specifically to "accommodate" the transfer students when the desegregation plan began. "The myth of inferiority is still alive and well," said one district administrator, referring to the practice of tracking African-American students into low-level classes.

Through classroom observations, in which we would spend an entire day or several hours with one teacher, we would see dramatic shifts in the racial makeup of classes, depending on what track level the class was that hour. The lowest-track classes tended to be half black in schools that were about 15 percent black. In fact, in one of the Parkway high schools, which is about 18 percent black, a science teacher told us that he had a basic class in which all students but one were black. The highest-track classes had two or three black students in them at the most; often there were no black students in the high-track classes.

While tracking practices are not new to these suburban schools, and while many educators will defend the racial balance within the classes given the underpreparedness of many of the transfer students, a handful of suburban schools have begun to experiment with various "detracking" reforms, such as placing all students in the same level of English class and then providing a second period of English, a tutorial, for those who need extra support (see Chapter 8). Still, many of the teachers who dislike the inter-district transfer program believe that any changes in the rigid tracking structure are a sign that the suburban schools are lowering their standards and watering down their curriculum. Among the county schoolteachers surveyed in the USML study by Jones (1988), 61 percent of the high school teachers said that the quality of the educational programs at their schools was the same as it had been before the inter-district transfer program began. Another 27 percent said the quality was worse, and 8 percent said the educational quality was better. Middle-school teachers were somewhat more optimistic, with 56 percent saying that the school quality is the same, 15 percent saying that it was worse, and 22 percent saying that it had gotten better since the desegregation plan began. Elementary schoolteachers, on the other hand, were more pessimistic, with 44 percent saying that the quality of education was the same, 31 percent reporting that the quality was worse, and 12 saying that it was better. In fact, the achievement test scores of white county students have not declined. A Clayton School District report to the community on the desegregation program (1989) indicated that the Scholastic Aptitude Test (SAT) scores of resident students had actually increased significantly during the first five years of the desegregation plan.

Still, an interview with a teacher at Mehlville High School illustrates how resegregation is created via the tracking system:

Q: Do you think that the curriculum at the school would be different if the transfer students were not here?

A: That's hard to say, it really is. We have created more remedial classes. We still need more remedial classes, because now to get into a remedial class you have to be really, really bad. You cannot be marginal anymore. If you are marginal, there is no room for you, because they take the worst first. And so we got a lot of kids who are just in regular curriculum that should be in remedial.

Q: Is this mainly for the transfer students?

A: Mainly . . . yeah, you go around the school and if you know which classes to look in, like Science Concepts, and that is a science class that starts on the fifth-grade level. That class is over 90 percent black. [The school is less than 15 percent black.]

Q: Do you think that in terms of the top-level courses it has changed very much?

A: No, I don't think it has changed too much. . . . But the standard joke in the school is if you want to teach in a curriculum where you don't have to deal with the transfer kids, do senior English comp. None of them ever get that far. Or teach, you know, physics, or teach, you know, one of the other college credit classes. My wife teachers over at [a nearby high school]. She teachers the junior- and senior-level English, and in her senior comp classes just once in a blue moon she will get a deseg kid. . . . So the teachers will fight to teach that. . . . The main reason they are fighting to teach it is that they do not have to deal with as many problems as in a deseg class.

It is interesting that many of the suburban teachers emphasize the problems of teaching the low-track or "deseg" classes in these schools and the joys of teaching the high-track classes, full of supposedly eager, motivated, polite, and courteous white suburban students—the best of the best. In our classroom observations we did not see huge differences between the behavior of students in the low- and high-track classes, try as we did. In fact, in several instances we found students in mostly white, high-track classes to be insubordinate and discourteous toward their teachers and classmates. Meanwhile, students in the low-track classes, while not particularly well behaved by traditional standards, were not nearly as disruptive as the teachers had portrayed them be in their interviews.

Moore's math classes were a case in point. He argued that in the lower-level math tracks it is important not to overload classes with black students. "This is a very informal observation on my part—no scientific data to back this up, but I've watched this and I know it's true. Usually if you go beyond one in three [black transfer students to white resident students] you're in trouble. If you can maintain under one in three VTS [voluntary transfer students], you get a reasonable chance—particularly the male VTS students. You must keep them separated. The noise level and the jiving around and the things that interfere with doing math just escalate. So you get beyond one in three, you can't physically separate the kids. . . . . Of course, in the upper level courses, you have hardly any of the [transfer] kids. And they would be nicer, so there's no problem."

Interestingly enough, sitting through Moore's high- and low-track math classes, we saw almost the exact opposite behaviors. In the low-track algebra I-B class during fifth period, about one-third of the students were African-American transfer students; the white resident students were mostly girls and mostly the students referred to in this school as burnouts. These are the "forgotten" low-achieving white students who often wear a lot of makeup, tight blue jeans, and rock concert T-shirts. These are the less successful students who were here during the glory days, though resistant teachers don't really talk about them.

While many of the students in this algebra class were not highly engaged in what Moore was covering on this particular day, the class as a whole was fairly sedate, with the worst disruption coming from two white girls sitting in the back of the room whispering and exchanging photographs. Several of the black students volunteered to put homework problems on the chalkboard and explain their answers to the class. One transfer student was particularly eager to explain the problems and how he had solved them; only some of his classmates were very interested. After class Moore made a point of saying that this was the second time this student was taking algebra I-B.

Moore's sixth-period pre-calculus class was another story. There were no African-American students in the class, nor was there much teacher control. Before the class began, the students had decided—without Moore's consent—that today was to be a pizza party day. Three of the students were not in the classroom when the bell rang because they had gone to pick up the pizza at a local pizza shop. The students had, in essence, taken over the classroom, and Moore laughed and went along with the students' plan. In his interview he noted that "I love those kids, I do, and it's [the pre-calculus class] fun and I truly enjoy it." He and the students spent the entire class period in a "dialogue" about the desegregation plan (see Chapter 9). Here, in his high-track, all-white math class, Moore felt comfortable leading a discussion that started with his proclamation that the desegregation plan has made him "more racist." In his low-track math class he did not facilitate a discussion of the program.

We are not saying that Moore's job is easy or that he intends to treat students unfairly. But he, like so many white suburban teachers, resents that the black students attend their otherwise "good" schools, an attitude that black students sense immediately and often react to negatively. It seems that even when black students do the right thing in their classes, these educators are sometimes blind to their contributions. Many of the transfer students we spoke to, as well as those interviewed in the focus groups (Public Policy Research Centers, 1993a), said that they thought the teachers in the suburban schools treated white local students better than the black transfer students. Meanwhile, 75 percent of all suburban teachers surveyed said that they believe white and black students are treated equally in their schools (Jones, 1988). These different perspectives on the same "reality" too often lead to a vicious cycle of black students "acting out" toward white teachers and administrators whom they believe to be racist. This behavior in turn confirms the resentful attitudes of the most resistant white teachers; some white women teachers told us that they are afraid of the black students.

According to a woman who had been working in staff development in one suburban district, 80 percent of all transfer student disciplinary referrals come from 20 percent of the teaching staff. These are the teachers whom many of the transfer and return students speak of when they try to explain why it is difficult for them to succeed in the suburban schools.

An African-American administrator at one of the suburban schools told us about a math teacher whose classroom was directly across from the main office. One day the administrator overheard this teacher yelling at students: "'You damn black kids, I'm just sick of this, I'm sick of this!' So he comes storming out of the classroom, sees me, comes over to me and confronts me right in the hallway. . . . 'I want you to get a bus right now and get all these black kids and put them on a bus and send them back to the city!'" Despite his shock over the teacher's behavior, the administrator said he realizes that African-American students who transfer from the city are not always easy to get along with because their parents often send mixed messages about the transfer plan: "They want their kids to get a good education, but they send the kid out the door saying, 'Don't take anything.' And that kid rides the bus anticipating white folks are going to do something, and they are just waiting for some white person to look at him the wrong way, to say something the wrong way, to hit on the wrong thing. Unfortunately, they are going to encounter some folks like that who are going to say some things to them."

One of the main conclusions to be drawn from interviews with the teachers and administrators, especially those who strongly dislike the transfer program and resent the transfer students, is that they tend to be the people with more negative attitudes toward teaching and students in general. As the principal of an elementary school in Clayton said, "You show me a principal who is doing an excellent job with the voluntary transfer program, and I will show you a principal who probably does an excellent job with any kind of problem-solving situations."

The more resistant teachers tend to be older teachers who are set in their ways. According to the principal of an elementary school in Mehlville, the teachers in his school, many whom have been teaching there for a very long time, like to stay where they have always been. "They like how it's been, and now in so many ways they have to change, and they don't like that. They have been here for twenty years and they did not enjoy changing that."

Resistant teachers also seemed to be more frequently found in the supposedly "black-and-white" fields of math and science rather than in the English and social studies departments. One older science teacher we interviewed noted that he was not planning to do anything differently in his classroom to help the transfer students succeed "unless they want to take me and retrain me and give me different tools. Maybe that is necessary."

Related to much of the tension between the suburban educators and the transfer students is the fact that they come from very different backgrounds. Nearly ten years after the desegregation program began, only two of the sixteen suburban school districts receiving transfer students—Kirkwood and Webster Groves—have teaching staffs that are more than 9 percent African American, and most have faculties that are less than 5 percent black (Hick, 1992). On average, about 4 percent of the teachers in these districts are African American. In terms of administrators, the numbers tend to be even lower, though there is a wide range. Four of the sixteen districts have no black administrators at all, but in all the districts combined, 5 percent of the administrators are black.

Suburban superintendents say that they are constantly trying to hire more black educators, but they complain that the pool of "qualified" applicants is far too small, and many of the districts end up competing for the same candidates. The principal of a large high school in one of the south county districts where there has been a great deal of tension and racial conflict noted, "We don't have any black teachers—we had one, and he left to go get an advanced degree."

THE PURSE STRINGS

The central paradox of all the resistance to the desegregation program on the part of suburban educators is that the districts have become extremely dependent on the money they receive from the state for every city student they add to their rolls. This money supports hundreds of teaching and administrative jobs. At a time when the resident school-age population in St. Louis County is shrinking, the transfer program has allowed the suburban districts to fill empty seats, balance their enrollments, and keep school buildings open (see table 7.2).

As one business education teacher in a large suburban school explained it, "If you plug them [the transfer students] into classrooms where you have empty spots anyway, it's sheer profit."

Yet what is clear from the table is that not all suburban districts are reaping equal rewards from the program. Under the settlement agreement, suburban districts receive an annual incentive payment for each transfer student that is equivalent to their per-pupil expenditure. Thus, the less affluent suburban districts receive far smaller reimbursements than the wealthier districts do on

Table 7.2.   State Fiscal Incentive Payments to County Districts, 1993–1994

County School District	Approximate Per-Pupil Cost	Number of Transfer Students	Amount of Fiscal Incentive Payments from state
Affton	$3280	407	1,334,744
Bayless	2500	170	424,788
Brentwood	6600	154	1,016,049
Clayton	7665	397	3,042,937
Hancock Place	1850	229	423,969
Hazelwood	1406	60	84,356
Kirkwood	4365	560	2,444,336
Ladue	7413	353	2,616,882
Lindbergh	4144	869	3,601,402
Mehlville	2700	1562	4,212,444
Parkway	4960	3402	16,867,524
Pattonville	5422	990	5,367,888
Ritenour	2130	409	870,600
Rockwood	3960	2319	9,184,632
Valley Park	3960	165	653,788
Webster Groves	3980	407	1,619,792

Source: Missouri State Department of Education

a per capita basis. It is a case, many suburban administrators admit, of the rich getting richer and the poor getting poorer.

Despite these disparities, suburban school boards and their superintendents have become financially dependent on the state-funded desegregation program, which most of their constituents do not like and do not understand. In addition, few Missouri policy makers support the inter-district desegregation plan or the court-ordered state expenditures on suburban or urban schools in St. Louis. In fact, most of the gubernatorial candidates for the last several elections have used their opposition to the desegregation program as a major campaign issue. Michael Fields, one of the lawyers for the Missouri attorney general's office, said that the city and county school districts have become "addicted" to the desegregation money. "If you took it out from under them, they wouldn't have any source to survive." Fields argues that the suburban districts receive much more state money than they need to educate the transfer students: "I don't know if you would call it a slush fund or not, but they have certainly been able to use the money for things other than voluntary inter-district transfers."

As one official in the Missouri State Department of Education noted, the incremental cost of educating one more student in a suburban school district is not as large as that district's average per-pupil cost due to economies of scale and certain fixed costs. "Once you have a class size of twenty-two pupils, you put one or two more students in that classroom, your costs are not increased by the amount that you receive per student." Educators and lawyers for the suburban school districts disagree. They argue that the schools have added special tutoring programs and teacher's aides who help serve the needs of transfer students. But perhaps the most contentious aspect of state funding of suburban school districts has to do with a provision in the settlement agreement that called for the state to cover "other costs" related to the transfer plan. These costs could include one-time extraordinary costs associated with the shifting student enrollments, including the cost of reopening a school that had been closed. In other words, if a school district could prove that it needed to reopen a school or add on to an existing school partly to accommodate the transfer students, then the state should help offset the cost to the district.

By the late 1980s the Ritenour School District had run out of room to house its resident student population and the nearly 400 transfer students it needed to achieve its plan ratio. When Ritenour lawyers and board members asked the state to provide the district with $300,000 to help reopen Buder Elementary School, the state refused. Ritenour took the state to court, and Judge Limbaugh, the district court judge overseeing the desegregation case at the time, agreed with the Ritenour lawyers and officials that the state should share in the cost, as the transfer program had necessitated the reopening of the school. The state appealed to the Eighth Circuit Court, which also ruled in favor of Ritenour. The state then appealed to the U.S. Supreme Court but was, as in every other Supreme Court appeal in this case, denied certiori. Thus, thousands of state tax dollars were wasted fighting a payment that was within the parameters of the settlement agreement, and in the end the state paid the Ritenour District the $300,000 to reopen the school.

The Ritenour superintendent said he was shocked that the state attorney general's office had spent so much time and legal resources to fight the district: "We took a very compromising position with the Buder School. I don't know why the state chose to fight this case. . . . We were fighting over $300,000, and they would take it to the Supreme Court! They [saw] it as a kind of crusade. I wish the state had taken a leadership role—so much of the money has been wasted."

Crusade or not, the attorney general's decision to fight the Ritenour request turned out to be bad legal strategy. The Buder case established a legal precedent regarding state payments to suburban school districts for capital improvements and school reopenings that would cost the state $36 million as of 1995 and greatly benefit suburban St. Louis taxpayers, who, since the mid-1980s, have paid relatively little for new schools in their home districts.

Yet many of the parents and voters in the suburban school districts do not realize that their districts receive hundreds of thousands of state dollars because of this program. Some even believe that the cost of the transportation and education of black students comes out of the districts' operating expenses. Moreover, they do not seem to realize that a sudden end to the program would would force administrators in their districts to lay off hundreds of teachers and, in many cases, to close schools. One administrator suggested that his superintendent talk to his constituents about these issues on a level that they would understand: "If the voluntary transfer program ended . . . tomorrow, we're talking 250 teachers, plus administrators in this building, plus central office jobs, plus secretaries, plus custodial, and we could just keep going right down the line."

One suburban superintendent explained it to us this way: "I do wake up sometimes in a cold sweat thinking that if all of a sudden somebody would say it is over—the kids are going back to the city—aside from the emotional problems that the kids would have, the logistics of reducing that number of teachers and the closings of buildings that would be a result would just be a nightmare."

The other aspect of the desegregation program that would be greatly missed is many of the black students' contributions to the athletic teams in the county schools—programs that also help to raise money for their schools. In fact, the superintendent of the Brentwood School District said that his tiny district has been able to maintain some sports teams that would otherwise be eliminated without the extra students from the city. One principal who had little positive to say about the desegregation plan did note, when asked if anything good had come of it, that "we've got one hell of a football team." The suburban school teams have gotten so good that many educators in the city accuse the suburbs of trying to illegally recruit their best athletes. The response to this acquisition in the suburbs is mixed. For instance, a teacher at Mehlville High School who assists in coaching the football team told us about the city teacher whom the school "hired" to help recruit football players from middle schools in the city.

> A: Well, in one way, it [the desegregation plan] has really helped our football program. . . . We used to be the doormat of the county. . . . Now we are the best.
> Q: Do you recruit for the football team?
> A: Oh, yeah, the football team hired this city teacher, Lester . . . That's the first thing that he did when he got out here he made up shirts for all the city kids, Lester's Molesters. . . . So we call him Lester the Molester, and he brings us our whole team, practically our whole team. . . . We have a school of 1,800, and we don't even have our 15 percent [black student enrollment], and you know, our football team was 85 percent black. Our starters were mostly black.

The teacher added that the coach's strategy is to "just pull out the white kids" when the team falls behind, but he always plays a "couple token whites."

Yet when we asked an administrator in the Mehlville School District about Lester and the process of recruiting transfer students who could help out the football team, he denied any such activity in his district: "We do not recruit for athletics. . . . I am sure that there are city individuals who think that we recruited certain students, [but] in some cases they have recruited some of their own students back. You know we are in a world now where everybody recruits everybody else. . . . Mehlville has had a good football team for the last number of years, and, yes, the transfer program has helped. No questions about it. But I don't think we are actively recruiting athletes."

This is the same school district that Denise in Chapter 6 attended until her brother, the star basketball player, graduated, after which she said she was not treated very well by the administration.

Although county residents like it when their local high school team is successful, many white suburban would-be jocks and their parents are angry that the slots on their team have been taken by black students from the city. One district administrator in the suburbs explained it this way: "I think sometimes people are sensitive to the fact that maybe if those students from the city weren't playing, then my son would be playing."

MORE LEGITIMATE COMPLAINTS

While the resistant educators tend to focus on the negative aspects of the desegregation plan, there are two areas in which the complaints seem to be more broadly substantiated by a wider range of people—that is, by the more visionary educators as well as the resistors. These areas are the increased disciplinary problems, especially violence and theft, in the suburban schools, and the many logistic problems of the program—including the long bus rides and the lack of access to the St. Louis public schools' records on the transfer students.

Violence and Theft

The attempted denial of the massive social transformation taking place in the suburban schools has not prevented the inevitable: the black inner-city students have substantially changed the climate of these suburban institutions. The noise level in the hallways has gone up, and so has the number of fights. Turf battles between rival gang members or other adversaries begin in the city over the weekend and then erupt in fights at a suburban school. Black girls frequently resort to violence—kicking, scratching, and hair-pulling—over a boyfriend or a spiteful comment. Theft rates are also up. Weapons—everything from steak knives to semiautomatic pistols—have been found on transfer students, though there have been few instances in which a weapon was used in a suburban school.

According to the Jones (1988) survey of teachers in the participating suburban districts, 20 percent of elementary faculty, 24 percent of middle school teachers, and 18 percent of high school instructors said that there has been a large rise in fighting and violence since the transfer program began. Another 41 percent of elementary faculty, 34 percent of middle school faculty, and 44 percent of high school faculty said there has been "some" increase in fighting and violence. The majority of teachers who said there has been either some or a large increase in fighting and violence reported that it is mainly the result of struggles among transfer students, not fights between transfer and suburban students. Furthermore, 32 percent of the elementary school teachers said that the transfer students require much more discipline than do local students, as compared with 26 percent of middle school teachers and 20 percent of high school teachers.

As we mentioned earlier, the Voluntary Interdistrict Coordinating Council's report (1995) demonstrates that the number one reason for transfer student suspensions was fighting, followed by insubordination and disruptive behavior. A special disciplinary report conducted by Parkway, the largest suburban school district, found that black students—most of whom are transfer students in this particular district—are far more likely to be involved in fights than are white resident students. But the study also found that the resident students are much more likely to be involved in drugs. "So they [the transfer students] may be bringing in somewhat different kinds of crime, but it is not like our county districts were free of it before they got here or will be free of it if they go back," said the Parkway administrator who conducted the discipline study.

But fights, often between two black girls and almost always between two black students, are something that white suburban educators and students were not used to in their schools. "It took us a while to figure out what was going on," said one suburban school principal, who added that he and the faculty had to learn more about rival neighborhoods and gangs in the city to understand why groups of students who did not even know each other would fight at school. He said that his "largely white staff" was not familiar with urban issues. "We didn't even know what was going on. All of a sudden, two groups of girls would get into open warfare and every time you came around, they were fighting."

Several of the suburban administrators we spoke to believe that transfer student fights often begin on the long bus rides between the city and the suburbs.

The fact that transfer students appear to be much more likely to fight with other students creates a kind of tension for suburban educators, especially those who do not subscribe to a strict assimilationists' or color-blind perspective but who do not want students fighting in their schools. The principal of an elementary school in Clayton argues that if fighting is acceptable and even necessary for survival in the city neighborhoods, then those students are going to have to learn when fighting is needed and when it is not: "And there are some things that I am not willing to give on, like fighting, and I think the only way that kids can survive is to behave one way in one place and another way in another place. . . . We have just given them another cultural language, we haven't changed their cultural language. They now speak two cultural languages, and we haven't taken away the other, nor do I think we should."

Logistics

The 1988 Jones survey conducted at USML for the *St. Louis Post-Dispatch* found that when asked what they like least about the interdistrict transfer program, suburban schoolteachers most frequently cite the length of the bus rides (19 percent), the differences in values and culture between the transfer and local students (11 percent), and the transfer students' disciplinary problems (11 percent). Educators in the suburbs complain constantly about the affect of the bus rides on the transfer students' ability to stay awake and concentrate in class. Suburban educators also have found that a fight or threat that is carried out on a bus on the way to school can ruin the entire day—or the week or year, in some cases. To minimize travel time for the African-American students, many of the suburban educators proposed that the shape and scope of the desegregation program change to allow students fewer choices by matching zones within the city to sections of the county. With a more specific zoning system, suburban educators argue, all the students from a given city neighborhood would transfer to the same suburban school or at least to the same suburban school district. This would shorten bus rides while allowing specific suburban and urban communities to create stronger bonds.

There are, in general, two distinct arguments against this type of arrangement: First, it would curtail the degree of choice available to African-American students in the city. And second, given that so many transfer students state that one of the main reasons they transfer is to avoid conflict with neighborhood peers, matching whole urban and suburban neighborhoods could lead to a "no escape" situation for some students.

A related logistical issue is the suburban administrators' complaints about the lack of cooperation from the St. Louis public schools in sending on accurate student records. As one administrator noted, "There are things like [student] records that you cannot get, and even when you do get them, you can't trust them." Principals said they had to estimate students' placements based on what the transfer students and their parents told them. "So the student would say 'I have had algebra,' but it became clear within a week that they had never had algebra," he said.

CONCLUSIONS

As the numbers of transfer students continued to climb, suburban superintendents and many of their more reform minded principals launched initiatives to help teachers discover new ways of working with diverse student populations, increase their sensitivity to racial issues and poverty, and broaden their curricula to include black history and the works of black writers. These efforts have been more successful in some schools and some classrooms than in others.

We have found in almost any suburban setting a minority of whites who are agents of change, those who have a greater sensitivity to the inherent inequality within our society and a broader critique of the system as a whole. Even though these individuals benefit in some short-term way from the current system, they have a longer-range view of the social problems and ignorance that stem from a racially divided society. Their framework goes against the grain and provides a critical perspective of the dominant culture as something that blacks and other minority groups should not try to assimilate into, but rather as something that has to be exposed for what it is and removed from its privileged place at the top of a cultural hierarchy.

Judges cannot order tolerance, understanding, and compassion in the face of a social structure that rewards attitudes and beliefs about the cultural, moral, and intellectual superiority of whites who are middle and upper middle class. But once a court order is in place, the people who live and work in the day-to-day reality of a changing social structure must reevaluate the attitudes and cultural preferences that upheld the prior segregated system. Whites must accept that not only did they and their ancestors create the separate and unequal society we live in, but they, in their everyday lives and prejudices, uphold that system and thereby thwart efforts to change it.

8

Visionary Educators and Their Reforms

Desegregation, to be termed successful, must have eliminated widely-held racial stereotypes, broadened the cultural values transmitted by the schools, and increased the access of minority children to quality educational programs— the conduit to preferred colleges and jobs.
—G. Orfield, *Law and Contemporary Problems*

The desegregation plan in St. Louis has had a very different impact on a small group of suburban educators who, unlike the majority of their colleagues, have come to see the program and the African-American students it brought to their schools as assets rather than liabilities. While these educators do not represent the "typical" administrators or teachers in their districts, they provide a unique view of how a court-ordered policy becomes an impetus for educational change at the school and classroom levels.

The educators profiled here tell us that when their mostly white and middle-class schools experienced a sudden influx of African-American students—many from low-income families—they began to reevaluate their views of what constitutes a "good school." The conclusion that this group of educators reached is that much of their schools' "business as usual"—that is, traditional teacher-student relationships, curriculum content, and practices such as tracking—not only alienates the black students who transfer from the inner city but also fails to meet the educational needs of hundreds of resident white students. Therefore, as a result of the desegregation plan, these teachers and administrators have become more critically aware of the negative impact of the procedures they used to accept as sound educational practice. Meanwhile, they have become increasingly attuned to the individual needs of every student whose life they touch. The meanings these educators make of the desegregation plan and their students echo much of the recent literature on educational change and racial issues within desegregated schools.

As we discussed in Chapter 7, in looking at the school-level impact of the desegregation plan we focused on four suburban school districts—Clayton, Kirkwood, Mehlville, and Parkway—that vary in size as well as in the wealth and political leanings of their constituents; all but Kirkwood had virtually all-white student populations when the desegregation program began. We base this chapter on the data from interviews with principals and teachers in these districts. We made a conscious effort to interview a broad cross-section of educators in these districts by visiting twelve schools—five high schools, two junior highs or middle schools, and five elementary schools. About forty-five of the teachers were selected from faculty rosters to ensure a balance of departments and gender at the schools; the other fifteen teachers were recommended to us as people we needed to speak with because they strongly opposed or strongly supported the desegregation plan. This is the story of those who support the plan.

VISIONARY EDUCATORS

When we set out to interview principals and teachers in suburban schools, we were seeking to uncover their general attitudes toward the desegregation program and toward the black students from the city, as well as views on how the program had affected their schools' academic standards. We anticipated both positive and negative responses, but we did not anticipate the degree of divergence between educators on each end of the spectrum. Furthermore, we did not expect to find teachers who said that the desegregation program has had a profound positive impact on their professional development—that it was the main catalyst behind their efforts to discover teaching techniques that would better serve all their students and that it profoundly enhanced their critical thinking about the way schools are organized and how teachers and their colleagues interact with students. These are the educators who perceive the desegregation plan as providing them an opportunity to reevaluate their approaches, practices, and ways of thinking about teaching and learning.

We called these teachers and administrators visionaries. Overall, of the more than seventy principals and teachers we interviewed from these four districts, only a small minority were adamant about the positive influence of the program on their schools, and several were more moderate in their visions of positive change. Still, even those suburban educators who held only moderately positive views of the desegregation plan were in stark contrast to those on the other end of the spectrum—the resistors who do little more than blame the desegregation plan and the black students for a decline in their schools' standards. But what is more significant than their numbers or percentages are the ways the visionary educators make meaning of the desegregation plan and the African-American students who come to their schools. The parallels between these meanings and the changing nature of the field of education—the questioning of fundamental assumptions about intelligence and learning—are quite striking, leading us to believe that desegregation policy can encourage educational innovation in classrooms and corridors when educators are open to rethinking old paradigms.

For instance, the visionary educators question the dominant views in our society of what constitutes intelligence and how it should be measured; they question the "banking" model of education, in which teachers simply deposit information and knowledge into the heads of students, without drawing on the students' own experiences; and they question textbooks and curriculum guides that do not reflect multiple standpoints and more multicultural "ways of knowing." In this way the practice of these teachers and administrators challenges the more traditional culture and structure of suburban schools in ways that could lead to far more meaningful experiences for all students. These more visionary educators validate the philosophies of some of the most important theorists in education, including John Dewey, Paulo Freire, and Jürgen Habermas—theorists who have stressed the emancipatory potential of education (see Young, 1990). These educators, as postulated by the theorists of a more critical tradition, provide students with the intellectual opportunities to question and critique the current condition of society, including how our society came to be racially polarized with so much poverty in the inner city as compared with the prosperity in the suburbs. Such a curriculum creates a critical awareness among students concerning various forms of oppression and the potential for change (Bell and Schniedewind, 1987; McLaren, 1991a; Sirotnik and Oakes, 1986).

Similar arguments are made by researchers who examine "second generation" desegregation issues, including the resegregation of black and Latino students in low-track classes, unfair application of disciplinary standards to students of different races, and insensitivity of teachers and administrators to the culture and history of nonwhite students (Metz, 1978; Oakes, 1985; Schofield, 1989). For instance, Orfield (1975) noted twenty years ago that school desegregation plans tend to underscore a growing "crisis" within the teaching profession, a crisis in which teachers realize, consciously or subconsciously, that they don't know how to teach children whose background is very different from that of the dominant group. He writes that "good" middle-class and predominantly white schools are often "rigid, unimaginative institutions that do violence to students who cannot conform to school norms." The suburban St. Louis educators discussed below could see this, and they decided to make changes.

Thus, the findings presented here focus on the attitudes and experiences of the visionary and more moderately supportive educators. In an attempt to organize the data from the in-depth interviews, we have categorized their responses to our questions into two broad categories: first, those answers that demonstrate how the desegregation plan has fostered their critique of the status quo within their schools, and second, how these insights have helped educators become more sensitive to the individual needs of students. The visionary educators argue that showing students, especially African-American students, that white educators believe in them and support them is half the battle in trying to improve their academic achievement. Most pronounced in the new meanings that these educators make of their roles in their desegregated schools are the ways that these approaches to understanding schools as organizations have had a positive impact on *all* students—black and white, wealthy and low-income. Thus, through the experiences of these educators the benefits of the inter-district schools desegregation plan for white and wealthy students become more apparent.

Critical Awareness of Inherent Inequality

The visionary educators' criticisms of the status quo were aimed mainly at the content of the curriculum and the "institutional rationality," or the structure of the school that serves the demands for efficiency and formality—that is, the way that students are tracked into separate and unequal classes (Oakes, 1985; Foster, 1986). The desegregation plan and the changing demographics in the schools helped these teachers better understand the mismatch between the needs of the students they were serving and traditional way that schools operate.

Knowledge as Power According to McLaren (1991b, p.21), the development of "contextual, critical knowledge and understanding" entails affirming the histories and experiences of students to the extent that their voices become part of the dialogue. The truly visionary teachers in suburban St. Louis knew that the standard curriculum at their schools did not account for the histories and experiences of their newest constituents—the African-American students. And they realized that denying these different perspectives was a disservice to white and black students. Even those teachers who said they had been aware of the Eurocentric curricular focus in their schools before the desegregation plan was implemented told us that they became increasingly uncomfortable with that focus when the black transfer students showed up.

For instance, Bonnie Doe, an energetic English teacher at Oakville High School in the large, working-class, and politically conservative Mehlville School District, was writing her doctoral dissertation on the English literary canon during the first few years of the desegregation plan. Through her research she learned that 74 percent of the works in five major anthologies were by white males, 14 percent by white females, 6 percent black males, 4 percent black females, and 2 percent others. She said that this information had a profound impact on her as a woman and as a teacher in a racially mixed high school who was trying to build better relationships with her African-American students.

In the late 1980s Doe began giving the students in her advanced, college-credit English composition course a list of 100 authors about whom they could write their research papers, and she reversed all the statistics. About 80 percent of the listed writers were female; there were more black than white authors listed, and a number of Latino and Native American authors were added. "I think the teacher has to break out of the Eurocentric mold and take the responsibility to move on. . . . I mean we are dismantling the Eurocentric canon. . . . I think that the greatest disservice is to white males, and I tell them you never have the opportunity to know what a woman thinks or feels because your literature is written by Hemingway. . . . And I had white boys doing the neatest things—writing about women's issues and going to black cultural events with me—white boys whose parents certainly would not approve."

Peggy Mack, an English teacher in the same district, at nearby Mehlville High School, made similar changes to her reading list—adding books by black writers, books that portray blacks as leaders and intellectuals, and books that look critically at white-over-black domination and the oppression of African Americans throughout American history. She said that before the desegregation plan began she would give students a list of mostly white male writers, "because that was what the textbook emphasized." In retrospect, she noted, it is one of "those subtle little things that we do that is very racist and very sexist.

"This morning I had four presentations, and three of them were on black writers," said Mack, adding that all of the students conducting the presentations were white. She said that one of the students presented on a book that a black woman had written about apartheid in South Africa. "She said she had never read anything like that and that she would never have appreciated what it was like to live under those conditions." Another student presented on Claude McKay, "and the students were throwing terms around like the 'Harlem Renaissance'—things that I probably would not have thought in terms of if I had not tried to overcome certain racist things by changing what they read."

Mack said that the influx of black students into her school and classroom has also forced her to reevaluate the language in the literature she assigns and the language she uses when talking to her students, "so that we are not talking about blackness as being wrong and whiteness as being right. . . . I work very hard to create a different language."

Janice Owens, an English teacher at Kirkwood High School, refuses to use textbooks in her classes, except when she and her students are critiquing the content of these books. "I use this as a lesson. This is our textbook, and we hardly use it. Now in a couple of weeks I'll have them really tear apart the book and take a look at it and tell me if they see what's wrong with it. There are only one or two women in the whole book and one or two blacks, and I'm teaching in the 1990s."

In place of the textbooks, Owens pulls together various readings from her cabinet full of "handouts, tear-outs, and run-offs." She said that she undoubtedly is violating copyright laws but that she really couldn't do a good job of teaching if she didn't photocopy from several different sources. "How could I teach out of the textbook?" She also has students select their own books to read, allowing them to follow themes and genres that they are interested in exploring.

Perhaps one of the most interesting aspects of our interviews with these suburban teachers is the degree to which they all stressed the importance of the desegregation program and considered the resulting racial mix of students in their schools as broadening the educational experiences of the white students. To teach a more multicultural curriculum is one thing, but to have a diverse student body to discuss that curriculum is another. Although these teachers are aware that not all of their white students like the desegregation plan and that many of them resent having black students in their schools, they emphasized that without the program the white students' lives would be incredibly sheltered. For many suburban students, the visionaries say, their world begins and ends within a five-mile radius of their subdivisions and the nearest shopping mall. When mostly white suburban teachers incorporate the culture, history, and oppression of other races and ethnic groups into the curriculum and introduce varied perspectives to a broad mixture of students in their classes, they help white suburban students understand the value of differences. Thus, the new discourse in the classrooms of these visionary teachers has brought the "marginal" issues and concerns to the center "by making the interests of the disadvantaged and excluded heard in the classroom and by including them in mainstream curricula" (McLaren, 1991b, p. 250).

Studies and reviews of research in school desegregation demonstrate the significant role that teachers can play in either demeaning or dignifying the culture, experiences, and contributions of various nonwhite groups through their selection of textbooks and other curricular components (Schofield, 1991, 1993). Research demonstrates that teachers in desegregated schools who honor and celebrate the different cultures of their students enhance intergroup relations as well as the academic achievement and self-esteem of black and Latino students (Schofield, 1993; Tate, Ladson-Billings, and Grant, 1993).

According to Sara Jones, another English teacher at Mehlville High School, "The program has been very good in that our curriculum on the sophomore level in American literature—one of the main themes is freedom and equality—and it has enhanced the general quality of learning in the classroom, because the white students seem to have more of an understanding [about racial issues and inequality]."

Jones cited an example from when her sophomore students read *Adventures of Huckleberry Finn* and had a long discussion about Twain's use of the word "nigger." The students discussed what Twain was trying to do by using the word and how they feel about it. Suddenly it was not just a bad word for the white students; they saw its real impact. "My whole theory of teaching had to do with 'everybody is somebody.' And no put-downs, not to discriminate. So the [desegregation] program to me is a real plus as far as what my teaching is trying to accomplish. . . . From my perspective I think it is better for the suburban kids than it is for the black kids because it breaks down walls. . . . It causes them to have a heightened awareness of the truth."

Similarly, Sally Smith, a social studies and history teacher at Parkway South High School, said the desegregation plan benefits the white resident students the most by changing the dialogue in the classroom and the content of class discussions. "We have to broaden our world, and I think it helps our county students, our white students, to see that up close—that 'Yes, indeed, this is a human being, just as I am a human being, with the same goals that I have and the same concerns and feelings that I have.' We can learn a lot from that."

These sentiments are echoed by Owens at Kirkwood, who argues that just as it is important for her male students to understand the importance of women's liberation, it is also important for white students to learn about the injuries society has inflicted on African Americans. That learning, said Owens, takes on new meanings in a racially mixed classroom. "I have to have the Caucasian students see the pain or the anger or the disgust on an African-American student's face when something is said, and there has to be a mediator there to say, 'Okay, did you see that expression? Now pay attention to that. Let's talk about that.'" She added that it is better for students to have these kinds of discussions and disagreements about race in her classroom than outside of school, where there is no one mediating and trying to create a broader understanding on both sides.

Critique of Business as Usual

Much of the visionary educators' critique of their schools and the ways that black students have been treated centers on the norms within the school that guide relationships between teachers and students in general and the African-American transfer students more specifically. For instance, the visionaries talk critically about teachers who assume that black students are less intelligent or "immoral" and those who, through body language and actions, communicate to black students that they are not welcome and that white teachers consider them to be inferior.

Owens said that the hostility that can develop between white teachers and transfer students often begins because most suburban teachers have not attempted to change their curricula to reflect the heritage or the suffering and oppression of African Americans or any other group. Thus, she said, many of the transfer students are angry—at whites in general and white teachers in particular for not relating to the experiences of people of color. If these students are not provided a space within the curriculum to work through this anger and redirect their energy toward learning more about the history and culture of the United States, she said, they will continue to act out in class. "Every time I have a kid who's really angry—and I do every year—unless you have a class where they can talk about it, there is no place for her to go with it. She has to keep sitting through history classes where they are halfway through the year, and they've never mentioned a black person."

The failure of many teachers to add various perspectives to their curriculum is often coupled with a stereotype that many white teachers have of African-American students as disruptive and unmotivated. Owens said that there is definitely such a stereotype among many teachers, that the students who are misbehaving are those who are "bused in" from the city. "There is no question about that attitude, and some of that is true, but . . . my experience is it is not the kids who are bused, it's that there are *certain* kids [who are unmotivated]." If these unmotivated or disruptive students are disproportionately African American, Owens and others concur, then teachers need to examine their curriculum and their relationships with black students and the kinds of messages they send to these students about whose history and whose knowledge is important.

According to Sally Smith, the social studies teacher at Parkway South, often the transfer students are highly motivated, but the white suburban teachers have not learned how to tap in to that. "We don't recognize it. We're frightened by it. We did not invite the black children out here, and so there is an underlying hostility towards them that may not be recognized [by most teachers]."

For example, she mentioned that the black children are often accused by the faculty and parents of bringing drugs in from the city and selling them in the high school. "I don't really see the black children as being as involved in using drugs as the white child," said Smith. She said that the transfer students who endure hour-long bus rides to and from school every day must be "pretty highly motivated, whether the teachers understand that or not. These children are really not into drugs."

According to data collected by the Voluntary Interdistrict Coordinating Council (1995), less than 2 percent of the total suspensions—68 of 4,012—issued to transfer students during the 1993–94 school year were for selling or possessing drugs. And as one administrator mentioned in Chapter 7, the drug problem in white suburbia did not arrive with the transfer students. White suburban students are more likely to have the money to purchase drugs than are the students from the city.

Peggy Mack, the English teacher at Mehlville High School, said that many of the problems that her colleagues have with the transfer students stem from the teachers' preconceived notions about black students coupled with resistance to change. "[You have] some people who would not make a change in a million years. And then you have other people who want to change but in their own framework. . . . Relinquishing control is very difficult, and when you make a major change like this one you have to change your tactics. You have to look at yourself—it's frightening. You have to look at who you are, and that can be scary for some people."

Bonnie Doe, the English teacher at Oakville High School, was chosen by the superintendent to conduct staff development and teacher evaluations for the Mehlville District. She said that few of the problems that the district has had with the transfer students stem directly from the behavior or attitudes of the students. She said that many more of the problems begin with teachers and school administrators who treat the black students as unwelcome visitors.

As we mentioned in Chapter 7, 80 percent of the black students who are sent to the principals' offices are referred by 20 percent of the teachers. "If [the desegregation plan] is working with some of the teachers, then it is not the kids. . . . The assistant superintendent and one principal suggested [staff development for] those teachers who had more at-risk kids. I said, 'No. Deal with the teachers who are sending the kids to the office. . . . And I don't care if that is a teacher who is in the highest [track] group. If I have twenty-four low-tracked kids, I'm not having problems because I am not using those behaviors that set kids off."

Doe said that Mehlville High School—the older, more established of the two high schools in her district—offers a particularly hostile environment for the transfer students, mainly because traditionally the administration there has condoned the type of behavior and attitudes that are sure to create conflict and tension in the school. "As long as the administration allows people to say 'nigger' in the faculty room, they will say 'nigger' in the school. . . . It is the responsibility of the administrator to stand up in front of the whole faculty and say 'I will not allow you to say "nigger" in this building. . . . I will not tolerate that behavior.' But then he would have to modify his own."

According to some of the more visionary educators we spoke to, there is confusion among suburban educators regarding transfer students' "ability" and their lack of preparedness. The principal of one west county high school notes that educators in suburban schools need to distinguish between when a student has what he calls an "academic limitation" and when a student simply has a gap in his or her academic background. Despite what many suburban educators believe, he said, "the percentage of kids who are academically limited in the desegregation program is about the same percentage as the kids in the residential population." But he added that there are more students from the city with academic gaps. "Those kids are the ones we have to be careful of," he said. "The suburban schools should focus on helping them catch up rather than labeling them incapable."

Owens at Kirkwood argues that much racial prejudice in the suburban schools stems from the outdated and narrow-minded ways that many suburban educators conceive of "intelligence." She argues that educators tend to think of intelligence as a definable and quantifiable entity that can be measured—something that some people have and others don't. This way of conceptualizing intelligence, says Owens, leads to stereotypes about different groups of people having more intelligence than others. "There are people who still believe that some of us are more intelligent, whether it be because of being female, male, whether it's because you're Italian or you're a Jew or whatever; there are those people who really believe that."

This paradigm for understanding intelligence—and who is and who isn't intelligent—is entrenched in U.S. society, said Owens, because a lot of people are very comfortable with it. "Well, let's face it. If you were raised under the system that said you were very intelligent and high achieving, you don't want anyone questioning that system."

But Owens sees many facets to the concept of intelligence, and she argues that some of her students who do not do as well on standardized tests are far more creative than are students who are good at recalling information in a testing situation. She described a white student named Brad in her American studies class whom we observed making insightful connections to various poems, books, and essays he had read. Yet because Brad does poorly on standardized tests he has been identified as a special education student. Owens' class is one of the only classes he has excelled in since he came to the high school. "I've gotten many phone calls and letters from parents who were overwhelmed with good feeling about the fact that someone understood. 'I always knew my son was intelligent, but I didn't know how to explain it.' Like a Brad, or any of the kids in that class. I mean the kid's sharp; you heard him. He makes connections like that all day long. Now he is totally frustrated because if he has to take an objective test, he has a hard time."

Narrow conceptions of intelligence not only fail to take into account the genius of students like Brad but they also legitimize school policies, such as tracking. When educators believe that some students are intelligent and some are not, and when they see a relation between whom they consider intelligent and race, tracking practices that result in resegregation within racially mixed schools make sense (Oakes, Lipton, and Jones, 1995). Thus, it follows that the visionary educators in the suburban St. Louis schools challenge not only the traditional conception of intelligence and genius but also the practice of tracking that is supported by it.

Interestingly, all of the visionary teachers we spoke to support efforts to detrack their schools. Several of these teachers have read the research detailing the negative effects of tracking and ability grouping on the educational opportunities of poor and minority students in desegregated schools (see Schofield, 1989). Others have learned these lessons from experience. Many of the visionaries, therefore, favor more research- and discovery-oriented assignments that allow students to follow their own interests and work at their own pace. They also like cooperative group learning strategies and a less competitive classroom environment. They are bothered by the reality of resegregation within their "desegregated" schools, but have been able to make only small changes thus far, in part because they are in the minority at their schools.

At Parkway South High School, Sally Smith praises her former principal, calling him bright, creative, and caring. She said that he worked toward changing the school climate and condemning attitudes and behavior that lead to racial conflict. He supported the efforts of some teachers to dismantle the school's tracking system. This principal has also attempted to create a school culture that promotes a more democratic, decentralized form of governance while raising teachers' consciousness about how schools solidify social relations that reflect the racial and economic stratification within the larger society (Foster, 1986).

The principal said that he had noticed shortly after the desegregation program began that there was a rapid increase in the number of white suburban students trying to get into honors English in ninth grade. When the percentage reached 50 percent he began to suspect that the requests for honors English were not all about students wanting a more rigorous English course but about white parents who did not want their children in classes with African-American students.

Yet even at Parkway South, where the principal and a core group of teachers favored movement away from tracking, change was thwarted by political forces. White parents in the suburban community protested when they learned that the principal and English teachers planned to do away with the honors English classes in the ninth grade, integrate students of all "ability levels" into common English classes, and then offer students the option of completing extra work or "weighted assignments" that would count toward advanced placement or honors-level credit. The parent group, comprising mainly the parents of honors students, went to the district superintendent to complain and threaten to pull their children out of the high school if honors English was not offered.

Hence, Parkway South's students remain tracked between honors English and the general-track English course. But Parkway South and the other Parkway high schools have done away with their lowest-track—remedial or "basic"—English classes and added "backup" or "tutorial" classes, an extra period once or twice a week with the same English teacher for students who need extra help and support in the general track. Although the move to two English tracks and a tutorial was a compromise, it was, according to the principal at Parkway South, better than the prior three-track system. "The tutorial works much better than putting students in a basic class. It's a whole issue of desegregation, too. If you put them [transfer students] in a basic class then you are dooming them to be in a black school within the school."

A principal of another Parkway high school said that English tutorials at his school are premised on the belief that all students can learn difficult material:

"It just takes some students more time if they have not had the background. . . . Rather than being in a basics class and being re-segregated, they are in regular English classes. But if they are at risk, we ask them to circulate back to that English teacher every other day for a tutorial with a small group of students. . . . They are taking the same work they had in regular class, but they're getting more one-on-one help with it."

While much of the tracking structure remains in place, this move toward a two- instead of three-tiered system in English is seen as a significant accomplishment, not only for the educational opportunities of African-American students from the city, but also for the white county students who had been relegated to the basic classes. "And what we have found is that all kids can learn, and we are taking kids out of tracks—all kids move on to English II. And this is not specific to the desegregation plan, but it is certainly appropriate to it," said another administrator.

Efforts to detrack the history and social studies classes at Parkway South have been more successful. According to Smith, students in history classes are "dispersed a little bit better," but they're still tracked. "[The] outcry from the community caused us to come back and try to placate the community, though we thought at the time—and still think—that most of it was an attempt to segregate—resegregate—the kids. So the social studies classes are not as heterogeneous as we would like them to be. . . . But we're not as bad as the English department."

In her own fairly heterogeneous classroom, Smith is doing a lot of group work and cooperative learning. During the weeks we visited, her tenth-grade students spent several days preparing group presentations on the fate of various American Indian tribes since the arrival of the Europeans in North America. On the day of the student presentations, every member of each group was responsible for a part of the overall presentation. Students brought in handmade visual aids, including maps and drawings of Indian clothing. Group projects such as these, Smith noted, allow the individual talents—map making, public speaking, researching—of all students to shine through while reaffirming the value and importance of non-European cultures.

At Parkway West High School, which serves a slightly more affluent area of the Parkway District, English teacher William O'Shea approved of the elimination of the remedial-track English classes. He said the addition of the tutorial program and the reading and writing center, where teachers can send students for help in a specific area, has strengthened his department. "Maybe the transfer students made us more aware of the need for these programs, but I think we are finding out now that all students are benefiting from it."

Other suburban high schools have eliminated some of their lowest-level or remedial courses in recent years, but they remain fairly rigidly tracked at the upper level, with several advanced placement (AP) courses for college credit that are virtually all-white. Thus, Owens' interdisciplinary course is more of a suburban anomaly because it attracts high- and low-track, white and black students. Owens argues that this kind of heterogeneous grouping is essential to the learning process, and because she individualizes the curriculum for her students—letting them choose much of their own reading and letting them work on research projects at their own pace—she does not feel that she is holding back the high-achieving students by having them in the same room with low-achieving students. In fact, she sees it as quite the opposite. For example, she described the benefit of the detracked classroom on one of her high-achieving white students from a very wealthy suburban family:

> Melinda is a perfect example. She'll come into class . . . and she is writing things down, and they [the other students] are still playing. And she'll say, 'You know that article I read,' or 'You know that poem?' And the next thing you know, while I am taking attendance, she's sitting up next to me, and we're talking about this poem. . . . Because it's not that I'm saying to her, 'We can't talk about that today, Melinda.' That would shut her down. But I'm not doing that. She comes up to me any time she wants. And in class, when I have a discussion and she makes a statement, everybody else hears it, and we talk about it. She gets to pontificate, she gets to make a statement about something very important. She also gets insight from somebody who hasn't had her experience, or doesn't own a horse or a place out in the country. A kid who gets on the bus every day and lives in two rooms. So when she defines self-reliance [the topic of recent class discussion on Emerson] . . . it's from the perspective of the kid who has it—who has a family that has given it to her and the financial security to maintain it. But she's got to hear from a kid who's had to struggle his little buns or her little buns to get it. Now if that is not a learning experience, I don't know what is.

By setting up her class in such a way that there is a lot of independent student learning going on, coupled with dynamic class discussions among students of very different backgrounds and academic strengths, Owens has created a learning environment in which she sees more students looking for what she calls the "genius within them"—insight into their own ways of knowing and learning. And when they do that, says Owens, she finds that they become highly motivated "students" in the broader sense of the word, thirsty for a greater understanding of the world around them. Researchers have found this more individualized approach to teaching especially helpful in racially and socioeconomically mixed schools, to which students bring their different "ways of knowing."

But Owens, with her desire and ability to teach a heterogeneous class, remains the exception rather than the rule in most American high schools. For instance, Bonnie Doe noted that the Mehlville District remains "rigidly tracked" and that this tracking system inhibits positive race relations within the desegregated school. She said that for the most part, the black and white students are segregated throughout the school experience, with black students always in the lowest-level courses. She noted that in her advanced, college-credit English class there were no black students, nor were there any blacks in any of their other "advanced" classes taken by these white students by the time they were seniors.

Doe said that while she and a handful of other teachers at her high school oppose the tracking system and believe that it increases white students' feeling of superiority and prejudice toward blacks, the idea of detracking is "not a priority except for a few of us." While Doe realizes that the rigid tracking system was in place before the transfer program began, the resegregation between tracks has made the inequity of the system more visible. "We start tracking in the first grade in many schools—reading and math are tracked all the way through. . . . But to me the most abominable of all these is that we begin tracking social studies in the junior high. I mean, there is no reason—no research, nothing—why we should do this."

Doe told us of a junior high social studies teacher she was supervising who gave an "incredibly boring" lecture about the Civil War to her students in the lower-track class and then allowed her honors students to study the same period by re-creating a plantation setting. The honors students went to the library to conduct research on plantation life and then acted out their scenes, playing the parts of different characters. "Of course, there weren't any blacks in this group," she said, noting that it was a "fabulous assignment, and the kids loved doing the research and the acting. So I said to her, 'Why did you not do that with lower-track kids?' And she said, 'Well they just could not handle it.'"

Doe said that when she was teaching her college credit English composition course about three years into the desegregation plan, there were no black students in her class. So she began recruiting transfer students for the class, and they did fine. "Then this teacher teaching the low-level classes came to me the second week of school and said I have this black senior in my sophomore lowest-level class, and he is just the brightest kid. I can't get over it. And he said what about putting him in you college composition class. So I said terrific. . . . That kid got in my class and was just fantastic, the kids just loved him. . . . He was just an asset to the class. . . . He was the leader. . . . I believe that kids rise not only to expectations, but to the level of their peers."

The footnote to the story is that this student did not get any college credit for the class because he had not yet passed sophomore English.

Criticisms of tracking practices are not restricted to the most reform-minded suburban teachers, such as Doe and Smith; even the more moderate teachers, such as Michael Mills, a business teacher at the small and very upper-middle-class Clayton High School, question such practices. Moore said that teachers have to be more creative in how they teach all students. "I know just from the things that I read, the only way to really make kids, all kids, learn is by raising expectations and not tracking them." But Mills, like the other teachers who want to change the current system, is aware of the political and structural barriers: "The thing of it is you're dealing with a political situation that is highly explosive—you're dealing with parents, and their kids are two years away from college . . . and it's tough to break down barriers."

Hence, even the small steps toward change—steps that do not radically re-structure but simply weaken the existing structure—are considered victories. Parkway's elimination of remedial English classes is one such example. Also, Stacy Phillips, a math teacher at Clayton High School, designed "low-level" geometry and algebra II courses for students who completed the school's low-track algebra course. Phillips said that before she created the new courses, low-tracked math students "were just dead ended" after algebra. They did not have the prerequisite for the regular geometry or any of the other high-track math courses, and there was nothing else available for them to take. Many of the students who benefit from new courses that allow them to go beyond basic algebra are black transfer students, but not all of them are. "We created these new, more advanced classes for the low-track students, and now they have math courses that they can take all four years of high school. . . . That should have been done whether there's a transfer program or not. . . . There were resident students who would have benefited from the classes before the transfer program. . . . They were just never there."

When we visited her newly created lower-level geometry class, less than half the students were black.

Meeting Individual Needs of All Students

Virtually all of the visionaries are guided by a humanistic view of what teaching and learning is all about. They strive to foster self-esteem and efficacy among their students, and they draw on students' thoughts, feelings, and experiences as rich and valuable resources that are relevant to learning (Bell and Schniedewind, 1987). In many instances, these teachers find themselves advocating the opposite approaches of those employed by their more resistant colleagues. And many of them are forced to try to make changes in the way they work with students behind the backs of school administrators. As Doe explains it, "I don't ask first, I just do what I know will work."

And, of course, these attitudes toward teaching and learning serve all students—black and white—but as with the issues discussed above, the desegregation plan has heightened the visionary teachers' awareness of what does not work. Because of the widely felt distrust between the transfer students and many of the white teachers in the county schools, issues of student efficacy and self-esteem become even more poignant to those who see them as part of the solution. According to the Voluntary Interdistrict Coordinating Council office, in-service staff development programs designed to help make white, middle-class teachers more sensitive to the needs and feelings of low-income African-American students have increased dramatically since the desegregation plan began. For instance, during the 1992–93 school year a series of nine workshops called the "Black Legacy Program" were offered through the council office to educators in all sixteen suburban school districts. In addition, several districts obtained funding for their own staff development programs, including "Multi-Cultural Emergence. What's It Like to Walk in My Shoes: Understanding Black Culture," "Multi-Cultural Sensitivity Training," and "Images and Others" (Voluntary Interdistrict Coordinating Council, 1993). Through programs such as these and their own understanding of the dynamics of a racially mixed school, the visionary teachers realize that they have to go out of their way to build trusting, nurturing relationships with the transfer students.

Believing in the Transfer Students In contrast to the more resistant educators, who emphasized their course content and whether the students were absorbing that content in a timely fashion, the visionary educators begin with a focus on the students—what knowledge and understanding they bring with them to the classroom and what trusting and safe conditions help students engage in learning.

"I don't teach English, I teach the humanities, I guess, is the way I look at it. Or, I teach . . . how to learn. You know, I teach a subject only as a vehicle for learning," said Owens at Kirkwood, where she teams up with another teacher for her interdisciplinary English and social studies course.

Stacy Phillips, the math teacher at Clayton High School who established the new geometry and algebra II courses, said she spends a lot of time working with kids, making sure that "they believe that I want good things for them. I really spend a lot of time at the beginning of the year making sure that they know that."

Phillips said that she eats lunch with her students and talks to them about what they do on weekends. She plays cards with them and attends their sporting events or plays. "I make sure that I know something about most of them—then I try to be visible and available." She said that she does this with all of her students but has become more aware of the need for such interaction because of the transfer students' tendency to distrust the suburban teachers.

Martha Irving is the warm and jolly former nun who taught English at Parkway West for several years before becoming the director of the school's interracial relations program. Reflecting on her teaching career, which spans two decades and includes five years at a Catholic school, Irving said that she changed her approach and philosophy a lot after working with the transfer students. "When I started teaching you just had to have a good unit, you had to know your business, you had to plan your lessons, and if you had a sense of humor—that was a plus. . . . We didn't talk about at-risk kids and we didn't talk about home problems and we didn't talk about counseling these kids."

When Irving returned to teaching after staying at home with her son for several years, the transfer program was in its third year at Parkway West. She returned to a student population that differed dramatically from those she had taught in the past. She found that her established teaching techniques did not work, especially with the transfer students. The students resented her authoritarian approach, and she was frustrated and exhausted. Irving decided that the problem was that she had not formed trusting relationships with the students, and she had not established methods of conveying that she liked them. So she started building relationships with her students and letting them know that she saw their strengths and did not dwell on their weaknesses. "I tried to convey that I knew they were nice people, and I came to realize that a lot of it [insubordination or acting out] was their [the transfer students] way of hiding feelings of being afraid and insecure and confused. And once I could put that together, I could understand better," she explained.

As Irving began building stronger ties with her students, she realized that the middle-class suburban white students, whom people always assume are well taken care of, were also in dire need of strong interpersonal relationships with adults. "I mean, when you take the statistics out here in west county on marriages . . . A white kid can be ripped up overnight and sent off to his father in another state because he had a fight with his mother. . . . Actually dealing with the black kids has made me more effective with the white kids because I've really had to change. I was into all of this assertive stuff. Well, forget all that stuff, you know, it doesn't work. . . . I think the success of any program is dependent on the relationships that you form with the kids. It's a relationship—it's not just presenting the materials."

In the past, Irving said, she had wanted to be in complete control of the materials, which she would feed to the students through lectures and handouts. "Now I break stuff into smaller parts and look at it from more points of view than I ever used to before. And I think, again, it's because I focus on the kids and not on the material."

As director of the interracial relations program, Irving remains highly focused on students. An hour in her office is an hour of constant interruptions as students—black and white, outgoing and shy—filter in and out. Some come by just to say hello and to update her on their latest relationships or upcoming test; others have more serious things on their minds—they feel that a teacher has not treated them fairly, or they are having problems at home. Irving also keeps tabs on the teachers who are not succeeding with individual students, especially transfer students. "It's usually because they're not relating to the kids as people. They think what they are doing is excellent, therefore anybody who doesn't measure up is inadequate. But are you really teaching if nobody is learning? I think the big difference in terms of education is the people who focus on the material and the people who focus on the kids. . . . [Many teachers here] focus only on scholarship   Well, I believe that a whole lot of what I do is in the affective domain. And that builds trust and it builds self-esteem. The kids need to feel that it matters to somebody."

She told of one math teacher who keeps perfect records, teaches perfect lessons, and uses his time extremely well. "The only thing that messes up his class is the kids," she said.

Stan Boxer, a math teacher at Parkway West, has gone through a transformation similar to that undergone by Irving. Boxer, a twelve-year veteran of the school, said that when he began teaching he used a sort of "dictatorial" approach: "I'm going to throw out this knowledge, and you should grasp it, you should pull it in—that's your job. Now, for me at least, I really push harder to make sure they have some retention of it—whether that's because of the transfer students being added in or whether I am just becoming more observant, I don't know. . . . I think [in part] it is just the nature of the child of the nineties. . . . Really getting them to think more is very much the challenge."

Similarly, Gloria McDonna, an art teacher at the Captain Elementary School in the Clayton District, said that if it weren't for the transfer students and the desegregation program, the teachers in her school would not be paying as much attention to individual differences. "I think it [the desegregation plan] has forced us to take another look at how children learn, and we had to vary our activities in a very expansive way in order to try and accommodate all of those cultural differences—not only in dealing with black kids but with white students as well. We have also had an influx of international kids that we never had before. So it is a different world of teaching than when I started. The world has expanded, and we have to grow with it or we will lose the students."

Bonnie Doe, working as a staff developer in the Mehlville District, holds discussion or focus groups for teachers who have been most successful in working with the transfer students. They compare notes and find that very simple but highly sensitive methods of working with students—showing respect for students and building trust—are what make them successful. Little things, such as kneeling down to be on eye level when talking to students instead of standing in a confrontational stance, help make all students feel more comfortable, but they particularly help students who are far from home and in a different cultural context. In the focus groups, the issue of touching students was discussed, along with the importance of not touching without permission. Participants talk about body language and what messages teachers send to students when, for instance, they lean toward students when talking to them instead of pulling back. "Body language is extremely important—that's the first indicator of a teacher's attitude toward students," said Doe. She said she had heard about teachers in the district who ignore the black students when they raise their hands but run over to help white students with questions.

Doe recalled a discussion with an assistant superintendent about the need for teachers to change their attitudes and ways of dealing with the transfer students. The administrator told her that there is no reason to do anything different for the transfer students as long as the teachers are doing "super teaching." Therein lies the problem, said Doe. Whose definition of super teaching is used? "I also think that a teacher has to be ethical and humane and has to know about black culture and reach beyond. I buy the teaching part, and that's true that black students would probably excel if the teacher were teaching in an excellent way, but I think we have to go beyond that. I think we have an ethical responsibility to our client population. If I have a kid from Pakistan, I have to bone up on what's happening [there]. I truly believe I do my children a disservice if I don't know who they are."

Doe said that given so much of what happens in her high school is skewed toward the needs and culture of white suburban students, she tries to think of activities in which black students would have an advantage over white students so that the blacks could gain more self-esteem and confidence. For instance, one day she had students draw a map of the route from south St. Louis County to the zoo in the City of St. Louis. She said that many of the white suburban students, who had spent little time in the city, were lost, but for the black kids, "that was their day to really shine."

As we mentioned in Chapter 7, Kirkwood School District has instituted efficacy training for all administrators and teachers in the district. The training, designed and implemented by Jeff Howard's Efficacy Institute in Cambridge, Massachusetts, helps educators recognize the talents of all students and focus on how they can improve students' self-esteem and school achievement. According to the district administrator who spearheaded this training, it has spurred a dialogue about how educators tend to pigeonhole kids, particularly black kids, and then become complacent about their lower achievement. "It's very much a strategy based from the point of view that we tend to expect kids to come packaged with self-confidence. When they don't demonstrate it, we don't know what to do."

CONCLUSIONS

The efforts of this small group of visionary educators may seem meek when one considers the barriers that they face in making systemic changes in their schools. But their stories, perhaps more than any other form of "data," should help policy makers and researchers make sense of the test score data cited in Chapter 5, which shows that when controlling for prior achievement, participation in the transfer program did not, as a whole, improve African-American students' performance on standardized tests until after eighth grade (Lissitz, 1994). Learning about how the suburban educators and the transfer students interact can help us better understand these aggregated, quantitative test results. If the visionary teachers are in the minority at most suburban schools, then what do we really expect black students' average test scores to look like? This does not mean that the goal of school desegregation is wrong, nor does it mean that the benefits of the desegregation plan—to students of all races and educators in these once racially isolated suburban schools—are not "worth," in some quantifiable sense, the cost of the program.

Perhaps what we can learn from the voices and stories of these visionary teachers and principals is that their ideas are contagious—more teachers in these and other schools in suburban St. Louis are becoming committed to change. For instance, the principal of Captain Elementary School in the Clayton District explained that she has tried to encourage teachers who "are not real focused on helping kids develop" to leave her school. Furthermore, beginning in the 1991–92 school year, she and her staff decided not to accept the failure of at-risk students any longer. "We are going to tackle that as simply not being acceptable. I think in previous years probably we accepted that by saying, 'Well, they come from a bad family background' . . . 'Well, they are not bright enough,' 'Well, whatever . . .' and I think that a change that is going on is that we are beginning to see that it is our responsibility to educate all of those kids."

In some suburban schools and districts the change will be greatly contested as more resistant educators struggle to hold on to old ways of doing things and thinking about children. According to one district-level administrator in Parkway, sometimes, there has to be a crisis before you make movement. "The pressure is on," she said. "The crisis in Parkway is that these kids are failures, and in the last thirty years, we [as a school district] have succeeded. Now we are not succeeding with these students—so now we have to change ourselves. The crisis will happen within each person."

The stories presented here suggests that the inter-district school desegregation plan provided an important catalyst for "the crisis" to happen in some of the suburban educators. As several of the teachers noted, the sudden influx of African-American students increased the teachers' critical awareness of the prevailing norms and practices in their suburban schools and made them more sensitive to the individual needs of all students. Their critique and experiences in seeking successful new strategies do not appear to be glimmers of insight that they will soon ignore or forget. Instead, these teachers and their counterparts in other suburban St. Louis schools will continue to speak out against injustices to African-American students. They will continue to pursue classroom- and school-level reforms that lead to greater success for all students.

Certainly there is growing evidence that more suburban schools, through their attempts to better meet the needs of the black transfer students, are serving their white resident students in more creative ways. New before- and after-school programs are cropping up in county schools, as are more support programs for parents. "We have not only changed the way we worked within the classrooms, but we began to expand outside of the school day to give children lots and lots of experiences," said the principal of the Merrimac Elementary School in Clayton.

One of the principals of a Parkway high school said that the plan and the arrival of the black transfer students has helped to uncover some attitudes that needed to be dealt with, and that has changed what teaching is like. "It has made for more creative teaching, and that has benefited everybody. But it has also given us an opportunity as a school to say, 'What does it mean to be a good citizen, and how do we accept that?'"

9

White Families in Flux:

Intergenerational Lessons on School Desegregation

And these children that you spit on as they try to change their worlds are immune to
your consultations. They're quite aware of what they're going through
—David Bowie, "Changes"

The professional and political risks that the visionary suburban educators take
every time they advocate the benefits of the desegregation plan or discuss
their changing understanding of intelligence and learning cannot be truly appreciated unless they are placed within the political contexts of their local
communities and the state of Missouri. In general, white voters in the St.
Louis metropolitan area "put up" with the court-ordered inter-district desegregation plan because they feel they have no choice. The attitudes toward the
plan among white suburban adults range from highly resentful to fairly accepting of the racial diversity that it brings to their schools; but strong advocates of the plan are few and far between, and it seems that only a small
number of the adults—particularly those with children enrolled in magnet
schools in the city—would be upset if the program went away. The scope of attitudes among white suburban students appears to be even broader, with
some students resorting to antiblack racial politics to express their disapproval
and others embracing the plan as a vital aspect of their education. In fact, as

the state's recent efforts to end the desegregation plan have filtered through the media and into suburbia, a fairly small but highly vocal group of suburban high school students have protested loudly.

In spite of the range of perspectives on the desegregation plan, few of the adults in suburbia are going to fight to keep African-American students from the inner city in their schools. Only a handful, at most, seem to understand and appreciate the complex history of race in America or the structural and cultural factors that have created and maintained the color line between the suburbs and the city. Few, if any, know the history of the court case, and most have forgotten why their suburban school districts signed on to the settlement agreement—why their lawyers were afraid they could lose at trial, and what was at stake if they did.

In the years since all of these issues were salient to the people of St. Louis County, most white suburbanites have heard nothing but disparaging remarks about the program from their state and local political leaders. In fact, most of these politicians have used the desegregation plan for their own political benefit—running against it in order to gain the support of Missouri voters from the smaller towns and rural areas. Even most of the local business "leaders" in the St. Louis area have been ominously quiet lest their support of the program be bad for business.

"If they [business leaders] get identified with a controversial position people might buy less Rice Chex or Budweiser," said Dean Jones of the University of Missouri–St. Louis, referring to two of the larger corporations in the St. Louis area—Ralston Purina and Anheuser-Busch. Jones, who conducted the 1988 metropolitanwide survey of opinions toward the desegregation plan for the St. Louis Post-Dispatch, said that outside of the educational community, where small numbers of suburban school administrators and teachers have spoken on behalf of the program and tried to pave the way for its acceptance, there is virtually no support from the local or state leaders. He said, in fact, that the reason so few of the teachers in the county schools see themselves as participating in a noble cause is that virtually no one in a position of power and influence sends that message to the suburbs: "There is no support from the leadership in the community outside of the educational community—county executive and mayors aren't saying good things about the program. The governor, of course, has been pretty active against the plan. Corporate leadership has not come out and said, 'Isn't this great, this is a sign of our maturing, we have recognized that we have a racist past, and we are trying to overcome it.' This was something which we could take pride in as a metropolitan area, and we run away from it and leave it in the hands of the educational professionals and let them take a lot of heat."

Of course, the 1995 Civic Progress report has changed this to some extent. The strong support for the desegregation program stated in this report by a task force of local leaders and businessmen represented a major shift in the relationship between the program and the business elite. After the release of the report, more business leaders came out in support of the program (Samuel, 1995). Still, some educators consider this newfound support to be too little too late. The heat that the educational professionals have had to take regarding the desegregation plan has been more difficult to bear around the time of statewide elections, when candidates for major offices from both political parties use the desegregation plan as a political tool, demonstrating that they know how to play the race card in U.S. politics and that they care less about the constitutional rights of African-American students than their own political advancement.

STATE POLITICS OF DESEGREGATION

The 1992 gubernatorial campaign trail was littered with one-liners about the "disaster" of the St. Louis and Kansas City school desegregation programs—that they cost too much and are considered failures. In fact, in the spring of 1992, six months before the election, the two leading Democratic candidates for governor—the then–St. Louis Mayor Vincent C. Schoemehl, Jr., and the then–Lt. Gov. Mel Carnahan, who would later win the election—both said that they if they were elected they would do everything in their power to end the desegregation programs in the two metropolitan areas. Speaking at a candidates' forum at the Democrat Days festivities in Hannibal, Schoemehl stated emphatically that "no one in this state has a better understanding than I of the disaster these programs have caused for urban, as well as rural, schools" (Mannies, 1992a). This is an incredible statement from a mayor of a city whose urban school system has received an estimated $411 million in additional state funding since the original intra-district desegregation plan began in the St. Louis public schools in 1981.

At the same forum, Carnahan reported that "those who have studied the Kansas City and St. Louis programs have concluded they are failures." He did not cite any specific studies of the programs.

Schoemehl and Carnahan blamed the then governor, John Ashcroft,[1] and his attorney general, William J. Webster, both Republicans, for many of the

1. Ashcroft was Missouri's attorney general at the time the settlement agreement was written. He is now a U.S. senator from Missouri. He declined several requests by us to interview him for this book.

problems associated with the desegregation plans, especially the high cost. Schoemehl said that Webster had failed to "adequately address the needs of the state by taking constructive court actions to fight the programs." Schoemehl was alluding to Ashcroft and Webster's political decision to fight every aspect of the court-ordered desegregation plan, a fight that has cost the taxpayers of Missouri an extraordinary amount of money in state legal fees. Between 1983 and 1991 the Missouri Legislature allocated an *additional* $3.72 million to allow the attorney general's office to continue to fight the school desegregation case. This funding, above and beyond the regular cost of staffing the attorney general's office, was used to hire Washington, D.C., law firms as outside council and for additional legal costs to fight the federal court order. All of these resources—tax dollars that could have gone to education—have been expended to prove to the voters of Missouri that these white politicians oppose a court-ordered school choice program that allows African American students from St. Louis to attend white suburban schools. Proving this may have become more important to the political futures of the politicians than it has to any of the taxpayers of Missouri.

In 1980 the Eighth Circuit Court of Appeals ruled that the state of Missouri had not taken proper steps to ensure that the schools in St. Louis were desegregated after the Supreme Court's *Brown* decision in 1954, and that in fact, the Missouri Constitution still contained an article calling for separate schools until twenty-two years after *Brown*. Over the nearly twenty-five-year course of the St. Louis desegregation case, all of the state's appeals to the U.S. Supreme Court have been denied. These judicial decisions, however, did not guide the state attorney general's office toward compliance with the court-ordered settlement agreement. Instead, the succession of attorneys general and governors have made much more political headway in the mostly rural and white state by using school desegregation as a political symbol of the federal government taking away local control and state's rights and spending large amounts of taxpayers' money on "busing."

The Confluence St. Louis Task Force report (1989) noted that "throughout the implementation of the order, the state of Missouri has opposed the desegregation plan, despite the finding that the system willfully violated the law of the land. Fiscal support for the plan by the state had been fought every step of the way, and leadership in Jefferson City [the state capital] is not supportive of the desegregation efforts" (p. 88). Even though Missouri was found guilty of violating the constitutional rights of the African-American students, the report argued, state leaders have resisted taking steps to rectify the problem. "Political maneuvering and campaigning at both the local and state level are significantly tied to the desegregation case and the larger issue of race. The issue of funding the desegregation plan has become a political football" (p. 35).

Over the years, the state of Missouri has fought with the St. Louis public schools over the cost and development of state-funded magnet schools and capital improvement programs. Throughout the late 1980s, for instance, the attorney general's office engaged in constant heated battles with the St. Louis public schools over practically every magnet school proposal put forth by the St. Louis school board. The former St. Louis superintendent, Jerome Jones, called the state's tactics "guerrilla warfare" ("Desegregation—The state," 1988).

And, as we mentioned in Chapter 7, the Missouri attorney general's office has also fought ferociously with suburban St. Louis school districts over their capital improvement programs, which the state is obligated to pay for under the terms of the settlement if the districts can demonstrate that the expansion is needed because of the influx of transfer students. The attorney general's office continually lost these battles, costing Missouri taxpayers thousands of dollars in the process. Even the governor-appointed state commissioner of education, Robert Bartman, admitted that the state has taken a "very narrow and adversarial position" on the desegregation plan. "We have tried to take a reasonably narrow look at the order and not provide everything that anybody ever thought was good under the guise of the court order," Bartman said.

Meanwhile, in all of their handwringing and speechgiving on the perils of "busing," these state politicians ignore the fact that less than 20 percent of the $135 million a year the state spends on the St. Louis desegregation plan (about $26 million) is actually spent on transporting students. The remaining money is spent on education within the St. Louis public schools and the six-teen suburban districts. In a state that ranks fiftieth in the United States in per-capita taxation and forty-third in per-pupil spending on public education, this hardly seems a complete waste of state tax dollars, as some politicians would lead voters to believe. In fact, state funding of education has been so low that in 1993 a state circuit judge found the Missouri finance system to be unconstitutional. The judge ruled that because the legislature had "massively underfunded" the state funding formula, school districts were left to support educational programs with local property taxes. This reliance on local wealth, the judge wrote, has produced a statewide system of schools that ranges "from the golden to the God-awful" (West, 1991).

In a stinging 1988 editorial the *St. Louis Post-Dispatch* questioned then-Governor Ashcroft's argument that the state could do a much better job of educating children if it were not forced "to spend those millions of dollars" busing and could instead spend the money on programs that "we know could bring excellence to our classrooms, such as paying good teachers more." The *Post* editors responded, "No one doubts that a big infusion of money would help schools statewide. But the governor has never pledged that if it weren't for desegregation, he would be lavishing that money on schools anywhere in the state, much less in the city." The editors went on to chastise the governor for wasting state funds to fight a case that the state had already lost once it was found to have been a "primary constitutional wrongdoer" in maintaining dual education for blacks and whites in the city. "Payments from the state rarely come without a fight, and the plan's progress has often been stalled by protracted court wrangling. This year [1988], for example, five new city magnet schools did not open as planned because of objections by the state" ("Desegregation—The state," 1988).

By 1988 the St. Louis Board of Education had, since the inception of the inter-district transfer plan in 1983, submitted twenty-eight proposals for new magnet schools, and the state had turned down all of them. Jerome B. Jones, the St. Louis superintendent at the time, contended that state officials blocked the proposals because they did not want to spend money on new schools for the mostly black city school system.

In an effort to explain the state's stance in fighting the desegregation plan, Assistant Attorney General Michael J. Fields said the state fears that the St. Louis public schools are trying to take advantage of the desegregation plan: "It is our perspective that when you are not playing with your own money, it is much easier to propose things that slop over into the area of general upgrade of your school system. If I had the opportunity to dip into the state till and do something on a districtwide basis, I'd probably do it that way. There are kids who are getting the benefit of this money who are not victims of segregation. That's not the goal of this case. It's not to say that the things that they are proposing are not educationally good ideas, it's just that we have a concern—we have a big concern about who's paying for these things."

Given the low level of state support for education, it would seem that the parents of school-age children in metropolitan St. Louis might see the desegregation plan as a court-ordered solution to a lack of funds. As one suburban superintendent noted, the incentive payments from the transfer program benefit the district, which, in turn, "benefits all students." But there has been no rallying cry around the plan as a significant source of state school aid. In fact, to the contrary, when Missouri voters rejected Proposition B, a 1991 ballot initiative calling for a tax increase to provide an additional $385 million for public schools and colleges, journalists and observers noted that the state's two expensive school desegregation programs "played a key role" in the defeat of the proposition. According to one article, "some opponents of the tax measure suggested the revenue [from the measure] could be channeled to desegregation" (Mosley, 1992; West, 1991).

State Commissioner of Education Bartman commented that despite the negative attitudes toward the desegregation plan, the state money that it has brought to the school districts in metropolitan St. Louis has helped. He said that even though the program is expensive, he has developed a greater appreciation for its impact on the educational quality in those districts and the improved opportunity of the people who are involved with the program.

The annual $135 million cost of the St. Louis school desegregation plan in 1993, which was about 3 percent of the state's $4.6 billion budget that year, comes off the top of the budget or from general revenue and is not drawn out of any one department or program. Thus, the funding for desegregation in Missouri does not come out of the existing education (kindergarten through twelfth grade) budget, which is usually about one-fourth of the state budget, or about $1.3 billion. Bartman noted that if the St. Louis desegregation program were to end tomorrow, and the state were no longer required to pay, the state education budget would probably only receive about 30 percent of the money saved to spend on schools across the state. The other option would be for the already low-tax state to cut taxes, which would give the desegregation savings "back to the people." Thus, the end of desegregation in St. Louis would, at most, add about $45 million, or about 3 percent, to an annual state education budget of more than $1.3 billion for 541 school districts—or about $85,000 per district. According to a school finance supervisor in the state Department of Elementary and Secondary Education, "You really can't say how much of that money that is being spent [on desegregation], what percentage of that should be going to schools."

But in 1992, Ashcroft and Webster argued in state court that they should be allowed to pay the state's share of the Kansas City desegregation plan by cutting funding to schools elsewhere. The lower court ruled against the governor, but the Missouri Supreme Court overturned this decision and ruled in favor of Ashcroft's plan, which led to unexpected mid-school-year cuts in school budgets across the state. These cuts came from budgets that were already very tight and thus did not increase the political popularity of school desegregation programs in Missouri. The former governor's decision to use state education dollars to pay for the Kansas City desegregation plan came after his administration had fought an order by the U.S. district court judge to raise local Kansas City taxes to pay for the plan ("Desegregation money is education money," 1992). The Missouri Supreme Court's ruling in favor of the state blurred the boundaries between state education funding and school desegregation funding, opening the door for voters to blame school desegregation for the state of their grossly underfunded schools.

"The rest of the state is paying for it—Joplin is paying for St. Louis' desegregation. How long does Joplin have to tax itself to have its own good school system, and then through state taxes, pay for St. Louis and also suffer a loss of other state services," said Michael Fields, the assistant attorney general who has been involved in fighting the desegregation cases on behalf of the state. "It is sort of like the St. Louis and Kansas City school systems like to be on welfare. They would like for everyone else to pay for their education."

Bartman admits that some policy makers and voters use the desegregation plans in St. Louis and Kansas City as excuses to not spend money on public schools: "I think in fairness to all sides that there are many people—there are some—who are not in favor of appropriating money to public schools . . . who use desegregation money as a reason not to. . . . If you don't want to do something, any reason is good enough."

In 1991, as he was gearing up his Republican gubernatorial campaign, Attorney General Webster made a settlement offer to the St. Louis public schools that would have given the city schools $162 million over a five-year period, plus $10 million in a one-time payment to help the city integrate its neighborhoods (Mannies, 1992b). In exchange for these payments, the city school system would wean itself from the state desegregation funding that it has received since 1980 and regain local control of its schools. African-American students would no longer have the option to transfer to suburban schools, although those students already attending the suburban schools could remain there until they graduated. The St. Louis public schools rejected the state's offer, which turned out to be just one in a long line of attempts by the state to end the desegregation plan. This motion for a settlement was particularly significant, however, because it became a focal point of Webster's 1992 gubernatorial campaign.

As the governor's race heated up that summer and fall, the two final candidates—Webster and Carnahan—squared off over the St. Louis and Kansas City school desegregation plans, each trying to prove to Missouri voters that he would get rid of the programs faster. One newspaper reporter noted: "The desegregation issue is so volatile and so hot among voters that it could overshadow other issues in the governor's race, including Missouri's lagging economy, abortion and the controversy surrounding Webster's involvement in a worker's compensation program" (Mannies, 1992b). Webster argued that the state should continue its court fight against the desegregation plans in both St. Louis and Kansas City. He ran TV campaign advertisements claiming that he would continue to fight to end "excessive desegregation payments" in St. Louis and Kansas City. Carnahan, who ultimately won the race, said that by "taking the hard line" against the desegregation plans, the state had cost the Missouri taxpayers millions of extra dollars. He criticized Webster's TV ads, calling them hypocritical, given that Webster had already spent so much of the state's money on fruitless legal challenges. Carnahan advocated reaching a settlement among all parties "to cut our losses" (Mannies, 1992; Bell, 1992).

Since winning the election, Carnahan has taken on a more conciliatory tone, writing in an opinion editorial in the *St. Louis Post-Dispatch* about the need for the state government to provide the federal courts "reason to believe that the state is making a good-faith effort to address the desegregation issue" (Carnahan, 1995). Still, he continues to use an antidesegregation argument to win votes by writing about the cost of the school desegregation plan while saying nothing about the state's role in the creation of the color line that makes a court ordered policy necessary. He also says nothing about how this program has improved the life chances of thousands of African American students in the city of St. Louis.

But Missouri's current attorney general, Jay Nixon, also a Democrat, is on a mission to end school desegregation in Missouri and reap as many political rewards as he can in the process. Since practically his first day on the job in 1993, Nixon has made his crusade against school desegregation the focal point of his term as an elected state official. "I am convinced the State of Missouri has done as much as is feasible and practical to ensure an equal system," Nixon said (Eardley, 1993b).

Nixon's office has filed several motions in district court to limit the state's involvement in the St. Louis plan, while appealing a decision in the Kansas City case, *Missouri v. Jenkins*, to the U.S. Supreme Court. In June 1995 the Supreme Court ruled on the Kansas City case, finding that the state of Missouri was not required to continue paying for the desegregation plan until the achievement rates of African-American students increased (Greenhouse, 1995). Nixon has since stated that the same standard should be applied to the St. Louis case, because, as he has maintained since he took office, the state's responsibility to pay for the settlement agreement must now come to an end (Little, 1995).

Carnahan's special council, Michael Wolff, in responding to the Kansas City ruling, has reflected the more conciliatory tone of his boss, stating that the governor wants to negotiate an agreement among the parties on how to end the desegregation case and perhaps maintain a smaller-scale parental choice program. Wolff said that the important questions at this juncture in the case would be "What is it that makes urban schools work, what kind of schools do we want and how quickly can we get to that?" (cited in Little, 1995).

In the political bantering between Republican and Democratic elected officials in their similar efforts to cut off state funding for the St. Louis school desegregation program, the racial segregation of African Americans on the north side of the city is treated as a historical accident. The lack of political will within the city to support a mostly black public education system is not seen as a consequence of race. The stories of the thousands of transfer students who describe how many opportunities are open to them in suburban schools—opportunities that they would not have in their politically bankrupt neighborhood schools—appear to fall on the deaf ears of state politicians.

In rural central Missouri, the region once known as Boonslick, about fifty school districts have banded together to oppose the desegration plans in both St. Louis and Kansas City. They have lobbied in Jefferson City to make their standpoint known. And once again, as when southern planters first brought African-American slaves to Missouri, the Boonslick region is driving the racial politics of the state.

But that is not to say that the whites of St. Louis County are defending the desegregation plan or the millions of dollars in state education funding it brings to their schools. Given the lack of support for the program at the state level and all of the political rhetoric that has been used against the plan by anyone trying to woo voters in central Missouri, most suburban St. Louisians may just assume the plan will go away. In our interviews with more than fifty white parents and students in four suburban districts, we found a range of perspectives reflecting some of what the survey and focus group data from researchers at the University of Missouri–St. Louis demonstrate: Basically there is a subset of whites in the suburbs who actively resist the desegregation program, and often in quite blatant racial (some would say racist) terms. These parents and students are more likely to live in the south county school districts of Mehlville or Lindbergh. But perhaps more common are the "sympathetic" suburbanites who pity the "poor black students" from the city but who, when pressed, will say that they would rather see the desegregation program end and have "all that money" that is spent on "busing" go to the city schools.

And then there are a few visionary white suburbanites, mostly students who have grown up with the desegregation plan and who know from experience that, no matter what the politicians tell them, young people on both sides of the color line have benefited as a result of the court order and the inter-district desegregation plan it created.

THE RESISTANT SUBURBANITES

The 1988 University of Missouri–St. Louis survey of suburban white parents and students reported that even though the desegregation plan was not as "bad" as they expected it to be, most respondents would prefer that the program end. Dean Jones, who conducted the survey, noted that whites in the county view the desegregation program as something forced on them by the federal court, but most will admit that it has not been as awful as they thought it would be, and most feel as though they can "live with it." But when white St. Louis County residents are asked whether they would mind if the program were taken away from them, they say they are eager to get rid of it. For example, one survey question asked whether "the money going to the voluntary program would be better spent on improving education in the all-black city schools?" An overwhelming 70 percent of local white parents strongly agreed, and another 14 percent partially agreed. Only 12 percent of the white suburban parents disagreed with this statement; 4 percent had no opinion.

Furthermore, Jones said, if you ask the suburbanites whether they want more transfer students in their suburban schools, they say no: "They want this cross lifted from their shoulder. They have no sense that making blacks' [educational experiences] better is an investment for the entire community—absolutely no sense of that at all."

As one suburban superintendent explained to us, some of his constituents believe that the word "voluntary" in the title of the program—Voluntary Transfer Program—means that the school districts, not the black students, are the ones volunteering. "So they call up and say why don't you just quit volunteering? Just send them [transfer students] back."

Resistance to the desegregation plan is complicated by the fact that suburban residents don't always know how the program is funded or why. When asked whether the program has had an impact on their local school district's financial situation, 26 percent said that it has hurt their district. Only 11 percent said that it has helped. The proportion of respondents who thought that the program has had a negative financial impact is highest in the west county, central corridor districts, where 33 percent of white parents agreed with that statement (Jones, 1988).

A very involved parent in the Kirkwood District said that the people she associates with are fairly aware of how the desegregation program is funded, but that does not change their attitudes toward it:

Q: Do people here realize that . . . there's money coming in from the state for the desegregation plan?
A: Yes. Yes, but they also realize that the money that goes to the state is from them.

That it's still tax. . . . I mean the state doesn't have any money. It's all taxpayer money. . . . People do realize that, that . . . without it, it would be very hard right now because we're given an enormous amount of money, but it's still taxpayer money. I think people like to see that money put into a neighborhood school instead of being used this way. There's just so much controversy about it, about how the money could be spent better. With people in the city, I think they'd much rather have that money back for their students.

Taxi Cabs

There is perhaps no truer example of "symbolic politics" than the white suburbanites' anger over the taxi cabs that frequently shuttle transfer students home in the late afternoon or evening after they have participated in a school activity. Because the transfer program guarantees students from the city one free round trip each day between their home and their suburban school, those students who stay after school for activities and do not ride the bus home directly after school are often picked up by taxi cabs instead of buses. The reason for the taxi cabs is economic: If there are only a small number of transfer students trying to get home from a given suburban school, it is cheaper for them to be picked up and delivered by a cab rather than a bus. This more economic approach to transporting students should please white county residents, who seem to worry incessantly about the cost of the desegregation program. But white parents in the county, especially those who have to come to school to pick up their son or daughter after an athletic event or other school activity, resent the fact that the black transfer students are being "chauffeured" home in taxi cabs. Thus, the taxi cabs have become a symbol for the desegregation program and the taxpayer money that it wastes. Many of the parents we spoke to mentioned the taxi cabs as factors that make them most upset about the desegregation plan.

A district-level adminstrator in the Parkway School District noted that parents and community members make few public objections to the desegregation plan, except when it comes to the taxi cabs. "It grates on the nerves of some parents when they go up at 10:00 at night to Parkway West after a basketball game [to pick up their child], to have a taxi cab waiting there for a student from the city. That makes them mad. . . . For some reason, a yellow bus does not irritate people as much as a yellow taxi cab does, even though it costs more than the cab. I would advise other school districts to stay away from the symbol of a taxi cab if they are able to—even if it is a yellow bus with two kids in it."

A teacher at Mehlville High School said that community reaction to the taxi cabs has caused the administration at his school to hold down the number of black students they assign to a "Saturday school" in-house suspension program because the students would ride taxi cabs to participate in the program. "I know the principal won't admit this, but it is true," he said.

In the wealthy central eounty districts, such as Clayton and Parkway, parents appear to be less likely to complain about having inner-city students in their neighborhood schools. But they do not hesitate to complain about the mode of transportation that brings those student to their schools. In the south county school districts of Mehlville and Lindbergh, parents and community members are likely to go beyond the use of symbols, such as taxi cabs, to complain about the desegregation program. They use much more straightforward language about race and "those black students."

White Racial Resistance

As one teacher in a south county high school noted, in contrast with the Parkway administrator's comment, the sight of the desegregation buses lining up in front of the school "makes people ill." He said that he and the taxpayers in the community do not want their tax dollars spent to bring black students from the city to their school. "The very fact that we had to go out to buy hundreds of buses and diesel fuel makes me crazy," he said.

The best pieces of data on the more blatant racial politics of the desegregation plan come from the south county newspapers. Here, many angry white residents do not hesitate to voice their opinions of the desegregation program and the transfer students. Someone who wrote a letter to the editor of the *Oakville Call* shortly after the uprising in Los Angeles in the spring of 1992 noted: "Yes, you can take the savages out of the jungle, but you can't take the jungle out of the savages. Just look at Los Angeles, Mehlville High School, Bernard School [another school in the Mehlville District] and others. The officials in charge always try to cover up the real facts. It's time to clean up this mess."

Another local paper, the *South County News Times*, ran a lengthy story in 1992 on the efforts of the National Association for Neighborhood Schools of Missouri, a group attempting to end the school desegregation program in the state. The group had proposed a federal constitutional amendment to limit the taxing power of judges, specifically those who call for tax increases to pay for school desegregation plans (Corrigan, 1992).

Some county parents dislike the desegregation program for less economic reasons—mainly because it keeps their children off the football field or basketball court. Several suburban educators and coaches mentioned this form of resistance. As one district administrator told us, the loudest resentment he hears regarding the desegregation program is from parents whose children would be playing a sport if it weren't for students from the city who have made the teams. "And I think people are sensitive to those issues. Coaches are going to find the players who are going to be the most help to the team . . . so there has been this quiet resistance." According to a science teacher at Parkway South, "If you were a white kid and you were six foot tall and a black boy was six foot four and playing basketball, you would resent it because you would want to be on the school athletic team, and the black students dominate many of the sports that the whites could be a part of."

It is interesting, in fact, how a white suburbanite's conception of what is fair or deserved shifts when it comes to black students "earning" a spot on an athletic team. Suddenly the hard work and dedication of these black athletes is diminished in the eyes of many who want their own often less talented children or students to have the opportunity to play on a school team.

But then perceptions of what is fair seem to shift a lot in suburban St. Louis. For instance, whereas some transfer students reported that the suburban teachers treat white students better than black students, some of the white suburban students see things the other way around. According to Jones' (1988) survey data, 64 percent of white suburban students agree with the statement that "teachers in their schools discipline the transfer students about the same as the local kids when they break school rules." But 24 percent say that the teachers are less strict with the transfer students, and only 10 percent say that the teachers are more strict with the black students from the city.

According to one angry white student we interviewed, the black students at his suburban high school get away with more because "they have a price on their heads," he said, referring to the state incentive payment his district receives. "It's okay for a black student to do something, but not a white student." One of the white eleventh-graders participating in UMSL's Public Policy Research Centers' focus group study (1993b) said, "If you do something bad and if you're colored, then they'll just say, 'Stop doing that.' But if you're white, they'll just totally go off on you. It's like, it's almost like they give the blacks a little more respect." This particular student attends Lindbergh High School, the school that Penny, a return student, would have attended had she not seen the white students outside the high school protesting the transfer program.

Another white student from a different suburban high school said that during his freshman year he got into a fight with a transfer student. He said that he walked away from the fight without throwing any punches yet still was suspended for three days. "I didn't do nothing to the kid. But they're afraid of him—everybody is—and they suspended me" (p. 16).

The resentment toward black students and the changes that the transfer program has stimulated in the suburban schools extends to curricular changes and the struggle over whose knowledge is valued in suburbia. The white Lindbergh student, for instance, disagrees with the high school's effort to incorporate more black history into the curriculum: "The principal comes over the intercom like once or twice a week, and like since it's black history month, we get a whole trivia about it. I was like, I don't want to sit and listen to it. I really don't. And that's not right to have to sit and listen to it, but you have to. And some teachers they like go on a twenty-minute trip about it. . . . It's like they're trying to regulate, they're so afraid of actually being accused of being racists that they take every step that's possible. So much so it's obvious that they're afraid of being called racists. Because when that happens then you have like all sorts of groups from the city like just [ragging] on you, you know."

In fact, Lindbergh High School has been the site of a great deal of racial conflict since the desegregation plan began. In the focus group study by the Public Policy Research Centers, the two Lindbergh High School students reported a great deal of racial tension. One noted that when a black speaker came to the school to talk about race issues, white students began walking out of the assembly. "He said Jesus was black," reported one of the students. The other Lindbergh student said that these symbolic issues, such as what race Santa Claus will be at Christmas, are extremely charged at their school. "Because we have a white Santa Claus, they should have a black one? It's like, that's not fair. And it's just, it doesn't work. It does not work at Lindbergh."

These two students reported that they know a "lot" of students at Lindbergh who are Ku Klux Klan members. "We have [Klan] fliers posted every month or so. I'm friends with probably ten guys that are in the KKK."

In another south county school district, an elementary school principal told us that when the desegregation program began, a group of white teenagers would stand on the corner near the 7–11 store and throw rocks at the buses carrying African-American students from the city to the schools in their community. She added, however, that over time, the adults and children in the community have become more accepting of the program and the black students.

Extreme views are not limited to students in south county districts. At Parkway West High School in a west county district, students in Lloyd Moore's all-white pre-calculus class spoke openly about their attitudes toward the school desegregation plan. One student noted that he thinks the program is "absolutely ridiculous," that the black transfer students just "come out here for the free food."

Another student, a thin, pale, and very freckled young man, noted that the desegregation plan had made him and his brother more racist. Most of these high-achieving white suburban students expressed a strong sense of entitlement in that dialogue session—a dialogue Moore did not engage in with his lower-track, racially mixed classes. They believed that their parents worked hard to afford a middle- or upper-middle-class standard of living and that the black students from the city just wanted a free ride—to benefit from the riches they had not earned. When asked, they said they really knew very little about the history of the St. Louis inter-district desegregation case or exactly why their school district participated, but most of the students in that classroom felt that the district had made a mistake. When asked whether they ever talked with the transfer students about why they travel so far to a county school each day, all but one student either said no, shook their heads, or looked down at the floor.

SYMPATHIZERS

In contrast with the more resistant county residents, there are many white parents and students who tentatively support the "concept" of desegregation and say that they appreciate the fact that their schools are more racially diverse and thus more accurately reflect the "real world" than a single-race school would. The more accepting or sympathetic white parents frequently comment on the benefit of exposing their children to people of different cultures: "The voluntary transfer plan was like giving us an opportunity to give our kids even more than we're giving them already because it exposed them to people that were different than they were, and I really want them to see that, I really want them to know that everybody isn't exactly like them," said one mother of two students in the wealthy Clayton School District.

These parents are also frequently "sympathetic" to the cause of rescuing black students from the despair of the city school system, and they see their school districts playing a crucial role in saving these students from the morass that is the St. Louis public schools. In a sometimes condescending way, these parents see the transfer plan as a form of charity rather than a remedy for past injustices. This attitude provides a more liberal middle ground on which white parents and taxpayers can feel better about the desegregation program without conceding white suburbia's role in creating the separate and unequal system that they live in. Such a view absolves suburbanites of any implication that they and the policies they endorse have contributed to the poverty from which the transfer students must be saved. Because most of these sympathetic parents and their children have not considered these larger, historical issues, they often conclude that the desegregation plan is a Band-Aid approach and that the state really should spend the "busing" money to fix up the city schools.

As one Clayton parent put it, "What I hear from most of our friends and neighbors both in the Clayton District and around from the public and the private sector is that if we took all that money and put it into the city schools, we could educate all of them. And what we are doing now is educating a very small percentage."

One mother of a senior at Kirkwood High School said that she believed in desegregation, "but I don't think it can be forced." This is an interesting statement, given that the St. Louis desegregation plan is a voluntary transfer program from the perspective of the black students and that only the suburban school districts are, in essence, "forced" to participate via the settlement agreement. This mother went on to somewhat contradict herself by explaining that white students do not necessarily have to go to school with African-American students in order to learn to like them. She said that although she grew up in a small town with no blacks, she does not feel that she is racially prejudiced. "I have nieces and nephews who grew up in Seattle and went to private schools, and didn't really go to school with [blacks]. And my one nephew does this program called City Year in Boston—it's like a volunteer service project kind of thing—and a lot of kids in there are black, and he's just . . . I mean, he loves them. . . . But he never really grew up around any."

The way that white suburbanites separate themselves from the reality of urban America and fail to relate their prosperity to the suffering of other, "less fortunate" people allows this mother to talk about African Americans as though they are a novelty, exotic people you meet on an adventuresome year doing charity work in the inner city. This view of African Americans as "the other" allows white suburbanites to distance themselves from the poverty and despair only twenty or thirty miles from their single-family homes and suburban schools. Because her daughter does not need to go to school with blacks to learn to like "them," this particular mother would prefer that the black students from the city go to school in their own neighborhoods.

This mother, with her comfortable suburban lifestyle and minivan, is representative of many white parents we spoke with. They are generally nice and likable people who mean well and want what is best for their children. They feel sorry for African-American students who come from low-income families and who have much less than their children do. But most would strongly prefer for these poor black students to have nice neighborhood schools in their own communities and not have to travel all the way to suburbia to get a quality education. They fail to acknowledge, of course, that nearly all the people with the money and political power to force changes in the St. Louis public schools have left the city or that the schools themselves, like the neighborhoods they are in, are so often evaluated by the race and wealth of the students who attend them. Thus, as long as low-income African-American students remain segregated and isolated in "urban" schools, the broader society will continue to perceive these schools to be "less than" suburban schools attended by white and wealthy students. And, as the past fifteen years in Missouri have proved, whites will continually resist spending more public resources for students left behind in urban schools. Once these societal perceptions are in place, the self-fulfilling prophecy of bad schools begins.

But the more sympathetic view of the desegregation plan appears to be the prevalent one among white parents in the suburbs, and there are signs that many of their children feel the same way. Like their parents, many of the white suburban students we spoke with appreciate the racial and cultural diversity in their schools. The vast majority—77 percent—of white suburban students surveyed by Jones (1988) either strongly or partially agree with the following statement: "I've really learned a lot about getting along with blacks because of going to school with kids from the city." Only 22 percent of the white students surveyed disagreed with this statement. When asked how much the experience of going to school with transfer students changed their attitudes toward blacks, 18 percent of white suburban students said their attitudes have changed a lot; 43 percent said they changed somewhat; and 38 percent reported no change. Of those reporting a lot or some change, 17 percent said that they liked African Americans more than they did before the program began, and 15 percent said that they liked African Americans less.

Like their parents, white suburban students are inclined to say that diversity in their school is good—it prepares them for life after high school—but they feel sorry for black student who must endure long bus rides, and thus they too say that fixing up the city schools is the solution. According to one white high school student, his parents and their friends "wish that they would fix up the city schools because they feel sorry for them—city students. And of course their feelings have kind of rubbed off on me, so that's where I get my ideas."

Another "real world" perspective on the desegregation plan was offered by a senior in one of the Parkway high schools, who noted that attending a desegregated school has helped him realize that he must compete with people of other races: "It hit me that black kids can be smart, and you better watch out because they might be better than you, and can compete with you and might graduate with a higher rank than you. And I think that's neat because that is how the real world will be."

When pressed on the issue, nearly all the county whites we spoke to say that the black students are better off in the suburban schools right now. But ideally, most of them believe that the city schools should be brought up to the level of the county schools so that black students could go to excellent neighborhood schools.

The prevalent tracking system within the suburban schools also helps to minimize white parents' and students' rejection of the desegregation program. Many of the parents we interviewed said that their children's education has not been affected by the desegregation program because they are in honors classes and the transfer students, as a rule, are not. One father in Clayton noted that his two sons are enrolled in the honors and advanced programs, in which the norm has not been brought down. "[The transfer program] has not really affected them."

A counselor at one of the west county high schools, when asked about community attitudes toward the desegregation plan, noted that there is a highly "elitist" contingent in her district "that believes in integration as long as it doesn't touch them." The tracking system in some of the suburban schools assures that the more elite white students, such as those in Moore's pre-calculus class, are hardly touched by the desegregation plan. They can have their diversity and their segregation, too.

Many of the white students we spoke to said that they did not generally have any transfer students in their classes. Even the white students who appreciate the cultural diversity that the transfer students bring to their schools do not think that the rigid tracking system should be altered to assure more racial integration within classrooms. One student noted the worst thing his suburban high school could do would be to say that a certain percentage of the city students have to be in honors classes. "Because I think it is a privilege that you have to earn to get into, it can't be done on figures, on numbers."

TRUST AND TENSION

As we mentioned in Chapter 7, some subsets of the transfer students act in ways that make it difficult for white students or teachers to like them. Since the transfer program began, the number of thefts and fights has increased in the suburban schools. This is not to say that white suburban students do not steal things or fight with each other, just that virtually all of the suburban schools have reported increases in these offenses since the program began. And then there are the transfer students who arrive in the county schools so angry and resentful over the relative wealth of the county students that they act out in very disruptive ways—for example, bumping into white students in the hallways and talking back to teachers—in an effort to elicit fear in suburban students and educators. Frightening whites may be the only real source of power these transfer students have in an environment far removed from the familiarity of their own neighborhoods. As one junior high school principal in the Parkway District explained, "The black kids tend to travel with two or three other black kids. They will walk down the middle of the hall so that everyone has to get out of their way. It's a form of intimidation."

But for white suburban students, many of who are empowered by a sense of optimism about their lives after high school and the privileges they will inherit from their parents, this behavior on the part of some of transfer students is frightening, not to mention annoying. The Jones survey (1988) found that when asked what they disliked about the transfer program, the suburban students were most likely—29 percent—to cite the disruptive behavior of the transfer students.

Rhonda, a student at Parkway West, said she had difficulty keeping the desegregation program in perspective because sometimes she gets very angry at some of the transfer students, like "the girls in the locker room who walk by you and just kind of shove you out of the way." Or the transfer students who scream at teachers and show them no respect. But on the other hand she is tired of hearing white students make insensitive comments about Black History Month and of teachers who seem prejudiced against black students and don't even realize the attitude they are projecting." When asked whether she and other white students in her school believe that Parkway West is the transfer students' school, too, she said, "There are times when I would just like to say take most of them and send them back. Let them get their education down there; let us get ours out here. And you know, I think realistically, and I truly believe that I have my moments like when my polo jacket was stolen and you say 'Go away.' But most of the time I would say this is as much their school as it is ours. But I don't think they feel that and sometimes we, the west county students, don't feel that either."

Furthermore, the white suburban students we interviewed were in elementary school or even preschool when the transfer program started. So they have no real memory of their schools before the desegregation program began. They are aware, however, of much less racial tension in their elementary schools as compared to what they find in their junior and senior high schools. Most of the students we interviewed noted that black and white students got along just fine until they reached seventh or eighth grade, and then they became more cliquish with people of their own race.

Some attribute this greater separation at the high school level to the tendency of students to form intimate relationships with students of their own race. Interracial dating in suburban St. Louis, based on what students and parents have told us, is far more acceptable today than it was ten or fifteen years ago. But this does not mean that students find dating someone of another race easy or well accepted by their peers. A suburban mother told us of her daughter's experience dating a black transfer student: "Jenny used to date a black boy freshman year, and then she . . . had a real positive attitude, you know, then about blacks. . . . But she really saw—and I think it was just an individual kind of taste, it had nothing to do with desegregation—but once . . . you're in high school there's like this separation, and I don't know why. But his black friends really gave him a lot of problems about him going with a white girl, and he broke it off. And she said he used to hang out with a lot of white guys, and he doesn't do that anymore."

In all of the suburban high schools we visited, lunchrooms are, for the most part, divided along racial lines. There are almost always a few mixed-race tables, but the trend is separate black and white areas within one room. A white tenth-grader at Kirkwood High School named Jeremy noted that black and white students do not, in general, hate each other at his school, but self-segregation occurs. "If you go in the lunchroom at lunch time, blacks are on this side and whites are on this side, and there's a little bit of mixing, but not much. So, I don't know if people are just afraid. . . . They're not their best friends, and that's fine because maybe a lot of them live in the city and stuff so you don't hang out with them 'cause they don't live by you and stuff. But there's not really that much tension, I don't feel. . . . Sometimes you'll feel it."

Yet as in all high schools across America, there are delineations other than race among students, so that in many suburban St. Louis schools white students have divided themselves into cliques, each with its own degree of status vis-à-vis the others. There are, as we noted in other chapters, several variations on the standard themes of jocks, preps, nerds, and "burnouts" or "lounge lizards" who spend much of their time in the smoking lounge doing drugs or smoking cigarettes. While the boundaries between the groups may be more fluid in some schools than in others, teenagers generally form such cliques, each with its own set of unspoken rules and admissions criteria (Eckert, 1989; Peshkin, 1991; Schofield, 1989). Similarly, the African-American students who attend the suburban schools create different cliques, some of which overlap more naturally with the white students' cliques than others. But while the transfer students see themselves as clustered into distinct social groups within the suburban schools, white students are more likely to say that all of the "deseg kids" hang out together.

In the focus group study conducted by UMSL's Public Policy Research Centers (1993b), eleventh-grade white students described the various cliques in their suburban high schools. According to one student, the lounge lizards and the "deseg kids" are the two groups in the school that don't mix in with other students very much. "Those groups stay pretty much to themselves, and then between all the other groups you've got a lot of sifting."

It seems as though, with or without a transfer program, these suburban schools are not easy places in which to get along with the different groups of people, even for a white student. For instance, other students in this focus group spoke of intense social competitiveness among the white students, particularly in the wealthier school districts, where students judge each other based on clothing or cars. According to one student, "There's like all the *[Beverly Hills] 90210* people, you know, who dress up like they wish they were on the show. And they separate themselves, people whose parents buy them really cool cars."

Another student noted the social competitiveness at her high school by saying that "you can't be different. If you're different nobody likes you. . . . Like, if you have your hair a different way, they don't like you. They'll kick you out of your group."

These descriptions of social competitiveness in suburban schools raise questions about how welcoming these schools can be not only to the transfer students but also to the "not cool" white students. Furthermore, many of the white female students we spoke to noted that it is often easier for the black and white boys to get along together because many of them participate on the same athletic teams. "The people who have a harder time are the girls," said an eleventh-grade girl at one of the Parkway high schools. The cultural clash around activities such as cheerleading and pompons works to keep many African-American girls out of these high-status programs. Stylistic differences in dance and cheering are more pronounced, the students say, than differences in how boys play football or basketball. This sets up a greater sense of competition and separateness between the white girls and the black girls.

THE MORE VISIONARY FUTURE

But some of the white suburban students (and perhaps some of their parents) see things from a different standpoint. These students have a rich understanding of the role of race in American society and how African-American students have been placed at a disadvantage. These students, like their more resistant counterparts, dislike when a transfer student acts out or pushes a white student in the hallways or brings a weapon to school or steals something, but they seem to have a deeper wisdom about how the many years of discrimination and isolation can create a sense of frustration in black people that can be triggered by even a minor incident in a suburban school—an incident that tells the transfer students that they are not welcome.

Back in Moore's all-white pre-calculus class, the only student who said that he had actually talked to transfer students about why they transfer to county schools was a big, athletic-looking young man who responded to the nickname Moose. He was quiet during much of the class discussion of the transfer plan as the more vocal students spoke very negatively of the program and of the transfer students in general. He looked out the window and down at his books as the classroom dialogue continued. When Moore called on him to state his opinion of the plan, he smiled slowly and thoughtfully, paused as the others waited, and said, "I kind of think the attitude here is self-centered, and I think you are stereotyping all black students." In his response to the question about talking with transfer students, Moose said that he runs track with a lot of transfer students, and he asks them whether they are sick of "coming all the way out here—but most of them are pretty positive." Somehow, Moose's gentler, more understanding comments slightly changed the tone of the rest of the class discussion, which was almost over at this point. Even those who were negative about the plan found something nice to say about at least one transfer student. And after class, several of the students who had remained silent told us that they like the desegregation plan.

A few of the eleventh-grade white students participating in the focus group study noted that white administrators or security guards in their suburban schools will follow or hassle a group of black students while they let similar sized groups of white students do whatever they like. One of these students described an incident in which some black teenagers came through the front door of his school and an administrator "got on them. He's like, you know, get someone down there to check them out. You know, like they're probably going to start causing trouble. And it's like, you know, you think that at least the administrators would have the decency to trust. . . . They should check everyone, not just, you know, the black kids" (p. 29).

These students argue that there is a tendency for whites in the suburban schools to stereotype black students as troublemakers. "There are a couple of troublemakers [in the desegregation program]. . . . People start stereotyping the deseg students and then it gets bad. Then the racism gets involved, just makes it incredibly big. Like Channel 5 [TV news crew] starts showing up," said a Parkway West student. The local media according to this white student, tend to blow out of proportion anything negative about the desegregation program. He said that one time the television crew showed up at Parkway West and reported that the racial problems at the school could lead to a race riot. He said the students at the school were more surprised than anyone to hear this news. "We're like, 'What the heck are they talking about?'"

In fact, several other suburban students and educators spoke of media bias in coverage of the desegregation plan. The superintendent of the Lindbergh School District noted that when the white students at the high school protested the desegregation plan after some transfer students had gotten into trouble, the media sensationalized the event and "made a much bigger deal about it." He added that whenever something happens involving a transfer student in the district, the south county papers will bring up incidents that had occurred several years ago—"events that most people had forgotten about."

The superintendent of Ritenour recalled the first day of school in 1983, when the inter-district transfer plan formally began. Even though his district had been participating in the pilot version of the program for two years, a flock of reporters showed up with their TV cameras. "The reporters were looking around and going 'Where's the story, where's the riot?'"

There are other signs that some members of the younger generation of white suburbanites may be eschewing some of the more negative attitudes portrayed in the media and held by people of their parents' generation and embracing a deeper understanding of racial difference and the history that has created it. The Jones (1988) survey also reported this inter-generational distinction. Slightly more than 50 percent of the suburban students said that it was a good idea to mix black city students with white county students, and another 27 percent said that they partially agreed with this statement. Only 18 percent of the students disagreed with this statement. The parents, on the other hand, were less likely to agree that it was a good idea, with only 24 percent strongly agreeing with the statement and 30 percent partially agreeing. A much larger percentage of suburban parents—41 percent—disagreed with the statement that bringing together the city and county students was a good idea.

This suggests that the in-school experience of living with the transfer plan is not as bad as people outside the schools perceive it to be. In addition, virtually every high school in all four of the districts we studied in depth has a biracial student committee that deals with the issues of race and integration. These committees, which are usually appointed by the principals, are often the forums for some of the most thoughtful dialogue on racial issues taking place in suburban St. Louis. Some of these committees, like the one called Connect at Parkway West, go on retreats together or mobilize schoolwide activities and events.

Melany, a white student from Mehlville High School, is a member of the student biracial committee, and she said that participating in that program has helped her to better understand where the transfer students are coming from. "Usually we meet and discuss things about different races." She said the committee was planning a trip to a city school. Melany noted that this trip would be a really different experience for the white county kids. "And that could be interesting, you know, just to get the feeling of how it is to walk in and you be the minority."

Melany also noted that Mehlville had a black homecoming king that particular year. "I'm aware of people who voted for him because he was black—because they wanted to see him win. It was important to a lot of people. . . . I think they realized that, wow, this is some sort of progress here."

In the focus group session, one student said she became frustrated with the negative comments the students from Lindbergh were making about the desegregation plan. One of these more negative students had said that if life in the city is so horrible and violent, why are "they" letting the black students bring it "out here to us." The young woman replied:

> They're doing it because everyone deserves an equal opportunity to learn, and the people in the city aren't given a chance—the opportunities that you have every day, you know. And I agree that there's a lot of people at my school that, I mean, if they just left and never came back, then I could be so much happier. . . . I mean, they make it really rough. But we can't just cancel the whole program, because there really are people that want to learn, and they really should be given an opportunity of a good education. I know if, you know, I lived in the city, and I went through that every day, I would be really resentful of the county students who I went to school with. I think that would be really hard. But you know, I have a friend, I have a lot of friends in the deseg program, and I mean, like she tells me horror stories about the bus ride and her neighborhood. I mean, it's like another world. Like, I couldn't even ever imagine it. And I think it's really, I think it's a good program for the people who work well with it. . . . I think everyone deserves school, opportunity for a good education.

That white students in suburban St. Louis are working through these complex questions and trying to weigh the experiences they have had with the transfer program and their African-American classmates is perhaps one of the greatest signs of hope to come out of our study of the desegregation plan. Not all of the white students are in favor of this desegregation plan and the inner-city issues and problems it has brought to their schools. But many have struggled, sometimes with the help of supportive educators, to make sense of the larger issues of race and inequality in the United States and in metropolitan St. Louis. And in the process they may be teaching their parents and other adults a thing or two.

Over the past several years, as Missouri politicians plot their legal strategy for ending the inter-district transfer plan and generate proposals to persuade elected officials in the city to go along with them, various groups of white students in St. Louis County have mobilized to protest these political maneuvers and the consequences for their suburban schools. For instance, high school students in the Parkway School District have circulated petitions in support of the desegregation program. One of the student leaders of this effort argued that to end the desegregation program "just wouldn't be right." He said that the transfer plan has allowed students to "grow up learning that blacks and white are equal" (Hick, 1992a). Similarly, the student council president of Marquette High School in the Rockwood School District wrote in a letter to the editor of the *Post-Dispatch* that "to this 17-year-old white male, desegregation is a success. . . . I may just be an idealistic and optimistic youth, but in my mind there is progress in solving today's prejudicial problems. One of the reasons is this program" (Blake, 1996).

One suburban mother we interviewed told us that her daughter, Jennifer, had some very bad experiences with the transfer program and the black students during her four years of high school. Much to the mother's surprise, her daughter wrote an editorial for the high school newspaper when she learned that the state of Missouri was trying to persuade the district court judge to end the desegregation program. "And she was saying, 'Hey, give us a chance, you know, we're the ones living it, and we're not ready to give up' . . . that just made me cry." Jennifer wrote, "The adults' opinion [is] that the project is extremely expensive and difficult so they can quit and not feel too bad because they at least tried. But what about the students of all races? We accepted this experiment and learned to try to make it succeed; we live with it every day and we don't want it to end."

Concluding Remarks

Of all the things that I have done since I've been on the court, I think that this [the St. Louis desegregation plan] is the best thing I have done—and God knows, it isn't perfect.

—Judge Gerald W. Heaney, Eighth Circuit Court of Appeals

Since 1991, the U.S. Supreme Court appears to have been moving in favor of ending federal school desegregation court orders in districts that prove they have removed the vestiges of segregation "to the extent practicable." What that means exactly is measured by judges who examine the history of student and teacher assignment practices, among other things, and determine whether a school district is "unitary," or no longer operating a dual system—one for white students and one for all others. If a judge finds the district to be unitary, the court order is removed and "local control" is restored. The school board of that district can, at that point, reassign all students to segregated and racially distinct "neighborhood" schools.

In this way, court-ordered school desegregation policy is a legal anomaly: once the constitutional violator—in this case, the school district—has proved that it has suspended the practice of creating racially identifiable schools for several years, it is then free to re-create racially segregated schools. As Michael Fields, the lawyer with the Missouri attorney general's office, noted, "When you have reached a point where [the vestiges] have been eliminated and that elimination has been sustained for a period of time—then it is up to the school district to either maintain that or let it slip away." But in the relatively few years that school districts have been under court orders, the problems of housing segregation and employment discrimination have not been resolved, so when the school desegregation orders end, everything is able to return to "normal"—that is, the state of affairs before the court orders were issued. Unfortunately, "normal" in this society is a social system of racial inequality. But normalcy is what most of the people we spoke with in St. Louis want to return to.

Time and time again educators, policy makers, parents, students, and "people on the streets" of metropolitan St. Louis told us that the millions of dollars the state pays to bring nearly 13,000 African-American students to suburban schools would be better spent "fixing up" the city schools. We have heard this argument from whites and blacks alike, though more often from whites in the suburbs. They say they feel sorry for black children who have to get up at 5:00 in the morning to take an hour-long bus ride to the suburbs. It is a shame, they say, that these students can't attend their neighborhood schools. What an odd state of affairs when the white suburbanites bemoan the inconvenience of the transfer plan more loudly than the students who make that trek to the county five days a week.

Furthermore, after examining the St. Louis inter-district desegregation plan—the history of the color line that made it necessary and the specifics of the implementation of the court order—we respectfully disagree with those who would just as soon see the plan go away. We disagree mainly because we do not believe that separate can ever be equal in American society. And we do not believe that in the negotiations to end the desegregation plan that the St. Louis public schools will ever get a long-term commitment from the governor and the attorney general to provide this beleaguered urban district ongoing additional state funding. The removal of the court order would no doubt be the beginning of the end of extra state resources to the city schools and thus the end to some of the most successful aspects of this rather unsuccessful school system, most notably its magnet schools. At most, the St. Louis school board will be bought off by the state with a set amount of money in return for agreeing to end the interdistrict program.

State and local politicians, as we mentioned, are on a mission to end the case for political and economic reasons. "We are in the case to get to unitary status as quickly as possible," said Fields. Thus, the idea that any state money not spent on desegregation would be spent on schools, particularly urban schools, seems a little farfetched.

And once the court order is revoked, we do not believe that many people living in the suburbs would really care whether the money saved from the inter-district plan ever got invested in the neighborhood schools in the city. In fact, many of these suburbanites would probably end up—after the memory of the desegregation plan had faded—protesting the extra spending on urban schools at the taxpayers' expense, just as they do now in the Boonslick region.

Furthermore, we are not convinced that the St. Louis public schools will ever offer African-American students the same educational opportunities that students receive in the suburbs. If we listen to Will and Gerald and other transfer students, we learn why a high school diploma from an urban school means so little in this society. Will knows why he got up before dawn each day and stood on a desolate corner waiting for a school bus to take him to the suburbs. It wasn't so that he could waste the taxpayers' hard-earned money, and it wasn't because he found so many of the teachers at the suburban schools to be friendly and welcoming. The reason Will and the other 30,000 black students who have participated in the inter-district program since it began get up so early and travel so far is that they know how our society perceives the schools in their neighborhoods. They know what the name, status, and reputation of the suburban schools mean to colleges and employers. They know that the suburbs offer hope and possibility—even if they have to put up with white educators and students who don't want them there—and they know that so few students in the city schools have any place to go.

What is "wrong" with the city schools is much larger than anything the St. Louis Board of Education or state funding can fix, though both are important factors. But the problems of the city school system are part and parcel of what caused whites to flee to the suburbs in droves after World War II. A major part of what is "wrong" with the St. Louis public schools is that it is an urban school system serving mostly poor and nonwhite children. This reduces its status significantly in the eyes of middle-class parents and the general society. We are not saying this is right, but we are saying that no matter how wonderful a principal or group of teachers are placed at the Patrick Henry Elementary School in downtown St. Louis, a school of black and white students who come mostly from very poor families is never going to have the status of a predominantly white and wealthy elementary school in the suburbs. With the concentration of poor students in the school, it will always be a school of last resort.

During the 1990–91 academic year, more African-American students in the city of St. Louis dropped out of high school (1,421) than graduated (996)

(Missouri Department of Education, 1994). Most of the high schools in the St. Louis public school system have neither a competitive college prep program *nor* a vocational education program. It is not at all clear to many of these students what kind of future their schools are preparing them for; so many we talked to and met on our visits to these schools seemed to be adrift and very uncertain about their futures. In the suburbs, more students have direction and the resources and connections to act on their choices. Transfer students in these schools, many of which send more than 75 percent of their graduates on to four-year colleges, attend school with white students who have been told by their parents since they were very young that they will go to college. To be in a school in which college is a reasonable expectation for the vast majority of students is very different from attending a school in which the majority of students are isolated from higher education institutions and people who have been to them.

The achievement and attitudinal data comparing the transfer students with black students in the magnet, integrated, and all-black schools in the city of St. Louis strongly suggests the effects that this different kind of academic environment has on African-American students. We believe that the transfer students are showing greater gains between eighth and tenth grades because they are in schools in which they feel more secure about their futures and their options for life after high school (Lissetz, 1993, 1994). They are connected to a network of college counselors and vocational training programs. Sixty-five percent of all transfer students who graduated from suburban high schools in spring 1993 went on to either two- or four-year colleges (Voluntary Interdistrict Coordinating Council, 1993).

Another reason we do not believe that the desegregation plan should end soon or that state desegregation dollars would be better spent exclusively in the city schools is that we are just beginning to see that the long-term effects of school desegregation are paying off in a number of ways for African Americans. Thus, despite the emphasis on the short-term effects of school desegregation—improvement in test scores after a few years, and so forth—the more recent literature on the long-term effects suggests that desegregated educational experiences have had more subtle, sociological effects on the social mobility and life chances of African Americans in particular. "Though there may be overwhelming evidence that schools have not equalized life chances[,] . . . such equalization remains a criterion worth using in asking the value of school desegregation. The research question that arises directly from this criterion is whether the life chances of blacks who attend desegregated schools are significantly improved over those of comparable blacks who do not. Because there is ample evidence that test scores and grades in school do not explain much of the variance in later income or status . . . these latter results must be studied directly" (Granovetter, 1986, p. 103).

Lawyers and civil rights advocates who presented constitutional and moral arguments for school desegregation believed that guaranteeing African Americans access to predominantly white institutions would enhance their opportunities for social mobility and thus improve their life chances. The NAACP desegregation cases preceding the landmark *Brown* ruling were predicated on the theory that degrees from prestigious, predominantly white universities were the keys to high-status employment, social networks, and social institutions. Without access to these universities and the status of the degrees they conferred, African-Americans, no matter what their level of educational achievement or attainment, would remain a separate and unequal segment of our society (see Kluger, 1975). This is a structural argument aimed at addressing barriers to social mobility.

As we mentioned in Chapter 2, arguments for school desegregation since the early 1950s have become more disparate as psychologists and educators maintained that providing black children with access to white educational institutions from which their parents had been excluded could lead to several short-term outcomes: greater self-esteem, academic achievement, and educational attainment for black students; and improved race relations among all students. After the Coleman report of 1966, an additional social-psychological rationale was added to the cause of desegregation: placing low-income black students in schools and classrooms with middle-class white students would enhance their educational achievement by exposing them to better-prepared and more motivated peers.

In part because of this shifting focus and in part because policy makers require instant feedback on program effects, most school desegregation research conducted during the late 1960s and early 1970s focused on the short-term effects—achievement test scores, intergroup relations, self-esteem of black students, and levels of white flight (Braddock and McPartland, 1982; Levin, 1975). Meanwhile, policy makers and researchers lost sight of many of the original theoretical underpinnings embedded in the long-term goals of school desegregation policy. As Prager, Longshore, and Seeman (1986) note, "Desegregation research has suffered because it has come to stand as a kind of scholarship guided largely by public concerns and public issues, not by theoretically generated empirical questions" (p. 4).

In an attempt to refocus the policy debate on the value of school desegregation on more theoretical and sociological arguments, we have examined the research on the long-term effects of school desegregation. This body of literature remains significantly smaller than research on short-term effects, but it is more recent. Much of this work was published in the 1980s and early 1990s as the long-term effects of desegregation plans implemented in the late 1960s and early 1970s became more apparent. Meanwhile, because of the ambiguous findings of the research on the short-term effects and the ongoing resistance of many white Americans to desegregation policies, school desegregation had already been declared a failure in many policy circles by the time much of this literature on long-term effects was available. Thus, the more positive findings in these studies were virtually ignored. At the same time, the data on the more short-term effects of school desegregation were looking more positive. In fact, since school desegregation policies were implemented on a broad scale in the late 1960s, the gap between the test scores of black and white students has decreased by nearly 50 percent—a phenomenon attributable to rising scores for black students, not lower ones for whites (see Grissmer, 1996). Furthermore, much of the research now suggests that African-American students who attend desegregated schools are less likely to drop out of school, get pregnant, or get into trouble with the law than those from segregated schools (Middleton, 1994).

We believe that in order to assess the impact of school desegregation policy on the life chances of African-American adults, researchers and policy makers need to look beyond the short-term effects, especially standardized test scores, and focus more on long-term social and economic outcomes. Because school desegregation must do more than raise black students' test scores; it must also break the cycle of racial segregation that leaves blacks and whites worlds apart. This is not to say that equal educational outcomes for all students is unimportant or that higher achievement levels for African-American students should not be a national goal. But these outcomes do not necessarily hinge on the racial makeup of a school. As we mentioned before, black children do not need to sit next to white children to learn, but they are more likely to have access to high-status knowledge if they do. Still, in our study of social networks we are inspired by the adage that *who* you know is as important (or even more important) in social mobility as *what* you know, and the lawyers and civil rights advocates of the 1950s were well aware of this. The social network advantage of desegregated schools for African-American students is real, even though it could not be measured in time to satisfy policy makers who lost sight of the original goals of desegregation.

Perpetuation theory, as it has been developed by Braddock (1980) and McPartland and Braddock (1981), states that segregation tends to repeat itself "across the stages of the life cycle and across institutions when individuals have not had sustained experiences in desegregated settings earlier in life" (McPartland and Braddock, 1981, p. 149). Drawing on Pettigrew's research on social inertia and avoidance learning, Braddock (1980) derived perpetuation theory by focusing on the tendency of Americans, particularly blacks, to self-perpetuate racial segregation. He notes that minority students who have not regularly experienced the realities of desegregation may overestimate the degree of overt hostility they will encounter or underestimate their skill at coping with strains in interracial situations (p. 181). These segregated students will, in most instances, make choices that maintain physical segregation when they become adults because they have never tested their racial beliefs. While Braddock's perpetuation theory does not preclude the existence of real structural constraints to racial integration, his focus is on how individual agents adjust their behavior to accommodate, and thus perpetuate, these constraints, and how exposure to integrated settings can change this behavior.

Expanding on Braddock's theory of perpetual segregation, we have added a discussion of social networks and argued that segregation is also perpetuated across generations because African Americans and Latinos lack access to informal networks that provide information about and entrance to desegregated institutions or employment. This explanation complements Braddock's writing on blacks' lack of information on which to test their racial beliefs. In applying network analysis to perpetuation theory, we draw from Granovetter's (1973, 1983, and 1986) work, which shows the strong impact of "weak ties"—less formal interpersonal networks, such as acquaintances or friends of friends—on the diffusion of influence, information, and mobility opportunities. These weak ties, Granovetter (1973) argues, are the channels through which ideas that are socially distant from an individual may reach him.

In connecting his work to the research of Braddock and others who study the effects of school desegregation, Granovetter (1986) notes the importance of weak ties in bridging the worlds of white and nonwhite teenagers. Desegregated schools may be the only institutions in which African-American and Latino students would have access to the abundance of college and employment contacts that white and wealthy students often take for granted: "School desegregation studies frequently show that cross-racial ties formed are not very strong. But even such weak ties may significantly affect later economic success. Because employers at all levels of work prefer to recruit by word-of-mouth, typically using recommendations of current employees, segregation of friendship and acquaintance means that workplaces that start out all white will remain so" (p. 102–103).

Other network analysts have argued (see Lin, 1990, and Montgomery, 1992) that people on the bottom of the social structure, including African-American students from low-income families, have more to gain than white and wealthy students through the use of weak ties because these ties will invariably connect them to more affluent and better connected people, whereas strong ties usually connect them to family and close friends who are also poor. Lin and others have found that "the advantage of using weaker ties over the use of stronger ties decreases as the position of origin approaches the top of the hierarchy" (Lin, 1990, p. 251).

As Wilson (1987, 1996) and other social scientists have noted, the greatest barrier to social and economic mobility for low-income, inner-city blacks is the degree to which they remain isolated from the opportunities and networks of the mostly white and middle-class society.

There are obvious and not-so-obvious ways that social organizations, especially schools, filled with white and wealthy students provide greater access to information about colleges and careers than do schools serving mostly low-income minority students. For instance, in St. Louis the transfer students benefit from access to informants and well-connected acquaintances that they would not have in all-black urban schools, where less than 20 percent of the students go on to college. In their suburban schools they attend college fairs, are constantly reminded by their counselors and peers about college opportunities and deadlines, have access to a wealth of information on the college application process, and are assigned to college counselors with strong ties to college admissions offices across the country.

A third and related issue that we would like to stress is that the degree of racial and socioeconomic segregation and isolation in our society today demands metropolitanwide solutions. It is not a problem created by cities alone, and it will not be solved by cities alone. Borders between city and suburbs are artificial and malleable, constructs of antiquated laws and regulations. In this postmodern era, the practice of dividing society into urban and suburban units no longer makes sense. The problems of the urban ghettos have spilled over the city-suburban borders, and the solutions will call for people on both sides of the dividing line to join together. The St. Louis inter-district desegregation plan is one example of how that might be done. In this way it is a model for the nation, and the African-American students who transfer to the suburbs are the border crossers that more of us must become.

And finally, we would like to discourage rushing toward a ruling of unitary status in the St. Louis desegregation case, as the attorney general of Missouri would like the district court to do. We hope that all the parties involved in this case will not move to dismantle the program and return the city and suburban school districts to the separate and unequal systems they were for many years before this case began. The state of Missouri violated the constitutional rights of African Americans for more than a century before it was forced to try and remedy that situation. "Ten, fifteen, twenty—however many years of interdistrict transfers don't strike me as undoing 115 years of state-imposed segrega-tion," said Bruce La Pierre, the special master to the district court judge on the St. Louis case. In addition, we would like to reiterate the point that, except for the money spent on transportation for transfer students, all of the money expended in the St. Louis desegregation plan goes to schools and children's education. In a state that ranks in the bottom ten for educational funding, the fact that this court order has forced the state government to invest more money in children is far from tragic. As many of the state officials we inter-viewed pointed out, there is no guarantee that the money currently spent on school desegregation will continue to be expended—on schools or anything else—if the plan is scrapped.

If you consider all the ways that the rights of blacks in Missouri, a former slave and Jim Crow state, and in St. Louis, its southern city with a "northern exposure," were denied for more than one hundred years, this voluntary cross-district school desegregation program seems a minor initiative with which to chip away at the major cultural and structural forces that have been built up over the years. But because of the hope and dedication of many of the people who make this program happen—especially the transfer students and the visionary educators in suburban schools—we have found that it is making a small difference.

There is evidence from some of these districts, for example, that white sub-urban communities are becoming more accepting of African Americans, not only as schoolmates for their children but also as neighbors. There has, for in-stance, not been massive white flight from the suburban public schools. In fact, a principal of a school district in southern St. Louis county told us that several black families have moved into the virtually all-white working-class community near the school since the mid-1980s, and there has been no public outcry. "I think the reaction of the community to having four or five black families living here is very different today than it would have been six or seven years ago," she said. "It didn't create a stir that I know about. It got no reaction whatsoever when they started moving in."

There is much more implementation to be done. Suburban educators and communities need to embrace reform efforts that will better serve all of their diverse students, and the St. Louis Board of Education needs to focus more intently on the all-black schools on the north side of the city. Rather than al-lowing these to become "schools of last resort" that are "chosen" mainly by students who choose not to choose, we suggest that the board move toward a more "controlled choice" system by requiring all of these schools to create vi-able school of emphasis programs and allow students who stay in the city school system a greater choice of schools by asking them to select the schools with the emphasis program they most want to attend. If the city school system is to move toward such a model, the Board of Education must provide parents with information and access to counselors who help them select which program best suits the educational needs of their children. The board must also provide all students with transportation to the school of their choice.

Several people we interviewed suggested creating zones within the city that would be paired with specific districts or regions of the suburbs to create a greater sense of community and partnership between them. Such a plan could be helpful, though it will limit to some extent the choice available to black students in the city and also limit their degree of "escape" from negative social forces within their communities. We think, however, that if the zones are large enough, they would allow city students a great deal of choice. The payoff of this zoning system for both black and white adults in urban and suburban communities would be great, as paired communities within a given zone could create strong partnership programs that would draw parents and community members from both sides of the color line.

We commend the people of urban and suburban St. Louis for being a part of what Judge Hungate once called the "greatest social experiment of our time." Although it has not been easy and the implementation is far from perfect, many people in this metropolitan area, with its odd north-south mix of racial problems, have tried to do the right thing by the court order. There were no protests or major boycotts of suburban schools, just incremental change that has weakened but not abolished the color line and has, in many instances, transposed the lives of a subset of African-American and white students, educators, and perhaps future generations. Paradoxically, many people who live in the St. Louis metropolitan area are unaware of the magnitude of their inter-district school desegregation plan and its distinction from programs in other cities. We sense that most do not realize what an important footnote in the history of American racial politics their schools and community have become.

"I don't think that historically the people of St. Louis realize that there is something different going on here that's really not going on in a lot of places," said Minnie Liddell, the mother of the original plaintiff in this case and, in many ways, the mother of this unique desegregation plan. She added, "I don't think that many people want them to know that."

Perhaps Minnie Liddell is right. If so, she helps explain why, at a time when conservatives and liberals alike are clamoring for new ways to provide parents with educational choices, it seems highly ironic that the state of Missouri is on the verge of dismantling one of the country's largest and most successful school-choice programs. The St. Louis inter-district desegregation plan is one of a very few such programs that give meaningul choices to students who have traditionally been very poorly served by the educational system. And as conservative advocates of school choice push harder for private school voucher plans for inner-city students—plans that do not provide students with enough funding to attend high-status private schools or with transportation to their schools of choice, assuming they are admitted—we have to wonder why these same advocates would not embrace the St. Louis inter-district desegregation plan as a model. If their goal really is to help low-income black and Latino students "escape" from bad urban schools, perhaps they should advocate a program like the one in St. Louis. As imperfect as it may be, it tackles racial inequality and the problem of the color line more than any voucher plan supported by conservative policymakers.

The distance between judicial decrees and the lives of the people they are designed to affect parallels the gap between what we, as citizens of a free democratic society, know in our hearts is just and our reactions to a social, economic, and political system that rewards separatism based on race. Nearly fifty years ago Gunnar Myrdal told us as much.

The time has come for our nation to do some soul-searching—to reexamine the American Creed and the prevalent cultural themes that it nourishes as well as our history and the structure of our society. This book is a window into that soul, a continuation of an effort begun by social scientists, educators, and other prophetic people before us. We hope that somewhere between the assumed purity of the Creed and the reality of race in America lies a deeper understanding of what policies such as school desegregation were designed to remedy.

Appendix

Methodology

In this book we present the findings from our five-year case study of the St. Louis inter-district desegregation plan. Our goal in 1989, when we embarked on the study, was to examine this unique urban-suburban student transfer program from the perspectives of the different people who helped create it as well as those who are involved in it and contribute to its success or failure. We did not conduct a policy evaluation from which we could conclude whether this program "works." Instead, we were interested in the complexity of the St. Louis desegregation plan and how it is shaped and limited by the political and economic forces that surround it. We set out to embed the desegregation plan in a deep understanding of the culture and history in which it is taking place and thereby qualify any conclusions we drew by illustrating the obstacles the program faces (Raab, 1994).

In this way we conducted a politics of education study, examining the process by which this program came to be and its successes and failures, as opposed to a straightforward policy study in which we would focus only on the "measurable" or quantifiable outcomes (Dale, 1994).

As with most case study research, our methods were varied; we strove to gather as much data as we could to help us understand the creation and implementation of the St. Louis desegregation plan (Yin, 1989). We conducted in-depth semistructured interviews with more than 300 people; observed classrooms and meetings; examined U.S. Census data on the St. Louis area; and gathered any and all documents on the plan, including other studies of it. Our underlying research question asked how this program came to be, who has benefited from the plan, and why.

All of the names of the students and teachers quoted in this book have been changed to protect their identity. The names of the schools and school districts have not been changed because we did not think it was fair to mask the identity of some of the school districts and their schools when others—the St. Louis public schools—were virtually impossible to disguise. Still, except for major public figures, we tried to conceal the identity of individual respondents.

INTERVIEWS

We made decisions about whom to interview in a variety of ways, depending on the category of respondent. Because we were conducting a case study of a desegregation program in one large metropolitan area, it was essential for us to interview politically powerful and influential players or local elites. Thus, we began our data collection by interviewing school district superintendents and some school board members in all but one of the school districts participating in the desegregation plan. (One of the small suburban districts on the south side of the county refused to participate in the study, though we were able to obtain data on this district through other sources.) In addition, we interviewed the superintendents or assistant superintendents in four of the suburban districts that do not participate in the desegregation plan because of their demographics. Three of these districts had predominantly black student enrollments; the fourth was more than 25 percent black and conducting its own intra-district desegregation plan.

In this early phase of the project we also interviewed political leaders from the state of Missouri and St. Louis metro area, as well as lawyers and judges who had been involved with the case. Members of the various monitoring committees (existing and disbanded) were interviewed, as were politically active community members in many of the districts. In all of these instances we wrote interview protocols for each category of respondent and then probed during the interviews with follow-up questions specific to each person.

Once we had interviewed state, city, county, and school district leaders, we began to focus in on individual schools and the educators, parents, and students associated with them. In the St. Louis public schools we visited six all-black schools: three high schools, two middle schools, and one elementary school. We also visited two of the integrated schools—one high school and one elementary school—and four magnet schools. We wanted a mixed sample of all-black or nonintegrated, integrated, and magnet schools so that we could better understand the impact of the settlement agreement on each category of school in the city. We chose these schools based partly on geography (we wanted to look at schools in a variety of neighborhoods) and partly on recommendations from district leaders and others, who said that these were examples of either the worst or the best of schools in the district. We chose the three all-black high schools because we wanted to look at neighborhood schools on the north side of the city and found that these schools traditionally have been strongly tied to their communities.

At each of these twelve schools we interviewed the principal, and in most cases—at all of the all-black schools, one of the integrated schools, and two of the magnet schools—we also interviewed two or more teachers and sat in on classes. Teachers were chosen randomly from the faculty rosters, though we often conducted additional interviews with particular teachers who had strong opinions—for or against—the desegregation plan.

The sample of students and parents from the city (see Chapters 4 through 6) were purposively selected from lists of tenth-grade students who lived in three fairly different neighborhoods in the city. Each of these neighborhoods was near one of the three all-black neighborhood high schools—Sumner, Vashon, and Northwest—that we were studying. We wanted to assure two things: first, that the city students we interviewed would be attending a nearby all-black neighborhood high school, and, two, that the three neighborhoods would differ demographically. The neighborhoods were identified by examining demographic data from the sixty-three predominantly black Census tracts that make up the north side of the city. Our goal was to interview students from three neighborhoods that varied in educational level or percentage of adult residents who had completed high school, unemployment rate, median household income, the percentage of people living beneath the poverty line, and the percentage of homeowners versus renters. Every tract was ranked from 1 to 63 for each of the five factors, with 1 being the highest rating for education level, median income, and percentage of homeowners, and the lowest ranking for unemployment and poverty rates. The tract with one of the lowest composite scores, which was near Northwest High School, was selected as the "middle-class" black neighborhood. The tract near Sumner High School with the composite score close to the median was selected as the "working-class" black neighborhood, and the tract near Vashon High School with the highest composite scores was our "low-income" neighborhood. These class labels are not based on a comparison of the neighborhoods to a national norm but are relative to the other all-black neighborhoods in the city of St. Louis, and thus are well below the national norm for these types of labels.

African-American students and parents from each of these three neighborhoods were selected when we matched the zip codes to the Census tracts and then selected tenth-grade students according to their zip codes. While their zip codes and Census tracts did not match perfectly, we were able to use the overlapping areas to select the students. We were looking for three sets of students—city, transfer, and return—from each of the three neighborhoods. From the Voluntary Coordinating Council and the St. Louis public schools, we obtained lists of students who lived in these zip codes and who were in tenth grade. The Voluntary Coordinating Council gave us two lists—of students who lived in those areas and were attending suburban high schools through the transfer program and of students from the same neighborhoods who had attended a suburban high school but who had since withdrawn from the voluntary transfer plan to return to city schools or drop out altogether. The St. Louis public schools gave us lists of students whose home addresses had the three selected zip codes and who were enrolled in the all-black neighborhood high schools—Northwest, Sumner, or Vashon. These student lists were obtained under an agreement that the names of all the students who were interviewed would be changed for publication to protect their identity.

We selected thirty-six students from the three lists by plotting each student's address on maps of the three neighborhoods where the zip codes and Census tracts overlapped. From each neighborhood we chose twelve addresses—four from each of the three lists—that were clustered closest to the high schools in those neighborhoods. We chose those students who lived closest to their neighborhood high school because we wanted to assure that the city students lived very close to the more familiar neighborhood school— close enough to walk in many instances—and that the transfer and return students we chose would have been assigned to that neighborhood school had they not chosen to transfer. This meant that most of the return students were reassigned to either Northwest, Sumner, or Vashon. Yet because of all the building renovation taking place in the St. Louis public schools in the early 1990s, some of the students attending Sumner High School had been temporarily reassigned to schools in other neighborhoods at the time we conducted the interviews. Still, we also wanted to assure that each set of city, transfer, and return students from the three neighborhoods would have somewhat similar neighborhood experiences.

This sampling resulted in three lists of twelve students—four city students, four transfer students, and four return students—from each zip code. Also, as we noted in Chapter 5, we interviewed eight additional transfer students whom we met on our visits to the suburban schools. Although these students were not part of the original sample, we sought them out because they further articulated the views and dilemmas of the transfer students in our sample and thus gave us additional descriptions of important issues. We interviewed the parents of only one of these additional transfer students, while we interviewed virtually all the parents or guardians of the students in the original sample of thirty-six. This meant that we conducted nearly eighty in-depth interviews with African-American parents and students about the inter-district desegregation plan and why they were or were not participating in it. These in-depth interviews complemented other quantitative data on these students from other researchers, which we incorporated into our analysis and describe below.

Although we do not claim that the views of these parents and students are necessarily representative of the views of all African Americans in the city of St. Louis, we believe that the in-depth interviews gave us rich data and a deeper understanding of the issues. We also feel that many of the perspectives of these interviewees are reflected in survey and focus group data collected by other researchers. In combining all of this data into one book, we feel that we have captured much of the essence of the struggles these families face.

In an effort to elicit discussions of sensitive racial issues from the interviewees, we hired three African-American women interviewers to accompany the first author on the parent and student interviews. All three of these women were graduate students at Washington University in St. Louis; one was studying education and two were studying social work. All three had some interviewing experience, and all were interested in the topic. One of these women also assisted us in contacting parents and students to set up interviews.

The parent or guardian of each student selected from the lists was contacted by telephone and asked to participate in the study. Most of the parents we contacted initially agreed to participate. They in turn either told the student that we were coming, asked the student if he or she would be willing to be interviewed, or told us to call back and ask the student ourselves. In order to interview the thirty-seven students (including the extra return student but not counting the eight additional transfer students) and the thirty-four parents who composed the final sample, we attempted to reach a total of 126 students.

Hence, the total number of students selected who were not interviewed was eighty-eight. Sixty-five of these failed attempts, or 75 percent, were the result of our inability to reach the student, their parents, or anyone who knew of them. Disconnected telephones and wrong phone numbers were common, particularly in the low-income neighborhood. Thirteen failed attempts were the result of information that disqualified the students for the study—that is, the student no longer lived there or the student had never really transferred to the suburbs and thus was not a return student. Only eleven of the parents or students we contacted refused to participate. Most of these refusals came from parents who said they were too busy or were not interested in talking about their children's schools. Despite our concerted efforts to change their minds, these parents did not participate. Parents who lived in the low-income neighborhood and whose children were attending the neighborhood high school—Vashon—were particularly hard to persuade. Seven of the eleven refusals came from parents of city students, four of whom lived in the low-income neighborhood.

We ended up with seventy-one interviews—thirty-seven students and thirty-four parents—in the first round of data collection from these three neighborhoods. (The additional eight transfer students and one additional parent were interviewed later.) The extra student in the original sample (thirty-seven students as opposed to thirty-six) was a return student from the low-income neighborhood who originally told us that he had never attended a suburban school—thus we thought he was a city student. But in the course of his interview we learned that he had attended a county school in junior high. Apparently he was not aware that the school is located in a suburban district, just that he took a bus to get there. This left us with an extra return student from the low-income neighborhood. But his mother, who was moving her family to another section of town, was not willing to be interviewed.

Two additional parents are missing from the sample (thirty-four instead of thirty-six). One of these parents was hospitalized, and her son, a transfer student, was living in a Catholic group home for boys. Her son, however, told us a great deal about his mother's involvement in his decision to transfer to a county school. The second missing parent was the mother of a city student in the low-income neighborhood; she kept postponing our visits and finally refused to speak to us on the phone. We interviewed the daughter after more than twenty failed attempts to find one last city student from this low-income neighborhood for our study because so many of the students for whom we had names and phone numbers no longer lived at the listed address or no longer had phones that were in working order.

The final sample of thirty-seven students consisted of twenty girls and seventeen boys. The parent sample, which should actually be called the guardian sample, consisted of twenty-seven mothers, one stepmother, two fathers, and four grandmothers. In two-parent families we interviewed whichever parent claimed the most responsibility for choosing the student's school and communicating with teachers and administrators in that school, usually the mother.

All interviews were conducted by two interviewers—one black and one white. Most of the interviews took place in the home of the respondents, though five of the students and one of the parents were interviewed in fast-food restaurants. One student and one parent (the schoolteacher) were interviewed at their school, and two other parents were interviewed at work. All but three of the student interviews were conducted out of the presence of their parents, and all but one of the parent interviews were conducted out of the presence of the students.

We developed semistructured interview protocols. This guaranteed that we asked each student about his or her background—age, number of siblings, number of people living in their household, number of schools attended. We also asked general questions about students' opinions of the transfer program and the city schools as well as their reasons for choosing or not choosing a suburban school. Students' knowledge of the transfer program and the suburban schools was recorded, and their opinions of these schools versus the city schools were solicited. More specific questions were asked of the students to probe them on these issues.

Parent interviews focused mainly on the quantity and sources of information they had on the transfer program and their opinions of the county versus the city schools. Special attention was paid to the degree of influence that parents had on the students' decisions to attend or not attend a county school and on their view of the role that they and the schools play (or should play) in preparing their children for life after high school. Data on parents' and students' racial attitudes were found in respondents' answers concerning city-versus-county schools and the benefits of integrated versus all-black schools.

In the suburbs, we began by interviewing about forty district-level administrators and school board members, and followed by interviewing more than seventy teachers and principals who work daily with transfer students. As we mentioned in Chapter 7, in our interviews with principals we focused on one or more schools in eight of the sixteen districts. We chose these eight districts based on their diverse demographics, size, and political climate.

We interviewed several teachers in each of twelve schools within four suburban districts—Clayton, Kirkwood, Mehlville, and Parkway. These districts represented to us the most interesting cross-section of geographic, demographic, and political standpoints (see Chapter 7 for more description). Within each of the twelve schools—five high schools, two junior highs or middle schools, and five elementary schools—we interviewed the principals, often one or more assistant principal or counselor, and at least three teachers. About forty-five of the sixty teachers interviewed were selected from faculty rosters in order to assure a balance of teachers across departments at the schools. We also wanted a mixture of male and female teachers. The other fifteen teachers were recommended to us as people we needed to speak with because they either strongly opposed or strongly supported the desegregation plan.

As we mention in Chapter 8, we do not claim to understand how all the educators in suburban St. Louis feel about the desegregation plan or what their experiences of working with the transfer students have been. But we do believe that our in-depth data, coupled with the available survey data from the University of Missouri–St. Louis, present some prevalent themes in the meaning that these educators are making of the desegregation plan and the African-American students who come to their suburban schools.

And finally, we interviewed more than fifty white parents and students in the four suburban districts. We selected students by asking principals and teachers to recommend white students who they thought had strong opinions—for or against—the desegregation plan. We also asked certain students who were in classes we observed if they would be willing to be interviewed. White parents were purposely drawn, based mainly on their involvement in their suburban schools and thus their influence on policy making and other school-level decisions. Because there are so many parents in these suburban districts, we could not hope to interview a representative sample, thus we sought out those parents who were most likely to have a major influence on the school. These parents often had a good understanding of general community attitudes toward the desegregation plan. We also conducted brief interviews with white parents after orientation meetings we attended. Once again, the UMSL (Jones, 1988) survey of county parents and the Policy Centers' focus group studies were helpful additional sources of information in our efforts to understand the suburban perspective on the desegregation plan.

We conducted only a handful of interviews with white suburban parents and students who had chosen to attend magnet schools in the city of St. Louis. While we found these interviews interesting, we did not pursue more such interviews for two reasons: first, we lacked the resources and person-power to conduct large numbers of interviews with these white transfer students and their parents, and second, because the number of white students transferring into the city is relatively small compared with the number of African-American students transferring out, we did not focus on this group. Because the court order and the resulting desegregation plan were designed to provide a remedy to black students in the city for the results of years of segregation, we thought that the stories of white transfer students to magnet schools was less important to this case study than the opportunities and experiences of the black and white students in the suburban schools. Another interesting study could be conducted on these white students and the reasons why they choose to attend urban magnet schools.

OBSERVATIONS

In about half of the instances in which we visited city or county schools and interviewed teachers, we also observed their classes. Much of this depended on the timing of our visits and the willingness of teachers to be observed as they taught. Still we did observe a range of classes—different grade levels and subjects—in various urban and suburban schools. These observations of teacher-student and student-student interactions helped us better understand animosities on both sides. We also became more aware of curricular and pedagogical distinctions within and between the schools we studied.

We also observed various meetings, including a meeting of the Voluntary Interdistrict Coordinating Council and orientation meetings for parents at suburban schools. Observing these meetings helped us to better understand political issues and concerns surrounding the desegregation case.

DOCUMENTS AND OTHER DATA

And finally, we gathered as much additional data from all of our respondents as we could by asking them for copies of reports, studies, and surveys they had conducted or collected. For instance, we spent an entire day at the law offices of one of the attorneys selecting various exhibits to photocopy. We also spent several days at the federal district court in St. Louis, examining and photocopying from the docket of the desegregation case. Daniel Schlafly, the former school board president in St. Louis, kindly shared with us important historical documents, including very old newspaper clippings.

In addition, several years' worth of clippings from local newspapers, including the *St. Louis Post-Dispatch* and several of the smaller suburban and black community newspapers, were available to us through the Voluntary Interdistrict Coordinating Council office. We also read various issues of the St. Louis Post-Dispatch from the early 1980s on microfilm at the UCLA University Research Library. The first author's parents, who live in the St. Louis area, regularly clipped local newspaper articles on the desegregation case for us.

Most important, we drew on the careful research of others who have studied aspects of the St. Louis plan, attempting to bring their survey, focus group data, and student achievement data into a dialogue with our rich interview data. Lissitz's (1993, 1994) studies on the achievement of transfer and nontransfer African-American students who live in the city of St. Louis was helpful to us in our efforts to understand how the experiences of the students that we were learning about were related to the academic performance of students in general. These studies were ordered by the U.S. district court and administered by the Voluntary Interdistrict Coordinating Council.

We also relied heavily on the important 1988 metropolitan-wide survey of 2,500 educators, parents, and students on their opinions of the desegregation plan. The survey was conducted by E. Terrance (Terry) Jones, dean of arts and sciences at the University of Missouri–St. Louis. This survey of randomly selected respondents was conducted for the *St. Louis Post-Dispatch's* special series on the desegregation plan. The findings from this survey helped us to verify that many of the attitudes and opinions we found in our in-depth interviews were reflective of broader concerns and beliefs in the St. Louis area.

And finally, another important source of data was the University of Missouri–St. Louis' Public Policy Research Centers' (1993) series of eleven focus groups with transfer students and parents, black students who remained in city schools, and white students in the suburbs. The focus group study was conducted under the direction of Mark Trannel, a senior research analyst at the Public Policy Research Centers. The facilitators for focus groups of African-American students were African American as well. White facilitators worked with the white student focus groups. Like the achievement studies by Lissitz, the focus group research was ordered by the U.S. district court and administered by the Voluntary Interdistrict Coordinating Council.

By bringing all of these data together with our qualitative and Census data we were able to synthesize findings and paint a more contextualized and comprehensive picture of the success, failure, and ongoing struggles inherent in this unique inter-district desegregation plan.

References

Adair, A. V. 1984. *Desegregation: The illusion of black progress.* Lanham, Md.: University Press of America.

Ahmad, I. April 19, 1993. The fate of Vashon is in the hands of the SLPS, judge says. *St. Louis American.*

Ahmad-Taylor, T. February 27, 1994. A movement driven by visions of a better place. *The New York Times.*

Annie E. Casey Foundation. 1994. *Kids count data book: States profiles of child well-being.* Baltimore: Author.

Anderson, J. D. 1988. *The education of blacks in the south, 1860–1935.* Chapel Hill: University of North Carolina Press.

Anderson, J. D., et al. 1994. Brief of amici curiae James D. Anderson et. al. in support of respondents. In the Supreme Court of the United States, October Term. *Missouri v. Jenkins.* On writ of certiorari to the United States Court of Appeals for the Eighth Circuit.

Apple, R. W. September 29, 1992. Missouri's word of advice to Bush: Jobs, jobs, jobs. *The New York Times.*

Armor, D. 1972. The evidence on busing. *The Public Interest* 28:90.

Aronowitz, A., and DiFazio, W. 1994. *The jobless future.* Minneapolis: University of Minnesota Press.

Babcock, R. F., and Bosselman, F. P. 1973. *Exclusionary zoning: Land use regulation and houring in the 1970s*. New York: Praeger.

Bartelt, D. W. 1993. Housing the "underclass." In M. B. Katz, ed., *The "underclass" debate: Views from history*, 118–157 Princeton, N.J.: Princeton University Press.

Bell, D. 1987. *And we are not saved: The elusive quest for racial justice*. New York: Basic Books.

Bell, K. September 9, 1992. Carnahan rips Webster on desegregation. *St. Louis Post-Dispatch*.

Bell, L., and Schniedewind, N. 1987. Reflective minds/intentional hearts: Joining humanistic education and critical theory for liberating education. *Boston University Journal of Education* 169(2):55–77.

Bennett, W. J. 1992. *The de-valuing of America: The fight for our culture and our children*. New York: Touchstone.

Berger, J. September 29, 1993. Settlement reached in suit on segregation in housing. *The New York Times*.

Berman, P. April 14, 1996. Redefining fairness: *The New York Times*, book review section, 16–17.

Berry, B. J. L., and Kasarda, J. D. 1977. *Contemporary urban ecology*. New York: Macmillan.

Blake, J. March 30, 1996. Letter to the editor. *St. Louis Post-Dispatch*.

Blauner, R. 1990. *Black lives, white lives: Three decades of race relations in America*. 1st paperback ed. Berkeley: University of California Press.

——. 1994. Talking past each other: Black and white languages of race. In F. L. Pincus and H. J. Ehrlich, eds., *Race and ethnic conflict: Contending views on prejudice, discrimination, and ethnoviolence*, 18–28. Boulder, Colo.: Westview Press.

Bobo, L. 1983. Whites' opposition to busing: Symbolic racism or realistic group conflict? *Journal of Personality and Social Psychology* 45(6):1196–1210.

——. 1988. Group conflict, prejudice, and the paradox of contemporary racial attitudes. In P. A. Katz and D. A. Taylor, eds., *Eliminating racism: Profiles in controversy*, 85–114. New York: Plenum.

Bobo, L., and Kluegel, J. August 1993. Opposition to race-targeting: Self-interest, stratification ideology, or racial attitudes? *American Sociological Review* 58:443–464.

Bourdieu, P. 1984. *Distinction*. Cambridge, Mass.: Harvard University Press.

Bourdieu, P., and Passeron, J. 1979. *The inheritors: French students and their relation to culture*. R. Nice, trans. Chicago: University of Chicago.

Bower, G. February 16, 1993. U. City residents will be surveyed on race, schools. *St. Louis Post-Dispatch*.

——. 1994a. High school is one of only three in Midwest on "Exemplary" list. *St. Louis Post-Dispatch*.

——. 1994b. Special college eludes city students; others seize challenge. *St. Louis Post-Dispatch*.

Bowles, S., and Gintis, H. 1976. *Schooling in capitalist America: Educational reform and the contradiction of economic life*. New York: Basic Books.

Braddock, J. H. July 1980. The perpetuation of segregation across levels of education: A behavioral assessment of the contact-hypothesis. *Sociology of Education* 53:178–186.

Braddock, J. H., and McPartland, J. M. 1982. Assessing school desegregation effects: New directions in research. *Research in Sociology of Education and Socialization* 3:259–282.

Braddock, J. H., Crain, R. L., McPartland, J. M., and Dawkins, R. L. 1986. Applicant race and job placement decisions: A national survey experiment. *International Journal of Sociology and Social Policy* 6(1):3–24.

Braun, S. November 16, 1993. A surprise roadblock for busing. *The Los Angeles Times*.

Brown, K. 1996. Revisiting the Supreme Court's opinion in *Brown v. Board of Education* from a multiculturalist perspective. In E. C. Lagemann and L. P. Miller, eds., Brown v. Board of Education: *The Challenge for Today's Schools*, 44–53. New York: Teachers College Press.

Brown v. Board of Education 347 U.S. 438 (1954).

Bryant, T. January 19, 1991. Judge strips city schools of vocational programs. *St. Louis Post-Dispatch*.

———. April 28, 1995. Jay Nixon: Cut funds for new classrooms. *St. Louis Post-Dispatch*.

Bryant, T., and Lindecke, F. W. September 28, 1993. Busing issue "comes down to money," judge says. *St. Louis Post-Dispatch*.

Bugel, T. S., Kiel, S. W., and Fister, L. P. February 18, 1993. Rights of whites. *St. Louis Post-Dispatch*, letters section.

Carmichael, S., and Hamilton, C. 1967. *Black power*. New York: Random House.

Carnahan, M. March 26, 1995. A good-faith effort on desegregation (opinion editorial). *St. Louis Post-Dispatch*.

Carter, S. L. 1991. *Reflections of an affirmative-action baby*. New York: Basic Books.

Christensen, L. O. 1988. Missouri. In J. H. Madison, ed., *Heartland: Comparative histories of the midwestern states*, 86–105. Bloomington: Indiana University Press.

Chubb, J. E., and Moe, T. M. 1990. *Politics, markets, and America's schools*. Washington D.C.: Brookings Institution.

Civic Progress Task Force on Desegregation. December 1995. *Desegregation: A report from the Civic Progress Task Force on Desegregation in the St. Louis Public School System*. St. Louis: Author.

Clayton School District. 1989. *Voluntary student transfer program: Report to community*. Clayton, Mo.: Author.

Coleman, J. 1961. *The adolescent society*. New York: Free Press.

Comer, J. P. 1980. *School power: Implications of an intervention project*. New York: Free Press.

Community Advisory Committee of the St. Louis Public Schools, February 14, 1985. *Phase I summary: The long-range plan*. St. Louis: St. Louis Public Schools.

Confluence St. Louis Task Force. 1989. *A new spirit for St. Louis: Valuing diversity*. A report of the Confluence St. Louis Task Force on racial polarization in the St. Louis metropolitan area with recommendations. St. Louis: Author.

Corrigan, D. March 20–26, 1994. Rebellion brews in Missouri. *South County News Times*.

Crain, R. L. 1969. *The politics of school desegregation*. Garden City, N.Y.: Anchor.

Crain, R. L., Peichert, J., Hawes, J., and Miller, R. 1993. *Finding niches: The effect of school desegregation on black students*. New York: Institute for Urban Education, Teachers College, Columbia University.

Dale, R. 1994. Applied education politics or political sociology of education: Contrasting approaches to the study of recent education reform in England and Wales. In D. Halpin and B. Troyna, eds., *Researching education policy: Ethical and methodological issues*. London: Falmer Press.

Dawson, K. S. May 7, 1981. Legal memoranda: Summary on interdistrict movement to St. Louis of black students attending high school until the 1950s. St. Louis: The law firm of Lashly, Caruthers, Thies, Rava & Hamel.

———. July 31, 1982. Legal memoranda: Summary of research on state laws, statutory changes, etc. St. Louis: The law firm of Lashly, Caruthers, Thies, Rava & Hamel.

DeParle, J. December 1, 1993. An underground railroad from projects to suburbs. *The New York Times*.

Desegregation money is education money. March 16, 1992. *St. Louis Post-Dispatch*.

Desegregation—The state. March 1, 1988. *St. Louis Post-Dispatch*.

De Witt, K. February 27, 1994. Black journeys: Many travelers along many roads. *The New York Times*.

Du Bois, W. E. B. 1969. *The souls of black folk*. New York: Penguin Books.

———. July 1935. Does the Negro need separate schools? *Journal of Negro Education* 4(3):328–335.

Eardley, L. September 29, 1993b. Longtime advocate still favors busing. *St. Louis Post-Dispatch*.

———. November 23, 1993a. Missouri asks court to end schools case. *St. Louis Post-Dispatch*.

———. November 22, 1993c. Suspensions from school vex NAACP. *St. Louis Post-Dispatch*.

Eckert, P. 1989. *Jocks and burnouts: Social categories and indentity in the high school*. New York: Teachers College Press.

Edsall, T. B., with Edsall, M. D. 1991. *Chain reaction: The impact of race, rights, and taxes on American politics*. New York: W. W. Norton.

Education Monitoring and Advisory Committee. April 1995. *Assessment of college prep and related programs: Final report pursuant to memorandum and order*. St. Louis: Author.

———. March 1994. *Interim report on the status of college prep and related programs*. St. Louis: Author.

Egan, T. September 3, 1996. Many seek security in private communities. *The New York Times*.

Eight school officials named aides to Hickey. July 5, 1962. *St. Louis Post-Dispatch*.

Epstein, J. L. 1990. School and family connections: Theory, research, and implications for integrating sociologies of education and family. In D. G. Unger and M. B. Sussman, eds., *Families in community settings: Interdisciplinary perspectives,* 99–126. New York: Haworth.

Faherty, W. B. 1976. *St. Louis: A concise history.* St. Louis: St. Louis Convention and Visitors Commission.

Farley, R. Winter 1975. Residential segregation and its implications for school integration. *Law and Contemporary Problems* 39(1):164–193.

Farley, R., and Frey, W. H. February 1994. Changes in the segregation of whites from black during the 1980s: Small steps toward a more integrated society. *American Sociological Review* 59:23–45.

Farley, R., Schuman, H., Bianchis, S., Colasanto, D., and Hatchett, S. 1978. Chocolate city, vanilla suburbs: Will the trend toward racially separate communities continue? *Social Science Research* 7(4):319–344.

Feagin, J. R. 1989. *Racial and Ethnic Relations.* 3rd ed. Englewood Cliffs, N.J.: Prentice Hall.

Feldmen, J., Kirby, E., Eaton, S. E., and Morantz, A. 1994. *Still separate, still unequal: The limits of Milliken II's educational compensation remedies.* Cambridge, Mass.: Harvard Project on School Desegregation.

Fine, M. 1993. [Ap]parent involvement: Reflections on parents, power, and urban public schools. *Teachers College Record* 94(4):682–710.

Finkenstaedt, R. L. H. 1994. *Face to face blacks to America. White perceptions and black realities.* New York: Morrow.

Fletcher found guilty of gross misconduct as school buildings chief. December 22, 1958. *St. Louis Post-Dispatch.*

Fordham, S. 1988. Racelessness as a factor in black students' school success: Pragmatic strategy or Pyrrhic victory? *Harvard Educational Review* 58(1):54–84.

Fordham, S., and Ogbu, J. 1986. Black students' school success: Coping with the burden of "acting white." *The Urban Review* 18(3):176–205.

Foster, W. 1986. A critical perspective on administration and organization in education. In K. A. Sirotnik and J. Oakes, eds., *Critical perspectives on the organization and improvement of schooling,* 95–129. Boston: Kluwer.

Franklin, D. 1988. Board head blasts programs for all-black schools. *St. Louis Post-Dispatch.*

Franklin, J. H. 1993. *The color line: Legacy for the twenty-first century.* Columbia: University of Missouri Press.

Freivogel, W. H. May 15, 1994. Forty years after ruling, city schools are failing. *St. Louis Post-Dispatch.*

———. December 4, 1995. Report calls for new desegregation plan. *St. Louis Post-Dispatch.*

Gayle, L. April 1, 1988. Board seeks to cut class sizes at all-black schools. *St. Louis Post-Dispatch.*

Gillerman, M. April 13, 1992. School chief paints grim financial picture. *St. Louis Post-Dispatch.*

Gottlieb, Harry N. May 1976. The ultimate solution: Desegregated housing. *The School Review,* 463–478.

Granovetter, M. 1973. The strength of weak ties. *American Journal of Sociology* 78:1360–1380.

———. 1983. The strength of weak ties: A network theory revisited. In R. Collins, eds., *Sociology theory*, 201–233. San Francisco: Jossey-Bass.

———. 1986. The micro-structure of school desegregation. In J. Prager, D. Longshore, and M. Seeman, eds., *School desegregation research: New directions in situational analysis,* 81–110. New York: Plenum.

Grant, C. A. 1996 Reflections on the promise of *Brown* and multicultural education. In E. C. Lagemann and L. P. Miller, eds., Brown v. Board of Education: *The Challenge for Today's Schools*. New York: Teachers College Press.

Greenhouse, L. June 13, 1995. Justices say lower courts erred in orders in desegregation case. *The New York Times*.

Grigsby, W. G., Stegman, M. A., Rosenburg, L., and Liechty, G. June 1970. *Housing and poverty*. Philadelphia: Institute for Environmental Studies, University of Pennsylvania.

Grissmer, D. W. April 1996. Perceptions and misperceptions about families, schools, and social/educational investment programs. Paper presented at the Education Writers' Association National Seminar, Minneapolis.

Grossman, J. R. 1989. *Land of hope*. Chicago: University of Chicago Press.

Hacker, A. 1992. *Two nations: Black and white, separate, hostile, unequal*. New York: Charles Scribner's Sons.

Hartman, R. October 6–12, 1993. In defense of deseg: Separate won't be equal. *The Riverfront Times*.

Heaney, G. W. 1985. Busing, timetables, goals, and ratios: Touchstones of equal opportunity. *Minnesota Law Review* 69:735–820.

Hendric, C. 1996. Mo., K.C. reach desegregation subsidy accord. *Education Week*, May 29.

Hick, V. June 1992a. Educations meet to discuss racism in schools. *St. Louis Post-Dispatch.*

———. May 19, 1992b. Parkway students more to keep desegregation. *St. Louis Post-Dispatch*.

———. March 5, 1992c. Seven city schools to close. *St. Louis Post-Dispatch*

Hills v. Gautreaux, 425 U.S. 284 1976.

Hirsch, A. R. 1993. With or without Jim Crow: Black residential segregation in the United States. In H. R. Hirsch and R. A. Mohl, eds., *Urban policy in twentieth-century America*, 65–99. New Brunswick, N.J.: Rutgers University Press.

Hirschman, A. O. 1970. *Exit, voice, and loyalty: Responses to decline in firms, organizations, and states*. Cambridge, Mass.: Harvard University Press.

Hochschild, J. 1984. *The new American dilemma: Liberal democracy and school desegregation*. New Haven: Yale University Press.

hooks, b. 1992. *Black looks: Race and representation*. Boston: South End Press.

Horton, B. W. March 18, 1991. *Exclusion and optimism: Black Americans keep their eyes on the education prize. A story of school desegregation in St. Louis 1954–1980*. Thesis submitted in partial fulfillment of the requirements for Senior Honors in History, Department of History, Washington University, St. Louis

Human Development Corporation of Metropolitan St. Louis. May 1970. *Social and economic poverty: St. Louis metropolitan area*. Research and Planning Document Number A-23. St. Louis: Author.

Hubler, S., and Silverstein, S. October 1, 1993. School doesn't close minority earning gap. *The Los Angeles Times*.

Hyde, W., and Conard, H. L. 1899. *Encyclopedia of the history of St. Louis*, vol. 4. New York: Southern History.

Jackson, K. T. 1985. *The crabgrass frontier: The suburbanization of the United States*. New York: Oxford University Press.

Jackson, T. F. 1993. The state, the movement, and the urban poor: The war on Poverty and political mobilization in the 1960s. in Michael B. Katz, ed., *The "underclass" debate: Views from history*, 403–439. Princeton, N.J.: Princeton University Press.

Jankowski, M. S. 1995. The rising significance of status in U.S. race relations. In M. P. Smith and J. R. Feagin, eds., *The bubbling cauldron*. Minneapolis: University of Minnesota Press.

Jaynes, G. D., and Williams, R. M. 1989. *A common destiny: Blacks and American society*. National Research Council. Washington D.C.: National Academy Press.

Joiner, R. August 8, 1971. From slaves to leaders. *St. Louis Post-Dispatch*.

Jones, E. T. 1988. Survey on St. Louis school desegregation plan conducted for the *St. Louis Post-Dispatch*

Jones v. Mayer Co., 392 U.S. 409, 427 1968.

Kansas City: Innovative, friendly. August 8, 1971. *St. Louis Post-Dispatch*.

Kaufman, J. E. and Rosenbaum, J. Fall 1992. The education and employment of low-income black youth in white suburbs. *Education Evaluation and Policy Analysis* 14(3):229–240.

Kirschten, F. 1960. *Catfish and crystal*. New York: Doubleday.

Klatch, R. E. 1990. To the right—the transformation of American conservativism. *American Journal of Sociology* 96(3):801–803.

Kluegel, J. R. 1990. Trends in whites' explanations of the black-white gap in socioeconomic status, 1977–1989. *American Sociological Review* 55:512–525.

Kluger, R. 1975. *Simple Justice: The history of* Brown v. Board of Education *and black America's struggle for equality*. New York: Vintage.

Kozol, J. 1991. *Savage inequalities*. New York: Crown.

Kunen, J. S. April 29, 1996. The end of integration. *Time*, 39–45.

La Noue, G. R., and Smith, B. L. R. 1973. *The politics of school decentralization*. Lexington, Mass.: Lexington Books.

La Pierre, B. D. 1987. Voluntary interdistrict school desegregation in St. Louis: The Special Master's tale. *Wisconsin Law Review* 1987 (6):971–1040.

Lareau, A. 1989. *Home advantage: Social class and parental intervention in elementary education*. London: Falmer.

Lemann, N. 1991. *The promised land: The great black migration and how it changed America*. New York: Knopf.

Levin, H. M. 1975. Education, life chances, and the courts: The role of social science evidence. *Law and Contemporary Problems* 39:217–240.

Levy, S. May 16, 1995. Board: Good report, but can we do better? *St. Louis Post-Dispatch*.

Lhotka, W. C. March 24, 1988. Neighborhood magnets suggested. *St. Louis Post-Dispatch*

Liddell v. St. Louis Board of Education, 72C 100(1). Consent Judgement and Decree. U.S. District Court, Eastern District of Missouri (1975).

Liddell v. St. Louis Board of Education, 620 F. 2nd. 8th Cir. (1980).

Liddell v. St. Louis Board of Education, 867 F. 2nd 8th Cir. 1158, 1989.

Limbaugh, S. N. September 4, 1991. Memorandum Opinion. *Liddell v. St. Louis Board of Education* (2–3).

Lin, N. 1990. Social resources and instrumental action. In R. Breiger, ed., *Social mobility and social structure*, 247–271. Cambridge: Cambridge University Press.

Lindecke, F. W., and Hick, V. May 16, 1992. St. Louis schools in line for break. *St. Louis Post-Dispatch*.

Lipset, S. M. 1963. *Political man: The social bases of politics*. New York: Doubleday.

Lissitz, R. W. January 1992. *Assessment of student performance and attitude: St. Louis metropolitan area court ordered desegregation effort*. Report submitted to the Voluntary Interdistrict Coordinating Council. St. Louis: Voluntary Interdistrict Coordinating Council.

————. December 1993. *Assessment of student performance and attitude year III— 1993: St. Louis metropolitan area court ordered desegregation effort*. Report submitted to the Voluntary Interdistrict Coordinating Council. St. Louis: Voluntary Interdistrict Coordinating Council.

————. December 1994. *Assessment of Student Performance and Attitude Year IV— 1994: St. Louis Metropolitan Area Court Ordered Desegregation Effort*. Report submitted to the Voluntary Interdistrict Coordinating Council. St. Louis: Voluntary Interdistrict Coordinating Council.

Little, J. September 30, 1993a. Class sizes are a lie, city teacher charges. *St. Louis Post-Dispatch*.

————. August 26, 1993b. Enrollment up at St. Louis magnet schools. *St. Louis Post-Dispatch*.

————. October 31, 1993c. Schools have far to go to meet court's goals. *St. Louis Post-Dispatch*.

————. November 15, 1993d. Shortages plague city classrooms. *St. Louis Post-Dispatch*.

————. June 16, 1994a. City schools join crowd in using detectors. *St. Louis Post-Dispatch*.

————. May 13, 1994b. New aid bypassing schools. *St. Louis Post-Dispatch*.

————. March 11, 1994c. School board flunks project courage. *St. Louis Post-Dispatch*.

————. November 21, 1995a. City schools "financially stressed." *St. Louis Post-Dispatch*.

————. June 13, 1995b. Impact in St. Louis questioned. *St. Louis Post-Dispatch*.

————. June 27, 1995c. 7 appointed to shape vo-tech district. *St. Louis Post-Dispatch*.

Little, J., and Mannies, J. January 5, 1996. Nixon files proposal to end school plan. *St. Louis Post-Dispatch*.

Little, J., and Todd, C. February 20, 1994. Discrimination in city school lives on. *St. Louis Post-Dispatch*.

Lowes, R. March 1990. Reading, writing and racial integrity. *St. Louis Magazine, 32,* 34, 35, 36, 37, 110–14.

MacLeod, J. 1995. *Ain't no making it.* 2nd ed. Bolder, Colo.: Westview.

Mannies, J., and Little, J. January 6, 1996. Nixon's plan called too much, too fast. *St. Louis Post-Dispatch*.

Mannies, J. March 8, 1992. Candidates attack school plan. *St. Louis Post-Dispatch*.

———. September 20, 1992. Desegregation a key campaign issue. *St. Louis Post-Dispatch*.

———. September 27, 1993. Mayor wants to end school busing. *St. Louis Post-Dispatch*.

Mannies, J., and Lindecke, F. W. September 29, 1993. Bosley remains firm on anti-busing stance. *St. Louis Post-Dispatch*.

Manning, A. June 12, 1995. The best, worst cities for children. *USA Today.*

Massey, D., and Denton, N. A. November 1988. Suburbanization and segregation in U.S. metropolitan area. *American Journal of Sociology* 93(3):592–626.

———. 1993. *American apartheid: Segregation and the making of the underclass.* Cambridge, Mass.: Harvard University Press.

McConahay, J. B. 1982. Self-interest versus racial attitudes as correlates of anti-busing attitudes in Louisville. *Journal of Politics* 44:692–720.

McLaren, P. 1991a. Critical pedagogy: Constructing an arch of social dreaming and a doorway to hope. *Boston University Journal of Education* 173(1):9–34.

———. 1991b. Decentering culture: Postmodernism, resistance, and critical pedagogy. In N. B. Wyner, ed., *Current perspectives on the culture of schools*. Boston: Brookline.

McPartland, J. M., and Braddock, J. H. 1981. Going to college and getting a good job: The impact of desegregation. In W. D. Hawley, ed., *Effective school desegregation: Equality, quality and feasibility,* 141–154. London: Sage.

Metcalf, G. R. 1988. *Fair Housing Comes of Age.* Westport, Conn.: Greenwood.

Metz, M. H. 1978. *Classrooms and corridors: The crisis of authority in desegregated secondary schools.* Berkeley: University of California Press.

Middleton, M. February 10, 1994. Why desegregate our schools? *Kansas City New Times*

Milliken v. Bradley, 418 U.S. 717 (1974).

Missouri State Department of Education. 1994. District Profile (supplements). Missouri Department of Elementary and Secondary Education. District Receipts and Expenditures. Jefferson City, Mo.: Author.

———. 1995. District Profiles. Missouri Department of Elementary and Secondary Education. District Receipts and Expenditures. Jefferson City, Mo.: Author.

Mohl, R. A. 1993. Race and space in the modern city: Interstate-95 and the black community in Miami. In H. R. Hirsch and R. A. Mohl, eds., *Urban policy in twentieth-century America,* 100–158. New Brunswick, N.J.: Rutgers University Press.

Montgomery, J. D. 1992. Job search and network composition: Implications for the strength-of-weak-ties hypothesis. *American Sociological Review* 57:586–596.

Moore, D., and Davenport, S. 1990. School choice: The new and improved sorting machine. In W. L. Boyd and H. J. Walberg, eds., *Choice in education: Potentials and problems*. Berkeley: McCutchan.

Morantz, A. April 1994. *Money, choice, and equity in Kansas City.* Cambridge, Mass.: Harvard Project on School Desegregation.

Morrison, P. A. 1973. *Small-area population estimates for the city of St. Louis, 1960–1972, with a model for updating them* (Report R-1373-NSF). Santa Monica, Calif.: Rand.

Mosley, J. January 1992. Kansas City's plush schools lure students. *St. Louis Post-Dispatch*.

Murray, C. 1984. *Losing ground: American social policy, 1950–1980*. New York: Basic Books.

Myrdal, G. 1962. *An American dilemma: The Negro problem and modern democracy.* 2nd ed. New York: Harper and Row.

Newman, K. S. 1993. *Declining fortunes: The withering of the American dream.* New York: Basic Books.

Oakes, J. 1985. *Keeping track: How schools structure inequality*. New Haven: Yale University Press.

———. 1990. *Multiplying inequalities: The effects of race, social class, and ability grouping on opportunities to learn mathematics and science*. Santa Monica: Rand.

Oakes, J., Lipton, M., and Jones, M. 1995. Changing minds: Deconstructing intelligence in detracking schools. Paper presented at the annual meeting of the American Educational Research Association, San Francisco, April.

Ogbu, J. U. 1991. Immigrant and involuntary minorities in comparative perspective. In M. A. Gibson and J. U. Ogbu, eds., *Minority status and schooling: A comparative study of immigrant and involuntary minorities*. New York: Garland.

Orfield, G. Spring 1975. How to make desegregation work: The adaptation of schools to their newly integrated student bodies. *Law and Contemporary Problems* 39(2):314–340.

———. 1978a. *Must we bus? Segregated schools and national policy*. Washington, D.C.: Brookings Institution.

———. 1978b. Research, politics and the antibusing debate. *Law and Contemporary Problems* 42 (Summer, no. 3):141–173.

———. 1980a. The St. Louis Desegregation Plan: A Report to Judge James H. Meredith. May 2.

———. 1980b. "School segregation and residential segregation": A social science statement. In Walter G. Stephan and Joe R. Feagin, eds., *School desegregation: Past, present, and future*. New York: Plenum.

———. 1981. The housing issues in the St. Louis case. A report to Judge William L. Hungate, U.S. District Court, St. Louis.

———. 1988. Race and the liberal agenda: The loss of the integrationist dream, 1965–

1974. In M. Weir, A. S. Orloff, and T. Skocpol, eds., *The politics of social policy in the United States*. Princeton, N.J.: Princeton University Press.

————. 1993. *The growth of segregation in America schools: Changing patterns of separations and poverty since 1968*. Washington, D.C.: National School Boards Association.

————. June 3, 1994. Beyond the rhetoric on desegregation. *St. Louis Post-Dispatch*.

————. 1994. Public opinion and school desegregation. In E. C. Lagemann and L. P. Miller, eds., Brown v. Board of Education: *The Challenge for Today's Schools*, 59–70. New York: Teachers College Press.

Orfield, G., and Ashkinaze, C. 1991. *The closing door: Conservative policy and black opportunity*. Chicago: University of Chicago Press.

Park View Heights Corporation v. the City of Black Jack, 605 F 2d 1033 1979.

Patchen, M. 1982. *Black-white contact in schools: Its social and academic effects*. West Lafayette, Ind.: Purdue University Press.

Pearce, D. M. 1980. Breaking down barriers: New evidence on the impact of metropolitan desegregation on housing choices. Washington, D.C.: Center for National Policy Review.

Pearce, D. M., Crain, R. L., Farley, R., and Taeuber, K. E. 1995. The effect of school desegregation in large central cities.

Peshkin, A. 1991. *The color of strangers, the color of friends*. Chicago: University of Chicago Press.

Pettigrew, T. F. 1988. *The sociology of race relations: Reflection and reform*. New York: Free Press.

————. 1994. New patterns of prejudice: The different worlds of 1984 and 1964. In F. L. Pincus and H.J. Ehrlich, eds., *Race and ethnic conflict: Contending views on prejudice, discrimination, and ethnoviolence*, 53–59. Boulder, Colo.: Westview.

Pfeifer-Harms, B. July 14, 1982. Atlanta law firm joins county desegregation fight. *West County Journal*.

Pope, S. H. August 8, 1994. Parents and boards should run schools, panelists say. *St. Louis Post-Dispatch*.

Prager, J., Longshore, D., and Seeman, M. 1986. The desegregation situation. In J. Prager, D. Longshore, and M. Seeman, eds., *School desegregation research: New directions in situational analysis*. New York: Plenum.

Primm, J. N. 1990. *The lion in the valley*. 2nd ed. Boulder, Colo.: Pruett.

Prost, C. July 15, 1994. Wreckers to clear space close to science center. *St. Louis Post-Dispatch*.

Prost, C., and Gest, T. December 26, 1975. "Magnet" schools to need U.S. aid. *St. Louis Post-Dispatch*.

Public Policy Research Centers. 1993a. *Perceptions of the transfer program: Focus group transcription: 11th grade city transfer students*. Report submitted to the Voluntary Interdistrict Coordinating Council. St. Louis: University of Missouri–St. Louis.

————. 1993b. Preceptions of the transfer program: Focus group transcription: 11th-grade white students who are resident students of county schools. Report submit-

368   References

ted to the Voluntary Interdistrict Coordinating Council. St. Louis: University of Missouri.

———. 1993c. *Perceptions of the transfer program: Focus group transcription: Parents of 11th grade transfer students*. Report submitted to the Voluntary Interdistrict Coordinating Council. St. Louis: University of Missouri–St. Louis.

———. 1993d. *Student/parent perceptions of the St. Louis voluntary interdistrict transfer program: Results of focus group discussions*. Report submitted to the Voluntary Interdistrict Coordinating Council. St. Louis: University of Missouri–St. Louis.

Raab, C. D. 1994. Where are we now? Reflections on the sociology of education policy. In D. Halpin and B. Troyna, eds., *Researching education policy: Ethical and methodological issues*. London: Falmer Press.

Rainwater, L. 1970. *Behind ghetto walls: Black families in a federal slum*. Chicago: Aldine Atherton.

Racialism creeps back in St. Louis. July 16, 1963. *The Times* (London).

Rist, R. C. May 1976. School integration: Ideology, methodology, and national policy. *The School Review*, 417–430.

Rivkin, S. G. October 1994. Residential segregation and school integration. *Sociology of Education* 67:279–292.

Rosenberg, M. 1986. Self-esteem research: A phenomenological corrective. In J. Prager, D. Longshore, and M. Seeman, eds., *School desegregation research: New directions in situational analysis*. New York: Plenum.

Rossell, C. 1990. *The carrot of the stick for school desgregation policy*. Philadelphia: Temple University.

Rusk, D. 1993. Suburban renewal. *The New York Times*.

St. John, Craig, and Bates, Nancy A. 1990. Racial composition and neighborhood evaluation. *Social Science Research* 19:47–61.

St. Louis Board of Education. August 1995. *Desegregation report and policy statement*. St. Louis: Author.

St. Louis Public Schools. September 1967. *Hard times . . . and great expectations: An account to the community of the condition of the St. Louis Public Schools*. St. Louis: Author.

———. 1968. *A tale of two cities: A blueprint for equality of educational opportunity in the St. Louis Public Schools*. St. Louis: Author.

St. Louis Public Schools, Division of Evaluation and Research. November 1990a. *Postgraduation activities of 1989 high school graduates*. St. Louis: Author.

———. May 1990b. *The role of instructional coordinators in non-integrated and magnet schools*. (Prepared in response to L [2737]) 90. St. Louis: Author.

———. April 1990c. *The school of emphasis program evaluation report, 1989–90*. (Prepared in response to L [2737]) 90. St. Louis: Author.

St. Louis schools in racial accord. December 27, 1975. *The New York Times*.

Salins, P. D. January 9, 1994. Cities in crisis: America can no longer afford ghettos. *The Los Angeles Times*.

Samuel, Y. December 5, 1995. Good grade report on schools. *St. Louis Post-Dispatch*.

Savage, D. G. JUne 13, 1996. Court deals blow to school desegregation rules. *The Los Angeles Times*.

Savageau, D., and Boyer, R. 1993. *Places rated almanac*. New York: Prentice Hall Travel.

Schlinkmann, M. June 4, 1994. Governor opposes Klan's plan to tend roadside. *St. Louis Post-Dispatch*.

Schneider, W. July 1992. The suburban century begins: The real meaning of the 1992 election. *The Atlantic Monthly*, 33–44.

Schofield, J. W. 1989a. *Black and white in school*. New York: Teacher College Press.

———. 1989b. Review of research on school desegregation's impact on elementary and secondary school students. Paper commissioned by the Connecticut State Department of Education.

———. 1991. School desegregation and intergroup relations: A review of the literature. In G. Grant, ed., *Review of research in education* 17:335–409. Washington, D.C.: American Educational Research Association.

———. 1993. Promoting positive peer relations in desegregated schools. *Educational Policy* 7(3):297–317.

Schuman, H., and Lawrence, B. September 1988. Survey-based experiments on white racial attitudes toward residential integration. *American Journal of Sociology* 2(94):273–299.

Sears, D. O., Hensler, C. P., and Speer, L. K. 1979. Whites' opposition to "busing": Self-interested or symbolic politics? *American Political Science Review* 73:369–384.

Seeman, M. 1959. On the meaning of alienation. *American Sociological Review* 24:783–791.

———. 1972. Alienation and knowledge-seeking: A note on attitude and action. *Social Problems* 20(1):3–17.

Selbert, P. November 16, 1992. Students get hands on the environment. *St. Louis Post-Dispatch*.

Separate and unequal. February 28, 1994. *St. Louis Post-Dispatch*.

Shapiro, M. February 2, 1004. High scores: Students improve on their college entrance exams. *West County Journal*.

Shelley v. Kraemer, 334 U.S. 1. 1948.

Shirk, M. December 31, 1975. Teachers union dislikes integration plan. *St. Louis Post-Dispatch*.

Sigelman, L., and Welch, S. 1994. *Black Americans' views of racial inequality: The dream long deferred*. 1st paperback ed. Cambridge: Cambridge University Press.

Simon, H. 1987. Rationality in psychology and economics. In R. M. Hogarth and M. W. Reder, eds., *Rational choice: The contrast between economics and psychology*. Chicago: University of Chicago.

Sirotnik, K. A., and Oakes, J. 1986. Critical inquiry for school renewal: Liberating theory and practice. in K. A. Sirotnik and J. Oakes, eds., *Critical perspectives on the organization and improvement of schooling*, 3–93. Boston: Kluwer Press.

Skocpol, T. 1988. The limits of new deal system and the roots of contemporary welfare dilemmas. In M. Weir, A. S. Orloff, and T. Skocpol, eds., *The politics of social policy in the United States*. Princeton, N.J.: Princeton University Press.

Sly, D. F., and Tayman, J. December 1980. Changing metropolitan morphology and municipal service expenditures in cities and rings. *Social Science Quarterly* 61(3–4):595–611.

Smith, B., and Little, J. March 24, 1996. School decision: 'I'm glad I'm not the one making it.' *St. Louis Post-Dispatch*.

Smothers, R. October, 18 1993. City seeks to grow by disappearing. *The New York Times*.

Sniderman, P. M., and Piazza, T. 1993. *The scar of race*. Cambridge, Mass.: Belknap Press of Harvard University Press.

Snyder, M. 1988. Self-fulfilling stereotypes. In P. S. Rothenberg, ed., *Racism and sexism: An integrated study*. New York: St. Martin's Press.

Sobel, M. G., and Beck, W. W. 1980. Phenomenological influences in minority attitudes toward school desegregation. *The Urban Review* 12(1):31–40.

Spitzer, D. L. August 8, 1971. Uneven course for education. *St. Louis Post-Dispatch*.

Spring, J. 1990. *The American school, 1642–1990*. 2nd ed. New York: Longman.

Stahura, J. M. Summer 1983. Determinants of change in the distribution of blacks across suburbs. *The Sociological Quarterly* 24:421–433.

————. February 1986. Suburban development, black suburbanization and the civil rights movement since World War II. *American Sociological Review* 51:131–144.

Stipak, B., and Hensler, C. 1983. Effect of neighborhood racial and socio-economic composition on urban residents' evaluations of their neighborhoods. *Social Indicators Research* 12:311–320.

Suburbs, rich and poor. June 21, 1989. *Education Week* 3.

Sussman, M. H. November 1990. Nondiscrimination in housing and education: Toward a coordinated federal policy. *Education and Urban Society* 23(1):50–60.

Sweatt v. Painter, 339 U.S. 629 1950.

Taub, R. D., Taylor, D. G., and Dunham, J. A. 1984. *Paths of neighborhood change: Race and crime in urban America*. Chicago: University of Chicago Press.

Tate, W. F., Ladson-Billings, G., and Grant, C. A. 1993. The *Brown* decision revisited: Mathematizing social problems. *Educational Policy* 7(3):255–275.

Terkel, S. 1992. *Race: How blacks and whites think and feel about the American obsession*. New York: Anchor.

Tobin, G. A. 1976. Suburbanization and the development of motor transportation: Transportation technology and the suburbanization process. In B. Schwartz, ed., *The changing face of the suburbs*, 95–112. Chicago: University of Chicago Press.

Todd, C. April 6, 1992. Housing integration group boosted: Group decision allows neighborhoods to seek racial diversity. *St. Louis Post-Dispatch*.

Troen, S. K. 1975. *The public and the schools: Shaping the St. Louis system, 1838–1920*. Columbia: University of Missouri Press.

University of Missouri–St. Louis (UMSL). 1988. Survey on St. Louis school desegregation plan.

U.S. Commission on Civil Rights. 1970. *Hearing on racism and segregation in St. Louis*. Washington, D.C.: Author.

Urban Land Institute. 1987. *Cities reborn*. R. L. Levitt, ed. Washington, D.C.: Author.

Vespereny, C. July 18, 1982. Desegregation case defense outlined. *St. Louis Post-Dispatch*.

Volland, V. June 6, 1994a. City schools vow to raise test scores. *St. Louis Post-Dispatch*.

———. March 11, 1994b. School program rewards high grades. *St. Louis Post-Dispatch*.

Voluntary Interdistrict Coordinating Council. September 1993. *Tenth report to the United States District Court, Eastern District of Missouri*. St. Louis: Author.

———. August 1994. *Appendices to the eleventh report to the United States District Court, Eastern District of Missouri* (Court filing G[1305] 94). St. Louis: Author.

———. January 1995. *Complete eleventh report to the United States District Court, Eastern District of Missouri* (Court filing G[1445] 95). St. Louis: Author.

———. December 1995. *Complete twelfth report to the United States District Court, Eastern District of Missouri* (Court filing C[1843] 95). St. Louis: Author.

Waters, K. (December 26, 1975a). No-busing school desegregation plan will go in effect next fall. *St. Louis Globe Democrat*.

———. (December 26, 1975b). School plan aim: Avoid violence. *St. Louis Globe Democrat*.

Wellman, D. T. 1993. *Portraits of white racism*. 2nd ed. New York: Cambridge University Press.

Wells, A. S. 1993. *Time to choose: America at the crossroads of school choice policy*. New York: Hill and Wang.

Wells, A. S., and Crain, R. L. 1992. Do parents choose school quality or school status: A sociological theory of free market education. In P. W. Cookson, Jr., ed., *The Choice Controversy*. Newbury Park, Calif.: Corwin.

———. Winter 1994. Perpetuation theory and the long-term effects of school desegregation. *Review of Educational Research* 64(4):531–555.

West, C. 1993a. *Prophetic thought in postmodern times*. Monroe, Minn.: Common Courage Press.

———. 1993b. *Race matters*. Boston: Beacon.

———. 1993c. The new cultural politics of difference. In C. McCarthy and W. Crichlow, eds., *Race identity and representation in education*. New York: Routledge.

West, P. December 11, 1991. Mo. weighs plan to aid districts facing bankruptcy. *Education Week*.

White, J. A. September 1994. Brown revisited. *Phi Delta Kappan*, 13–20.

Willis, P. 1977. *Learning to labour*. New York: Columbia University Press.

Wilson, W. J. 1996. *When work disappears: The world of the new urban poor*. New York: Knopf.

———. 1987. *The truly disadvantaged: The inner city, the underclass, and public policy*. Chicago: University of Chicago Press.

Witte, J. F., Baily, A. B., and Thorn, C. A. 1993. *Third-year report: Milwaukee Parental*

Choice Program. Madison: Department of Political Science and The Robert La Follette Institute of Public Affairs, University of Wisconsin.

Wright, John A. 1994. *Discovering African-American St. Louis: A guide to historic sites*. St. Louis: Missouri Historical Society Press.

Wyant, W. K. 1966. Study praises city schools' desegregation. *St. Louis Post-Dispatch.*

Yes for city schools. May 26, 1992. Editorial. *St. Louis Post-Dispatch.*

Young, R. 1990. *A critical theory of education: Habermas and our children's future.* New York: Teachers College Press.

Yudof, M. G., Kirp, D. L., and Levin, B. 1992. *Educational policy and the law*. 3rd ed. St. Paul, Minn.: West.

Zweigenhaft, R. L., and Domhoff, G. W. 1991. *Blacks in the white establishment?: A study of race and class in America*. New Haven: Yale University Press.

Index